HART CRANE
A Biographical and Critical Study

HART CRANE

BROM WEBER

HART CRANE

A Biographical and Critical Study

THE BODLEY PRESS · NEW YORK

Designed by Nettie Weber

Manufactured in the United States of America for The Bodley Press, 104 Fifth Avenue, New York 11

FIRST EDITION

PREFATORY NOTE

This book is concerned with the life and work of Hart Crane, because it was found that neither could be separated from the other if we were to understand either. The book is, therefore, neither orthodox criticism nor orthodox biography, but rather a fusion, a genetic study. In the course of writing I found myself compelled to probe deeply. I would not wish the candor of my approach, however, to obscure the great admiration I bear for Crane as unquestionably the major poetic talent of twentieth-century America, nor the intense sorrow evoked in me by his brief and tragic existence. I have attempted throughout to "heed the negative" in Crane without denying him the "mastery" which he achieved.

I am alone responsible for the use to which any information, documents, and photographs have been put in the book, but I wish to thank those who graciously helped me assemble them: Eleanor Anderson, Nicholas Bessaraboff, Peter Blume, Ludwig Bromberg, Malcolm Cowley, Caresse Crosby, Lorna Dietz, Walker Evans, Herbert Fletcher, Waldo Frank, Shlomo Grodzensky, Solomon Grünberg, David Ignatow, Matthew Josephson, Isabel Lachaise, Samuel Loveman, Harry F. Marks, Henry A. Moe, Gorham Munson, Dorothy Norman, Richard and Charlotte Rychtarik, Carl Schmitt, Israel Solon, John L. Sweeney, Allen Tate, Eda Lou Walton, Charmion Wiegand, William

Wright; the late Claude Bragdon, Guido Bruno, Paul Rosenfeld, Joseph Stella, Alfred Stieglitz; the New York Public Library; and the Libraries of Brown, Harvard, Ohio State, and Princeton Universities. For permission to use copyrighted quotations not elsewhere acknowledged I am indebted to the following: Twice A Year Press for Crane's prose writing from *Twice A Year* (XII-XIII); Coward-McCann, Inc., for Crane's "Modern Poetry" reprinted from *Revolt in the Arts*, edited by Oliver M. Sayler, copyright, 1930 by Brentano's, Inc., 1933 by Coward-McCann, Inc.; The Macmillan Company for "On the Seashore" from *Collected Poems and Plays of Rabindranath Tagore*; Malcolm Cowley for his *Exile's Return*; Liveright Publishing Corporation, and Waldo Frank for his *Our America* and *Salvos*, for Gorham Munson's *Waldo Frank*. Unless otherwise indicated, poems by Crane quoted in the text are reprinted from *The Collected Poems of Hart Crane*, published by Liveright Publishing Corporation, New York. Since continual references are made to poems and prose by Crane, the reader should familiarize himself with the *Collected Poems* and the *Appendix* of my book. Special thanks are due to: Mrs. Grace Hart Crane for authorization to quote from her son's poetry and prose; Harold Holden and Jack McManis for enabling me to study their edition of Samuel Greenberg's poems before publication; Samuel Loveman and David Mann for suggesting that I write the book and for cooperating throughout the ordeal of composition. It would be impossible to ignore my debt to the many writers whose works have obviously or indirectly influenced me. In preparing my bibliography, however, I selected only those who concerned themselves directly with Crane, believing that such a list would ultimately prove most valuable for the reader.

B. W.

May 15, 1947

CONTENTS

ILLUSTRATIONS

I

"I DRIFTED HOW MANY HOURS"

1. EMERGENCE

IN DECEMBER 1916, HART CRANE ARRIVED IN NEW York City determined to be a poet and bearing in his baggage such spiritual resources as the Bible and Mary Baker Eddy's *Science and Health with Key to the Scriptures.* Behind him in Cleveland, Ohio, he left his father; his mother, meanwhile, was in Chicago waiting for the outcome of a divorce action which she had instituted against Mr. Crane. The New York City to which sixteen-year-old Hart Crane came with enthusiasm was hardly the place anyone would have suggested for the peaceful development of an incipient poetic talent. The nation was on the verge of entering the military conflict being fought in Europe, and the Eastern metropolis was already burgeoning with preparatory activity of a distracting nature. Hart's family, however, was in too upset a condition to consider this question. In any case, they took comfort from their decision to entrust him to the care of Carl Schmitt, a young Ohio painter and friend of the Crane family who was now a resident of New York. It was the second of Crane's many flights and, despite the war, also the most peaceful.

3

The childhood and early adolescence from which he
thus escaped had not been happy.† Even without biographical data, the clouded atmosphere of his youth is
deducible from Crane's poetry. A passage from his major poem, *The Bridge*, dealing with childish play is
strangely surrounded by an aura of cruelty, as though
the boy were taking revenge for pain inflicted upon
him:

> Remember, remember
> The cinder pile at the end of the backyard
> Where we stoned the family of young
> Garter snakes under . . . And the monoplanes
> We launched—with paper wings and twisted
> Rubber bands . . . Recall—recall
>   the rapid tongues
> That flittered from under the ash heap day
> After day whenever your stick discovered
> Some sunning inch of unsuspecting fibre—
> It flashed back at your thrust, as clean as fire.

From this background Crane emerged a sensitive and in-
trospective child. Though he engaged in the usual boy-
hood activities of skating, ball playing, and swimming, he
very early drifted away from children of his own age.
He derived more pleasure in the pursuit of solitary activities which enabled him to exercise his love of color
and sound. Under the influence of his mother, who enjoyed singing and music, he learned to play the piano.
At the age of nine, he appeared one day on the porch
of his home and displayed an oil painting on which he
had been working in secret. Lack of companionship
did not depress him, however, since he was content with
a few friends who shared his interests.

The absence of harmony between Crane's mother and
father was a more potent cause of unhappiness, for the

† *Hart Crane was born on July 21, 1899 in Garrettsville, Ohio. He
was the only child of Clarence Arthur and Grace Hart Crane.*

boy was caught in the web of tumultuous emotion which
enshrouded his parents' married life. In the struggle
which eventually culminated in separation and divorce,
the boy sided with his mother, thereby laying a foundation for the major maladjustment of his life:

> Your mother sang you out of a stuffy parlor
> one summer day in a little town where you
> had started to grow.
> And you ran outside afterward as soon as you
> could get free from the company,
> and brought back the only rose on the bush
> in the front yard.
> You will never forget the song nor the rose.

Mr. Crane, an active man whose creative energies were
concentrated in the furtherance of his business plans,
naturally took this partisanship without good grace. Whether from this time on, or gradually from an earlier date
is difficult to determine, but Mr. Crane in any event became overtly less affectionate to his son than the latter
could desire. In later life, Crane was to typify this
relationship in the only passage of poetry which refers to
his father directly:

> Is it the whip stripped from the lilac tree
> One day in spring my father took to me . . . ?

When the boy's stubborn youthful decision to become a
poet could not be shaken, Mr. Crane's hope of seeing his
son in the family business had to be discarded. His disappointment drove him to see signs of effeminacy in the
boy's affection for his mother and in his literary ambition, and he did not spare his son these conclusions to
which he was drawn. Thereafter, the father became for

Crane a symbol of oppression and masculine virility which he strove to surmount and conquer.

In an age distinguished by the rapid decline of belief in a divine being and his agencies, Hart Crane stood apart as one who saw God ("Elohim, still I hear thy sounding heel!") and who dedicated his major work to God's glory:

> O Sleepless as the river under thee,
> Vaulting the sea, the prairies' dreaming sod,
> Unto us lowliest sometime sweep, descend
> And of the curveship lend a myth to God.

Crane's spiritual life was non-institutional:

> But since the Cross sank, much that's warped and cracked
> Has followed in its name, has heaped its grave.
>
> Oh—
>
> Gallows and guillotines to hail the sun
> And smoking racks for penance when day's done!
>
> No—

The secret of his faith and its particular nature is to be found in these early years. One of the temperamental disagreements between Hart's father and mother which preceded their final rupture resulted in a nervous breakdown for Mrs. Crane when Hart was nine years old. In her desire for solace to alleviate the pain she was suffering, Mrs. Crane became an adherent of Christian Science. With its pronounced emphasis on the healing aspects of Christ's teachings, this religion extended to her the consolation she needed. The congress of religions presented in 1893 at the World's Fair in Chicago, the city in which Mrs. Crane grew to womanhood, had been a revelation to many in the Middle West as well as the rest of the United States of the diversity of religions

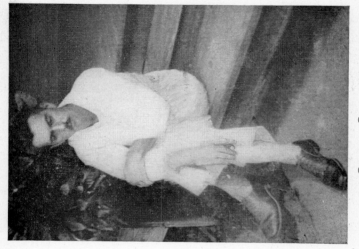

Crane as a Child, 1908

Crane in Cuba, 1926

Religious gunman! that died too soon
in other ways than as the wind settles
on the sixteen thrifty brudges of the city--
your capped and hidden eye succeeds the faun's
as arbiter of beauty in these streets
darkly spread out before the motor dawn.
What did you ask for; what were you refused?
The privilege of a gift, a goose, tobacco
and cologne; or belles and voices?

O thief of time! sing in the new year;
laugh out the meager penance of their days
who dare not touch the cup that sings!
Clink in with me the praise of all
assembaled near the gasp of desperation
that floods the mind with lovliness released.

Impossible if I deny -- yet know
it so that love gives you more than than them.....
The quenched breath, the substance drilled
shall prophesy your soul in heaven
by the sigh Astarte- of Astarte, mother of beauty---
mother of saints!

The lavish heart shall win the rape, in sight,
of ever-virgin Beauty, untouched, untouchable.
It shall see, beyond the cautious scan
of mortal wisdom, navel and womb.

The aged fire leaps up again, as always,
clearing away the mists of measured hours.
Forgoteen measures are retraced on the grass,
and ancient feasts beabd down the boards.
Primeval presences lick the dews:
inviolable, the soul has twanged its bow!

                @   @   @   @

There is no light on all the street
to echo now the shimmer of my lamp
against the blackened window pane....
Tower against tower, to build the skies
glooms out before me in my dreams!
Accuse the wind that sails the sun
into your sight, and dawn...It is the same.
I do not accuse. Fools come in the dark
to pipe complaints against this dawn
that brings dismay and Beauty to the world.

"FAUSTUS AND HELEN" MANUSCRIPT, 1922

which existed in the world. The effect of this knowledge, when coupled with the pessimism generated during the nineteenth century by the failure of traditional Christianity to meet the problems of materialism and industrialism, was to strengthen a spirit of religious restlessness in a nation already distinguished for its origination of new religions. It is not unlikely that Mrs. Crane was affected spiritually by this breakdown of tradition and rendered amenable to Christian Science. Although the Crane family was a member of a Methodist Episcopal Church, the elder Cranes and their son did not adhere strongly to the doctrine and rituals of that church, and indeed did not regularly attend church. The religion of Christ Scientist soon occupied a dominant spiritual position in the Crane household. Where his parents and his maternal grandmother, who lived with them, showed the way, their son followed. For a short time, therefore, Hart attended the sessions of a Christian Science Sunday School, at which family discussions of the religion were supplemented for him by more formal instruction.

But for a boy with the sensuous propensities of Hart Crane, the basic tenets of Christian Science could be nothing other than unattractive. Feeling and sensation were subordinated by Christian Science doctrine to their supposed source of origin, the consciousness, to be evoked or effaced at will by states of consciousness, and therefore without reality in themselves. This could hardly satisfy someone who took delight in musical sounds or the interplay of color against color, a boy engaged in the process of discovering the world in its physical and emotional aspects. Grounding her faith in the New Testament, the founder of Christian Science (Mary Baker Eddy) had postulated the principle that causation was mental, and that the only true "Mind" was God. Since everything "which He creates is good, and He makes all that is made," matter, which had shown itself because of sin, death, and disease to be bad, could not have been created by God. Matter was therefore unreal; it possessed a simulated reality only because "unrealities seem real to human, erring belief." But error was not intrinsic in the human mind, since it was part of the Divine Mind and shared His divinity and immortality, a thoroughgoing pantheistic belief. Once spiritual harmony between human minds and the Divine Mind (variously identified as God, Good, Spirit, Infinite Person, Love, Truth, etc.) was established, error was automatically banished. Although Christian Science did not imbed itself in Crane, its exaggerated idealism continued to exercise a strong influence over him for many years to come. With regard to Christian Science as church and ritual, he was too young to crystallize a reasoned opposition; in addition, the affection he felt for his mother and his grandmother, since they had been the first to welcome and continue the family allegiance to the Science, discouraged him from rebelling overtly.

During the summer of 1914, Hart successfully managed to spend a few weeks, with his parents' reluctant approval, at Roycroft, the East Aurora, New York establishment of Elbert Hubbard. It was the first of his flights, and resulted from a meeting with Hubbard, who had come to Cleveland to write a success story about the Crane chocolate business. The career of Hubbard is one of the low points in American cultural history. A shrewd and imaginative entrepreneur with a gift for debasing art and literature in the service of the highest bidder, he capitalized upon the contradictory and confused American temper at the turn of the century by clothing materialism with an atmosphere of romance and culture. As advertising copywriter, vaudeville actor, columnist, and publisher, he fought vigorously for the principles of conservatism. At the same time, his "artistic" appearance with its Windsor tie, long hair, and unpressed clothes . . . his surface obeisance to the ideas of William Morris . . . his sponsorship of Stephen Crane's free verse poems . . . his reports of visits to the home of writers like Emerson, Poe, and Ruskin and of his meeting with Whitman, as well as his frequent quotations from their works . . . gave an air of ingenuousness to his commercial activities. To Hart, he was a fresh and liberating figure as he made his habitual scoffing remarks about businessmen, attacked Christian Science, and perhaps impressed him with his friendship for Stephen Crane. At East Aurora, Hart lived with the Hubbard family, eating at their table, and participating in their discussions. In accordance with Hubbard's baronial ideas, Hart worked in the Roycroft bookbindery mornings and spent his afternoons on the Roycroft farm doing odd jobs in the open air. Though the days spent in Hubbard's company speedily destroyed the illusion of the man as a literary genius, there is no doubt that Hart's decision in the 1920's to enter advertising as a profession, as well as his familiarity, if not his initial acquaintance, with the works and ideas of America's classic poets, were encouraged by this summer interlude.

The following year, after Hart returned with his mother and grandmother from a trip to the family plantation on the West Indian Isle of Pines, Mr. Crane spoke to Mrs. Harriet Moody of Chicago about his son's future. Still unreconciled to Hart's choice of a literary career, he sought for advice which might enable him to cope with

the problem. Mrs. Moody, in addition to operating the
catering business which had brought her into contact with
Mr. Crane, was a leading figure in Chicago's artistic and
intellectual life and the wife of the late William Vaughn
Moody, one of America's important turn-of-the-century
poets. It was Mrs. Moody's opinion that Hart should be
permitted to continue with his poetic development, and
Mr. Crane apparently accepted her recommendation. Mrs.
Moody's advice was practically implemented on her part
by a subsequent meeting with Hart and invaluable letters
of encouragement and stimulation. The friendly association which grew up between Hart and the older woman
had other consequences. Mrs. Moody, like her husband,
was deeply concerned with questions of spiritual faith,
and Hart's mother has related that she invigorated his
interest in Christian Science. From Mrs. Moody, too,
Hart heard news of the poets and novelists in and about
Chicago, many of whom shared her hospitality while in
that city. One of these writers was Rabindranath Tagore of India, whose first visit to Chicago had occurred
in 1913, shortly after several poems from his *Gitanjali* collection appeared in an issue of the newly-founded *Poetry*.
When Tagore came again to the United States in 1916,
he stopped off at Cleveland. One of the few interviews
he granted at that time was to Hart, who returned home
impressed with the serene dignity and acute observations of the Indian writer and philosopher. Hart was now
at a stage where he easily appreciated Tagore's insistence
upon the fusion of religion with everyday life, as well as
his distaste for the supremacy of American business and
scientific ideals over the values of art. Undoubtedly he
read the cadenced English translations of Tagore's Ben-
gali poems and responded to the poet's pantheistic concep-

tion of God's immanence, his imagery of infinite sky and bottomless ocean depths, and his faith in the motive-power of love. In later years, one of Tagore's poems was to make a strange re-appearance in a poem written by Crane.

The atmosphere which enveloped Crane upon his arrival in New York in 1916 reflected the peculiarity of the city. Unlike most other American urban centers in so many ways, the passion for social reform and the struggle against convention were bound up with the progress of highly-individualistic artists. The focal point of these fused forces was in Greenwich Village, where Crane found himself a host of new friends and a room in which to live. Through the neighborhood's narrow streets, restaurants, and apartments passed individuals who could not be confined within traditional channels—anarchists, socialists, vegetarians, birth control advocates, sexual deviants, free lovers, poets, musicians, and painters—many of whom became Crane's friends. Few young provincials escaped the impact of these cosmopolitan influences, and Crane was no exception. Unlike Rimbaud, whose bad manners attracted hostility and prevented him from being welcomed by the Parisian intelligentsia, Crane's evident youthful insecurity was inoffensive to the Village artists and amenable to the pressure of their ideas and emotions. The nature of these influences acting upon Crane shaped to a considerable extent his future role as a poet.

It was in October 1916 that Joseph Kling's *The Pagan*, a new literary-art magazine in New York, printed a letter written by Crane a few months earlier in Cleveland: "I am interested in your magazine as a new and distinctive chord in the present American Renaissance of literature and art. Let me praise your September cover; it has some suggestion of the exoticism and richness of Wilde's poems." This initial contact with *The Pagan* was continued in New York and, with but a few exceptions, Crane's poems from 1916 through 1919 appeared regularly in Kling's periodical. *The Pagan's* editorial policies typified in miniature the amalgam of art and social theory which now surrounded Crane. A few months before the United States entered the war, the magazine unleashed an attack against those who wanted to hurry the nation into military allegiance with the Allied powers. "We say further to you jingo-politicians, ammunition-makers, and slaughter-seekers in general," *The Pagan* announced in March 1917, "that if you want to peddle your powder and shells undisturbed, want to coin blood into money without let or hindrance, want to lie and deceive, breed hatred and blood-lust to the applause of multitudes, go to Hell!" This intransigency was counterbalanced, however, by the magazine's genial enjoyment of life undisturbed by practical issues; this is seen in its creative contents, as well as in its subtitle: "A Magazine for Eudaemonists." The September 1917 issue defined the editorial conception of its hoped-for readers in the following words:

"A eudaemonist is one who realizes that the will-to-be-happy is an evolution of the will-to-live (though both are identical, sometimes); hence its universal manifestation in spite of repressive legal, social, and religious codes. A eudaemonist also believes that maximum of happiness is attainable through the satisfaction of one's (cultivated) senses and mental faculties; in other words, through the pleasures of the flesh and the spirit."

Manifestly Crane subscribed to the amorphous philosophy of *The Pagan*, for with the April-May issue of 1918 he became an associate editor of the paper, then located in the East 15th Street headquarters of the Socialist Party.

Like Kling, most of the editors and writers whose acquaintance Crane made were not revolutionaries despite their rebellious mien. If anything, they were artists pure and simple, and the majority were bohemians. Through the agency of Mrs. Moody, for example, Crane was introduced to Padraic Colum, Ridgely Torrence, and other prominent poets; he also met Alfred Kreymborg and Maxwell Bodenheim, and before long became intimate with Margaret Anderson and Jane Heap of *The Little Review*. Threads of some significance tied these individuals to movements which, in greater or lesser degree, strove for the amelioration of social, political, cultural, or economic sores in the structure of society. Colum supported Ireland's struggle for independence against England; Kreymborg was a member of the old Liberal Club, a gathering-place for intransigents, and contributed to *The Seven Arts*; Bodenheim wrote for *The Soil*; Anderson and Heap espoused the philosophy and accomplishments of anarchism in their magazine. It was Kreymborg who became involved in a tussle with the law enforcement authorities of New York City the very month in which Crane stepped off from his Cleveland train. The same Guido Bruno who had sponsored the first published poem of the unknown Harold H. Crane in the September 23, 1916 number of *Bruno's Weekly* was Kreymborg's partner in the affair. *Bruno's Weekly* having expired a few issues thereafter, Bruno's periodical-publishing activities were at a temporary lull. Suddenly more than Philistine indifference overwhelmed him and Kreymborg too. On December 13th, an agent of the Society for the Prevention of Vice arrested Bruno for selling copies of

Kreymborg's brief "true" story of prostitution, *Edna*: *The Girl of the Streets*. Haled to court, Bruno was held in $500 bail, only a fraction of which he was able to raise before Frank Harris interested himself in the case. Within a short time thereafter, the necessary funds were gathered, and George Bernard Shaw wrote from England in support of Bruno's defiance of the censors and materially aided the "inveterate foe[s] to the Powers that Prey." It was some time before the case was settled, and meanwhile Kreymborg could add the censor's crown of thorns to the laurels won as founder of experimental poetry magazines *Glebe and Others*. But the reason for which Kreymborg's work aroused the ire of the law was far less explosive than the socialism and anti-war sentiment which brought *The Masses* to trial in a Federal court in 1918, and which had caused its exclusion from the United States mails in 1917.

When one turns to consider the other men listed among Crane's new friends, and the periodicals for which they wrote, their radicalism also dwindles into thin air. Colum, for example, in an article on Ireland which appeared in *The Seven Arts* (September 1917) foresaw that subjugated nation as a median point between a future socialized Europe and an individualistic America: Ireland was to be a co-operative nation, "democratic for production, aristocratic in leadership," and as precursor of that leadership Colum envisaged "The literary movement of today . . . a prophecy of or perhaps a preparation for that brotherhood." Though this might be anti-imperialistic in its revolt against British rule, its faith in an aristocratic leadership arising from the people and its mystical reliance upon the cultural nationalism of the Irish Renaissance kept it at a far remove from a radicalism based upon the rise to power of new economic and political forces which would upset established interests.

The anarchism and general social iconoclasm which had distinguished *The Little Review* turned out to be a passing fancy. Upon the magazine's arrival in New York early in 1917, the combined interests of the new foreign editor, Ezra Pound, speedily replaced the former policies of Margaret Anderson and her associate Jane Heap. The pages of *The Little Review* began earnestly to promote, despite protest from so-called "reader-critics," Pound's profound affection for Wyndham Lewis, James Joyce, T. S. Eliot, and Ezra Pound . . . Pound's detestation of American culture . . . and Pound's determination that American writers must familiarize themselves with the best European writers of all ages.

Periodicals like *The Seven Arts* and *The Soil*, both of which were founded in 1916 and passed out of existence in 1917, were not essentially more radical, though not because of the fickle aesthetic and intellectual conceptions which motivated Misses Anderson and Heap. *The Seven Arts* and *The Soil* were expressions of a sense of maturity which the American intellectual had been feeling since the turn of the century, the accompaniment to the artistic renewal launched by Theodore Dreiser, Robert Frost, John Gould Fletcher, and Edgar Lee Masters. The assumption of a dominant world role by the United States, which roused them, was also to culminate in the financial and political adventure of participation in the European war of 1914-1918. The men who organized these magazines, however, were primarily concerned with nurturing an American expression stemming from the organic, untrammeled substance of American life. The declaration with which *The Seven Arts*

group, in their first issue, announced their consciousness
of an American Renaissance is also broadly applicable to
The Soil: "It is our faith and the faith of many, that we
are living in the first days of a renascent period, a time
which means for America the coming of that national
self-consciousness which is the beginning of greatness.
In all such epochs the arts cease to be private matters; they
become not only the expression of the national life but
a means to its enhancement."

Each magazine served as an unconscious complement
to the other. *The Seven Arts*, the responsibility of James
Oppenheim, Waldo Frank, and Van Wyck Brooks, represented the theoretical approach, though Oppenheim was
a poet, Frank a novelist as well as a critic, and only
Brooks a critic solely. Robert Coady's *Soil* was never to
formulate an organized aesthetic beyond a statement of
the editor's likes and dislikes and critical remarks made at
random. Further to distinguish *The Soil* from *The Seven
Arts*, it was weak in its literary pages; as compensation,
however, its issues were lavishly strewn with reproductions of paintings, sculpture, and photographs of the
phenomena of American life. In the pages of *The Seven
Arts* a serious effort was made to evoke a spiritual re-
birth, to find an expansive "American legendry and mythology" in the events and personalities which had preceded the twentieth century and had been distorted by
the effects of industrialism and Puritanism, to evolve a
communal sense in the American artist, and to develop
an optimism based on understanding and emotion which
would counteract the pessimism and frustration prevalent in the sensitive artist. Revolutionary developments
in Russia were welcomed, American foreign and domestic policy and the opportunism of liberalism were analyzed

and decried by Randolph Bourne—but *The Seven Arts*
was primarily romantic in its approach and emotional in
its effect. The trail-breaking character of the magazine
was soon revealed, however, when its financial subsidy
was withdrawn and the project ceased; it stands in noble
contrast to the acquiescent war-time record of other
liberal magazines like *The New Republic*. *The Soil* boldly expounded the thesis that the art of America is
everything distinctively American; under the influence of
the European futurists, it celebrated indigenous machinery, business, films, window displays, ships, bridges,
rivers, vaudeville, skyscrapers, and prizefighters with Whitmanian inclusiveness and enthusiasm. It was typical, for
example, that the first issue carried an article by film-actor
Charlie Chaplin on comedy. Coady's glorification of
popular art antedated the expatriates who were to return
from Europe in the early 1920's and extol the genius
behind flashing electric signs and giant sewers. But he
was not insensitive to other trends, and gave space to the
sophisticated art of Picasso and other European artists.
In this mixture, even the decadent could find room, and
one of the last issues of *The Soil* devoted a section to
Oscar Wilde which included an article by a man claiming to have seen the Irish poet after the date established
for his death.

From a milieu such as has been briefly described, Crane
derived a sensitivity to the social world and a reinforce-
ment of his artistic will. Any antagonism which had
arisen in him to business and industry as a result of his
father's positive contempt for literary expression of a non-
commercial character was sharpened by his contact with
ideas and individuals who proudly, often successfully, defied bourgeois values. It did not, however, ever develop

into an adherence to a revolutionary party or doctrine.
The bedrock was laid down in Crane for a later recog-
ntion of the potential merit and beauty of American
life and tradition. He was far more immediately respon-
sive to the aesthetic and personal freedom sponsored by
Others and *The Little Review,* and the nationalistic af-
flatus crystallized in *The Seven Arts* and *The Soil* would
be accepted in due time. With this perspective in mind,
it becomes clear why Crane's rebelliousness, which had
primarily arisen from a chaotic childhood and the desire
for artistic expression, was fed upon streams of emotional
and social discontent in which political and economic
motivations were subordinate, and found itself chan-
nelled accordingly into psychological spillways. So we
find Crane in 1918 impatiently and seriously criticizing
preparedness parades and ruefully calling attention to a
pacifist artist's successful war propaganda. But more revealing as to the actual state of his mind was his brief
article entitled "The Case Against Nietzsche," which
appeared in *The Pagan* for April-May 1918.†

To Friedrich Nietzsche must unquestionably be assigned a considerable share in the development of Hart
Crane. That Nietzsche's aesthetic and philosophical ideas,
particularly as expressed in *The Birth of Tragedy,* received an opportunity to display themselves concretely in
Crane's career is evident. Crane's faith in the myth, his
desire to transmute music into his poetry, his disregard
for cause and effect logic, his affirmation of life's joy
coupled with an affirmation of suffering and tragedy,
his belief in metaphysical inquiry as the artist's task—the
entire Dionysian complex of dance, ecstasy, and triumph

† *See Appendix.*

of the will which Nietzsche portrayed formed the backbone of Crane's life. It is even possible that Nietzsche's
call for "a rising generation . . . with bold vision . . . to
desire a new art, the art of metaphysical comfort . . .
to claim it as Helen, and exclaim with Faust" in *The Birth
of Tragedy* contributed to the genesis of "Faustus and
Helen." However, except for a brief quotation from
Human-All-Too Human in his article, there is no record
indication that Crane actually read any of Nietzsche's
other works. On the basis of the article itself, one might
conclude that he had read *Ecce Homo*, for Crane's assertions that Nietzsche "declared himself a Pole in all his
views and sympathies" and that Nietzsche's "favorite novelists were French; Pascal and Montaigne were sources
which he frequently mentions as potent influences in his
development" may be based on the opening sections of
Ecce Homo.

But if Crane's reading of Nietzsche is undetermined,
he was nevertheless exposed to and colored by Nietzsche's
powerful ideas. Although the philosopher had died as
recently as 1900, by the second decade of this century
his ideas and personality had begun to permeate many
writers and intellectuals, among them Lewis, Pound, Margaret Anderson, and John Gould Fletcher, who reacted
antagonistically to the genteel dogmatism of the nineteenth century and the aimless brutality of the twentieth.
In page after page of their work and in the magazines
they edited—*The New Freewoman, The Egoist, Blast, The
Little Review*, and the other magazines from which Crane
received the basic education that supplemented his broken
schooling—the emancipating message of Nietzsche was directly and indirectly stressed in ringing tones.

From the very beginning of the Nietzschean effect, when the master was already beyond the possibility of welcoming the appearance of disciples, his messages had thrilled the artist more than anyone else. As Crane Brinton writes in his study, *Nietzsche* (1941): "Nietzsche appears first . . . in the history of opinion as the complete anti-philistine, the emancipated poet of dionysian joy, the master of those who live." To his banner swarmed writers and critics of various opinions and nationalities, and as early as the 1890's such men as George Bernard Shaw, André Gide, Franz Mehring, Havelock Ellis, and Georg Brandes had begun to evaluate and praise Nietzsche. The posthumous publication of *The Will to Power* early in this century, with its explicit statement of a necessary transvaluation of values—"The aim should be to prepare a transvaluation of values for a particularly strong kind of man, most highly gifted in intellect and will, and, to this end, slowly and cautiously to liberate in him a whole host of slandered instincts, hitherto held in check: whoever meditates about this problem belongs to us, the free spirits—though not to that kind of 'free spirit' which has existed hitherto . . . "†—brought about an intensified response to the Nietzschean doctrine. The battle for converts was waged in America by book and article. H. L. Mencken's *The Philosophy of Friedrich Nietzsche* was brought out by a Boston publisher in 1908, and proved so popular that Mencken edited a small volume of selections from Nietzsche in 1910, and in 1913 issued a third revised edition of his earlier critique. The joint editorship of *The Smart Set* from 1914 to 1923 by Mencken and George Jean Nathan gave Nietzscheism an important

† *Aphorism* 957.

magazine outlet, for which Willard Huntington Wright, a predecessor editor, had already paved the way. The appearance of Wright's *What Nietzsche Taught* in 1915 continued the pro-Nietzsche battle with a painstaking examination of the philosopher's argument volume by volume. Both Mencken and Wright were contributors to *The Seven Arts*, where Crane may have read them, although it was in the pages of *The Smart Set* that Crane first made his intimate acquaintance with Mencken, for a brief time one of his youthful idols.

The boy who left his Cleveland home behind him in order to become a poet in New York had much of the attitude that could find Nietzscheism an attractive philosophy. A letter he wrote to his mother in 1917 is illustrative of his determination to strike forth as a free and unshackled individual: "I am beginning to see the hope of standing entirely alone and to fathom Ibsen's statement that translated is, 'The strongest man in the world is he who stands entirely alone!'" Four years later, in 1921, Crane designated Nietzsche as one of his favorite authors, coupling him with such important figures as Eliot, John Donne, Joyce, and Pound. At the close of the same year, he used the term "Nietzschean" as an accolade of distinction in describing Ernest Nelson, the dedicatee of "Praise for an Urn." "A mutual friend of our's here recently died," Crane wrote to Gorham Munson, " a Nietzschean and thorough appreciator of all the best, who has pursued his lonely way in America since the age of fifteen when he left his family in Norway on account of religious differences." This is the Nietzschean at his loneliest peak of intellectual aristocracy, high above the slave-morality which Nietzsche despised. Crane, furthermore, seems to have believed quite thoroughly in

the transvaluation of values which Nietzsche urged, for
he wrote to Munson in 1922 praising Joyce's *Ulysses*
and Waldo Frank's *Rahab* as novels which possessed "a
strong ethical and Nietzschean basis." There was no
element of paradox intended by Crane in these few words.
The first expression of his affinity with Nietzsche is
found in the 1918 article wherein Crane disagreed with
those Frenchmen who, in the heat of war fever, arraigned
Nietzsche as the prophet of the German militarists. From
the mass of contradictory writings which Nietzsche
scorned to explain, Crane found enough evidence to
convince himself that Nietzsche was being unjustly accused. "How paradoxical . . ." he wrote. "Nietzsche,
Zeppelins, and poisoned-gas, go ill together." The reasons
offered by Crane were that the philosopher had always
spoken of the Germans with contumely, that he had considered himself a Pole, that the French such as Montaigne
and Pascal were more influential in Nietzsche's life than
German thinkers and novelists, and, finally, that Nietzsche's exposé of bureaucratic militarism ("Here the autocratic machine is cooly exposed. He cites the direct control by the state over all educational institutions; the
inaccessibility to all personal distinction except through
some service, sooner or later, to the state; compulsory
military training; the supremacy of the army . . .") obviously rendered untenable any assertions that he was a
Prussian "herald."

While Hart was developing in terms of ideas, he was
drifting away from Christian Science. His mother had
arrived in New York City in the spring of 1917, and he
left his room to live with her in an apartment on Gra-

mercy Park. Mrs. Crane was still under the influence of Christian Science, and received customary therapeutic treatments from a Christian Science practitioner. Although Hart did not trouble to disillusion his mother, the copy of *Science and Health* given him by his grandmother and which he had brought from Cleveland had not performed its hoped-for function of keeping alive his faith in Mrs. Eddy's doctrines. This decline of belief is easily understandable in view of his close association with Joseph Kling and others who viewed Christian Science cynically. It was Kling who had written in *The Pagan* for September 1916 (the same issue which Crane had praised in his letter) that Christian Science was "a rotten, idiotic creed," and he mercilessly attacked the Science in other issues as well. The crux of Crane's approach to Christian Science at this time was that it seemed to be exercising a beneficial effect upon his mother by assisting her to overcome the emotional disturbances resulting from the divorce from her husband; therefore, he would not openly align himself against it so long as she depended upon her faith and his approval thereof. Actually, Hart's primary dissatisfaction with the Science stemmed from the movement's mandate that all believers in its healing aspects must also regard the Science as their form of religion. "I have unbounded faith in its efficacy," he wrote his friend William Wright in 1919. "Not that a normal optimism will not accomplish the same wonders,—it is a psychological attitude which will prevail over almost anything, but as a religion, there is where I balk. I recommend it to you if you are nervous, etc., though, as a cure, and the best and only one to my knowledge. What it says in regard to mental and nervous ailments is absolutely true." Upon returning to Cleveland in 1919, where his mother then lived, he continued the fiction of his belief. As he grew progressively less and less able to live harmoniously with his mother, however, his increasing distaste for the Science became more overt. "The weight of this terrible Christian Science satisfaction [of his mother and grandmother] I feel growing heavier and heavier on my neck," he wrote Gorham Munson in 1920. Thereafter, it was not long before his opposition was obvious to his family.

Crane's distrust of Christian Science as a way of religious faith was grounded in his inability to accept its dictate that matter was unreal, whereas mental life was real. "It is the total denial of the animal and organic world which I cannot swallow," he wrote in the letter to Wright. He needed a religion which included every phase of life and denied none. A portion of this more positive approach to the problem of religious belief was evidently contributed by Carl Schmitt, under whose guardianship Crane had been placed in December 1916.

In addition to being a painter, Schmitt possessed a more than ordinary devotion to poetry. He was a friend of poets—Conrad Aiken, Alfred Kreymborg, and Padraic Colum, among others—and wrote poetry for his own pleasure. A devout Catholic, he was intimately acquainted with the works of the great Catholic poets of the past and present. The works of Dante, for example, and the poems of Gerard Manley Hopkins, with which Schmitt was familiar before the book publication of Hopkins' poetry by Robert Bridges in 1918, were among his favorites, and there were long discussions between Hart and Schmitt in which the latter analyzed the work of Dante, Hopkins, and other poets and interested Crane in their ideas and technique. It was perhaps inevitable that,

among other issues, Catholicism should have been one of
the new areas to which Crane was introduced by his contact with Schmitt. Mrs. Crane relates that Hart found
himself attracted by the ritual and pageantry of the Catholic Church, with its emphasis upon symbolism, its admixture of miracle and mystery, and its use of incense,
holy water, vestments, lights, music, and the plastic arts
as accessories of worship. But he did not enjoy the
prospect of submitting to the discipline which the Church
required from its believers. This was not unexpected,
of course, from a personality as emotional, unrestrained,
and spontaneous as the one which was slowly beginning
to emerge from beneath the superficies of Crane's conventional appearance and behavior. (It was at this time,
too, that Crane, with the approval of Schmitt, came to
the conclusion that the imaginative fire which characterized his interest in poetry would be dampened by the
pedantic routine to which a college career would subject him, and both Schmitt and Crane managed to convince Mrs. Crane that her anticipations of a college education for her son were injurious to his best interests.)
Thus the spiritual pattern of Crane's life, already exposed
to three varieties of religion, was crystallizing: a mode
of apprehension and appreciation of God which would
be personal and without the benefit of an established
church or theology. Certainly William Blake, whose
poetry Crane had begun to read at length in early 1917
and which thereafter exercised a profound fascination
over him, contributed no little to this emergent faith.
Though Crane was not converted to Catholicism, the
fusion of religious feeling and artistic method which Blake,
Dante, and Hopkins had successfully effected in their
poetry, a contrast to the unimaginative aridity of Chris-

tian Science, left its mark upon him. It demonstrated
that the religious tendencies of his being might properly
find their way into his poetry as major factors; the self-
consciousness and cynicism which striated the spiritual
faith of his contemporaries in the 1920's was therefore
less pronounced in Crane. The Catholic poets' technical
freedom was also in consonance with the vast expansion
of Crane's artistic knowledge taking place in New York.

Crane returned to Cleveland for the first time in May
1918, at the request of his mother. It was now that the
impact of his experiences in New York assumed its true
weight upon him. For the war, with its regimentation,
intruded itself upon him more personally than before. Like
others who were too young to wear the uniform, Crane
was pressed into industrial war service in a munitions
plant. Personal freedom was no longer an aesthetic concept, but a living necessity which haunted him as he
performed his repetitive bolt-tightening operation on an
assembly line. At first he undoubtedly fancied himself as
another young Joycean artist enmeshed in a cycle of social and personal relationships conspiring to thwart his
artistic development. For in a letter written shortly after
his return, he referred to Joyce's *Portrait of the Artist
as a Young Man*: "The character of Stephen Dedalus is
all too good for this world. It takes a little experience—
a few reactions on his part to understand it, and could
this have been accomplished in a detached hermitage,
high above the mud, he would no doubt have preferred
that residence."† Despite the bitter tone of these re-

† *See Appendix.*

marks, they also serve to point up Crane's affirmation of experiences which, as he wrote of Joyce and Baudelaire, had brought on "a penetration into life common to only the greatest." But if the transplanting of the poet from Greenwich Village's expansive atmosphere to the mechical confines of a factory appeared psychologically enriching at first, by mid-August it began to assume the aspects of forced slavery. The glow of satisfaction Crane had derived from the confirmation in New York of his belief that he was made of superior stuff and designed for a life of art began to wear thin. It was a crucial moment in his career. Several possible courses were open to him: adherence to radicalism; rejection of all social commitments, and an alternate concentration on aesthetics; complete apathy and disinterest.

Paradoxically enough, Crane chose none of these alternatives. With the dramatic perversity characteristic of him in later years, he defiantly gave up his job, thrust all thought of poetry out of his mind, and marched off to enlist at a recruiting office. Without any doubt, the flood of contradictory and nerve-racking draft announcements, alternately stating and withdrawing policies and procedures, had much to do with this sudden act of self-immolation. A partial explanation is found in a letter to his school friend William Wright. There Crane carefully dissociated himself from the conventional motives for enlisting: "Let me clear myself. Heat and conditions at home (both of which you comprehend, I'm sure) drove me to the deed from which I was frustrated this morning. I take no credit for patriotism nor Bravery." In any case, it was a startling decision akin to embracing malignant fate with a vengeance. Ironically enough, the guard at the door refused him admission to the recruiting office because of the latest official announcement prohibiting minors from volunteering and providing that, if drafted, minors would be assigned to service jobs in industry. Thus rebuffed in his desperate effort to rid himself of the responsibility for making those personal decisions which would affect his maturity, Crane again foresaw an uncertain future in which the issues compelling him to enlist were still unresolved. To Wright he wrote: "I may go to New York, I may remain here, I may explode, Lord knows. Thank your stars that you have a settled course to follow, and write soon."

Though the situation in which he found himself was untenable for long, Crane made a determined effort to adjust himself in Cleveland. There were a few weeks of riveting at a Lake Erie shipyard, interrupted one day by an official announcement ordering him to prepare himself for induction into the Army. With justifiable bitterness, he failed to welcome this reversal of former policy, and could only see in it the haphazard workings of a vast, unthinking apparatus of the sort he had earlier mentioned in his article on Nietzsche. Before he could be drafted, however, the influenza epidemic raging in the army camps had killed more soldiers than the combined efforts of all enemy agents operating in this country and the shipment of recruits for mobilization was temporarily halted. In November the Armistice brought an end to the Army's need for additional manpower, and with it any necessity for a further decisive step on Crane's initiative. For several months, he worked as a newspaper reporter without attracting any attention to himself as a writer. This job soon came to an end, and he returned to New York early in 1919, fulfilling the second of the three possibilities earlier outlined for Wright. The explosion he had also hypothesized was reserved for the future, and then it came with finality.

The events of these Cleveland days afforded Crane little happiness. But they were profitable insofar as they speeded up the process by which his personality and philosophy were assuming a recognizable outline. Factory and shipyard mechanization woke him to an understanding of the nature of industrialism. It did so more effectively than the cartoons and articles of the New York radical magazines, for the ideas which they had reiterated were now seen to be more substantive than his inexperience had previously led him to appreciate. Abstractions became realities. Thus he wrote early in 1919 of Lola Ridge's *The Ghetto and Other Poems* (1918) that "Extremities in the modern world clash in a close proximity, so that there is a finer, harder, line than usual to divide them."† This was a retrogression from his enthusiastic championing of Baudelaire and Joyce in 1918 as great artists because "The principal eccentricitiy evinced by both is a penetration into life common to only the greatest," since it implied that Crane did not have confidence in his ability to successfully resolve the questions pregnant in reality. His Nietzschean hope of "standing entirely alone" in the world bolstered by "the equilibrium maintained by two opposite forces, equally strong"—so he had written his parents in 1917—was proving itself illusory. There were too many forces—personal, social, literary—and it was impossible to understand and subdue them in his present circumstances. He did not possess the sharp insight requisite for dissection and evaluation of the myriad factors complicating his world. Of this he was aware,

† *See Appendix.*

and in its stead there matured a sense of social isolation
and antagonism, a feeling all the more poignant because
it had not arisen voluntarily and he knew it as the reflection of his helplessness. This feeling was still inchoate,
however, and Crane was trying to keep him from losing
touch with the world.

Despite his growing bitterness and confusion, the few
months which Crane spent in New York during 1919
were passed in a spirit of eagerness for conventional social
adjustment, a primary aim now. But his search for a
remunerative occupation remained fruitless until his father
extended his aid and found a job for him toward the end
of his stay. Publishing houses, newspapers, feature syn-
dicates, advertising agencies—all turned him down when
he applied for a position. For a few months in the spring,
he ambitiously undertook to manage the advertising and
new subscription departments of *The Little Review*, having
concluded that the magazine offered the prospect "of
affording me over four thousand per year on commissions
if I can fill up the allowable space . . ." But it proved
impossible "to even break into some of these huge and
ominous mechanisms, New York Offices," let alone to
sell them magazine space. In the end, he obtained only
a few advertisements. His father inserted the series advertising "Crane's Mary Garden Chocolates" which appeared
during 1919 and 1920; it is likely that Crane obtained the
advertisement of "Stanislaw Portapovitch — Maitre de
Danse" which appeared in the June 1919 issue, and in
whose honor Crane wrote "To Potapovitch" (*Modern
School*, February 1919). In order to develop his abilities
as salesman and businessman, Crane decided to take a
summer course in business and advertising at Columbia
University.

"I agree with you," he wrote Wright, a poet who was working in a retail store, "that for such as ourselves business life is not to be scorned. The commercial aspect is the most prominent characteristic of America and we all must bow to it sooner or later. I do not think, though, that this of necessity involves our complete surrender of everything else nobler and better in our aspirations. Illusions are falling away from everything I look at lately. At present the world takes on the look of a desert,—a devastation to my eyes and I am finding it rather hard at best. Still there is something of a satisfaction in the development of one's consciousness even though it is painful. There is a certain freedom gained,—a lot of things pass out of one's concern that before mattered a great deal. One feels more freedom and the result is not by any means predominantly negative."

Though Crane did not study at Columbia as he had intended, the note struck in that letter marked his mood. The "series of experiences intense and rather savage" which he underwent in New York were satisfying albeit excruciating. The finale of Joyce's *Portrait* with its eager spirit undoubtedly recurred frequently to him: "Welcome O life! I go to encounter for the millionth time the reality of experience and to forge in the smithy of my soul the uncreated conscience of my race." In the prose written by Crane during this period, the reviews of Ridge and Bodenheim, this is the theme which is stressed. On the one hand, therefore, his relish for life evolved a strong compulsion towards a positive, organic relationship with the complex world. Opposed to it was his despair, which took refuge in people, events, and emotions that stimulated his sensibility, heightened his capacity to enjoy fresh stimulation, and increased the store of emotional experience which he could express in poetry.

2. "SONG OF MINOR, BROKEN STRAIN"

BY DECEMBER 1916, THE FIRST VOLUMES OF MANY new American poets who swept aside the post-Victorian traditions stifling literature in all its phases had been issued: Carl Sandburg's *Chicago Poems* in the same year . . . Robert Frost's *A Boy's Will* in 1912 . . . Ezra Pound's *A Lume Spento* in 1908 . . . John Gould Fletcher's *Fire and Wine* in 1913 . . . Vachel Lindsay's *General William Booth Enters Heaven* in 1913 too. Numerous magazines which offered their pages to new poets were going concerns, some of them for several years: *Poetry* since 1912 . . . *The Little Review* since 1914 . . . *Others* since 1915. In these magazines and their fellows, the work of lesser-known figures such as T. S. Eliot, Wallace Stevens, William Carlos Williams, and Richard Aldington began to appear. These poets and magazines were before long to become the predominant names in Crane's letters, and their critical and creative achievements were to exercise a molding effect upon Crane's poetry and ideas. Yet despite the abundance of literary activity stirring the country's readers, the issuance of a new advance-guard magazine did not escape the attention of Crane. In August, 1916, he wrote the letter commending *The Pagan* which has been quoted earlier.

Yet if Crane was aware of the "American Renaissance," if he realized that the scratchy pens and hairless brushes were being replaced with adequate instruments, he had not yet brought his own voice fully into tune with the times. He had been able to compliment *The Pagan* with no greater distinction than to crown it with the flavor of Oscar Wilde. His own work, the poems written from 1916 to 1920, reveal more of the *fin de siècle* influence of Wilde, for example, and other nineteenth century poets such as Swinburne, than they do the spirit and form of the more modern poets. One of Crane's poems, the first to be published, appeared in *Bruno's Weekly* for September 23, 1916. Entitled "C 33," which was the prison letter and number assigned to Wilde during his incarceration in Reading Gaol, the poem was placed on a double-page spread honoring the memory of Wilde with a drawing of the dead writer and a mass of poems by other Wilde enthusiasts including Lord Alfred Douglas, William Salisbury, Allan Norton, and someone cheerfully named Jubal Agmenon. "C 33" is quoted in full in the appendix to this book, as is another poem written prior to August 1916, "Carmen de Boheme," neither of which has ever been reprinted.

Although "Carmen de Boheme" appeared in the March 1918 issue of *Bruno's Bohemia*, there are at least two reasons why I have concluded that it was composed prior to August 1916. Stylistically, it is inferior to poems printed in 1916, 1917, and 1918. The poem is, furthermore, credited in *Bruno's Bohemia* to "Harold H. Crane," the manner in which Crane's name had been appended to "C 33" in the 1916 *Bruno's Weekly*, although by 1918 his poems in *The Pagan* and elsewhere were being signed "Hart Crane." The likelihood is that Crane submitted both "C 33" and "Carmen de Boheme" to Guido Bruno in 1916, but that Bruno, who edited *Bruno's Weekly*, *Bruno's Bohemia*, and other magazines in an accentric fashion, simply withheld the second poem until he used it to accompany two articles on Bohemia which appeared in the issue of *Bruno's Bohemia* containing "C 33."

Both "C 33" and "Carmen de Boheme" show clearly that the "stormy, husky, brawling" spirit of Sandburg, the oratory of Lindsay, and the more delicate sweep of Fletcher had not yet affected Crane. This may have been the result of his contact with Mrs. William Vaughn Moody who, although she was in close touch with the new American and British poets contributing to *Poetry*, probably was under the influence of the classic conventional form and diction with which her husband had clothed his essentially modern themes. Another agent which encouraged Crane to employ conservative forms of poetry was *Bruno's Weekly*, which Crane undoubtedly read as carefully at this time as in later years he was to pore over *The Little Review* and *The Dial*. Guido Bruno was enamoured of the poets of the 1890's, and the works of Wilde and Ernest Dowson are reprinted in issue after issue, often accompanied by articles and sketches lauding Wilde's writing and life. The title and subject of Crane's "C 33," for example, were no doubt suggested to him by an article in a January 1916 issue of *Bruno's Weekly* which related Wilde's prison experiences with great sympathy. From Wilde, Crane derived the tone of his early poems, and his language, too, upon occasions. Thus, the first stanza of Crane's "Echoes" carries reminiscences of two poems by Wilde, "Symphony in Yellow" and "La Mer," the last one of which appeared in *Bruno's Weekly* for April 1, 1916:

> Slivers of rains upon the pane,
> Jade-green with sunlight, melt and flow
> Upward again: they leave no stain
> Of storm or strain an hour ago. ("Echoes")†

* * *

> The yellow leaves begin to fade
>   And flutter from the Temple elms,
>   And at my feet the pale green Thames
> Lies like a rod of rippled jade. (from "Symphony in Yellow")

* * *

> The shattered storm has left its trace
>   Upon this huge and heaving dome,
>   For the thin threads of yellow foam
> Float on the waves like ravelled lace. (from "La Mer")

Before long, however, the impact of the new poetry had burst upon his consciousness, and by the close of 1916 Crane was already writing verse like "October-November" without rhyme and measure. *Bruno's Weekly* was again a factor in this development, for in addition to poems by Poe, Wilde and Dowson, it presented in its columns the early work of figures such as Aldington and Kreymborg, who sponsored free verse and imagism; Stephen Crane, an early vers librist and imagist; and Marianne Moore. Furthermore, the magazine carried a regular review of the contents of advance-guard magazines like *The Little Review*, *Poetry*, *The Egoist*, and *The*

† *See Appendix.*

Pagan, as well as frequent literary letters from Chicago, London, and Paris. The hotly-debated issue in many of these reviews and reports was the form and content of the new anti-Victorian poetry being composed in French and English. Had Crane not read the books or magazines containing this poetry, *Bruno's Weekly* would have brought it to his attention. But the tenets of imagism and free verse, except for one, did not develop to any great extent in Crane's poetry before 1920. The abhorrence of the abstract, the resolution to employ rhythm in terms of a phrase rather than a steady beat, the determination to utilize only those words directly related to the subjective or objective "thing" presented in a poem—except for "October-November" and "Forgetfulness," these reveal themselves only as a subcurrent in the poems written during Crane's period of poetic apprenticeship. More than anything else, it was the brilliant color and description of imagism which attracted Crane, and this was so because of the dominant place which the sensuous and exotic maintained in his personality and in the poetry of his masters. Crane's love of the gorgeous and the colorful found fertile play in the plastic and musical arts, and these interests are given varying expressions in some of his early poems: opera in "Carmen de Boheme," ballet in "To Potapovitch," painting in "The Bathers." But not much more of imagism remains in his poetry because of the training he was shortly to receive.

After Crane arrived in New York in December 1916, he worked for many months on his poetry under the direction of Carl Schmitt. Schmitt was acquainted with a number of poets who were largely conventional in a literary sense, men such as Colum, Aiken, and William

Vaughn Moody's friend Ridgely Torrence. It was Aiken, for example, who had viewed with horror in 1913 the crimes against poetry which were being committed by Harriet Monroe and the contributors to the early issues of her *Poetry*. Possibly under the influence of these conservative poets, who seem to have been mainly concerned with techniques of versification, with rhyme and with meter, and on the basis of his own belief that craft is fully as important as meaning, Schmitt immediately sensed the rough music of Crane's poetry and realized that it was an outstanding fault in the boy's poems. Under his direction, Crane worked industriously at the subtilizing of his rhythm, employing the resources of verbal virtuosity wherever possible. Any tendency he may have had to write in *vers libre* was thus subjugated and explains the preponderance of rhymed verses over free verse poems for the next two years. Out of seventeen known poems written by Crane from the beginning of 1917 until the early months of 1919, only five were in free verse. An important feature of Schmitt's teaching was the composition of nonsense verses in which meaning played no part; the main purpose was to exploit the sounds of words and letters as if they were musical notes. Both Schmitt and Crane composed these verses, declaiming them aloud upon completion, and listening carefully for variations in meter and tone color, for alliteration, rhyme, assonance, and onomatopoeia. Under this careful training, the crudities of "Carmen de Boheme" gave way to the smooth workmanship of "In Shadow" (*The Little Review*, December 1917), a poem which Aiken was to praise ten years later in a review as one of the best pieces in *White Buildings* (1927), Crane's first collection of poetry.

Crane was learning the music of poetry from Schmitt's instruction. He was also learning from poets who preferred suggestion and allusion to the blatant use of description which dominated "Carmen de Boheme." Whereas the imagists had decided "To use the language of common speech . . . to present an image . . . to produce poetry that is hard and clear," these new influences introduced Crane to the French Symbolists, who had chosen the communication of complex emotional states by means of indirect devices including symbols, compressed metaphors, and subtle music which suggested rather than stated or described. An affinity with the Symbolists was inevitable for an individual of Crane's lush emotional nature. The externality of imagism could never have been sufficient alone for Crane, even though it did satisfy his sensuosity. The most important agents in this development were *The Little Review* and its editors, Margaret Anderson and Jane Heap. An anecdote related in Margaret Anderson's autobiography *My Thirty Years' War* (1930) indicates the nature of the criticism both she and Miss Heap gave to young poets like Crane and which inclined them to the Symbolist school: "The younger poets came for talk. We had long discussions on the making of poetry—stamping it indelibly with the element of one's self, measuring the area of one's personal existence, searching the specific gravity of emotions, weighing the content of one's thoughts, checking up on one's observation. Hart Crane came in with one of his first poems. It contained a vague reference to the immaculate white ice of Norway. Immaculate is a dirty word to use, said Jane. That ice is so white it looks black." Apparently these criticisms were taken seriously, because Crane's

"North Labrador" gives us neither white nor immaculate ice, only "leaning ice/Hugged by plaster-grey arches of sky." Under this guidance, the echoes of Keats (compare Crane's "Modern Craft" [1918] with Keats' "Modern Love"), the Swinburnian notes of "Carmen de Boheme," and the imagism of "October-November" were dispersed, to reappear in less obvious guise and dominated by overtones of the Symbolist poets.

Because Crane had for so long been concerned with the technique of poetry, the emphasis in Symbolist poetry upon the revelation of inner emotional meaning was a progression beyond the training he had received under Schmitt. Since most of the Symbolists—Verlaine and Mallarmé, for example—had not dispensed with rhyme and meter in their poetry, they did not influence Crane to turn to the cadenced phrases of free verse. But they did inspire him to revolt against the empty dominance of form and flair in a poetry devoid of reference. The expression of these ideas took form in his Joyce letter of 1918, wherein Crane defended Joyce, sections of whose *Ulysses* had been running in *The Little Review*, against the attacks of a reader who had criticized Joyce. The general import of Crane's letter was that literature must contain a meaning, that this meaning must be derived from an experience of all aspects of life, and that Joyce adhered to both requirements. The organic relationship of an artist with varieties of human experience does not lead to "decadence," Crane went on to say, nor to "immorality and obscenity." The artist must search into the heart of things for spiritual meanings, Crane implied, and regardless of the flotsam and jetsam which he brings to the surface, there is no other way in which he can function vitally and with integrity, no other way in which he can obtain the dra-

matic quality often absent in a self-centered art. The
artist may suffer, as did Stephen Dedalus or the Wilde of
"C 33," but in the end he achieves a spiritual reward—
"Mercy, white milk, and honey, gold love . . ." — and the
pity and understanding of the "Materna." Crane's belief
that an artist must enter wholeheartedly into experience
was a serious one. In his 1919 review of a book of poems
by Lola Ridge, for example, he praised her poetry for
its "dramatic 'awareness,' or a kind of sharp recognition,
of . . . [the] dominating aspects of her time . . . She is
seldom immersed in herself,—she seems never to lose consciousness of surroundings." And in a review of Maxwell Bodenheim's *Minna and Myself*, which appeared
shortly after the Ridge review, Crane took issue with
Bodenheim's assertion that human interests could not form
an imaginative groundwork for poetry.†

His intense desire for experience outside of art did not
mean, however, that he was opposed to further experimentation, or that he believed that he had achieved as full a
command of the medium of poetry as necessary and would
now devote himself to theme only. He was acute enough
to declare that Bohenheim's poetry, despite its brilliance of
language and image, was deficient as poetry precisely because the latter negected his meter and rhythm: "His
poems are often little heaps of images in which the verbal
element is subordinated, making for an essentially static
and decorative quality." (Crane may have been especially
sensitive on this point because his own "Forgetfulness"
and most of "C 33" are aptly described by that sentence.)
Like a good student, Crane attacked his old teachers
when he came to discover their flaws. Swinburne was
castigated in the Joyce letter on the grounds that he had

† *See Appendix.*

over-done the very same "verbal element" in his poetry:
"I am not yet aware that Swinburne ever possessed much
beyond his 'art ears,' although these were long enough,
and adequate to all his beautiful, though often meaningless mouthings. His instability in criticism and every form
of literature that did not depend almost exclusively on
sound for effect . . . are notorious." The wit of Wilde,
which he had regarded so highly only a few years
before, was now seen to be sophistical in a derogatory
sense. "And as to Wilde," he wrote in the same letter,
"—after his bundle of paradoxes has been sorted and
conned,—very little evidence of intellect remains. On
the other hand, he believed that those who flung "decadence" as a term of opprobrium at Joyce did not do so
because his work reflected an actual decay of moral and
intellectual standards; their abuse was motivated directly
by the innovations of his prose, and he could not agree
that a "change in form, viewpoint, or mannerism" deserved such treatment. It had much better be reserved
for those who could not or did not dare to advance their
art. "Sterility is the only 'decadence' I recognize," he
wrote.

Crane was striving for an expressive relationship in
which technique was organically fused with sense. What
this sense might be he had not yet discovered. As indicated earlier, factory experiences and the nervous strain
of the pre-Armistice months had reduced his confidence
in his ability to develop a coherent pattern from the
seething chaos which composed his world. His inability
to rationalize conflicts did not swerve him from his desire to be one with the "animal and organic world,"
and he had a distaste for pure aestheticism. Since he could
not himself impose an intellectual control over his envi-

ronment, he very naturally saw no value in so-called "propaganda" art or in the sort of poetic journalism which Amy Lowell had written in the topical *Can Grande's Castle*. The answer to Crane's problem came to him buttressed by his spiritual and social experiences. It envisioned the possibility of transcending the mundane by means of imaginative perception and creation, while at the same time maintaining a relationship with it through the technical constituents of his craft. Crane's review of Sherwood Anderson's *Winesburg, Ohio* contains an implicit formulation of this theory, important in Crane's mature religious mysticism.† The weight of Anderson's achievement in the short stories which compose that book was measured against that of Edgar Lee Masters in *Spoon River Anthology*. Although the bare statement and harsh realism of Masters was a potential source of fruitage, Crane reacted with disfavor to the emotional barrenness of his method. It was the realistic observation of a Balzac which Masters employed in his depiction of the particular. But Anderson had outstripped Masters, combined the realistic detail of Balzac with his own imaginative insight and emotional sympathy, and had thus been able to present a "sustained inner illumination and bloom" which could not be found in the *Spoon River* poems. "The Puritan that stalks through the swamps of 'Spoon River' is manifest also in 'Winesburg'," Crane wrote, "but he is here a little less gaunt; I will not say more or less historically 'true,' although I do maintain that Sherwood Anderson, while typifying him strongly in local garments and habits, has nevertheless somewhat modified him with a certain beauty and suggestiveness of his universal recurrence in many ages." Masters had given a convincing rep-

† *See Appendix.*

resentation of the temporal structure of reality, its thwarting aspects. It was Anderson, however, in Crane's belief, who had transcended the temporal and spatialized
man's predicament, thereby alleviating the pain which
might otherwise destroy us if we believed these tragic
aspects to be ultimate reality. As manifestations of a
greater reality, the phenomena of human life dwindle in
importance and gain a more tolerable perspective; thus
Crane could remain attached to the reality of matter
while passing beyond it to join in harmony with a superior world of universal forms. Crane wished, then, for
more than the portrayal of phenomenal existence in art, for
more than the "static and decorative quality" which exclusive devotion to the physical world allowed.

Something of this quest for universal realities is to be
found in the poetry written by Crane during his 'teens.
The timelessness of "eternity" is indicated in "North
Labrador" by consideration of the nature of time, which
is said to be non-sequential in movement . . . units of
temporal duration simply alternate their position with one
another, but do not follow one behind the other, just as
a person shifts his weight from one foot to the other
and back again but does not move forward or backward
("there is only the shifting of moments/That journey
toward no Spring—"). "North Labrador" reveals a
hopelessness, a sense of nihilism, about the universe ("No
birth, no death, no time nor sun/In answer"). In "Meditation," however, Crane is anxious to pierce the veil
cloaking the universe:

> I have drawn my hands away
> Like ships for guidance in the lift and spray
> Of stars that urge them toward an unknown goal.
> Drift, O wakeful one, O restless soul,

Until the glittering white open hand
Of heaven thou shallt read and understand.†

The poetry written by Crane prior to 1920 may be considered to constitute the first period of his literary development. As in the case of "Carmen de Boheme," the date of publication in a periodical does not provide an accurate index of the date of composition. Crane was not satisfied with the poems of this first period, and included only two of them ("North Labrador" and "In Shadow") in *White Buildings*. Considered as a group, the quality of these early poems is uneven. Most of them deal with personal feelings ("Fear," "Echoes," "Carrier-Letter," "Interior,"‡ etc.), but the complexities of Crane's emotions are not encompassed in his lines. This vagueness is traceable, in part, to his emotional immaturity; he had not yet reached the age of twenty when they were written. Thus he can only picture over and over again "An imagined garden grey with sundered boughs" ("Postscript"). Those poems in which physical description is a paramount concern ("In Shadow," for example) are far more successful than the poems of feeling. In matters of technical import, Crane is not always happy either. Thus he is given to "poetic" diction ("wine-hot lips," "dove," "night's chorister," "the heron has passed by"), to classical mythology ("Venus," "Medusa"), to inversions of language ("And he tented with far truths he would form"), to sloppy rhyming ("shiver" and "shiver" in "Annunciations"; "Pierrot" and "Chloe" in "To Potapovitch"), to affectations in titles of poems ("Legende," and a variant

† *An unpublished poem.*
‡ *See Appendix.*

title of "Carrier-Letter": "Exile (After the Chinese)"), to poor taste in language ("A gypsy wagon *wiggles, striving* straight;" my italics, B. W.), and finally to the use of carelessly-chosen words ("Falls like slow rain that whispers to forget . . . It laves with coolness *tarnished* lips and eyes;" my italics, B. W.).

Yet, against this roll-call of sins, there can be no doubt about the truth of Gorham Munson's statement in *Destinations* (1928) that "at sixteen he [Crane] was writing on a level that Amy Lowell never rose from . . . " The internal rhyming ("sensed" and "descent" in "Annunciations"), the gorgeous relevant colors of "October-November," the synesthesia of "C 33" ("you who hear the lamp whisper thru night"), the fertile range of similes ("Forgetfulness"), the movement of "To Potapovitch," the delicate mood of "In Shadow," and the passionate interest in metaphor ("The Hive")—these more than overbalance and compensate for deficiencies which his lines also carry. It is difficult to find another poet in the pages of *The Pagan*, for example, whose work is comparable with these early poems by Crane.

If these poems are examined for their specific relationship to Crane's later work, many foreshadowings of his mature style and subject are in evidence. It is true that his major themes of insecurity ("Fear"), love, the preconscious ("Annunciations"), and the affirmation of suffering ("C 33" and "The Hive") are found in these poems; death, however, had not yet become a component of his poetry. Although the language of these poems is generally simple and direct, some esoteric terms like "predestiny" ("Annunciations") are employed. A positive love-note may be seen in "In Shadow," which bears comparison for mood with Eliot's similar "La Figlia che Piange." The juxtaposition of disparate detail and allusion which must be united in the reader's mind, a characteristic of Symbolist poetry and a chief device of the mature Crane, distinguishes the lines of "Annunciations," a poem which might just as easily be said to concern itself with the dream-world as with the moment in which a man rouses himself from sleep. Indeed, some of the poems are genuinely obscure, as in "Modern Craft" where it is almost impossible to decide whether Crane is viewing a living person or the representation of a woman in sculpture or painting.

Fortunately, additional light can be thrown on Crane's obscurity by virtue of the existence of several versions of some of the poems written in this first period. It would seem that the revisions which he made, while they undoubtedly improved the lines in which the changes occurred, often shrouded the original meanings and invoked ambiguity. This can be seen from a brief glance at "Legende."† A 1918 version of the poem, entitled "Naiad of Memory," is quoted here:

> The tossing loneliness of many nights
> Rounds off my memory of her.
> Like a shell surrendered to evening sands
> Yet called adrift again at every dawn,
> She has become a pathos,—waif of the tides.
>
> The world has had its way . . .
> Though the smiles of many an adolescent moon
> Have held her,
> The sand of time flows barren through my fingers
> And even memory will be erased
> As a cameo the waves claim again.

† *See Appendix.*

The 1919 version had no changes in the first stanza which
were of any significance, but the second stanza was radically rewritten:

> The sand and the sea have had their way,
> And moons of spring and autumn,—
> All, save I.
> And even my vision will be erased
> As a cameo the waves claim again.

The transformation of form and substance is striking.
Roughly paraphrased, the 1918 version of the second
stanza relates that society, custom, events ("world") have
followed their routine pattern and effectively separated
the poet from his memory; though the adolescent poet was
able to maintain a communion of spirit with the feminine subject, the passage of time has destroyed this relationship and left his life empty. Soon the particular details which constitute his memory will disappear in the
same manner that the ceaseless friction of the sea smooths
out the raised surface of a cameo. In the 1919 version,
the first line has been integrated with the central metaphor of the poem and strengthened thereby. The second
line, however, has become ambiguous. The reader can conjecture that "moons of spring and autumn" refers to the
flow of time, but he may legitimately question whether
Crane meant that "the sand and the sea have had" the
"moons" in addition to "their way," or if the "moons,"
like "the sand and the sea," also "have had their way."
The second interpretation, of course, is the correct one.

Another interesting aspect of Crane's early method of
writing is the beginning of his mosaic work, his habit of
constructing new poems interlaid with fragments rescued
from older poems. Whenever Crane discarded a poem
for any reason whatever, he made it a point to extract there-

from lines and phrases which he thought worthy of preservation, and these he used again in some new composition. Some examples are in order. The third and fourth
lines of "Carmen de Boheme" read: "Plaintive yet proud
the cello tones resume/The andante of smooth hopes and
lost regrets." When the poem was junked by Crane,
the fourth line found its way into "Meditation," as follows: "The andante of vain hopes and lost regret/Falls
like slow rain that whispers to forget." When "Meditation" was discarded by Crane, the image assumed its last
resting-place in 1921 in "A Persuasion."† Accompanying
it, furthermore, was another line from "Meditation" ("I
have drawn my hands away"), so that its final appearance
took this form:

> She has drawn her hands away.
> The wind plays andantes
> Of lost hopes and regrets,—
> And yet is kind.

Other lines from "Meditation" ended up in "Faustus and
Helen" and in "Porphyro in Akron."

The self-consciousness of an artist is often a criterion
of the extent to which he will bring his potentialities to
their fullest point of realization. The inferior artist re-
gards the last piece of work completed as his best, with
the result that he feels no compulsion to polish, to chip
away, and otherwise bring the production to a finer state
of achievement. He is rarely aware that there is any possibility of improvement, and often he is too obtuse to detect the flaws which exist. Thus he does not grow in
quality. Crane was decidedly of that other breed which
pitilessly views each finished work of art as a stepping-

† See Appendix.

stone to better work, to work which will encompass more of that perfection which the artist may never actually achieve. Therefore, he subjected each poem to ruthless scrutiny, and a poem was never completed until it had taken all the retouching and revision which his critical faculties found requisite. Crane's self-critical attitude is manifest in a letter written in November 1918 to an amateur publisher whom he was anxious to interest in the printing of a small volume of his poetry, and to whom he had sent a bundle of poems: "While I am certain that you will be the first to detect any flaws and aberrations in these lyrics, I know that you will be alive to whatever beauty they may contain . . . There is still hope, as I am yet under twenty."

II

"THE TECHNIQUE OF ESCAPE"

3. "PORPHYRO IN AKRON"

PROLOGUE

IN A LETTER WRITTEN TO GORHAM MUNSON LATE IN 1922, Crane described with sympathetic compassion an individual who had impressed Munson unfavorably. It was at Crane's recommendation that this man had visited Munson in New York, so he endeavoured to explain why he possessed a considerable degree of liking for the man:

"Poor . . . [X]!" he wrote. "I feared you would not like him very much. My affection for him is based on a certain community of taste and pursuit we have which you will understand. Because he has been mewed up so long with unpleasant work . . . in a city where conversation and letters never existed—he has, out of sheer ennui, been forced to find entertainment in ways which have taken the best of him to feed what has become a sort of obsession . . . in his letters and on his favorite topic you get as strong a satire as Petronius'. Life has tamed him him terribly—yet he has lived a great deal if the senses mean anything."

With a revision of some of the biographical details in the above paragraph so as to bring them into accord with the facts of Crane's life, the lines would serve equally well to indicate the nature of Crane's development from 1919 until the spring of 1923. Indeed, the second clause of the last sentence may be taken as a leitmotif of the accumulated result of these years: "***He has lived a great deal if the senses mean anything." Pressed by an uncongenial social environment, guided by friends and other influences into paths of isolation, filled with an unbreakable need for poetic creation, he blended these opposing forces into a sensuous and abstract harmony that was centrifugal in nature and could only be maintained by ever-increasing admixtures of the intrinsically-destructive elements. Thus he became a vessel of fragility.

"INFLUENCE OF MERCANTILE LIFE"

In November 1919, Crane returned for the second time to Cleveland from New York; this time he bore with him the promise of a job in his father's expanding enterprises. It appeared likely to him that his adjustment to business life, which he now considered an inevitability, would realize itself in Akron, for soon after his arrival he was sent to that city to begin working in the drug store branch of the family business. The first weeks in Akron generated a mood favorable to the course of events. "The size of my father's business has surprised me much," he wrote Munson. "Things are whizzing, and I don't know how many millions he will be worth before he gets through growing. If I work hard enough I suppose I am due to get a goodly share of it, and as I told you, it seems to me the wisest thing to do just now to join him." This optimistic "Billy Sunday" spirit, as he defined it, was motivated by the belief that before long he would be away from Akron, located in another metropolitan center like

New York, possibly San Francisco, Kansas City, or New York itself. The elder Crane's plans for his business were ambitious and expansive, and he had intimated to Hart that he might soon receive a promotion as an out-of-town salesman. For now Hart felt more like a New Yorker than a Middle Westerner, and spoke with light mockery of Ohio's "great expanses of cornfields"; the "fresh growth" of Akron, with a treble increase in population since 1910 because of the automobile industry's demand for the products of its many new rubber factories, he viewed as if it were like the western frontier to which his ancestors had journeyed from the eastern coastal states: "It looks, I imagine, something like the western scenes of some of Bret Harte's stories."

Almost from the very beginning, however, Crane evinced dissatisfaction with the arrangements under which he worked, and with some justice. The seventeen hours he spent in the drug store, from six in the morning until eleven at night, allowed little remaining time for more than routine duties. "New theories" were filling his head every day as he eagerly scanned the work of the experimental poets, but there was neither "time or the proper mood" available in which he might transcribe his ideas and emotions to paper. Yet, as he plaintively wrote Munson: "I like to keep on writing a little, at least, of good quality . . . " By the middle of December, however, he had done no more than complete one poem which he had begun early in November, while still in New York, in addition to several random lines. This poem was "My Grandmother's Love Letters," one of Crane's few efforts in free verse and pre-eminently an example of his increasing willingness to experiment with poetic technique. One finds Crane using end rhymes, sight rhymes, assonance, and a phrasal cadence quite unique in his work; the "s" sound running through the lines serves as a beautiful reminder of the murmur of "soft rain" with which the poem opens and closes. Although "My Grandmother's Love Letters" is one of Crane's minor poems, it far outshone his earlier efforts and he was pleased with his mastery of the free verse technique, superficially freer than his habitual meter and rhyme form but actually as difficult to carry off successfully. His sense of achievement was also stirred because he had been able to adhere to the dictate he set himself when beginning the poem, not to be too sentimental and not to be too sophisticated, both of which dangers he faced because of proximity to his grandmother and the nature of his subject. "My Grandmother's Love Letters" is noteworthy, further, because it is one of the few poems Crane ever wrote in which he departed from the subjective realm to explore the content of another person's emotional life. Although he did not succeed in realizing this aim, there is an air of detachment in the poem which follows as a result of his selflessness of purpose; the poem is strangely ironic in flavor. Upon bringing the poem to completion, Crane sent it off to *The Little Review;* after being rejected, the poem was accepted by *The Dial.* When it appeared in the April 1920 issue of that magazine, Crane wrote Munson that it had been inspired by some poems of Charles Vildrac. Crane's sense of dependency upon other writers, perhaps natural in a poet of his young years, reflected an actual state of affairs. Not only Vildrac, but traces of William Vaughn Moody ("The Daguerreotype"), Paul Verlaine ("Ariettes Oubliées V"), and John Gould Fletcher ("Ghosts of an Old

House") may be detected in the lines of "My Grand-mother's Love Letters." During the two years which followed this poem, he was to continue under the influence of writers whose work affected him with their style and themes, only shaking loose from subordination in the latter part of 1921.

The days and nights in Akron were barren for Crane. They might have overwhelmed him were it not, among other salutary factors to be described, for the correspondence he was carrying on with his literary friends. To the state of frigid despair in which he was often immersed in the drug store or in his little room at the Hotel Akron and later the Hotel Bond, the frequent New York letters of Gorham Munson and Matthew Josephson were like birds from a warmer region. Literary news and gossip . . . advice to read the plays of Marlowe and Webster . . . sincere and enthusiastic praise and criticism of his poems and ideas . . . manuscripts of poems, plays, and translations written by Munson and Josephson themselves—these and other evidences of sympathy and consideration combined to give him the pleasurable sensation of continued involvement in the intellectual currents which had made the metropolis so enlivening. Before leaving New York, Crane had received a letter of thanks from Sherwood Anderson, whose *Winesburg, Ohio* he had reviewed so favorably in the September 1919 issue of *The Pagan*. This epistolary friendship, opened so pleasantly for Crane, was now continued with mutual enthusiasm. Evidently the sensitive older Anderson was deeply moved at the efforts of another Mid-western youth to achieve literary expression in the same hostile environment from which he had with difficulty and determination wrested his creative existence many years before. The poetic impulse he sensed in

the prose "flesh and bone" of Crane's letters, where the
younger man honestly laid bare the mainsprings of his
thought and the emptiness of his Akron days, was as moving to him as the poems which accompanied the letters, and
Anderson devoted himself to personal encouragement of
the spirit which he could not bear to see extinguished.
With great tact, he related his own unhappy business
experiences in nearly Cleveland and Elyria, obviously
intending to demonstrate that Crane's present difficulties
were not insurmountable, nor at all unusual for the artist in twentieth-century America.   At the same time,
he further strengthened Crane's artistic resolve by directing his attention to the critical work of Van Wyck
Brooks, whose *The Ordeal of Mark Twain* was on the
verge of being published, and whose earlier studies had
stressed the importance for American culture of that
imagination and feeling which Anderson detected in
Crane.

Crane also found compensatory relief when the stream
of customers to his counter ceased for intermittent periods.   In these brief respites, he managed to satisfy his
thirst with the poetry of Eliot, the criticism of Pound,
and the varied contributions of *The Dial* and *The Little
Review*.   Reading became one of the primary vehicles
by which he managed to make palatable the tedious
working hours and the lonely nights spent in his room.
"I have 'gone to books for the doctor' so much that I
know the remedial shelves quite well," he wrote to William Wright.   In addition to the experimental poets and
the little magazines, Crane read widely in other fields,
thereby forming one of the important habits of his life.
His tastes in literature are indicative not only of his tem-

per at the time, but also foreshadow his mature personality, and they can be divided into several loosely-drawn
categories.

Early in his Akron stay, Crane's tortured spirits found
some relief in humorists like Mark Twain and Rabelais,
as well as in lesser iconoclasts like Mencken. The boisterous nature of these writers evoked a kindred hilarity
in Crane. It seemed to him that a sense of the ludicrous
was a quality which an artist could use in order to assert
himself against an oppressive foe. With true Menckenian spirit he wrote Munson: "Humor is the artist's only
weapon against the proletariat . . . I pray for both of
us,—let us be keen and humorous scientists . . . I would
rather act my little tragedy without tears . . ." There
is very little humor in Crane's poetry ("Bacardi Spreads
the Eagle's Wings" might be considered such, for example,
but is really ironic and bitter), and he was never able
to adhere to the resolve in life as well. What did remain was a form of Rabelaisian gusto which never deserted him, and which relieved the smouldering depth of
despair into which he was increasingly flung as his life
drew to a close. If this humorous propensity often took
on the shape of hysterical outbursts, it was only so because of the thwarting effects of experience upon Crane.
Another form of escape from Akron was the path of
romance . . . the story of Gauguin as told by W. Somerset Maugham in his novel *The Moon and Sixpence* and
by Gauguin himself in his autobiographical *Noa Noa*
is typical. Maugham's book struck Crane as presenting
a suitable course of action for the modern artist. From
Gauguin's own story of his life in the South Seas, which
may have helped foster Crane's interest in tropical land-

and seascape, he learned that the artist must rebel against
bourgeois values without regard for social consequences
whenever his artistic integrity is in jeopardy. In *Noa
Noa*, too, Gauguin expressed his belief in the primacy of
instinct over reason, and this was a thought that remained with Crane in view of his life-long devotion
to the primitive in art and life. Samuel Butler's novel
of revolt against father and authority, *The Way of All
Flesh*, was a book which brought the theme of rebellion
closer to home, and it made a profound impression upon
Crane in the crystallization of his opposition to his father.
But the most important category of Crane's reading was
his interest in psychological fiction. He first made the
acquaintance of Nietzsche's favorite, Stendhal, in *The
Charterhouse of Parma*, and later enlarged his knowledge
of the Frenchman's masterworks with a reading of *The
Red and the Black*. Dostoyevsky was even more exciting,
for in his work Crane's neuroticism could bathe deeply,
glut itself in the schizophrenic Russian personalities with
their uninhibited emotional spontaneity, and find itself
portrayed with more understanding and pity than his
father offered. "He *does* give one more life than my
mundane world supplies,—and stimulates," he wrote Munson, while reading *The Possessed* in the latter part of
1920. "He makes you forget yourself (should I better
say, lose) in the life of his characters for days at a time.
And how few writers can do that!" He had already
read *Crime and Punishment* by this date, and after completing *The Possessed* was still so enthused that he followed it with *The Brothers Karamazov* and Middleton
Murry's study of Dostoyevsky. In addition to the intense personal interest which Crane felt in the works,

he was overwhelmed with Dostoyevsky's psychological insight. "A careful reading of 'Dosty' ought to prepare one's mind to handle any human situation comfortably that might ever arise . . ." he wrote, revealing thereby the problem which was uppermost in his own mind.

Whatever reading Crane accomplished was effective only in temporarily removing him to a more refreshing locale peopled by more kindly or stimulating characters. Within a few weeks, his discontent had additional sustenance for growth. Christmas "with its usual inhuman rush in candy-selling" brought a horde of "discourteous people to wait upon," and the constant opening and closing of the drug store doors visited drafts of icy air upon Crane's tense and nervous body. When he could reflect calmly about his predicament, he sustained himself with the knowledge that his father was well pleased with his efforts in the Akron store, and in January would grant him the promotion he had promised. Then, at least, his evenings would be free for poetry. But even these prospects could not compensate for the ominous conclusion that his present life was "barbarous" and thwarted the intense urge he felt for poetic expression. Gradually Crane's former desire for integration into the dominant pattern of American life became subordinated to an intense rebellious ferment. The enthusiastic words he had addressed earlier in 1919 to William Wright about the beneficial values to be discovered in American business were discarded as he wrote to his friend (now a student at Columbia University) about "the stolid and narrowing influence of mercantile life." He could also remember with bitterness his rejection of his mother's anxious efforts to send him to college in 1918; nor was it pleasant to recall the casual dismissal of the plea she made in May 1919 that he enroll as a journalism student at Columbia, supported in his refusal by the reason that he would be required to spend two preliminary years in college before becoming eligible for journalism school. The reaction he now experienced against the success formula which had spurred him on to welcome a business association with his father was, of course, stimulated in great part by his own wretched experiences in Akron and Cleveland. The attitudes of Munson, Josephson, and Anderson also contributed a goodly portion to this negative state. Yet these men were neither united in a common program nor sufficiently powerful each in his own right for Crane to follow them implicitly; nor was Crane himself prepared at this period to personally synthesize the various impulses which each of his correspondents evoked in him.

"THIS CLEAVING AND THIS BURNING"

The cultural atmosphere of Cleveland presented a dismal face to Crane when he came back from New York in November 1919. Not one of the little magazines in which Crane's poems had appeared was at all popular in the city. From Richard Laukhuff, the bookseller at whose outpost Crane had previously been able to read and buy most of the advance-guard periodicals, he was unpleasantly surprised to learn that the eccentricities of *The Little Review* made it unpalatable to most Clevelanders, while *The Pagan* suffered a similar neglect because of its mildness. As for *The Modernist*, neither Laukhuff nor any other dealer in town had ever seen a copy. Akron, however, was another matter entirely. In the hurlyburly of its rapid climb to prosperity, it had

unintentionally given shelter to a group of dissident intellectuals who represented the antithesis of the ideals of
material success boosted by the Akron Babbitts at their
luncheon meetings.

This amorphous group centered itself, as in many
other American cities, on the island of a bookstore.
Managed by Herbert Fletcher, whom Crane had met several years earlier, the shop was located next door to
the Crane drug store in which Hart worked. Before
long, Crane became one of the bookshop's regular habi-
tues. Here he could forget the drug store and enjoy the
acid witticisms of Fletcher and other characters with
unconventional tastes and a talent for riotous story telling.
Although several of the men had ties of some kind with
the weakened strain of political liberalism remaining in the
United States, on the whole the so-called "Cleveland-
Akron gang" was not inclined to concern itself with
practical problems of social reform and protest. Instead,
the prevailing disillusionment with middle-class standards
of morality and culture which permeated American intellectual life in the post-war years seems to have affected
them too. They probably regarded themselves, as indeed
they were, as emancipated cultural rebels against the contemporary milieu. Like Anderson, these older men were
sympathetic to the young poet tied down by a wealthy
father to a tedious job a what Crane called "starvation
wages." They enjoyed the irony which had been visited on
the middle-class manufacturer, that of having an aesthete
for a son instead of a go-getting salesman, and regarded the
situation as symbolic of the inevitable futility of bourgeois
values. When Mr. Crane was upset to learn that Hart
had been described in an Akron newspaper interview as

the poet-son of a reputable Ohio businessman, they were gleeful at this "anachronism in Akron."

For his own part, Crane hungrily welcomed the attention and interest of these men as compensation for the lack of understanding he received from his family, and as a more immediate satisfaction than the long-distance friendship he maintained with his New York friends. It mattered little that some of his new friends were not artists; of greater significance was the mutual sense of isolation from a congenial environment in which cosmopolitan individuality could flourish and aesthetic pleasures be pursued with devotion. This common feeling of involuntary restriction attracted him to one of these intellectuals, for example, who as the son of an indulgent woman had been able to satiate his esoteric tastes in literature, art, and social pleasures to their full extent. Underlying the mutuality of interest between Crane and his new friends was his insecurity, which made him overly-impressed with their erudition and their sophistication, deferential and impressionable in his contacts with them.

"I was suddenly surprised last evening," Crane wrote of one of these men to Munson, "to hear him mention the Baroness [Loringhoven]. It seems he knows her very well. Knew her before she came to the Village and Margaret Anderson got hold of her at all, and believe me he had some surprising tales to tell. He goes on for hours telling of exotic friends of his and strange experiences. He know[s] Europe well, English country house parties and Washington society,— prizefighters, cardinals, poets, and sculptors, etc., and the wonderful thing is to find him here in Akron . . ."

In Hervey Minns, whom Crane introduced in *The Little Review* in 1920,† he had a more creative but none-the-less cosmopolitan figure. Supposedly a friend

† *See Appendix.*

of Eugene Victor Debs, as well as a self-styled an-
archist, Minns was a photographer of distinguished achievement and uncompromising integrity; his career represented for Crane a vindication of the thesis that the
artist is thwarted in America. Of him Crane wrote:

"A marvelous photographer, the only one in this country to hold the
Dresden and Munich awards, and who has several times been 'written
up' in the *International Studio*. Authorities rank him with Coburn
and Hoppé of London and there is no one in New York who com-
pares with him. He used to read *The Little Review*, knows Marsden
Hartley,—and lives in a tumble down old house in the center of
the city. I expect the pictures of me he takes to be wonders. He
refused to take the 'rubber-king,' F. H. Seiberling, for love nor money,
simply because he thought his face without interest."

From the wide-ranging interests of Minns and the other
men, Crane was to absorb new ideas and experiences involving art, literature, and society. It was Minns, for
example, who encouraged Crane to discard the Dadaist
"theory of interesting 'accidents' " and to remain firm
in the belief that "There is little to be gained in any art
. . . except with much *conscious effort*." From another,
Crane was made aware of the beauties of Oriental sculpture and painting, and so on. The bitterness and contempt which these men felt for their surroundings expressed itself frequently in the form of sardonic humor.
As amateur bibliophiles, their reading tastes were catholic,
especially so in fields whose propriety and validity were
questioned by the genteel tradition. Thus Crane became
familiar with the satire of Swift and Cervantes, the lustier
classics of Catullus and Petronius, the bawdiana of Eugene Field and Mark Twain, the grostesqueries of Rabelais, and the contemporary wistfulness of James Branch
Cabell and braggadocio of H. L. Mencken. Hart's

new acquaintances also encouraged his opposition to continued adjustment with the social forces represented by his father. They, of course, were not the only ones to heighten his antagonism, for even at the drug store Hart's fellow employees resented the presence of the boss' son and made him acutely uncomfortable (I have a kind of tacit quarrel with everyone at the store, in spite of smiles, etc. . . ."). He first attempted to escape from the aimless wretchedness of existence in petty ways which were essentially inconclusive and unsatisfying, taking refuge in fictitious headaches which permitted him to stay away from the store, or else daydreaming about possible illnesses which would furnish the "time to read and 'work' a little more." But the atmosphere of rebellion and decadence enveloping the circle in which he was moving offered more positive forms of escape, and nourished the conception of himself as a sensitive artist. From his contacts with his new friends and the other people he was meeting, emotions were aroused, facets of his personality unfolded themselves, and he formed new habits. In general, the implications of these new flowerings, and the strengthening of the old sprouts, may be summarized as a heightening of his sensuous need and capacity, and the assumption of a Dionysian pattern of life.

The Dionysian achieves release from restraint by a variety of procedures, all of which strain and torment to excess the mental and physical organism. In the case of Crane, the chief devices became alcohol, emotional excitement, erotic passion, and music. A simple procedure by which the rebellious spirit of the nineteen-twenties could simultaneously gratify his sensuousness and concretize the gap that existed between himself and the proletariat-middle class (disdain for the "booboisie" was a component factor of the élite configuration) was to consume as much liquor as might be stealthily obtained in violation of the then-effective prohibition laws. The 18th Amendment to the United States Constitution, and the laws which enforced it, were regarded by many as violations of personal liberty. Some resented the curb on liquor manufacture and sales as insulting because it placed so many upright characters in the same category as the beer-swilling, saloon-frequenting laborer. Others, discontented for different reasons perhaps, fore-saw a complete breakdown of the traditional alliance of wine and art: was all of Greek mythology, the poetry of Swinburne, and the inspirational effect of the fermented grape to be crushed by cheap politics? Luckily for Crane, some of his friends knew their way about Akron, and could obtain home-made liquor from the immigrant element of the city. Now a "debauch" became something of which Crane could write with pride to Munson: "Akron has afforded me one purple evening . . . I got dreadfully drunk on dreadful raisin brew, smoked one of the cigars made especially for the Czar, defunct, of Russia . . . You will believe me an ox when I tell you that I was on the job again next morning, and carried the day through with flying colours." And on another occasion: "I went to visit my Akron friend armed with two bottles of dago red. That didn't suffice after we got started, and a quart of raisin jack was divided between us with the result that the day proper (after the night before) was spent very quietly, watered and Bromo-Seltzered, with amusing anecdotes occasion-

ally sprouting from towelled head to towelled head."
In moments like these Crane enjoyed the "bath in the
unconscious" which alcohol could provide. The sprees,
at first haphazard and without reference to his interest
in poetry, soon became more premeditated in character
when he learned that his imaginative faculties were stimulated to a higher pitch by alcohol. They form the basis
for Crane's later addiction to liquor, by which time he
could no longer free himself from the innocently-acquired
habit. The emotional exacerbation to which he subjected
himself is illustrated in a description of a prize-fight which
he attended with a friend.

"Many matches are boresome," he wrote Munson, "but provide two
sublime machines of human muscle-play in the vivid light of a 'ring,'—
stark darkness all around with yells from all sides and countless eyes
gleaming, centered on the circle,—and I get a real satisfaction and stim-
ulant. I get very heated and shout loudly, jump from my seat, etc.,
and get more interested every time I go. Really, you must attend a
bout of two in N. Y. where a real knock-out is permitted."

The sadistic element in that dramatic picture was balanced
by a delight in suffering, as if the mortification of his
mind and body unlocked a world of joy for him.
"Beauty has most often appeared to me in moments of
penitence and even sometimes, distraction and worry,"
he wrote in 1920.

But undoubtedly the most effective method by which
Crane simultaneously increased and discharged nervous
and physical tension was his newly-evolved and accepted
sexual status. All the letters written by Crane prior to
December 1919 which I have seen give no indication that

sex was a problem in his life, although with the advantage of hindsight one can discern evidences of conflict in seemingly-innocent passages. His first mention of a love relationship with anyone occurs in a letter to Munson written during December 1919. It was an ambiguous remark—"I . . . have embarked on a love affair, (of all places unexpected, here in Akron)"—which probably aroused little curiosity on Munson's part. A letter which followed closely thereafter was more revelatory, since Crane anticipated moving to Cleveland shortly after Christmas, and a separation from his lover was therefore imminent. With the usual lack of personal reticence that marked his letters, he was impelled by his anguish to break the following news to Munson: "This 'affair' that I have been having, has been the most intense and satisfactory one of my whole life, and I am all broken up at the thought of leaving him. Yes, that last word will jolt you." The letter implied quite clearly that this was not Crane's first love affair, whether heterosexual or homosexual is not made clear. In any case, it was not Crane's first contact with homosexuality; in the letter to Munson, Crane appears to be announcing the culmination of a predisposition rather than a discovery. Some time before 1917, while Crane was still a student in high school, a friend relates that Crane had had intimate relations with an older man whom he greatly admired. There is no evidence to indicate the nature of these relations, but Crane expressed himself strongly at that time in support of tolerance for the older man, who had been accused of homosexuality, and gave a number of arguments in favor which occur frequently in the self-justifications of deviants. This incident occurred at the time

when Crane was under the influence of the 1890's. The
decadent quality infiltrating into English literature and art
of the *fin de siècle* period had produced a favorable climate for sexual experimentation, and in the formulation
of this tolerance Oscar Wilde was a prime mover. Favorably inclined by his own nature and experiences, as
well as by a literary movement whose principles and productions he respected, Crane entered Greenwich Village
where, then as now, a profound revolution in morals
and taste had created an interest in experiences bursting
the bounds of convention. A writer who was friendly
with Crane in 1919 relates, although he did not recognize
it at the time because of inexperience, that Crane's attitude to him was almost that of a man courting a lover.
By December 1919, when Crane returned to Cleveland,
he was fully prepared to bring to fruition the inclinations which had been germinating within him. Yet surely this submission to a powerful urge would not have
been precipitated were it not for the painful craving
for affection which animated him. Working at an unpleasant occupation, living in a tiny hotel room, he did
not receive from anyone that love which involved an
awareness of his individuality and an acceptance of his
innermost creative nature. When a person appeared who
possessed similar interests and could offer him the consuming warmth and attention which he desired, it was with
little hesitation that Crane bridged the gulf dividing
the deviant male from the dominant heterosexual pattern
of Western culture. "I have never had devotion returned before like this, nor ever found a soul, mind, and
body so worthy of devotion. Probably I never shall
again," he wrote. This requited love became the source

of a deep satisfaction which smoothed the grating surface of reality and enriched its pallid texture:

"My love affair is affording me new treasures all the time. Our holi-
days are spent together here in Cleveland, and I have discovered new
satisfaction at each occasion. The terrible old grind . . . is much
relieved by this. I live from Saturday to Saturday . . . Perhaps
this is the romance of my life,—it is wonderful to find the realization
of one's dreams in flesh, form, laughter and intelligence,—all in one
person. I am not giddy or blind, but steadier and keener than I've
ever been before."

The fulfillment of Crane's need for giving and sharing love brought with it certain inevitable consequences.
The invert in Western society becomes a member of that
tragic group described so well by Marcel Proust: "Lovers
from whom is always precluded the possibility of that
love the hope of which gives them the strength to endure so many risks and so much loneliness." The impossibility of forming a stable relationship was clearly demonstrated to Crane within a few months after the beginning of his love affair, when he sorrowfully informed
Munson that he had "seen love go down through lust
to indifference, etc." Despite the disillusionment which
attended the demise of this and subsequent early attachments, he was compelled to continue searching each time
for the person who would break the vicious certainty of
failure, and he did so with an idealism slated finally to
be replaced by a bitter disappointment encompassing every
cell of his being. "I'm caught dead tight in a new affair
de coeur that at least keeps me stirred up in some ways,"
he would write to Munson, buoyed by the excitement of
a new affair. Lurking in his mind, however, was the
realization that it would never be possible for him to
achieve the perfect love-relationship which his nature re-

quired, and the denouement would follow thereafter as
if ordained: "I don't know how much blood I pay for
these predicaments,— but I seem to live more during them
than otherwise. They give the ego a rest. I may sound
like an utter profligate,—but there is much sincerity, too
painfully much, for me to laugh." As a result of the
unrelenting persecution and opprobium which Western
society's barbaric moral principles provides for sexual
inverts, these unhappy people often huddle together so
that, to quote Proust again, "they form in every land an
Oriental colony, cultured, musical, malicious . . . the ex-
ceptional character of their inclinations making them regard themselves as superior to the other sex, look down
upon women, making homosexuality the privilege of great
genius and of great epochs of history . . ." Thus comes
about an estrangement from society and its mores which
is almost ineradicable. Crane, too, found comfort in pro-
jecting himself backward into previous eras when his form
of sexuality was not considered abnormal. It was easy
for him to do so, because of his introduction at the time
to the esoteric classics of Greek and Roman literature
which treated homosexuality without fear or shame. When
he described his lover as "Gold and purple. Anti-
noüs at Yale," referring to the boy who was loved by
Emperor Hadrian and frequently depicted in Roman art
and decoration as the archetype of youthful male beauty,
Crane, besides drawing on his knowledge of the historian
Dio Cassius, also revealed an implicit understanding of
the anachronism of such passion in his world. There is a
tone of defiance implicit too, as if his inclinations contained an exotic fabric of richness which twentieth-century America could neither equal nor appreciate proper-

ly. By 1923, Crane had reached the conclusion that he was out of time and out of place, and even the occasional moments when he might let himself be elated over seemingly-adequate love affairs did not serve to dissipate the core of tragedy which pervaded him. Early in 1923 he wrote Munson:

"I am in a very unfavorable mood, and just after having congratulated myself strongly on security against future outbreaks of the affections. You see, for two or three years I have not been attacked in this way. A recent evening at a concert some glances of such a very stirring response and beauty threw me into such an hour of agony as I supposed I was beyond feeling ever again. The mere senses can be handled without such effects, but I discover I am powerless as ever against those higher and certainly hopeless manifestations of the flesh. O God that I should have to live within these American restrictions forever, where one cannot whisper a word, not at least exchange a few words! In such cases they almost suffice, you know."

Social isolation, because of the impossibility of being permitted to enjoy a deviant love relationship, fostered a sense of guilt within Crane, since he was essentially a person who believed confusedly in bourgeois values and in the ethical precepts which govern Western society. His sense of guilt was more intense because of the seeming inevitability of his deviation from the code, and showed itself in the excessive masculinization of his appearance and personality: thus he over-emphasized his predominantly-masculine characteristics in an effort to compensate for and mask the seemingly-feminine . . . he smoked heavily, and cigars almost to the exclusion of cigarettes . . . his clothing and bearing were conventional and contrived. Herein, too lies another reason for his excessive drinking, the accomplishment of which might be expected to demonstrate the strength and capacity traditionally assigned to the masculine sex. As a result,

Crane was not a feminine personality, as one commonly conceives of it in a heterosexual culture. Although he did not engage in many sports, he loved exercise and played tennis frequently with enjoyment; nor did he fear the physical exertion and strain connected with hard work or privation. As a sensitive individual, however, let us even say a poet, Crane's personality contained some aspects, a few of which are listed, that are considered feminine; he was generous and sympathetic, fond of children, fastidious in his grooming and devoted to cleanliness, anxious to make each furnished room and apartment in which he lived colorful and attractive with pictures, curtains, and other decorative materials. Throughout his life he found great beauty in flowers and all vegetation, whose colors and shapes he studied with endless satisfaction. These attributes and emotions found expression in his letters as in his poetry, whether it was the cripple of "Moment Fugue," the wretched boy of "The Idiot," the small animals of "A Name for All," or the children of a fragment which he wrote in 1923.† These characteristics would not be found amiss in the heterosexual male, especially if he were an individual possessing greater sensitivity than ordinary. But they posed a unique problem for Crane, since his deviation threw a different and unsavory light upon them; of this predicament he was unhappily aware. Writing to Munson early in 1923, he said apropos this matter:

"And now to your question about passing the good word along. I discoved that I have been all-too easy all along in letting out announcements of my sexual predilections. Not that anything unpleasant has happened or is imminent. But it does put me into obligatory relations to a certain extent with 'those who know,' and this irks me to

† *See Appendix.*

think of sometimes. After all when you're dead it doesn't matter,
and this statement alone proves my immunity from any 'shame' about
it. But I find the ordinary business of 'earning a living' entirely too
stringent to want to add any prejudices against me *of that nature* in
the mind of any publicans and sinners. Such things have a wholesale way of leaking out! Everyone knows now about B—, H—,
and others—the list too long to bother with. I am all-too free with
my tongue and doubtless always shall be—but I'm going to ask you
to advise and work me better with a more discreet behaviour."

His poetry, and its fate, was affected as well. "Episode of Hands,"† a poem which might be construed to
have homosexual implications, was never printed in magazine or book; a similar poem was altered to eliminate
such implications, as the following pages will show.

But the most important result of his sexual personality
was the dominant place which the concept of love as an
abstract ideal began to play in his life. It has often been
observed that those who find it impossible because of
circumstances to experience a full flowering of love, and
Crane was now one of them, tend to idealize love and to
make it the most powerful concern of their lives. For
Crane, love became inextricably interwoven with the
creative drive, the ground swell which carried on its crest
the sparkling expressions of the poetic imagination. He
had no patience with the Freudian theory that the unsatis-
fied sexual libido is converted by the unconscious into
artistic or intellectual productivity. "My continence,"
he wrote, "has brought me nothing in the creative way,—
it has only tended to create a confidence in me along
lines of action,—business, execution, etc. There is not love
enough in me at present to do a thing. This sounds romantic and silly,—you understand that I mean and refer
to the strongest incentive to the imagination, or, at least

† *See Appendix.*

the strongest in my particular case." The theme of love
is one of those most prominent in Crane's poems; the
"Voyages" series of love poems is an example. The
stress placed upon love in the mystical system of P. D.
Ouspensky was responsible in great part for the devotion
which Ouspensky's ideas aroused in Crane.

Two poems on which Crane was working during the
first half of 1920 confirm the hedonistic quality developing in his temperament and life. They do this not only
in their own substance, but in the close indebtedness they
acknowledge to the influence of Wallace Stevens, a poet
whose lines, although with lesser masculinity than Crane,
celebrate many of the themes which we find in the latter's
poetry. "Garden Abstract" was begun in January; Crane
saw in it a means of combining symbolism with the more
familiar effects of imagism. Its earliest versions were in
free verse, as the following specimen indicates:

> The apple on its bough
> Is my desire,—
> Shining suspension,
> Mimic of the sun.
>
> The bough has caught my breath up,
> And its leaves
> Pulse with their possession
> As they mock it.
> I am a prisoner of the tree
> And its green fingers.
>
> Like scimitars
> The green leaves shine.
> Like serpent tongues they twine
> Around the bough,
> Around the fruit.

The poem is an early statement of one of Crane's major themes, the power and ecstasy of desire; the symbolism is obviously sexual in nature. Probably Crane became somewhat uncomfortable at the homosexual implications of the poem; in any case, its phallic symbolism had been called to his attention by a friend who read it. The final version of "Garden Abstract" which appeared in *The Little Review* of September 1920 had been radically revised. The subjective consciousness of the poet was eliminated in favor of a woman objectively described, and the form was altered from free verse to blank verse. In making the first change, Crane may have been influenced by a Sherwood Anderson sketch in the May 1920 issue of *The Dial* which is substantively related to the final version of "Garden Abstract." Both the earlier and last drafts of "Garden Abstract" possess the frank delight we have mentioned in the joys of physical living, in lust and passion, in the caress of the wind and the warmth of the sun.

"The Fernery" is more particularly related to Stevens than "Garden Abstract"; its lines are strongly reminiscent of the first stanza of Stevens' "Sunday Morning." It is less physical than "Garden Abstract," for example, being almost as metaphysical as "Sunday Morning"; at this time more than at any previous period, Crane was drawn to the color, sensuousness, and other physical qualities of Stevens' work. In "Sunday Morning" itself, readers will recall, the metaphysical tone is thinly cast upon the more vigorous primitivism which lies beneath, and the poet's delight in odor, color, light, and sound is expressed lavishly throughout. Like "My Grandmother's Love Letters" and "Garden Abstract," "The Fernery" is a poem of extern-

ality. As such, it is a true product of imagism, for it
presents whatever emotional connotations there are in the
form of physical images. The poem was probably begun
sometime in 1919, before Crane left New York for Cleveland in the fall of 1919. An early undated version of
the poem follows:

PORTRAIT OF AUNTY CLIMAX

The light that travels on her spectacles
Will sometimes meet a mirror in her eyes.
I've seen it so in lifting up a shade
Beside her ancient fernery . . . And the dies
In zig-zag motifs round her wide mouth
No longer argumentative, show there
Sleep many runes within the crimped and furled
Grey wreathes of more-than-human-faithful hair.

Throughout 1920 Crane worked intermittently on the
poem, but by December of that year had not brought the
poem materially closer to its final version:

AUNTIE CLIMAX

The light that travels on her spectacles,
 Will seldom meet a mirror in her eyes.
I have watched when lifting up the shade
Beside her thriving fernery,—and there lies
A wreath of zigzags fast around her lips
Composed to darkness,—meshes that will wear—
Outlasting words that will flicker in the curled
 Grey crown she wears of perfect, borrowed hair.

"The Fernery" seems never to have been published in a
magazine; in the company of "North Labrador" and "Emblems of Conduct," it is one of the three poems in *White
Buildings* which fall into that category. It reveals the
emotional shallowness of "My Grandmother's Love Let-

ters," to which it is very similar in its inability to evoke a comprehension of the older person's feelings, and Crane may have been averse to seeing it printed because of its obvious inferiority to that poem.

4. FLIGHT FROM AUTHORITY

I N MAY 1920, CRANE WROTE TO MUNSON: "THIS 'business life' is getting me in a terrible way,—and I am beginning to feel that I must contrive a jolt for myself soon." Events had not proceeded in accordance with the promises made to him by his father. There had been no salesman's job for him after Christmas, and it seemed more likely that he would soon begin working in a restaurant annex to the drug store in Akron. Meanwhile, he returned to Cleveland and waited, uncertain of the future and unhappy. Towards the end of January, his father finally reached a decision and put him to work in the Cleveland factory warehouse where the materials employed in the manufacture of the Crane Company candies were stored. To Hart's chagrin, his new job involved manual labor of the most difficult kind: "I am packing cases and moving heavy cases of chocolate, barrels of sugar, etc. for my living at present . . ." The only consolation was the elimination of the long boring hours spent standing behind the Akron drug store counter, for the warehouse job kept him busy. But even this minor satisfaction was counterbalanced by Crane's belief that his father was persecuting him in a fixed intention to make him adhere to the conventional saga of American success, without any regard for his individuality. Instead of complying with his father's wishes, therefore, he reacted with emotional antagonism that alienated him from still another basic element of the dominant social mores. To William Wright, studying at Columbia University and participating in New York cultural pastimes, Hart wrote with unconcealed envy in February:

"Take a layman's word of advice and remain in your present surroundings as long as possible and extract the full amount of enjoyment from them while they last. It is not very exciting to arise and essay forth to ten hours dull and exasperating labor every morning at five-thirty and return home at night with a head like a wet muffin afterward. And that is the routine that I am enmeshed in at present, to say nothing of trying to exist on starvation wages. It's the old bunko stuff about 'working from the bottom up' and 'earning an honest dollar' in practice, and if there are not some enlivening changes in it soon, I am liable to walk into the office and tell the amused and comfortable and rich and thriving spectator that 'the joke's up.' "

The belief that it was futile to hope for a satisfactory business relationship with his father became an integral part of his thought.

Under such circumstances, he lost even the small amount of affection which he had previously possessed for his father. His mother having left the city for a trip during which she closed the family home, Crane did not live with his father. Instead, he spent a portion of his meager earnings for a small and unpleasant bedroom in a Euclid Avenue rooming house, from which he emerged only to work all day and eat catch-as-catch-can bites at lunch counters and cheap restaurants. With unrestrained eagerness, he looked forward to the imminent return of his mother, for he contemplated that then he would once again be able to occupy his own room and enjoy some form of per-

sonal stability.   However, the anticipated pleasures of
home life failed to materialize when he was once again
installed in the family domicile.   His divorced mother
and aging grandmother were naturally concerned with
practical problems of household finance, as well as with
considerations of business ventures which might enable
them to supplement their slender income; they had little
free time in which to extend themselves for him.   An
additional source of conflict lay in Crane's inability to sub-
merge his own personality and respond as fully to the
emotional needs of the two women as they might have
wished.   More warmth and stimulation were derived by
him from infrequent meetings with his lover and friends
in Akron or Cleveland, as well as from sporadic efforts to
enjoy a sense of fraternity with fellow employees in his
father's factory, a Whitmanian comradeship which he described in "Episode of Hands" in April.†   But any allevia-
tion of his depressed state of mind by these means was
slight in value, and he gradually came to realize that
he must stand alone.   Thus he continued to fortify an
inner refuge, drawing ever closer within himself the ideas
and emotions which a hostile environment found repugnant, and validating in the course of time those forms of
experience which had demonstrated their power to furnish the "balm, spiritual and fleshly" demanded by his
being:

"I don't know . . . whether I'm strong and hardened or not. I know
that I am forced to be very flexible to get along at all under present
conditions. I contrive to humanize my work to some extent by much
cameraderie with the other employees and this is my salvation there.
Of course I am utterly alone,—want to be,—and am beginning to rather
enjoy the slippery scales-of-the-fish, continual escape, attitude. The few

† *See Appendix.*

people that I can give myself to are out of physical reach and so I can only write where I would like to talk, gesture, and dine. The most revolting sensation I experience is the feeling of having placed myself in a position of quiescence or momentary surrender to the contact and possession of the insensitive fingers of my neighbors here. I am learning, just beginning to learn,—the technique of escape, and too often yet, I betray myself by some enthusiasm or other."

However unpleasant and difficult, Hart managed to continue a perfunctory performance of his duties. This seeming devotion, together with "an incipient rupture caused by the incessant heavy lifting at the factory" resulting in a week's vacation, finally caused Mr. Crane to look favorably at the commercial progress of his son. A talk between them early in May resulted in the promise that Hart would be permitted to spend a few weeks during the summer in the New York office of the business in lieu of a vacation. Summer arrived and Crane's elation was shattered when it turned out that he would not be sent to New York as contemplated. In anguished desperation, he was ready to look for a literary job in New York, follow the lead of Matthew Josephson who had announced that he was taking a shipboard job as a steward in order to obtain passage to England, and only as a last resort considered continuing in his father's employ. Before he could embark upon a decisive action, however, his father arranged to promote him to the position of company representative in the territory surrounding the District of Columbia. The future began to look promising, and the working arrangements were more generous than expected: "I shall more or less freely govern my own operations, rise and retire at late hours, and have a drawing account at the bank at my own disposal in addition to a good percentage commission on everything I sell." It flattered his pride and dignity that Mr. Crane, in announcing his decision, not only expressed his

"appreciation" of Hart's work but "even made the un-
hoped-for concession of mentioning that he had chosen
this territory for me on account of the better sort of
business type that is in Washington, and also on account
of Washington's 'literary and journalistic associations.' "
With an ingenuous impetuousness, his spirits soared as the
situation brightened, although just a short time before he
had been depressed because of misunderstanding or persecution. He seemed incapable of soberly evaluating his
experience, and the emotional fluctuations of which he
partook sapped his emotional resources, decreased the
possibility of initiative on his part.

Crane's transfer to Washington staved off the threatening rupture with his father by liberating him from the
"smug atmosphere" of Cleveland. He was not confident
about his "capacities for 'salesmanship' etc." as the time
drew near for his departure in September, and in this
doubtful state he arrived in Washington. Before more
than a week had elapsed, any latent doubts that he would
fail as a chocolate salesman were completely vindicated.
The city of Washington, possessing a permanently high
rate of employment and a lethargic dullness in the atmosphere which encouraged a taste for extravagant delicacies,
was already well supplied with chocolate manufacturers.
In addition, the varieties they sold were far cheaper than
the Crane candies in order to attract the great number of
low-paid clerks. As if to crush him completely, the tor-
rid heat of Washington's Indian summer had turned his
sample chocolates "grey with sweat." Yet he ventured
forth in good faith until he learned after a few visits that
most of the wholesale candy buyers came to their offices
late in the morning. So he too slept late, and the total
result of his efforts was that he opened only two new
accounts for his father.

He made the best of his visit, however, and spent many hours walking about the city, observing the wide tree-lined streets which he believed to be modelled after Parisian boulevards, the numerous parks, and the plethora of monuments. The vast impersonality which characterizes Washington in peace-time intensified his conviction of failure and he felt "a terrible vacuity about me and within me." Armies of clerks poured out of government offices, rushed past him bound for restaurants and motion picture theatres, and thereafter made straight to their rooms, apartments, and houses. Not being in touch with the upper stratum of Washington social life, as he wrote, he was regrettably unable to participate in any sort of "cafe life" which might have enlivened the hot afternoons and evenings. In the end, he found some pleasure in the companionship of soldiers and sailors from the local military establishments who wandered about the city on leave, and like Whitman before him was fascinated by "a strange psychology of their own that is new to me." But he did make a lasting friendship with Wilbur Underwood, an elderly government employee and literary enthusiast, to whom he had been directed with a letter of introduction by a mutual friend in Ohio.

Like Crane, Underwood had been forced by economic needs to adjust himself to an occupation which did not satisfy his creative impulses. The author of two volumes of poetry which had been published in England and a contributor to various magazines, Underwood was now engaged in working as the chief of a minor governmental administrative office. From the monotony and boredom of his work and milieu, which effectively prevented him from developing his imaginative gifts more than sporadically, he turned with eagerness to literature as a reader and collector of books which would stimulate his spirit and his senses. Among these were such insufficiently appreciated men as Herman Melville and Edgar Saltus, esoteric writers like Rabelais, Apuleius, and Petronius; they were read and discussed by the two new friends. Underwood also encouraged Crane in his bent for spiritual questioning, as we can judge by reading extracts from the letters which Crane sent him after his departure from Washington. To few of his other friends did Crane write in this vein. In one such letter, Crane wrote: "I am too happy not to fear a great deal, but I believe in, or have found, God again." And in another: "I long to go to India and stay always. Meditation on the sun is all there is. Not that this isn't enough." Underwood not only assisted in crystallizing Crane's inclination for the esoteric and the spiritual, but lent himself as well to a confirmation of the truth that was being forced upon Crane: the independent creative artist cannot survive as such if he reconciles himself to American society.

Despite the pleasant hours which Washington provided after Crane met Underwood and through him other people with similar interests, he evinced no regrets when his father asked him to return to Cleveland in late October. For his father professed to be satisfied with Hart's devotion to business in the face of the obstacles encountered and, further, promised that Hart would be returned to Washington the following January when it would be more appropriate to sell chocolates. Nor had Washington turned out to be a very substantial substitute for Cleveland. On the contrary, Crane had found it peculiarly "restricted and bigoted," a state symbolized by the eloquent predicament of Underwood. Typically optimistic again, he welcomed a mingling of his spirit with the bustling vitality of the industrial Midwest, even though he felt keenly that he could not survive as a poet if he were to be physically involved in its turmoil. "Yes," he wrote to Munson upon his return to Cleveland, " 'Jurgen' has been breathing his native *Ohio* air for two weeks now ... "

Unfortunately, Crane returned to Cleveland at a time when his father's factory was concentrating all its efforts on meeting the large orders received for Christmas. Again the old conflict between Crane's job and his writing arose, but now with greater ferocity because of the weeks of freedom and irresponsibility passed in Washington. When Munson drew his attention with unconscious irony to an article in *The Freeman* in which Van Wyck Brooks had advised the writer to pursue "outside interests" in the intervals between actual literary production, Crane was stung to protest: "With me, there are no poems for 'doldrums' to lag between, and no time, literally, for poems, to say nothing of energy." Again there were the long hours of work, and piled on top of them the aggravating "disgust and boredom" which the uninteresting work engendered. Yet one must also assign some blame for the lack of time in which Crane was able to work creatively to the habits which he had developed as remedial for his predicament. "Passions of this kind," he wrote about a love affair, "completely derail me from anything creative for days,—and that's the worst of it." The same story was applicable to his occasional drinking sprees, to the excessive amount of time he devoted to playing musical recordings on his phonograph, to his intensive round of social visits and entertainments. They stimulated him and thereby assuaged the "morose and irritable" state of his nerves, but they also consumed time and physical energy. All these factors combined served to bring him perilously close to the verge of a nervous breakdown, and he found himself coping with nervous symptoms and indigestion. Though his condition did not develop into collapse, he seems to have been suffering from a condition of hysteria which aggravated his already neurotic state of mind. From his friends in New York who wrote that they were leaving for Europe, he received an additional impetus to bring about "a clean and final break" with his father, whom he suspected of encouraging the factory employees to persecute him. When his father volunteered to send him to Chicago on a sales tour after Christmas, he regarded the offer as additional intrigue which would enmesh and tie him down. Fantastic schemes involving the accumulation of money for two years, one year, or even for shorter periods, and then flight from Ohio and the United States to foreign countries, began to appear as the only possible solution: "***Then embark once and for all for foreign lands, Italy or Russia or Paris, and not come back until I want to. Literature and art be hanged!—even ordinary existence isn't worth the candle in these States now." Essentially Crane was horrified at the increasing sterility which had been the predominating aspect of his creative life for so long a period. To Munson he wrote with undisguised bitterness: "I am filled with a kind of bleakness of mind and spirit lately . . . I should like to be able to see and talk to you,—the mere technical mechanics of writing have become so foreign to me from long neglect, that I feel awkward at best." It was the same desire for a transfusion of creative vitality which animated him to plead with Sherwood Anderson, in Chicago at the time, that the latter pay him a visit in Cleveland, as if otherwise he would succumb to the beaten frustration of his spirit: "You don't know how much I appreciate the encouragement your letters give me—although I am not at present doing anything creatively, I have not sunk too much into despair or indifference to hope."

But actually Crane had been continuing with his poetry. "Porphyro in Akron," written during 1920, concentrates within its Baudelairean lines considerable information bearing upon Crane's mood and ideas.† It was first announced to Munson in June: "I'm started on a set of sketches connected with Akron life now, and enclose a sample." The enclosure consisted of thirty-four lines in three sections:

> A shift of rubber workers presses down South Main
> Like a wave of muddy water,
> Dwindling at the cross lines
> Until you feel the weight of many cars
> North-bound, and East and West,
> Absorbing and conveying weariness,—
> Rumbling over the hills.
>
> *   *   *
>
> AKRON, "high place,"—
> A bunch of smoke-ridden hills
> Among rolling Ohio hills . . .
>
> The dark-eyed Greeks grin at each other
> In the streets and alleys.
> The Greek grins and fights with the Swede,—
> And the Fjords and the Aegean are remembered.
>
> Above their jokes and contraband
> Niggers dream of Kentucky melons,
> Yellow as gold,—golden as money.
> And they all dream of money.
>
> *   *   *

† *See Appendix.*

And some of them "will be Americans,"—
Using the latest ice-box and buying Fords;
And others,—

I remember one Sunday noon,—
Harry and I, "the gentlemen,"—seated around
A table of raisin-jack and wine,—our host
Setting down a glass and saying,—

"One month,
I go back rich . . . I ride black horse . . .
Have many sheep."

And his wife, like a mountain, coming in,
With four tiny black eyed girls around her,
Twinkling like little Christmas trees.

And some Sunday fiddlers, Roumanian "business men,"
Came and played ragtime and dances before the door,
And we overpayed them because we felt like it.

Although he did not make any great number of changes
in them later, Crane was dissatisfied with the first two
sections. One may conjecture that he reacted so because
of his feeling of inadequacy before the more sweeping
observation required in these sections than in the third,
more personal, part. The first section portrays the sinuous
flow of workingmen on foot and in vehicles to the burgeoning rubber factories at Akron. The slow linked progression of their movement is wearisome to observe; it
evokes the nature of their lives and work, and also the
boredom and routine of the poet's existence. The second
section introduces the contradictory elements in the city's
industrial pattern, the Southern Negroes and European
immigrants who labor in the rubber factories. These
aliens have not been absorbed into the life of Akron;
their thoughts are clotted with memories of the "golden"

past. In the final section, the transition between the laborers and the poet is effected. The opening lines express contempt for the American standard of living, traditionally embodied in mechanical appliances. From this bleak picture of progress, the poet turns with alacrity to a foreigner who has remained unseduced, whose spirit is still close to the soil and the sensuous. The personal experience of the poet begins to predominate in the supplementary lines sent by Crane to Munson in August, at which time Crane also gave the poem its title:

> Tumult of weariness from a basement cabaret
> splashes up into my room.
> Bucket of blood. Peggy dancing her guts out.
> Sweat and powder and rubber-dust on her sash.
> Whoops, my dear!
>
> Her usual morning remonstrance over the soda-bar
> Will again be muffled by what her
> fellow's teeth are letting out,—
>
> "You're the clev'rest girl I know . . .
> How do you do it?"
> For, sure, her father preaches up at Norton,
> and sends her money every week.

*   *   *

> Pull down the hotel counterpane,
> and hitch yourself up to your book.
> *"Full on this casement shone the wintry moon,*
> *And threw warm gules on Madeleine's fair breast,*
> *As down she knelt for heaven's grace and boon: . . ."*
>
> Connais tu la pays. . . . ?
>
> Your mother sang you out of a stuffy parlor
> one summer day in a little town where you
> had started to grow.

And you ran outside afterward as soon as you
could get free from the company,
and brought back the only rose on the bush
in the front yard.
You will never forget the song nor the rose.

But look up, Porphyro,— your toes
are tapping too ridiculously
the spindles at the foot of the bed.

The stars are drowned in a slow rain,
and a hash of noises is slung up from the street,
and you ought to remember how the bell-hop
shoved you, dazed, into the elevator as you were
looking toward the desk for mail.

You ought, really, to try to sleep, Porphyro,
even though, in this town, poetry's a
bedroom occupation.

The first twelve lines of this group were dropped from
the final version of the poem, and their subject was later
incorporated into the second part of "Faustus and Helen."
Continuing the picture of Akron (American) life, Crane
depicts the vulgarization of love, ironically subsidized by
a father who "preaches." The poet in his small hotel
rooms hears the cabaret noises while reading Keats' "The
Eve of St. Agnes," from which three lines are quoted by
Crane. The vision of Madeline to Porphyro ("so pure a
thing, so free from mortal taint") is an ironic contrast to
the chorus girl and her lover. The figure of Madeline
blends into that of the poet's mother, who occupies a
similar position in his heart. Unlike Madeline, his mother
is unattainable. The poet then ironically draws attention
to the sordidness of his present surroundings, the futility
of his childhood memories, and the incongruity of his
desires.

In September, prior to leaving Cleveland for Washington, Crane deleted the lines about the Kentucky Negroes and added the bitter stanza about the worthlessness of poetry in Akron. The poem was sent to *The Dial* and *The Little Review*, both of which rejected it; finally it appeared in *The Double Dealer* of New Orleans in August 1921.

For three months, from October 1920 until the end of January 1921, Crane wrote little more than two lines of poetry. It was if he were resting quietly, summing himself up, endeavouring to ascertain just who and what he was. He recognized his incongruity—a pathetic romantic clown, the artist striving for expression, who also combines in his makeup the enormous positive exuberance of a Rabelaisian hero:

> The everlasting eyes of Pierrot,
> And of Gargantua,—the laughter.

Yet he was determined to be remembered for himself, no matter how incongruous an amalgam he might be. In "Black Tambourine," which he wrote in February 1921, he felt that he had for the first time welded the "contradictory" elements of his personality into a distinctively individual poetry. "Something definitely my own," he wrote with pride to Munson, and he dismissed with contempt a quatrain he had begun as a poem on adolescence because "it savours too strongly of Eliot and Huxley for me to take further interest":

> "The mind shall burst its aquarium vagueness,
> Its melon opacity of graduate dawn;"—
> Wise-youthful prophecy to the tired pillows
> Resentful of the room and shades,—still drawn.—

But we must examine it with some care, since this quatrain is the first sample of Crane's mature style. Furthermore, Crane did not really abandon the lines; the eleventh and thirteenth lines of "Faustus and Helen I" are a recasting of the quatrain. The first point of interest is the syntactical freedom with which nouns ("acquarium" and "melon") are used as adjectives, a practice which induces some confusion, although it may enrich the implications of the poetry. The construction "aquarium vagueness" will serve as a demonstration of the latter point. The noun "aquarium" denotes an artificial pond or glass receptacle in which living aquatic animals or plants are kept. By referring back to "mind," we realize that the poet considers the mind to be floating within the skull cavity in the same manner in which fish float in the aquarium. But we can proceed back still further, for we have been informed by Crane that this quatrain deals with adolescence. A second explanation, therefore, would be that the poet has regarded the mind as an embryo desiring to burst forth from the womb. The result of this unusual juxtaposition of words has been to add layer upon layer of meaning to the line, whereas a lesser poet would have been satisfied to say something like "The mind shall burst its vagueness." Yet the proceedure used by Crane requires pains, or else needless obscurity may result. To illustrate this point we shall consider the construction "graduate dawn." Here it appears that Crane has not used the adjective "graduate," but has instead dropped the suffix "d" of the past participle of the intransitive verb "graduate," one of whose definitions denotes a gradual change or a shading off, so that the construction conveys the picture of a gradually-unveiling dawn. If "graduate" is considered as an adjective, the construction "graduate dawn" is meaningless. The increasing mastery of Crane's style can be seen in the deftness with which he plays with light and shape in these few lines. Although "mind" and "aquarium" do not indicate shape, as soon as we read "melon" we think of something round, and this thought carries us back and gives a roundness to both "mind" and "aquarium," almost as if Crane had been hinting all along at a round head and a round fish bowl. The play on light is very subtle, from the darkness of "mind" through the murkiness of "aquarium vagueness" and the reddish-yellow of the "melon . . . dawn" back to the darkness of the "room."

The Dial, to which Crane had sent "Black Tambourine" in February, confirmed Crane's fears that "such a Baudelairesque thing" would not be "acceptable *anywhere* in U. S." by rejecting it. But Crane had so much faith in the poem that, after a few revisions, he sent it off to *The Double Dealer.* There the editors liked it well enough to accept it for publication in their June 1921 issue. The poem was probably inspired by the Negro boy Pip in Melville's *Moby Dick,* who loses his mental balance and becomes a visionary, as well as by Crane's own experiences with Negroes in his father's factories and warehouses. The pre-*Double Dealer* version is quoted:

> The interests of a black man in a cellar
> Mark an old judgment on the world.
> Gnats toss in the shadow of a bottle,
> And a roach spans a crevice in the floor.
>
> Aesop, driven to pondering, found
> Heaven with the tortoise and the hare:
> Fox brush and sow ear top his grave
> Even though mankind was his care.
>
> The black man, forlorn, in the cellar,
> Sees two ways, too,—with less gay eyes.

> There's a tambourine stuck silent on the wall,
> And in Africa, a carcass quick with flies.

Crane's explanation of the poem is interesting in itself, and in its larger implications.† Throughout his life, Crane was entirely too eager to explain his poems to both friends and enemies alike, thereby giving rise to the logical conclusion that his difficult poems required such exegeses if they were ever to be fully comprehensible to a reader, or at the very least that he often failed to completely realize his purposes in a poem and was acutely aware of his failure. A later famous example of this lack of reserve was the long letter written to Harriet Monroe by way of explaining "At Melville's Tomb."‡ In actuality, such attempts at rationalization were nothing more than signs of poor judgment on Crane's part, since he should have realized that his poem did all the talking and explaining required. In attempting to forge a new language for poetry, however, Crane must have felt like an explorer who writes long reports to a patron about the validity of his original ideas while they come true on a day-to-day basis. There is a further reason to doubt these elucidations by Crane, since often they revolve about words not to be found in the original version of a poem, and a first version frequently contains the germ, if not the major portion, of a poem. So that when Crane talks about "mid-kingdom," he is referring to a word absent from the first draft of "Black Tambourine." The meaning of "Black Tambourine" is obvious afer a careful reading. But the poem *is* difficult, and testifies to Crane's growing involution.

† *See Part II, Section 6, this book.*
‡ *See Appendix.*

The neurotic feverishness which ran riot in Crane could not long remain quiescent. In January 1921, the expected denouement with his father took place, at which time his father confessed his inability to understand the "enigma" and generously offered to let him continue in his employ until Hart found "a job at some more 'literary' work." Mr. Crane even went so far as to place his son in a more responsible job as overseer of a warehouse. For a brief period, Crane was reasonably contented, especially since, as he wrote Munson, "My present job allows me more time while at work." It was indeed more satisfactory, for during this period he was able to complete the first version of "Black Tambourine." But when he was transferred in the latter part of April to a basement storeroom, the old feelings of persecution which were temporarily suppressed burst forth with unrestrained resentment and he finally left his father's employ. The severance of physical relations brought with it an exuberant sense of freedom. "The best thing is that the cloud of my father is beginning to move from the horizon now," he wrote Munson in the letter announcing his dramatic rupture from his father. "You have never known me when it has not been there— and in time we *both* may discover some new things in me. *Bridges burn't behind!*"

It was not really as Jurgen, the poet-pawnbroker who ventures forth into time, space, and myth in search of ideals and returns home disillusioned and reconciled with the mundane, that Crane had come back from Washington to Ohio in 1920. That interlude had only been a digression from the main route on which he was travelling, but now he had completed a decisive stage of his journey. In breaking away from his father ("the image of his overbearing head leaning over me like a gargoyle"),

Crane defied the symbol which represented the direct touch of authority upon him. In the course of a human being's development, such a revolt from the family over-lord is a progressive move towards the assumption of full maturity. Crane's rejection of the father-symbol, however, could not be profound because of his homosexual neurosis. For the remainder of his life, he was haunted by the image of his father laughing at his love for poetry and taunting him with his supposed lack of virility. Just as he did not banish his father's psychological influence from his mind, in like manner his rejection failed to sever him from the code of bourgeois values and morality which his father represented. Crane felt guilty because he was a non-conformist morally and socially, and his guilt haunted him. The repeated flights which he undertook failed to separate him from the burdens of conscience and a sense of failure. The pattern of surrender to experience, which he should have outgrown, continued to solidify and exert its destructive influence upon him.

FLIGHT FROM THE QUOTIDIAN

CRANE LEFT HIS FATHER'S EMPLOY IN THE SPRING of 1921 with the prospect of unemployment a real problem. The nation was suffering from an economic depression which had replaced the more joyful days of war-induced prosperity; like many others, Crane found it impossible to obtain a job. For a time he contemplated becoming a helper in a garage; his long-range plans were centered about a friend's promise of an advertising copy job. But meanwhile he was being supported by his mother, and this proved irksome after a year and a half of financial semi-independence. Having cut himself off from his father, he now began to regard his mother as a restraining influence. The more depressed he felt about being economically dependent upon her, the more exasperated he became. Since he was now confined to his home for days at a stretch, he naturally received more admonitions and advice than hitherto, and this was resented by him. Smarting with humiliation, he wrote Munson that in order to "escape constant interruption" all his writing had to be accomplished in an isolated attic room of the house, and that the only emotional solace for him in this nerve-wracking situation was to go on "an occasional

spree as a protest." When Munson hastily replied, urging
him not to lose his spirit and "not to be ridiculously
bourgeois in accepting bourgeois standards" about such
questions as being an economic failure, he was reassured
only slightly.

As Crane's personal life grew more intricate, he became
disgusted with the condition of the times, and with those
who, like the writers attached to *The New Republic*, *The
Freeman*, and other "liberal" magazines of the period,
formulated and applied principles of liberalism applicable
to the problems worrying the nation: "Sometimes I get
so exasperated with the 'intellectual' attitudes of these
papers . . . where everything is all jumbled together,—
politics, literature, painting, birth control etc., etc., etc.,
that I ignore them for a time and probably miss some
good things." But his irritation with the New York intellectuals was not directed against their eclecticism and
superficiality. From his point of view, it was useless to
concern oneself with practical problems when the outlook for reform appeared worse than hopeless. Far better,
he thought, to cultivate a little garden of the self wherein
it was possible to raise a pure aesthetic experience, and
he expressed this attitude specifically with regard to
politics:

"How tired I am of the perpetual ferment of the *New Rep*. Those
fellows are playing a canster game nonsense. Does anything they ever
say have any concrete effect? Old Washington goes on just the same
on the old rotten paths. These gentlemen are merely clever at earning their livelihood in clean cuffs. But hear me rant on!!! I don't care
two pence for the whole earth and heavens and least of all for politics. It's only when the political gentlemen (Irish potatobeds) ob-
struct my view of my petunias and hollyhocks that I'm thus aroused,—
and even that is a small complaint in the long list of larger ones I
have."

His contempt for remedial action, nevertheless, did not bring him closer to an overt compromise with American tastes and standards, which he depised with an increasing sense of isolation. As more and more of his friends departed on the grand post-war tour of Europe, he looked about him and could see only a perversion of beauty that was appalling:

"The 'march of events' has brought upon us Cleveland's 125th anniversary with all its fussy and futile inanities and advertisements to make hideous the streets. Blocked, and obliged to wait while the initial 'pee-rade' went by today, I spent two hours of painful rumination ending with such disgust at America and everything in it, that I more than envy you your egress to foreign ports. No place but America could relish and applaud anything so stupid and drab as that parade—led by the most notable and richest grafter of the place decked out in Colonial rags as the founder of the city Moses C. Ah—the Baroness, lunatic that she is, is right. Our people have no *atom* of a conception of beauty—and don't want it. One thing almost brought tears to my eyes, (and I hope you do not think me too silly in mentioning it)—the handful of Chinese who came along in some native and antique vestments and liveries to prostitute themselves in the medley of trash around them. To see them passing the (inevitable) Soldier's Monument ablaze with the aristocratic barbarity of silk gold and embroideries *was* an anachronism that could occur *only* in America. And the last of their 'section' brought a float with a large 'melting pot'—its significance was blazoned in letters *on* it!!! . . . If ever I felt alone it has been today."

Keyed by his revulsion from the American scene, he turned with strenuous effort to recapture the "mental and spiritual status" which had been his before 1919, before he fell a dupe to the siren-song of material success: "What I want to do is gather up the threads again and go on . . . I have reached such blind alleys and found no way out of them that there is nothing at present for me to do but laugh a little and *endure*—which I hope to do." As always when in the pit of despair, he received some succor from friends. Unlike the acquaintances he had made upon his arrival in 1919, these new friendships were with people who participated in the arts as active creators —William Sommer, the artist; Samuel Loveman, the poet and critic; Gordon Hatfield, the composer; Richard and Charlotte Rychtarik, artist and musician respectively; William Lescaze, the architect. At frequent meetings held in houses and restaurants, this group formed a lively circle in which Crane's interests in the plastic arts and in music were sharpened, and in which he was able to discourse at length about mutual concerns. Thus buoyed, he buckled down to his writing again, and searched eagerly for new themes about which he might write.

After completing "Black Tambourine," Crane returned to the simpler style of his earlier poems, and he may have done so as a reaction to his friends' inability to grasp the meaning of that poem.† The quiescent nature of his social life reflected itself in his static literary life. He marked time, rescuing lines from discarded earlier efforts, assembling patchworks like "The Bridge of Estador" (April)‡ or insignificant little works like "A Persuasion" (May)‡ or "Pastorale" (Summer 1921). None of these poems gave him a sense of accomplishment. Although his spirit of dissatisfaction was strong, however, it was not powerful enough to .drive him forward in the acquisition of a mature technique and subject.

"The Bridge of Estador" is the most interesting of these minor poems. It contains an explicit statement of the theme of beauty which forms the backbone of Crane's first major poem, "For the Marriage of Faustus and Helen," in addition to the first important utilization of

† *See Part II, Section 6, this book.*
‡ *See Appendix.*

the sea in Crane's poetry since "Meditation." The poem carries within itself fragments extracted from earlier pieces and lines which were soon to find a more permanent resting place in later poems: lines 10-15 stem from "Episode of Hands" and lines 31-32 from an unpublished couplet; lines 19-21 may be found in "At Melville's Tomb," lines 22-23 in "Faustus and Helen," line 24 and lines 31-32 in "Praise for an Urn." Subtitled "An Impromptu, Aesthetic Tirade," Crane felt "far from satisfied with it" as he wrote Munson after *The Dial* rejected the poem. The lack of finish he was conscious of may be seen in the rhyming which ends the first four lines and is then dropped except for a few lines in the fourth stanza. The poem is disjointed, a strange mixture of conventional literary imagery ("The slant moon with the slanting hill"—"Beauty's fool") and banality ("follow your arches/To what corner of the sky they pull you to") with the moving quality of the beautiful pair of lines closing the fourth stanza. The imagery is in parts vital and keen-sighted, as in the first stanza where Crane sees the light on the lake's ripples "lapped under" the water, or where the smoke coiling from chimneys is viewed as "cords" which tie the buildings together "bundle-wise."

The poem continues the exploration of the worldly position of the poet begun in "Porphyro in Akron." It can be considered stanza by stanza for its meaning. "Estador" appears to be a coined word of Spanish construction meaning roughly "he who views or measures." "The Bridge of Estador" probably connotes an elevated structure on which someone is observing and evaluating. No one has ever walked on the bridge before, but he who undertakes to cross it may see a natural object like a sunlit lake, or man-made objects like gloomy industrial buildings streaked with smoke. Both classes of phenomena contain a spiritual essence. Equally, nature and civilization partake of the essence of beauty. All objects, all experiences, are potentially beautiful, even those which are superficially ugly. There are those to whom the experience of walking over the bridge will be valueless, for that which is to be seen ("vision") depends on whether the observer is capable of intuitive sight, whether he does not still have to wait for a mysterious activation of his powers such as those by which the moon brings about the rise and ebb of the tides. The poet, however, has already seen his "vision" of "things irreconcilable" in a Dionysian ecstasy, and he is ironically "twisted" with his love for the beauty they contain. This beauty will always be a part of him. Man must search for this visionary beauty which Crane has found, even though he may thereby become as incongrous and contradictory as the poet.

In "The Bridge of Estador," Crane reconciled himself to being an outcast. Between heaven and earth, a resident of neither realm, a bridge-walker, he aspired skyward for a vision and looked below him for the few glimpses of beauty which the earth's ugliness might relinquish to him. The sea in this poem assumed a more positive character than it possessed in the earlier "Meditation," where the poet floated like a ship on the sea surface looking "for guidance" to the stars above. Here the sea is more than a beneficial medium in which one can float while waiting for the desires of heaven to make themselves known The sea has its own mystery and madness . . . it is linked with the moon, toward whose beautiful light it rises and by which it is repelled. In its watery depths the "dreams" of man are wrecked, and are then "cast up on the shore" after being stripped bare by the beating waves. Yet this cruel and mysterious sea gives vision, vision compounded from the bitter truths which appear to man when his earthly dreams are destroyed and he must find new ways of apprehending beauty and reconciling himself to life.

Although Crane was discontented with his poetry, his literary output was nevertheless receiving appreciative attention. *The Double Dealer* asked Crane for an article on Sherwood Anderson at the same time that it accepted "Black Tambourine." The piece† appeared in July, and a few months later *The Double Dealer* printed his "Porphyro in Akron." Probably as a result of the intercession of Padraic Colum, Crane's old friend who had written from New York of his admiration for "Black Tambourine," *The Measure* accepted Crane's "A Persuasion" for its October issue. When *The Dial* capped this series of acceptances by taking his "Pastorale" for its October issue after previously rejecting "The Bridge of Estador," Crane's confidence in his creative power was refreshed. He planned a short story, made some translations from the French, started to write an article on Ezra Pound, and finished two new and important poems.

During September, Crane completed "The Bottom of the Sea Is Cruel" which, after rejections by *The Dial* and *The Little Review*, was printed in *Secession* in 1923, and finally took its place in *White Buildings* as "Voyages I." The poem treats the sea as the same cruel agency of "The Bridge of Estador." It is difficult to tell when Crane began to write the poem, for it is strikingly reminiscent of Tagore's "On the Seashore" (*The Crescent Moon*, 1913), which Crane probably read many years before.

† *See Appendix.*

Tagore describes children playing on the beach with "empty shells" and "withered leaves" who are aware only that "the sea surges up with laughter"; they fail to observe that the "death-dealing waves sing meaningless ballads . . . like a mother while rocking her baby's cradle." In Crane's poem, too, the sea is an ambivalent force, alternately attracting and repelling with surges of maternal love and clutching death. The poet watches colorfully-dressed children playing on the shore. The enveloping mood is one of gayety, crispness, and brightness, but underneath the sunlight boom the waves with portentous clamour as they crash upon the shore. The waves trickle off into delusive "ruffles" as they reach the children. Do not be deceived, the poet would like to say. The sea is a mother, warm and maternal, which welcomes you to its bosom. But it is also treacherous—it has "too wide a breast" to be satisfied with its love for you; you will be engulfed and destroyed in its embrace. Yet he knows that those who approach the sea innocently, as children do their mothers, will not heed his warning. Subordinated in the poem is a lament for his childhood, an awareness of the distance which separates him from the happy children ("And could they hear me I would tell them"). The sea both as loved one and enemy rises to full prominence in Crane's later "Voyages"; "The Bottom of the Sea Is Cruel" is ironic and nostalgic, however, not profoundly passionate as are the later seascapes.

The self-pitying mood of 1920 and 1921 reached its climax in "Chaplinesque," where the symbol of clown-poet assumed its largest dimensions since it was used slightly at first in "My Grandmother's Love Letters," and with increased proportions in "Porphyro in Akron" and "The Bridge of Estador." It is quite evident that the inclination of Crane to a romantic and ironic view of himself was fostered by his experience. It was also nurtured by his readings in the French poets who devoted themselves to that approach in their poetry, as well as by his respect for the poetry of those, notably Eliot and Pound, who followed in their path. Although Crane was familiar with the French poets in translation and in criticism prior to 1920, it is fairly certain that he did not read extensively in the original French until the fall of 1920, when he ordered volumes of the poetry of Arthur Rimbaud, Charles Vildrac, and Jules Laforgue from a Parisian bookdealer. Thereafter, however, and even after his visit to France in 1929, he was unable to handle the French language with facility. He laboriously translated with the aid of a dictionary, a process which, as Elizabeth Foster has noted, led to a concentration on words and phrases rather than to the over-all grasp which a more developed knowledge of a foreign language provides. During 1921, Crane made several translations from the French. These included a poem by Vildrac, de Gourmont's comments on Poe and Baudelaire, and three poems by Laforgue;† the last items listed were printed in *The Double Dealer* of May 1922, and foreshadow the Laforguean tone of ironic self-deprecation in "Chaplinesque."

Crane began to write "Chaplinesque" late in September 1921. Although the poem was directly inspired by the motion picture *The Kid*, in which Charlie Chaplin starred with Jackie Coogan, it was with himself as poet that Crane was concerned. To many of those who have not seen the films in which Chaplin played during the second and third decades of this century, it may seem

† *See Appendix.*

strange that Chaplin should have inspired Crane to write the poem. Chaplin has, however, consistently appealed to many an intellectual as a symbolic representation of contemporary man lost and bewildered in a maze of social restrictions, the purity of whose heart is all the more poignant because of the simple humor in which it is clothed. Chaplin portrays a naif, the Tramp, too innocent to be able to comprehend the nature of the forces oppressing him, and too innocent not to continue along the road which he believes will lead to the fullfillment of his desire for love and security. Thus, in Waldo Frank's *Our America* (1919), Chaplin was regarded as the expression of the "serious beauties which America elsewhere may not approach . . . simple, poetic . . . infantile . . . fluent and elusive . . . the Puck and the muse of a harried people who find in his antic loveliness a mirror for their own wistful and forbidden gaiety, a glimmering invitation to respite and abandon." For Crane, Chaplin stood forth as a "dramatic genius that truly approaches the fabulous sort," as "the prime interpreter of the soul imposed upon by modern civilization"—and with "Chaplinesque" he tried to evoke "the buffooneries of the tragedian" . . . "some of the Chaplin pantomime, so beautiful, and so full of eloquence, and so modern." The version sent to Munson on October 1st contained the lines which form the first three stanzas of the final poem:

> Contented with such random consolations
> as the wind deposits
> in slithered and too ample pockets,
> we make our meek adjustments.
> For we can still love the world, who find
> a famished kitten on the step, and know
> recesses for it from the fury of the street,
> or warm torn elbow coverts.

We will side-step, and to the final smirk,
dally the doom
of that inevitable thumb
that slowly chafes toward us the puckered index,
facing the dull squint with what innocence
and what surprise!

A week later, Crane sent along another draft which, with only a few changes in syntax and words, was the version of "Chaplinesque" as it appears in *White Buildings*.

Although Munson was to arrange for the publication of "Chaplinesque" in the December 1921 issue of *Gargoyle* (Paris) after it had been rejected by *The Dial*, *The New York Post Literary Review*, and *The Double Dealer*, he was not at first impressed with the poem and failed to grasp its meaning. With Munson, as well as with another friend who had confessed to the obscurity of the poem's meaning for him, Crane fell into the same pitfall as with "Black Tambourine." He wrote them at length, carefully explaining that the poet was merged with the figure of the actor to form the "we" of the poem. This identification was valid, Crane held, because the clowning of Chaplin was a tragic mask equivalent to the futile visage worn by poetry in the modern world. The "famished kitten" represented the human feelings, or poetry, and took the place of the waifs whom Chaplin was always assisting in his films. Once it is recognized that the "inevitable thumb" belongs to the policeman who continually checks the warm-hearted intentions of Chaplin, its symbolic applicability to the poet is self-evident, and the poem is easily understood. These comments invite the observation that any difficulty which may be experienced in understanding the poem is due not to complexity of language or idea, but solely to the paucity of the material provided by the poet, as in the case of the policeman's thumb. Indeed, although Crane felt that in "Chaplinesque" he had made a noticeable advance, he had done so only with regard to "Pastorale." He had not outdone "Black Tambourine" in terms of language and imagery, though it must be granted that in terms of realized emotional implications "Chaplinesque" is finer. As the emotions thicken, so does the weight of the language, and in this respect it is quite a feat to encompass the light "sidestep" of Chaplin. Nevertheless, some of the imagery is strained and sentimental; the "kitten," for example, becomes a sentimental object "in the wilderness" . . . the entire last stanza employs a weak and poetic imagery of moon and grail which is shallow and dated.

The same fault of mawkishness marks "Praise for an Urn," which Crane wrote in the spring of 1922 after attending the funeral and cremation of his friend Ernest Nelson in December 1921, and which appeared in *The Dial* of May 1922. The poem is superior to "Chaplinesque" in its emotional impact, but the effect is lessened because of such images as "delicate riders . . . slant moon on the slanting hill" and the "Pierrot-Gargantua" unity. The last three stanzas, free of immature carryovers, are powerful in the manner by which they overcome the first three stanzas to bring the poem to a brilliant conclusion. These twelves lines, and a few from the preceding stanzas, contain the style of Crane at its positive best; they point the way to "Sunday Morning Apples" and "For the Marriage of Faustus and Helen." One of Crane's symbols for love makes its first appearance in this poem. I am referring to "gold hair," which thereafter is to be found in "Faustus and Helen III," "Virginia," "The Tunnel," and as "bright hair" in "Voyages V." It is of interest to note that many of the people whom Crane loved, including his mother, had blonde hair.

Although most of the poems written in 1921, and the Anderson article too, were accepted by magazines, Crane was too realistic to imagine that his successes had launched him on a free-lance writing career. He was convinced that poetry, not fiction or criticism, was his metier; in any case, the poems published heretofore had brought him not more than thirty dollars. Expecting to receive employment as a copy writer in June, he began poring over advertising books and commercial publications early in the spring. When June arrived, the general level of prosperity had not risen, and the firm which had expected to hire him found itself without sufficient business to warrant the engagement of a new writer. Crane had anticipated this disappointment somewhat, since other promises of help had likewise failed to materialize. "Most friends and friendly offers have proved such slippery fish," he wrote Munson. By October, he realized that his lack of experience in the advertising field was an important cause for his failure to be hired, and in order to overcome this obstacle he enrolled in an evening session course in advertising. "I am now sure of making advertising my real route to bread and butter," he wrote, "and have a strong notion that as a copy-writer I will eventually make a 'whiz'." His prediction came true. Although the course was not scheduled to end until May 1922, in January of that year he was hired as a copywriter by a Cleveland advertsing agency.

Crane was enthusiastic about his new job from the start, since it gave him an opportunity to work with words. In addition, it surprised him to find a business house functioning as this one did on "a decent basis" of courtesy and consideration for the individuality of its employees. "They actually will come of their own accord and tell you that they are pleased with the work you are doing for them," he wrote with unfeigned amazement to Munson. The heightened regard with which he was treated was so pleasant a contrast to the strained attentions of his father that he could, as he wrote further, exultantly "pass my goggle-eyed father on the streets now without a tremor!" Like many other young writers pressured by the need to earn a living, he was unable to foresee that in fashioning advertising slogans and paragraphs he would of necessity be weakening his integrity as a writer, as well as sapping his creative energies.

Before a few months had elapsed, however, Crane began to be discontented with his new work. At first his dissatisfaction was financially motivated, and undoubtedly his mother's need for a sizeable slice of his weekly salary of twenty-five dollars was a prime factor in this. As a result, he asked his firm for a considerable salary increase in July, which they were unwilling to grant. He had been feeling right along that the company was making him undertake too much "mail clerk work," duties which simultaneously hurt his pride and lowered his economic value. He had undoubtedly asked for the increase as a way of showing that his own idea of his value was still high, although as an apprentice he probably did not expect a sympathetic response from his employers. In August, therefore, he negotiated a transfer, at an initial raise of ten dollars a week and the promise of an additional increase within two months, to a newly-formed advertising agency.

Before he took over his new job in August 1922, however, Crane was facing a nervous breakdown, a physical
and mental distress which by now was common to him.
As he wrote to Munson: "For several days this week
I have been unable to retain food and have felt that at
any moment something would snap and I would go into
a million pieces. I haven't felt as 'dangerously' for several
years." It was his inability to find time in which to
write which brought him so close to demoralization, and
this was more important than any financial consideration.
At first, it had seemed logical to sidetrack his writing and
expend all his energies in his advertising work. "My
work takes up much of my time," he had written in
February. "I am giving satisfaction, I guess, and am
learning a trade that is the only possibile one for me so
far as I have discovered. It will get me back to New
York again sometime, and that is a considerable prospect.
I haven't done anything in poetry for some time, but may
resume again when I get a breeze in my sails." Within
a short time, he began to report that "I've been . . . puzzl-
ing my head over blueprints and figures until I have become somewhat dull." And again: "My present work . . .
demands the most frequent jerks of the imagination from
one thing to another . . ." And again, when Munson
asked him in September for contributions to *Secession*,
Crane could only sigh wearily: "Frankly, I'm tired to
death. The new job has been beyond expectations in
many ways, but it simply keeps my imagination tied down
more than ever. I have so much to do." The only poem
produced by Crane during these hectic months was
the weakly-satirical "The Great Western Plains,"† which
appeared in *Gargoyle* for August 1922.

†*See Appendix.*

But even time became unimportant under the impetus derived from reading the writing of P. D. Ouspensky.†
Cranes self-pitying mood of 1921 was replaced with a more positive quality which stimulated him in May 1922 to begin work on "For the Marriage of Faustus and Helen." Before long he was entirely preoccupied with the poem. "I have had a somewhat long poem on hand all summer," he wrote William Wright, "that has taken the kick out of everything else for me—and will continue to until it is finished. I never have had as steady an interest in my writing as lately . . ." An immediate result of Crane's return to poetry was the short piece "Sunday Morning Apples," which he wrote in August "out of sheer joy" after visiting the country studio of his painter-friend William Sommer. In the course of this writing, Crane slowly became aware that the question of time in which to write paled into insignificance alongside the far greater issue of creative energy. For now he wrote copy during the greater part of the day, and when he sat down in the evening or over a weekend to fashion his poetry, it was with chagrin that he found himself unable to write on a level which satisfied his high standards. This failure, he understood, resulted from his expenditure of thought and language on advertisements, catalogs, and folders. "There are birth pangs to go through with, even in so staid a thing as advertising copy and ideas," he wrote in October 1922 to Charmion Wiegand. "I hammer my forehead for hours somedays trying to get some idea that will be read, and loosen purse strings." In contrast to the creative doldrums in which he found himself now, the freer months of 1921 must have seemed

† *See Part II, Section 7, this book.*

preferable, even though he had been unemployed then and desperately in need of funds.

As always in Crane's life when the survival of his poetry was placed in jeopardy, his initial concern was to ensure its preservation. The efforts of young writers like Matthew Josephson who, under the influence of European writers impressed with skyscrapers and flashing electric signs, asserted in *Broom* that advertising was the most creative American art of the time, were scornfully dismissed by Crane. But it was not for any intellectual reason that he was antagonized. Indeed, advertising played the role of a "modern science" for him, and he firmly believed that it could sharpen the forensic eloquence of prose writers. But if advertising might be a suitable training ground for prose, it infringed too closely upon poetry to be tolerated. He therefore faced the dilemma of being disgruntled with an occupation into which he had acclimated himself so adequately that by October he had received a second raise in salary and was given full responsibility to write all the copy needed by his company.

Twisting and turning in his predicament, Crane directed his tortured mind outwards. The first manifestation of distemper was an intensification of the incipient estrangement with his mother. In mid-December, he suddenly left his home for a hotel, where he was determined to stay, as he wrote Munson, "until I talk to my mother about some things that will determine whether or not I shall continue to live out at the house any more. They are little things, mostly, but such little things accumulate almost into a complex that [is] too much for me to work under. There is no use in discussing them here, but just the constant restraint necessary in living with others, you may appreciate, is a deadening thing. Unless something

happens to release me from such annoyances I give up
hope of doing any satisfactory writing." Nor did Crane
limit his annoyance to those who surrounded him most
closely, for he had never fundamentally abandoned his
antagonism to the anti-cultural bias of America. The
visit of Isadora Duncan to Cleveland just before Christmas
gave him the pleasure of vicarious rebellion against the
city's smug insensitivity:

"You, as well as some of my local friends, must share in my excitement at seeing Isadora Duncan dance on Sunday night. She gave the
same program (All Tschaikowsky) that she gave in Moscow for the
Soviet celebration and, I think, you saw it in New York recently. It
was glorious beyond words, and sad beyond words too, from the rude
and careless reception she got here. It was like a wave of life, a
flaming gale that passed over the heads of the nine thousand in the
audience without evoking response other than silence and some mad-
dening cat-calls. After the first movement of the 'Pathetique' she came
to the fore of the stage, her hands extended. Silence —the most awful
silence! I started clapping furiously until she disappeared behind the
draperies. At least one tiny sound should follow her from all that audience. She continued through the performance with utter indifference
for the audience and with such intensity of gesture and such plastique
grace as I have never seen although the music was sometimes almost
drowned out by the noises from the hall. I felt like rushing to the
stage, but I was stimulated almost beyond the power to walk straight.
When it was all over she came to the fore-stage again in the little
red dress that had so shocked Boston, as she stated, and among other
things told the people to go home and take from the bookshelf the
works of Walt Whitman and turn to the section called, 'Calamus.'
Ninety-nine percent of them had never heard of Whitman, of course,
but that was part of the beauty of her gesture. Glorious to see her
there with her right breast and nipple quite exposed, telling the audience that the truth was not pretty, that it was really indecent, and
telling them (boobs!) about Beethoven, Tschaikowsky, and Scriabine."

Yet he could see no way of escape for himself. Sometimes
he felt that the age in which he lived—"A period that is
loose at all ends, without apparent direction of any sort"

—had paralyzed his limbs and frozen his mind, and that the wisest course would be to lie supine caught in the flow of its aimless current.

Ironically, his poetry served Crane as the agent of release from his torment, whereas his desire for poetic creation had originally caused it. By dint of much labor, he managed to complete "Faustus and Helen" in January 1923. Dispatched to Munson in New York, the poem so enchanted the latter that he quickly showed it to Waldo Frank, who was much moved by its lines. The praise Frank accorded the poem was duly transmitted by Munson to Crane, whose restlessness was thereby increased. For months Crane had been dreaming of living in New York, where he believed he would find himself free to write his poetry under the beneficial stimulation of writers who divined his spirit and appreciated his accomplishment. The urge to express himself in poetry, so long confined almost exclusively to the bounds of a single work, burst forth with vigorous character in the first two months of 1923.

Two of the four poems Crane wrote then are of insignificant character; although intended to be humorous, they are really not. "America's Plutonic Ecstasies" (January)† fails as satire . . . one has only to consider it alongside Cummings' "Poem, or Beauty Hurts Mr. Vinal" to sense the failure of Crane's poem and grasp its essential heaviness and lack of clarity. "Euclid Avenue" (February)† offers a bit more in terms of revealing Crane's pessimism, but is a confused and confusing effort as well. "Belle Isle" (January-February),† which Crane did not consider a finished poem, and later revised to form "Voyages VI," is another matter. It marks a further develop-

† *See Appendix.*

ment in Crane's handling of the sea, and foreshadows the love and death symbolism of the "Voyages" sequence. The river flow is the suspenseful passion of the lovers; fulfillment ("That instant white death of all pain") takes place on an island blooming like a flower in water. Time has dissipated the "absolute avowal" of love, but the memory of the island and ecstasy it bore is timeless.

The separation of lovers is also the theme of "Stark Major" (January-February). "A strange psychoanalytic thing," Crane wrote of it to Munson. Its title, he added, "came to me quite freely as *the* right thing." The poem appears pre-eminently simple in contrast to "Faustus and Helen." The opening stanza introduces the idea that the arrival of each new day heralds the parting of lovers. The second stanza is reassuring, offering the information that the lovers will be reunited at the close of day. The next three stanzas return to the anguished note of the first four lines. The psychoanalytic aspect of which Crane wrote enters in the observation that the birth of a child (like the birth of day) inevitably separates the two lovers who have conceived it, and emphasizes the suffering of the lover who is thinking the thoughts which compose the poem. The finality of the last stanza seems to contradict the hopefulness of the second stanza, and appears to be out of place in the poem, although it may be true from a psychological point of view. Though the poem is adequate enough technically, it does not penetrate into the emotional heart of the theme. Few images, except for "broken eyes" and "mound of undelivered life," approach a direct expression of feeling; the obliquity of treatment negates what effect these few have.

When in response to a note of thanks which Crane sent Frank he received a cordial answer, his desire to leave Cleveland grew more avid. By February 1923, his life had become, as he wrote, "entirely too febrile." An additional cause for his tension was his conception for a new poem, "The Bridge," which fired him with the grandeur and scope of its theme. Now it became positively repugnant to write advertising copy, and it was with furious resentment that he marched to work every day. He felt that it was "a repressive *fate*" which made it necessary for him to "munch ideas on water heaters" while his mind was "burgeoning with ideas and conceptions of the most baffling interest and lure . . ." During the second week of February, Crane was confined to bed with an attack of the grippe. A period of illness and convalescence is frequently the time when important decisions concerning the future are made, and there is every reason to believe that it was on his sickbed, away from his desk and with sufficient time and peace in which to reflect, that Crane determined to leave Cleveland for New York without much ado. Rendered confident by the success which had attended his past year of advertising work, and bearing in mind the rising economic prosperity of the country, he was quite certain that it would not take him long to locate a new berth in a New York advertising agency. A few weeks later, Munson received a package of booklets and clippings; these were samples of Crane's advertising work, which he intended to use as samples when hunting for a job in New York. Shortly thereafter, Crane himself arrived.

6. THE APPEARANCE
OF LITERARY PERSONALITY

THE DEVELOPMENT OF CRANE'S POETRY FROM the closing months of 1919 until the spring of 1922 may be viewed as a picture in miniature of the movement of modern art between the "expressionism" of Matisse and the "cubism" of Picasso. Indeed, it was to the works of plastic artists like Picasso and Matisse that Crane felt himself closely allied in spirit as a mature artist. If we substitute for the name of Matisse that of Sherwood Anderson, and for that of Picasso the name of T. S. Eliot, we are in a position to consider the two major literary forces between which Crane was propelled. From each of them he drew certain conceptions and standards of aesthetic propriety, and eventually emerged from their shadows with a full-fledged aesthetic system of his own in which, as it turned out, there was more of Eliot than Anderson, and a good deal of something new.

Crane was aware of the contrasting forces acting upon him. As early as December 1919, he wrote Munson in a letter dealing with Anderson: "He and Josephson are opposite poles. J., classic, hard, and glossy,—Anderson, crowd-bound, with a smell of the sod about him, uncouth. Somewhere between them is Hart Crane with a kind of

120

wistful indetermination, still much puzzled." If we engage in some more substitution and replace Josephson's
name with that of Eliot, we have the two points which I
have mentioned. Between the opposite principles which
these two men represented, Crane was to move slowly,
alternately writing and thinking under the guidance first
of one and then the other, never clearly cutting himself
away from either until the time arrived when he found
a third figure, Ouspensky, whose ideas enabled him to
reconcile the theories which he had taken from Eliot and
Anderson into the individual quality of Hart Crane.
There were imaginative attributes in both Eliot and Anderson which attracted him, approaches to the composition of art which in quite different ways gave him the
feeling that they had satisfactorily accomplished their
artistic aims. They were models of performance whom he
could emulate. Thus, when at one time he considered a
theme that he believed would require a freshness of mood
that was rare, he wrote: "T. S. Eliot does it often,—once
merely with the name 'Sweeney' and Sherwood Anderson,
though with quite different method in a story of his in
The Smart Set, some time ago, called, 'I Want to Know
Why,' one of the greatest stories I ever expect to read,—
better even than most of the *Winesburg* chapters." Each
man was original in his art, each was absolutely modern
in his subject, and in each Crane sensed a genuine poetic
spirit such as he felt within himself. It was a period of
rapid growth for Crane, still in his early twenties, and
in the face of the rapidly-changing poetic scene with its
strident quarrels between imagists, vers librists, symbolists, and conservatives, he might well have felt confused
although elated when, as he wrote; "New theories are
filling my head every day . . ." For this reason, it took

time before he could determinedly assert that this and
that, such and so, were to be the principles by which he
would manage his own work.

Anderson's friendship with Crane went beyond the discussion of similar experiences in business. Anderson cor-
responded frequently with Crane after 1919, criticising
the poems which Crane sent him, informing Crane of the
progress of his own work, and writing his impressions of
people seen and areas visited in the course of his travels
over the country. One such letter from Alabama, in
which Anderson discussed the Negro as a subject for
literature, may well have been the inspiration for Crane's
"Black Tambourine." "The Negroes are the living
wonder of this place," Anderson had written. "What a
tale if someone could penetrate into the home and life of
the Southern Negro and not taint it in the ordinary superficial way." In the summer of 1922, when Anderson
visited Crane at the latter's home in Cleveland, the two
finally met.

Crane's review of *Winesburg, Ohio*, the individual
stories of which he had read as they appeared in *The
Little Review* and other magazines, declared that Anderson had performed the Balzacian feat of sympathetically
vivifying every character in the book.† Anderson had
been able to achieve such understanding, Crane wrote,
because his approach was restrained without an accompanying loss in genuine emotional content: "The style is
flawless. I know of no finer selection of 'significant material,' combined with proper treatment and economy of

† *See Appendix.*

detail." The poetical quality of the book he likened to that of Lucretius. Anderson's work continued to excite Crane with its poetic overtones; *Poor White*, so he wrote Munson in 1920, pleased him as much as the earlier Winesburg stories:

"I wish, after you have read it, that we could have a fireside chat on the exquisite work of such scenes as the description of the murderer-saddle-maker sitting by the pond and rocking gently to and fro (the simplicity of A's great power of suggestion is most mocking to the analyst)—and the scene where the sex-awakening girl hears the men in the barn in speaking of her say,—'the sap is mounting into the tree.' Nature is so strong in all the work of Anderson—and he describes it as one so willingly and happily surrendered to it, that it colors his work with the most surprising grasp of what 'innocence' and 'holiness' ought to mean. Also, his uncanny intuition into the feelings of women (a number of women have remarked to me about this) is very unusual."

It seems Crane was imbued with a respect for the impressionist method out of all proportion to its true nature. By ignoring or failing to observe the essential formlessness of Anderson's style, Crane made it easier for himself to fall under the influence of impressionism as a method of literary workmanship.

Undoubtedly this acceptance was motivated in part by Crane's absorption of the spirit of emotional efflorescence generated by such magazines as *The Soil*, *The Seven Arts*, and *The Little Review*, which he had encountered directly while in New York. Another factor was an interest in avoiding didacticism, which in 1920 apparently was a more important literary issue to him than form. He was averse, for example, to the presentation of social ideas or programs in a piece of literature on the ground that the functionalization of art was a rank heresy: "Of course you cannot take it seriously as a work of art after the first page," he wrote at this time about a play which a friend had composed. "It is stark propaganda . . ." Nor did the verity of the didacticism presented in a poem or play alter his fundamental antagonism to "propaganda." He failed to distinguish formlessness as a defect so long as the work of art which contained it did not serve also as a vehicle of propaganda. This critical error is expressed in his doubt that Theodore Dreiser, Anderson, and Robert Frost wrote with deliberate ideological purpose. "After all," he asked Munson late in 1919, "has not their success been achieved more through natural unconsciousness than with a mind . . . thoroughly logical or propagandistic . . . " This was, of course, an error in judgment, for Dreiser, Anderson, and Frost consciously express their individual conceptions about human problems in their poetry and prose. A few steps further in analysis, and Crane would have understood that their "natural unconsciousness" was not of idea at all, but of the experimental technical manipulation of their medium instead.

Actually, it seems doubtful that Crane's primary interest in poetry during these years was one of form at all. His earlier poems had been chiefly composed in conventional rhymed moulds, and there existed in him a quiescent unconcern about the necessity for experimentation in new forms. Free verse, which he had already utilized in "North Labrador," seemed sufficiently experimental to him. When he did become aware of structural innovations, in the poetry of Wallace Stevens for example, his enthusiasm was restricted to "the novel rhyme and rhythm effects" rather than to other more daring qualities in Stevens' poetry. This interpretation is borne out further by his attitude to the forms of other artistic media. Henry James, whose work Crane enjoyed, is a case in point. In his 1921 article on Anderson, Crane showed his contempt for James' engrossment with the technical niceties of his vehicle by terming it a "pattern-making preoccupation." "And what a satisfaction this is," Crane went on to say about Anderson, "to read stories over and over again without a bundle of dry bones and cogwheels of 'situations' and 'plots' spilling out into one's lap."

Crane's method of composition also made it possible for him to look with favor on the impressionists. As early as 1919, he admitted that sudden inspiration guided him in the setting-down of a poem's preliminary lines. Thereafter, when he had exhausted the potentialities of this initial impetus, he would return to the draft and "hammer it into shape." This procedure, of course, was in accord with the theory of composition which Romantic poets have upheld since it was enunciated in Plato's *Ion*:

"For all good poets, epic as well as lyric, compose their beautiful poems not by art, but because they are inspired and possessed. And as the Corybantian revellers when they dance are not in their right mind, so the lyric poets are not in their right mind when they are composing their beautiful strains: but when falling under the power of music and metre they are inspired and possessed; like Bacchic maidens who draw milk and honey from the rivers when they are under the influence of Dionysus but not when they are in their right minds."†

How was the writer to fortify himself before he sat down to write? He must, like the impressionist writers, make himself into a full and enthusiastic observer of all phases of man and his life, Crane believed, and when filled with the "details of existence, plain psychology, etc." he began

† *Quotations from THE DIALOGUES OF PLATO, Jowett translation, on this and subsequent pages reprinted by permission of Oxford University Press.*

to write, all his knowledge, craft and insight would well up from within him and he would "create spontaneously."

It was Ezra Pound as poetic technician, critic, and symbol of the independent artist to whom Crane at first declared allegiance. Pound, after Yeats, appeared to him in 1917 to be the greatest living poet using the English language. Although Crane's admiration for Pound never entirely left him, the figure of Eliot soon began to assume a more commanding position in the hierarchy of living poets than either Pound or Yeats. In October 1919, for example, Crane turned to Pound and Eliot for standards of poetic achievement. A year later, it was Eliot alone whom he saw as the dominating influence in English poetry and upon himself as well. It was not merely that Crane sensed the greater poetic intensity and philosophical depth of Eliot. The levity and strained recondition of Pound began to pall upon him, and Crane expressed this dissatisfaction when he said apropos Pound's article on Brancusi in *The Little Review* (Autumn 1921) that Pound would engage in any antics in order to avoid being obvious. A good portion of Pound's criticism and poetry was too perilously close to the blatant high-pressure of Crane's American surroundings to be attractive, and the more earnest nature of Eliot's manner offered a pleasing contrast. Yet it was from both Pound and Eliot that Crane was learning . . . from their poetry as it appeared in *Poetry, The Egoist, Others, Arts and Letters,* and *The Little Review*, as well as from the acute essays which accompanied the poems, rationalized them, and built up a framework of critical theory.

In October 1921, Crane wrote to William Wright: "I . . . do not greatly care for Mme. Browning. And on the top of my dislike for this lady, Tennyson, Thompson, Chatterton, Byron, Moore, Milton, and several more . . . But you will notice that I *do* run joyfully towards Messrs. Poe, Whitman, Shakespeare, Keats, Shelley, Coleridge, John Donne!!!, John Webster!!!, Marlowe, Baudelaire, Laforgue, Dante, Cavalcanti, Li Po, and a host of others." With a few adjustments, the exclusion of Poe and Shelley from the second list and the inclusion of Henry James for example, one might have had a fairly accurate list of the writers whom Eliot and Pound had condemned on the one hand and lauded on the other for the five or six years prior to 1921. For it is obvious that Crane received his literary education from Eliot and Pound. Through them, he came to Laforgue and the French symbolists, the minor Elizabethans, Blake, Vaughn, and other writers who became his favorites.

Crane said in 1922 that he had read Eliot's "The Love Song of J. Alfred Prufrock" at least twenty-five times, and his "Preludes" many more times than that. Evidence of this reading can be found in Crane's poetry. One has but to place poems side by side: "Chaplinesque" and "Prufrock" . . . "In Shadow" and Eliot's "La Figlia che Piange." And there is textual evidence, too: the "old women" of "Faustus III" and the "ancient women" of "Preludes." Crane had read Pound carefully, as well. Lines from Pound occur frequently in Crane's letters as illustrations. Thus, a Hervey Minns photograph was linked by him to Pound's "A Virginal," and Crane described his own temper in 1920 with citations from Pound's "The Rest." Pound's influence upon the lines of Crane's poetry, however, was minor, although it is possible that the theme and imagery of Pound's "A Girl" infiltrated into "Garden Abstract," the spirit of his "In Durance (1907)" into Crane's "Episode of Hands." A further portion of Pound's influence upon Crane's direction may have been his little poem "A Pact," in which Pound acknowledged Whitman as the poet who "broke the wood" on which Pound would do the "carving"; this celebration of Whitman's rough modernity may have been one of the stimuli for Crane's later expression of a Whitmanian spirit in an antithetical form.

It is well to clarify Crane's primary concern in poetry during this period before we proceed, since it will explain many aspects of his future development. In September 1921 he wrote about a fellow-poet: "He seems afraid to use any emotion in his poetry,—merely observation and sensation,—and because I call such work apt to become thin, he thinks me sloppy and stupid . . ." The expression of emotion was the purpose urging Crane on to write poetry. It might be his emotional reaction to the atmosphere of a boxing match, slowly becoming heated under the impact of the crowd's savage cries for blood, the violent contrast between the arc-lighted ring and the surrounding darkness from which gleam the shining eyes and teeth of the audience. Or it might be his response to a package of old letters, as in "My Grandmother's Love Letters." Unfortunately for the completeness of his realization, it was only his own emotions that he understood. When he tried to convey another's feelings objectively, he failed, and so he asked himself ironically: "Are your fingers long enough to play/Old keys that are but echoes . . . ?" The black man of "Black Tambour-ine" wandered in a "mid-kingdom" where Crane could not reach him.

Crane recognized this subjectivity as a defect, and wrote in November 1921: "I have never, so far, been able to present a vital, living and tangible,—a positive emotion to my satisfaction. For as soon as I attempt such an act I either grow obvious or ordinary, and abandon the thing at the second line. Oh! it is hard." But he finally realized that his greatest successes in the capture of emotion were achieved when he explored his own depths, and he believed that in "Chaplinesque" he had performed well as an actor displaying his own feelings. "Praise for an Urn," "Sunday Morning Apples," and "The Bottom of the Sea is Cruel" were the products of further exploration in the realm of his own sensibility, and they paved the way for his self-analysis in "For the Marriage of Faustus and Helen," the first masterful justification of this knowledge.

The "interpretation of modern moods," with himself as protagonist, became his aim. At first he was not clear in his own mind about the nature of the moods he wished to concern himself with. In 1920, he had confessed to a liking for decorativeness and richness. At the same time, he found himself enthralled with emotions of purity and simplicity. Under the influence of Eliot and Laforgue, the incongruity of his pristine emotions in their uncongenial environment provided one direction, the ironic contrast in poems like "Porphyro in Akron" and "The Bridge of Estador," and Crane described this sort of juxtaposition as he found it in Gogol's *Taras Bulba*: "Human emotion in it is like delicate pastel tinted flowers on a background of midnight black. The black terrific power

of the forest and winter threatens continually behind
every word in the action." But simultaneously and at
an increasing pace, his own emotional propensities took
new forms. Intense and violent experiences which submerged his ego became more necessary if he were to be
able to survive the threat of those forces directly oppressing him: he had passed far beyond innocence and it could
no longer truly satisfy his emotional appetite. He found
the measure of his needs in the poetry of John Donne,
which stood for him as "a dark, musky, brooding, spec-
ulative vintage, at once sensual and spiritual, and singing rather the beauty of experience than innocence."

The texture of Crane's emotional sensibility determined
his reaction to other American poets among the advance-
guard. "American poetry is on a slump or vacation at
present," he wrote in 1920. Marianne Moore he found
overly precious, unexciting in a way he believed poetry
should not be. He more than admired the technical
ingenuity of Wallace Stevens ("There is a man whose
work makes most of the rest of us quail," Crane wrote
in 1919) and the meticulous precision of William Carlos
Williams. But the total impression their work left on
him was that it was over-refined, as though they had
strained their feelings through a sieve and fastidiously
selected those which passed through on the score of deli-
cacy.

The robust quality which Crane missed in the experi-
mentalists he found in the poetry of Edgar Lee Masters,
Vachel Lindsay, Carl Sandburg, and Whitman. He was
reinforced in his affection for them by his respect for
Anderson, in whose work he found emotional nuance
a distinguishing feature. Poems like "Episode of Hands"
with its comradely theme, "Porphyro in Akron" with its

industrial detail, stem from the language and spirit of Whitman and the Midwestern poets. The colloquial language, the direct and forceful diction, and the speech rhythm of "Porpyhro in Akron" is a derivation of the Midwestern school, although it may be presumed that the greater trace of Sandburg to be found therein is due to Crane's response to Sandburg's lyrical qualities. A comparison of a few lines from Sandburg's "Mamie" and the early draft lines of "Porphyro in Akron" clearly illustrate the influence of the older poet.

The example set by Sandburg, Masters, and Lindsay, and followed by Crane during 1920, inevitably led to the inclusion in his poetry of that didactic comment which Crane despised. The subject and detail of "Porphyro in Akron" and "Episode of Hands" revealed his point of view in his selection of the details comprising the poems. These subjects were in the social arena, not restricted to the secret mind of the poet, and he could not avoid displaying an intellectual position when handling them. Under the inquiries of friends who persisted in seeing socially-conscious attitudes ("propaganda" as Crane considered them) in "Episode of Hands" and "Porphyro in Akron," Crane gradually became aware that the impressionist method was at variance in its fundamental nature with his goal of emotional expression. In drawing upon non-psychological materials, the impressionists could not avoid becoming embroiled in the social-economic implications of those materials. When Munson asserted in 1920 that "Episode of Hands" was a failure, Crane replied:

"The poem fails, not because of questions, propagandistic and economic, which you mentioned, but because of that synthetic conviction of form and creation, which it lacks. It is all too complicated an explanation to attempt leastwise on paper at this time of the night,—but perhaps you will miraculously be able to penetrate through to my meaning. As it stands, there are only a few fragments scattered thru it to build on, but I may make something of it in time. However,—if it does evolve into something,—it will be too elusive for you to attach sociological arguments to at least in the matter of most of the details you have mentioned."

His revision of "Black Tambourine" in the early months of 1921 will furnish an illustration of his determination by that date to eradicate any so-called propaganda from his work. The original version refers to our lack of knowledge of Aesop's life and death ("Fox brush and sow ear top his grave"), and alludes bitterly to mankind's neglect of Aesop by its failure to provide him with a more suitable monument, i.e., accurate knowledge of him as an individual by posterity, despite his concern with the problems of man ("Even though mankind was his care"). This last line stands in the final version as "And mingling incantations on the air." Thereby Crane struck out the moral condemnation contained in the original version. In explaining the poem to Munson, who had prodded him for such an explanation, Crane avoided any elucidation of his position on the status of the Negro:

"Excuse my apparent evasion of your request for an explanation about 'Black Tambourine' The Word 'mid-kingdom' is perhaps the key-word to what ideas there are in it. The poem is a description and bundle of insinuations, suggestions bearing on the negro's place somewhere between man and beast. That is why Aesop is brought, etc.—the popular conception of negro romance, the tambourine on the wall. The value of the poem is only, to me, in what a painter would call its 'tactile' quality,—an entirely aesthetic feature. A propagandist for either side of the negro question could find anything he wanted to in it. My only declaration in it is that I find the negro (in the popular mind) sentimentally or brutally 'placed' in this mid-kingdom, etc."

Crane made a gallant effort to confuse Munson, but his sympathy for human suffering, perhaps vague and unpolitical, was nevertheless present in the lines of the poem.

Crane's awareness of impressionism as a method more suited to the expression of externals rather than emotions was linked to a growing belief that the form of his poetry was inadequate because of the impressionists' influence over him. From New York, Matthew Josephson wrote letters in which he belabored "Porphyro in Akron" for its crudity of form, and Crane could offer no defence because he admitted the justice of the criticism. Meanwhile, he had been reading the French Symbolist poets—Rimbaud, Baudelaire—as well as more modern poets like Vildrac, Eliot, Pound, Huxley, and Edith Sitwell, finding ever-increasing delight in their subtle revelations and their technical mastery of poetic music. He saw no structural rawness in their poetry, rather a conscious use of traditional metrical pattern and variation. They had managed, despite their self-imposed boundaries of obliquity, to plunge deeper into shades of emotion than had men like Sandburg with their artless presentations. It has been stated earlier that Crane was never averse to working with great patience and effort on the revision and finishing of his poems. Because of this attitude, he found it particularly simple to return to the traditional limits of poetry, and indeed it was a step that he took with a great deal of determination. Crane, as it happened, had used meter and rhyme in poems written during 1920 and 1921. "The Bridge of Estador" and "Black Tambourine" are examples. But now it was a weighed and measured intention to bring himself within the bounds which Eliot had posited in 1917 in a discussion of poetic pattern: "The ghost of some simple meter should lurk behind the arras in even the 'freest' verse; to advance menacingly as we doze, and withdraw as we rouse. Or, freedom is only

true freedom when it appears against the background of
an artificial limitation." In acceptance of this theory,
Crane wrote in November 1921: "I may even be carried
back into 'rime and rhythm' before I get through provided I can carry these encumbrances as deftly and un-
self-consciously as, say, Edward Thomas sometimes did."

Crane's movement to the camp dominated by Eliot was
precipitated as well by a gathering antagonism to the
forces of impressionism on the part of younger American
writers. By reason of his personal contact with Matthew Josephson and Gorham Munson, Crane was close
to the center of the revolt against the methods of critical
and creative writing utilized by those whom the first issue
of *Secession* castigated in the spring of 1922: "It hopes
that there is ready for it an American public which has
advanced beyond the fiction of Sinclair Lewis and Sherwood Anderson and the criticism of Paul Rosenfeld and
Louis Untermeyer." The crux of the attack was a revulsion from the so-called formlessness of these writers as
typified in their seeming disinterest in language and structure. In Ernest Boyd's praise of *Winesburg, Ohio*, the
attitude which men like Anderson and Dreiser embodied
for Josephson and Munson may be seen concisely. "They
have so much to say," Boyd wrote in an introduction to
the book, "that content is often unrestricted by mere form
. . ." Other manifestations, in addition to the creative
writings of the impressionists, were statements of artistic
negation such as Anderson gave forth with in *The Triumph of the Egg* (1921): "I have a wonderful story to
tell but know no way to tell it." With Crane's interest

in the problem of form at its peak, his confidence in Anderson, the figure who more than any other writer stood forth as a personal symbol of impression, began to leave him. *Marching Men* (1917), an early Anderson novel which Crane read in 1921, proved a sad disappointment to him. His doubt broadened into disillusionment later in the year after he read Anderson's latest book, *The Triumph of an Egg* (1921), which he considered a decisive book in terms of Anderson's career. "I feel in an odd way," he wrote in December 1921, "that he has, like a diver, touched bottom in a certain sense, and that his future work must manifest certain changes of a more positive character than the bare statement of reality, or conclude his promise." Extracts from Anderson's forthcoming novel, *Many Marriages*, which ran serially in *The Dial* during 1922, seem to have destroyed Crane's respect for him as a craftsman, for he considered them banal and stupid. "Anderson's naivete . . ." he wrote Munson after reading the chapters, "becomes very aggravating."

While drawing away from the American impressionists insofar as form was concerned, Crane did not follow in the extremist paths of those contemporaries like E. E. Cummings and Josephson who swallowed without a gulp the more violent impressionism of the European Dadaists. The Dadaists and their American adherents did not gain Crane's favor. They struck him as being more brittle than writers like Williams and Moore, and their constant preoccupation with superficial effects was not encouraging to a poet like Crane who desired an intensification of sensibility and its revelation. His negative reaction to what he called the "flamdoodle" of Dadaism was a manifestation of Crane's regard for form as a means and not an end in itself.

News about the Dadaist uproar, which had begun in Europe as the first World War drew to a close, started to seep into the United States in some quantity in 1920. In that year, for example, John Rodker announced to the readers of *The Little Review* that Baroness Elsa von Freytag-Loringhoven, whose incredibly-incomprehensible "poems" had been appearing in that magazine's pages for some time, was an original Dadaist, the first in New York City. Excerpts from Dadaist poems, as well as a complete Dadaist manifesto that had been issued in Paris, were reprinted in various numbers of *The Little Review*. In the same issue of *The Little Review* (September-December 1920) which contained Crane's "Garden Abstract" and his comments on Hervey Minns,† Louis Lozowick contributed a note on Russian Dadaists and translated sections from their amazing poems. We must bear in mind that Crane had seen this article in order to appreciate the full implications of a letter he wrote to Josephson in January 1921:

"I hear [that] 'New York' has gone mad about 'Dada' and that a most exotic and worthless review is being concocted by Man Ray, billets in a bag printed backwards, on rubber deluxe, etc. What next! This is worse than The Baroness. By the way, I like the way the discovery has suddenly been made that she has all along been, unconsciously, a Dadaist. I cannot figure out just what Dadaism is beyond an insane jumble of the four winds, the six senses, and plum pudding. But if the Baroness is to be a keystone for it,—then I think I can possibly know when it is coming and avoid it."

When Munson sent Crane some representative examples of Dadaist literary production from Europe, the latter commented unenthusiastically that they were "tres amusant,—but-well-alright56789————*!!" The Dadaist poet recognized few limitations controlling the extent to

† *See Appendix.*

which the form of his medium could be distorted. Absolute freedom for any form of surface experimentation, whether in typography, punctuation, or syntax, was permissible, even if it meant the grand elimination of words entirely and their replacement by groups of typographical symbols, numerals, or meaningless jumbles of letters as in the quotation which follows:

> "aeggov aaa crépuscule
> derrière le pastel le perforatrices les perforatrices
> hhhaa   il a signé le quadruple
> bregan   aeaeaeaeaeaaaa"

Despite Crane's antipathy for Dadaism, Josephson attempted to convert him to a finer appreciation of the liberty provided by Dadaism for the venturesome artist. He had correctly sensed in Crane, almost from the time they first met in 1919, that the latter tended toward conservatism where matters of poetic form were concerned. Accordingly, Josephson felt it his responsibility to convince Crane that he ought to break away from the patterns used by the more conservative poets such as Stevens and Eliot, and thereby free himself of a self-imposed restraint. Crane, however, had observed Dadaist work at close hand in the English translation of Jean Cocteau's long poem, "The Cape of Good Hope" (*The Little Review*, Autumn 1921). He found Cocteau's poem, as well as other Dadaist poetry, to be a capricious welter of uncontrolled detail which he could not adopt as a guide for himself, despite his high regard for Josephson as one of the most "acute" critics of poetry he knew. "Dada," he wrote with perspicacity to Munson late in the fall of 1921, "(maybe I am wrong, but you will correct me) is nothing more to me than the dying agonies of this movement, maladie moderne." Actually, of course, despite its nihilistic behaviour and ideology, the Dadaist movement served a useful purpose when it forced poets to re-examine their tools—words—from the individual letters which composed them to irrational combinations of these letters until words were finally reconstructed with a deeper perception of their organic constitution. The prime defect of Dadaism from a technical viewpoint lay in its mistaken demonstration of workshop exercises as completed works of art.

Despite his recognition of Eliot's stature, Crane could not avoid dissenting from the spirit of his work. With Eliot's recognition of the chaotic aimlessness of the age, he was in full accord. But he felt that Eliot had been overwhelmed by the emptiness he sensed and experienced after the war, and had taken refuge in a temperamental sterility. On these grounds, Eliot's spiritual influence over younger poets such as Aldous Huxley could not be other than harmful. "Is real poetry so obviously clever?" Crane asked Munson about Huxley in October 1920. "Modern life and its vacuity seems to me to be responsible for such work. There is only a lime or lemon to squeeze or a pepper-pot left to shake . . . He comes in the line of Eliot." A few months later, in March 1921, Crane discarded a poem he had begun because "it savours too strongly of Eliot and Huxley for me to take further interest." Crane's desire to avoid being marked with the stamp of another contemporary poet undoubtedly figures in the generation of his desire to strike out in another direction than the one Eliot had taken. But he was fundamentally motivated in this divergence by his habitual op-

timism and his spiritual beliefs, which impelled him to
search for a means of integrating the happy phases of his
existence with the bleak vistas of the wasteland. So he
wrote to Allen Tate in May 1922: "The poetry of negation is beautiful—alas, too dangerously so for one of my
mind. But I am trying to break away from it . . . one
does have joys. The vocabulary of damnations and pros-
trations has been developed at the expense of these other
moods, however, so that it is hard to dance in proper measure." About a month later, Crane amplified his conception of the relationship between Eliot and himself in another letter to Tate.

"I have been facing him for *four* years,—" he wrote, "and while I
haven't discovered a weak spot yet in his armour, I flatter myself lately
that I have discovered a safe tangent to strike, which if I can possibly
explain the position,—goes *through* him toward a *different goal*. You
see it is such a fearful temptation to imitate him that at times I have
been almost distracted . . . In his own realm Eliot presents us with an
absolute *impasse*, yet oddly enough, he can be utilized to lead us to,
intelligently point to, other positions and 'pastures new.' Having absorbed him enough we can trust ourselves as never before, in the air
or on the sea. I, for instance, would like to leave a few of his 'nega-
tions' behind me, risk the realm of the obvious more, in quest of
new sensations, *humours*."

By the time Crane read *The Wasteland* in a fall 1922
number of *The Dial*, Eliot's overpowering influence was
a bygone phenomenon. "What do you think of Eliot's
'The Wasteland'?" he asked Munson. "I was rather disappointed. It was good, of course, but so damned dead.
Neither does it, in my opinion, add anything important
to Eliot's achievement."

Crane's motives in seeking to incorporate the hopeful
and joyous aspects of his experience into poetry are not
impugned in the revelation that he desired originality as

a creative artist, and that he set himself off from Eliot on both these counts. The desire for a harmonious relationship with a universe in which he found himself frustrated and discontented was a powerful one, and far transcends any appetite for novelty on its own score. Thus he wrote to Tate in July 1922 about a poem the latter had composed: "I would like to see you follow out the directions indicated in this poem—not their downward slant (interesting enough), but (if you get what I mean) their upward slant into something broadly human. Launch into praise. *You* are one who can give praise an edge and beauty, Allen. You have done so well in a couple of damnations, that I feel confident in you." That Crane did not want to shock the bourgeoisie we observed in the discussion of Dadaism. But it is also true that an artist who strives to express a spirit contrary to that which animates those artists whom he most admires from a technical viewpoint, will often find it necessary to assert the individuality of his thought in garments equally individual. A more encompassing view would lead to the assertion that the artist is always searching for a technique whose total effect will be in rhythm with his purpose.

As early as 1920, Crane had said that he wanted to acquire a poetic tone which would possess "an extreme freshness that has nothing to do with the traditional 'dew-on-the-grass' variety." Like Baudelaire, Whitman, and Rimbaud before him, Crane was entranced with the need for originality, the new, and the modern. This effect could be obtained from a combination of form, language, and substance that was unique, and Crane demonstrated his awareness of this truism when he wrote in October 1921 that "I am only interested in adding what seems to me something really *new* to what *has* been written." He had stated earlier in 1921 that there seemed to exist a "kind of critical stricture that won't permit me the expression of the old asininities." The new substance that Crane intended to incorporate in poetry was his interpretation of universally-recurring Platonic themes such as love, death and beauty ("some new, intensely personal viewpoint . . . on the eternal feelings") with an emphasis upon the positive quality of these ideals and realities. But there would be no subject that was unsuitable per se as a poetic theme, unless it was hackneyed through "poetic" usage. The language in which these themes would find being must likewise be new, filled with all the rich resources of an extensive vocabulary ("One must be drenched in words, literally soaked with them") until it was entirely the "personal idiom" of its creator. "Be your own language—in so pure a way that it will be noticeable, and you will do well enough," he wrote in this vein to Tate in 1922.

Crane's determination to express a new viewpoint in a new idiom meant that he must inevitably face a restricted circle of readers, since there would be none of the recognizable hooks in his work upon which the mass of hidebound fanciers of poetry could hang their hats and make themselves at home. He had no fear of this limitation, and wrote in 1921 that "I realize that the audience for my work will always be quite small." He understood that a way to avoid it was to proceed in the path cut by Edna St. Vincent Millay: "With her equipment Edna Millay is bound to succeed to the appreciative applause of a fairly large audience." The lack of a wide range of readers did not disturb him, however, since the unalterable gulf between himself and this vast appreciation consisted of his own high standards of taste. In his 1921 article on Anderson, for example, Crane carefully explained that Anderson had been able to outgrow his propagandistic strain only because he had never pandered to the public: "In Anderson there has been some great sincerity . . . that has made him refuse to turn aside to offer the crowds those profitable 'lollypops' that have 'made' and ruined so many of our writers." The public did not appreciate the truth when it was offered, Crane said further, and in order to obtain its attention the artist had to incorporate in his work "universally obvious understandings" which falsified the artist's conceptions and wrecked his integrity. He was not prepared to sacrifice his integrity for the plaudits of a mass mentality which he fully despised, even though in 1920 he had assigned the artist a front-rank role among those who fight the Philistines. Indeed, he was satisfied now to ignore the crowds and please himself alone if need be. "What I seem to want to do more and more as time goes on," he had written in 1920, "is to preserve a record of a few thoughts and reactions that I've had in as accurate colors as possible for at least private satisfaction." He anticipated charges of extra-sophistication which would be thrown at him by those who, as Louis Untermeyer before long did in *American Poetry Since* 1900 (1923), would accuse him of overconcern with verbal craftsmanship and insufficient concern with what was to be said, but he was determined to adhere to his stated goal.

The form which Crane took as he shook free from the spirit of Eliot was the blank verse that had been brilliantly employed by Eliot and Wallace Stevens, and before them by the Elizabethans. Other modern poets had employed blank verse since its first proud appearance in Marlowe's lines, but never with the confidence and sustained achievement of the Elizabethans until Eliot. Under the influence of Eliot and Josephson, Crane had begun to read intensively in the Elizabethan playwrights. There he discovered an amazing opulence of language, a sense of ironic contrast, and an emotional sensibility which overwhelmed him with its universality and depth. In addition, the lustiness and expansiveness of the Elizabethan temper was akin to the psychological frame-work of his make-up. Stimulated by these interests and similarities, he decided to follow Eliot's lead and adapt the Elizabethans to the perfection of his own work:

"There are parts of his 'Gerontion' that you can find almost bodily in Webster and Jonson. Certain Elizabethans and Laforgue have played a tremendous part in Eliot's work, and you catch hints of his great study of these writers in his 'Sacred Grove.' I don't want to imitate Eliot, of course,—but I have come to the stage now where I want to carefully choose my most congenial influences and, in a way, 'cultivate' their influence."

At last he had found a solution for "the problem of form" which, as he wrote, "becomes harder for me every day." It was in its way a happy medium for Crane. His experience with free verse had made him impatient with what he designated as "that mechanical insistence of certain formal patterns that can sometimes infuriate me . . . tiresome repetitions of sound or rhyme . . ." In blank verse there was a measure of metrical discipline, but it could be balanced with run-on lines and verbal variations in sufficient quantity to provide a field of activity for musical exuberance and the full note of which Crane was enamoured. Crane's choice of this pattern for his major work presaged the freedom with which he would experiment in the formal avenues of poetry, whether the sonnet form of "To Shakespeare," the poem in prose ("Havana Rose"), or the Dadaist calligramme of "The Mango Tree."

7. "THE BRIGHT LOGIC IS WON"

WE HAVE SEEN IN THE PRECEDING SECTION that Crane intended to present "a new viewpoint" in a new idiom. It is the purpose of the pages which follow to trace the formulation of this viewpoint and the aspects of the idiom in which it was expressed, so that we may be enabled to trace its operation in his poetry and life. For the sake of convenience in clarifying the issues involved, the material is presented in terms of three men who influenced him—Rimbaud the poet, Ouspensky the philosopher, and Frank the novelist-critic.

ARTHUR RIMBAUD

It is probable that Crane's first direct acquaintance with the poetry of Rimbaud came from an article by Ezra Pound. Pound had taken it upon himself to put an end to "the time when the intellectual affairs of America could be conducted on a monolingual basis," and in the February 1918 issue of *The Little Review* he presented a little anthology of modern French poetry ranging from nineteenth century poets like Tristan Corbière and Jules Laforgue to contemporaries like Jules Romains and Charles Vildrac. The poems were interspersed with lively comments in which Pound called attention to the qualities he discerned

144

in them. Unfortunately, for Crane did not know French,
the poems were not translated into English. It must have
been Pound's critical statements then, rather than the
poems, from which Crane could learn about Rimbaud.
The three poets ranked by Pound above all the others were
Corbière, Laforgue, and Rimbaud; only in Rimbaud did
Pound find a pure poetic genius. Pound's observation that
the key to Rimbaud's accomplishment was the utilization
of intense emotional feeling, with direct entrance by the
poet into the subject as the method, undoubtedly was significant to Crane.

The opportunity to read the writings of Rimbaud in a
quantity sufficient for Crane to understand the man and in
a language he could understand was provided by J. Sibley
Watson's article on Rimbaud in *The Dial* of June 1920.
This article was followed in the two succeeding issues by
Watson's translations from Rimbaud's *Une Saison en Enfer*
and *Les Illuminations*. Crane did not pay too much attention to the development of Rimbaud, from disillusionment
and bitterness through disgust to final despair and renunciation, which Watson so carefully demonstrated. Watson's conclusion that Rimbaud was culpable, in part at
least, for the tragedy of his career and life ("Like some
noble animal caught in a garden, he ignored the things at
hand and persisted in butting his head against the wall")
demanded a different attitude to suffering and tragedy
than Crane possessed in order for him to treat the example
of Rimbaud with caution. It was sufficient for Crane to
read that Rimbaud was "one of the founders of a new
school of poetry" and to place that alongside Pound's
enthusiasm; thereafter, Rimbaud's poetry, and not the
moral implication of his existence, remained meaningful

for Crane. Evidently the farthest point Crane reached along the line charted by Watson for Rimbaud was the one at which Crane was himself located, and that was "without illusions . . . as to the pleasures of service and of making his way in the modern world . . . "

Watson's quotations in his article from Rimbaud's letter of May 15, 1871 to Paul Demeny, one of the two famous "letters of the seer," offered a succinct collation of the ideas which guided Rimbaud. In the first place, "the I is *somebody else*." The poet is a medium for the transmission of his song, he exists apart from his self, and it is this self which is his song. Therefore, he must study this self in all its phases: "The first subject for a man to study who wants to be a poet is his own consciousness, all of it. He searches his soul, inspects it, tries it, learns it." Rimbaud implies that the consciousness which has been entrusted to man is timeless, linked both to the past and to the future. In order to study it, one must adopt the methodology of the prophetic visionary, and "The poet makes himself a *seer* by a long, immense, and reasoned *derangement* of *all the senses*. All the forms of love, suffering, folly, he searches in himself, he boils down in himself so as to keep nothing of them but the quintessences." Having distilled the senses, he must convey them in the literary form which is organically inevitable: "If that which he brings back from down there has form, he gives form; if it is unformed he gives unform." [1] This form must be embodied in a language which is adequate, not an exhausted vehicle of the past, but something new that transcends logical construction by depending on the association of thoughts for a total meaning. "Find a language . . ." Rimbaud wrote. "This language will be of the soul, for the soul, summarizing everything: smells, sounds,

colours . . ." In another passage, Rimbaud includes tactil-
ity as a sense which the poet must embody in his work; it
was the tactile sense of the reader that Crane intended to
arouse with "Black Tambourine."

Watson's translations of *Une Saison en Enfer* and *Les
Illuminations* were the concrete evidences of Rimbaud's
achievement, and Crane was deeply stirred by their beauty.
This response never left him. Crane had Watson's translations well in mind or else carried a copy of *The Dial* with
him on his trip to Washington, for on September 24, 1920
he wrote to Munson from that city about certain political
scandals and concluded his observations with a quotation
from "Délires I" in Watson's words: "Amusing Household!" To this Crane added: "As Rimbaud would say."
No further references to Rimbaud occur in Crane's letters
until December 20, 1923, when he described Samuel
Greenberg in complimentary fashion as "a Rimbaud in
embryo." Thereafter, the references become more frequent. There is every reason to believe that Crane, whose
knowledge of the French language was always inadequate,
drew closer to Rimbaud after 1923 because of *Rimbaud*
(1924), the study in English by Edgell Rickword. It is
from Rickword's translation of *Bateau Ivre* in that book
that Crane quoted in a letter to Stieglitz written on December 27, 1926: "There were cloud epics, great jeremiads
and götterdämmerungs, and 'distances cascading to the
gulfs' as Rimbaud puts it." Miss Elizabeth Foster, in her
excellent dissertation on Rimbaud and Crane, has found
many parallels between Rickword's translations of Rimbaud's poems and the vocabulary and imagery of various
poems by Crane. As editor of the English magazine *Calendar of Modern Letters* (1925-27), Rickword later recognized the Rimbaldian element in Crane's poetry, and it was

he who published "At Melville's Tomb" in July 1926
when no American magazine had yet been willing to accept it. In 1926 Crane's interest in Rimbaud had reached
a new peak; Waldo Frank relates that on the trip which
he took with Crane to the Isle of Pines in May 1926, and
during the course of his stay on the island, Crane and he
spent much of their time in reading and discussing Rimbaud's poetry. It is significant that the impress of Rimbaud's work upon Crane's poetry is to be seen most clearly
in the poetry which Crane wrote while on the Isle of
Pines.

Among the numerous distinctions and observations made
by Rickword in his book, there were two among others
which have a direct bearing upon Crane's future development. One of them may have started, or at the very least
confirmed, a belief in Crane that he was one of those
poets who Rimbaud had predicted would arise after him
to carry on the work he had begun. This was Rickword's
union of Marlowe's intentions in *Doctor Faustus* with
those of Rimbaud, the effort of both men to obtain their
desires in a pure form unhampered by human restrictions
and imperfections: "The impulse which Marlowe translated so superbly in the physical symbolism of *Dr. Faustus*
was the same as that which tormented Rimbaud in a metaphysical hell" (XII). Crane, as we know, had by 1924
built an entire poem about the Faustus symbol in "For the
Marriage of Faustus and Helen." The second point made
by Rickword was an approving reflection on Rimbaud's
disregard for logic in his letter of the seer. According to
Rickword, Rimbaud's aesthetic theory and his poems in
prose, *Les Illuminations*, had come much closer to actually
apprehending the course of human thought than conventional logic could ever hope to do. "Logic is a good ser-

vant," Rickword went on to say, "but the method of linking effect to cause which has resulted in material triumphs, has created grotesque monuments in the world of thought. May all poets be defended from the illogical, which is detestable, and may all critics recognize that the mental world is non-logical" (153). This idea, of course, was one of the keystones of Crane's aesthetic theory, and it is significant that the language which Crane used in a letter†️ to Harriet Monroe, where he expressed his poetic preference for "the so-called illogical impingements of the connotations of words on the consciousness," is probably derived in part from Rickword's description of Rimbaud's artistry: "a swifter style of writing which should, corresponding to his vision, impinge directly on the senses, and not, like the contemporary art, elaborately reconstruct the illusion of reality" (11).

Crane's indebtedness to Rimbaud is more than problematical, of course. There is textual evidence that Crane read Rimbaud's poetry as carefully as any writer can ever read another, although it was Rimbaud's aesthetic theory that influenced him at first. It is even possible to construct interesting relationships on the further basis of biography. The general import of these exhibits would not greatly alter the conclusion we can draw from a similar consideration of Crane in relationship to Marlowe, Blake, Vaughn, Laforgue, Corbière, Melville, Poe, and a host of others with whom Crane has biographical and literary ties. The assignment of cause and effect is a dangerous venture to undertake precisely because it seeks to pin down in a prosaic logical manner those delicate threads which were apprehended imaginatively. We must note that in Rimbaud's

† *See Appendix.*

life there exist many aspects which Crane found to be duplicated in his own; that Rimbaud's aesthetic theory was amenable to someone of Crane's temperament, ideas, and ambitions; that Rimbaud's poetry constituted a high point to the equalling of which a poet might well devote himself; that Rimbaud's spirit was one with which Crane felt a powerful affinity. More specifically, Crane did employ the method of Rimbaud; and there is in his poetry much of the symbolism, imagery, and vocabulary of Rimbaud, although transmuted and re-worked in accordance with an individuality that is unmistakably Crane's own.

P. D. OUSPENSKY

Many of the concepts, even some of the language and imaginery of Crane's poetry and prose, may also be found in P. D. Ouspensky's *Tertium Organum*. Two immediate examples may be cited at this point. One of these is found in a letter by Crane written to Munson on June 18, 1922:

"Did I tell you of that thrilling experience this last winter in the dentist's chair when under the influence of aether and *amnesia* my mind spiraled to a kind of seventh heaven of consciousness and egoistic dance among the seven spheres—and something like an objective voice kept saying to me—'You have the higher consciousness—you have the higher consciousness. This is something that very few have. This is what is called genius'? A happiness, ecstatic such as I have known only twice in 'inspirations' came over me. I felt the two worlds. And at once. As the bore went into my tooth I was able to follow its every revolution as detached as a spectator at a funeral. O Gorham, I have known moments in eternity."

The relationship in this paragraph reposes in the phrase describing Crane's perception: "the higher consciousness." This same phrase recurs frequently in *Tertium Organum* as a description of the new man who, awakened to a realization of the cosmos, is moving "into a higher order

of intuition, into a higher consciousness which will reveal
to us a marvelous and mysterious world" (152).† A sec-
ond instance of Ouspensky's intimate relationship with
Crane is to be found in the poem "Sunday Morning
Apples," which Crane wrote in the summer of 1922. The
third stanza probably refers to a painting by his friend
William Sommer, to whom Crane dedicated "Sunday
Morning Apples":

> A boy runs with a dog before the sun, straddling
> Spontaneities that form their independent orbits,
> Their own perennials of light
> In the valley where you live
>
> (called Brandywine).

It is just as likely that Crane received the initial impetus
for the stanza from Ouspensky's statement that positivism
is limited to an understanding of matter, and cannot penetrate into the mysteries of consciousness, space, death, and
life:

"IN ORDER THAT OBJECTIVE KNOWLEDGE SHALL TRANS-
CEND THE LIMITS OF THE THREE-DIMENSIONAL SPHERE,
IT IS NECESSARY THAT THE CONDITIONS OF PERCEPTION
SHALL CHANGE . . . It is impossible to convey to a dog the idea
of the sphericality of the earth; to make it remember the weight of the
sun and the distances between the planets is equally impossible. Its
objective knowledge is vastly more *personal* than ours; and the cause
of it lies in the dog's more limited psyche"(214).

In an earlier portion of his volume, Ouspensky had
stated that the dog is unable to understand the principle
of recurrence, and that consequently the sun which rises
anew every morning is perceived by the dog as "a new

† *Reprinted from TERTIUM ORGANUM by P. D. Ouspensky,
by permission of Alfred A. Knopf, Inc. Copyright 1920 by Manas
Press. Copyright 1922 by Claude Bragdon. Page references are to the
Third American Edition (1945).*

sun." If we did not know that Crane read *Tertium Organum* carefully, if we did not keep seeing correspondences in thought and expression between Crane and Ouspensky, the two parallels above would be interesting and no more. Actually, they are indicative of the profound extent to which the dogmas elucidated by the Russian philosopher and cosmic theorist infiltrated into the poet's life and work.

I have deliberately cited instances of Ouspenskian influence upon Crane which indicate that he read Ouspensky by the summer of 1922. The only specific reference to Ouspensky which I have seen in Crane's letters occurs in one to Allen Tate dated February 15, 1923: "Frank has the real mystic's vision. His apprehensions astonish one. I have also enjoyed reading Ouspensky's 'Tertium Organum' lately. Its corroboration of several experiences in consciousness that I have had gave it particular interest." Presumably Crane is referring, among other incidents, to the experience of anaesthetic revelation about which he wrote Munson. Crane's statement that he had recently been reading *Tertium Organum* does not imply, I believe, that he had not also read it previously.

Crane came to Ouspensky through a fortuitous combination of circumstances. One of the many customers who patronized the Akron bookstore managed by Herbert Fletcher during the early 1920's was Nicholas Bessaraboff. At that time, Bessaraboff was an employee of a rubber plant located in Akron. Prior to his arrival from Rochester, New York, he had independently translated *Tertium Organum* into English from the author's original Russian. Bessaraboff had shown the translation in 1918 to Claude Bragdon, well-known as an architect and a writer on mysticism. Bragdon revised the translation together with

Bessaraboff, and undertook to publish the translation on his own initiative. In 1920, therefore, the first American edition of *Tertium Organum* appeared under the imprint of the Manas Press of Rochester. In Akron, Bessaraboff presented a copy of the first edition to Fletcher. After reading the book, Fletcher loaned his copy of *Tertium Organum* to Harry Candee, a friend of Crane. When Candee finished with the book, he in turn loaned it to Crane. From all indications then, it can be asserted that Crane read the book before the end of 1921 at the very latest, if not earlier.

Crane's interest in Ouspensky was undoubtedly stimulated by contact and correspondence with his friends, many of whom were interested in problems of mystical insight and philosophical speculation. On November 26, 1921, for example, Crane wrote to Munson in terms which indicate the interest of his friend William Sommer in the Kantian theory of art and genius:

"One must be drenched in words, literally soaked with them to have the right ones form themselves into the proper pattern at the right moment. When they come, as they did in 'Pastorale' (thin but rather good) they come as things in themselves; it is a matter of felicitous juggling; and no amount of will or emotion can help the thing. So you see I believe with Sommers that the 'Ding an Sich' method is ultimately the only satisfactory creative principle to follow."

Other friends like Candee and Underwood were also concerned with the metaphysical problems treated in *Tertium Organum* and the solutions which Ouspensky offered to harmonize the conflicting positions of the idealistic philosophers. It was not friendship alone, however, which drew Crane to Ouspensky's work. Spiritual questionings were no novelty to him, as we have shown. But he always refused to subject himself to the discipline of a particular

religious faith, despite his desire for a supernatural interpretation of life. *Tertium Organum* offered the possibility
of experiencing spiritual truth without a corresponding
loss of personal identity in the mysticism which it pro-
pounded. An affirmative, self-centered personality like
Crane found a mode of reconciliation therein.

Although mysticism generally presupposes a gradual
extinction of the self, it can approach the state of self-
annihilation either through denial of aspects of the physical and mental self (asceticism, for example) or else
through an intensification of the consciousness of mind
and body. The mysticism which Ouspensky presented as
a course of action fell into the second category. It fitted
in neatly with Crane's way of life by virtue of its high
praise for the Dionysian pattern as a stepping-stone to
mystical experience. Another resemblance to Nietzsche
was Ouspensky's belief that the mystic who adhered to
the ideas in his volume would become a "Superman." In
the high praise which is accorded to art, and especially to
poetry, as a means of learning spiritual truth, *Tertium
Organum* provided a dignity for Crane as a poet which
his family and society had refused to accord him, a status
more secure than that which had been his in the course of
writing "Porphyro in Akron."

Tertium Organum is not a disciplined nor a well-organ-
ized book. It is rhapsodic, unorganized, oracular, written
in the intuitive manner espoused by Ouspensky. I have
thought it appropriate, therefore, to briefly present the
ideas of *Tertium Organum* in a systematic fashion not to
be found in the book; but in order to convey the flavor
of the book and the style in which it is composed, I have
quoted at some length. Students of Crane and those in-

terested in mysticism will, of course, find no substitute for *Tertium Organum* itself.

Tertium Organum, audaciously subtitled "The Third Canon of Thought: A Key to *The Enigmas of the World*," is an ambitious effort to construct a new ontology and a new epistemology, in accordance with post-Newtonian concepts of a four-dimensional continuum developed in the theory of relativity and other revolutionary scientific speculations. Although the book is studded with mathematical, physical, and psychological reasoning and references (at one point Ouspensky implies that Einstein is in agreement with the statement that matter is a finite illusion in an infinite world), the aura of occultism which pervades the book indicates that it was not written primarily, if at all, for the scientific rationalist. It would be difficult for the latter to cope with the book at all in the light of Ouspensky's statement that "That which can be expressed, cannot be true" (108).

From the welter of repetition and rhetoric, a certain pattern emerges clearly. Ouspensky accepts the Kantian belief that empirical perception can never enable us to apprehend ultimate realities or noumena. Space, time, and other conceptual and experimental devices are adequate only for the grasp of phenomena. But he pursues the matter still further in accepting Hegel's belief that there is a noumenal world, and that it can in some way be perceived. The question then becomes: how can we know this ultimate reality? Ouspensky's answer is to turn to Neo-Platonism and its mystical intuition as the only possible approach to the supernal world.

According to Ouspensky, the noumenal world is composed of our conventional three dimensions plus the fourth dimension. The fourth dimension lies in time, but a radically-different time than we are accustomed to consider. This is a new time without duration, in which all is co-existent. ("This will be the universe of the *Eternal Now* of Hindu philosophy—a universe in which will be neither *before* nor *after*, in which will be just one present, *known* or *unknown*" [105].) The noumenal world has certain characteristics. Cause and effect simply cannot exist in that world. There cannot be any three-dimensional measurement; size and position are inoperative, replaced by subjective reactions of " 'affinity' or 'remoteness' . . . sympathy or antipathy." Matter and motion find no place in the noumenal world, nor do other physical phenomena such as color and odor. Death and unconsciousness are replaced by eternal life in which everything partakes, unlike the positivistic belief that the inorganic has no psychic life. Everything is infinite and variable, and three-dimensional mathematics cannot exist. The logic which stems from Aristotle is unsuited for the noumenal world; a supra-logic has been invented. ("This higher logic may be called *intuitive* logic—the logic of infinity, the logic of ecstasy" [235].) There is no individuality or separateness; all share a common self ("Everything is all." 236). The dualism which characterizes the three-dimensional world is left behind. ("There being is not opposed to *non-being*. *Life is not opposed to death.* On the contrary, the one includes the other within itself . . . *Everything subjective is objective, and everything objective is subjective.* That world is the world of the *unity of opposites*" [242].) In the world of more than three dimensions, there cannot exist a difference between real and unreal; nevertheless, it is necessary to believe in the illusoriness of this world and the reality of that world. There is no dividing-line between this world and that world, except that this world is only a narrow imperfect glimpse of the wonderful noumenal world.

The positivist cannot hope to reach the noumenal world, the world of reality and causes, because his logic and his investigation is inapplicable in a four-dimensional world (*"science must come to mysticism*, because in mysticism there is a new method" [230].) There must be an expansion of consciousness, for "The new knowledge is *direct knowledge*, by an inner sense" (209). The emotions of man serve as "Organs of Knowledge" in their apprehension of that which reason cannot understand. Anything which enlarges the emotional grasp of noumenal knowledge—occultism, yoga, hypnosis, narcosis, trance, ecstasy, sleep—will bring about a mystical "illumination" in which "the angle of vision will enlarge . . ." At the moment of "illumination," the mystic experiences "This sensation of *light* and unlimited joy . . . the sensation of infinity" (233). He participates in the higher world, he tastes the eternal, he returns with distaste to the unreal world of three dimensions. But he has also returned from these "Mystical states . . . [with] knowledge WHICH NOTHING ELSE CAN GIVE . . . knowledge of the *real world* with all its signs and characteristics" (251).

Ouspensky forthrightly tackles the problem of transition from the rudimentary shackles of three-dimensionality to the mystical state of expanded consciousness. In this connection, we shall consider the particular applicability of these theories to Crane as a poet, since it was undoubtedly because of the high rank accorded poetry and poets in the hierarchy of Ouspenskian values that Crane felt so powerful an affinity to the thesis of *Tertium Organum.*

Ouspensky represents the artist as a being who is advancing on the road to the higher consciousness at a faster rate than the ordinary being. This is so, because the operations of imagination involve "creating *new conceptions* and augmenting *the faculty for perceiving analogies*" (19). In the perception of analogies, the artist discovers the hidden meanings of four-dimensional reality; "the symbols and metaphors of art . . . are often revelations of the world of reality" (143). Therefore, symbol and metaphor attain a vision of reality and are themselves entirely real. Their construction is, in the Greek sense, the process of making. Art is able to transcend matter because "all art is just one entire illogicality . . . the axioms of logic are untrue even in relation to emotions, to symbols, to the musicality and *the hidden meaning of words* . . ." (223) As a result of his creative ability, the "thought of a poet contains enormous potential force, like the power confined in a piece of coal or in a living cell, but infinitely more subtle, imponderable and potent" (126). The combined power and creativity of the poet give him the authority, like that enjoyed by prophets, teachers, and lawgivers, to "speak in the name of the people . . . stand out to represent the nondescript multitude behind them, to speak their thoughts and to express their sentiments" (245). Near the close of his book, Ouspensky quotes a passage from Max Muller's *Theosophy* which states in part that "the founders of the religions of the world have all been bridge-builders," and he himself observes that "religion is the bridge between the *Visible* and the *Invisible*, between *Finite* and *Infinite*" (25). In the light of the role which Ouspensky has assigned to poets and all artists, it is not inconceivable that they too are "bridge-builders" in their work, and that Crane's conception of *The Bridge* may have been stimulated by this interpretation.

But "art is *the beginning of vision*," Ouspensky asserts. Neither symbols nor metaphors can ever embody reality completely. The task of the poet is particularly difficult, because truth is inexpressible in words; it can only be approximated. Therefore, there is a driving need for a new language. "In art we have already the first experiments in a *language of the future*" (73). This revolution in language must proceed at full pace ("The language for the transmission of the new temporal relations must be a language without verbs. *New parts of speech* are necessary, an infinite number of new words" [108]). But the poet can overcome the handicap of an inadequate language, and he does so by increasing the emotional range of his consciousness. This is not a compromise, but a fuller utilization of that which he must employ in his attempts to create metaphor ("The interpretation of emotional feelings and *emotional understanding* is the problem of art" [73]). Emotions in Ouspensky's scheme of three-dimensional life are tools in the acquisition of knowledge which no physical devices can accumulate. The emotional deepening and widening of the poet is carried on under the guise of a hunt for beauty ("Art serves *beauty*, i.e., emotional knowledge of its own kind. Art discovers beauty in everything, and compels man to feel it and therefore *to know*" [207]). The poet's work is a failure, however, once he becomes satisfied with the beauty captured in his lines and ceases his quest for new beauty ("Just as soon as art begins to take delight in that beauty which is already *found*, instead of *the search for new beauty* an arrestment occurs and art becomes a su-

perfluous estheticism, encompassing man's vision like a
wall.   The aim of art is *the search for beauty*, just as
the aim of religion is the search for God and truth" [207]).

   The poet is, of course, a mystic by virtue of his discovery of beauty and his illogicality, his use of metaphor
and his revelation of noumena. But he, like all mystics,
must induce mystical states in himself in order to utilize
his emotional resources and his technical facility to their
fullest advantage.   In a passage worthy of Rimbaud,
whom Crane had read by this date, Ouspensky calls for
activation of the poet's soul: "In art it is necessary to
study 'occultism'—the hidden side of life. The artist must
be a clairvoyant: he must see that which others do not
see; he must be a magician: must possess the power to
make others see that which they do not themselves see,
but which he does see." (145).

   Ouspensky's significance for Crane may be considered
from two more angles—one, that of subject, and the
other, that of prophetism. According to Ouspensky, there
are certain aspects of our phenomenal existence in "which
we come into direct contact with *eternity* . . ."   These
are death and love, the first of which Ouspensky claims
to have been more absorbing always to the mystic than
the second. On page 157 of *Tertium Organum*, Ouspensky quotes with approval a statement by Schopenhauer
that love and death are closely related, the beginning
and end of life, and that " 'Death is the great reservoir of
Life.' "   There is, therefore, no fear of death by a mystic,
but rather a feeling of welcome to the newness which
will uncover itself to the dead. This is in accord with
Ouspensky's statement that the life of man is a circle.
In the three-dimensional world, we see only a small section of that circle in its revolution, beginning with birth

and ending with death. Between death and birth, there is a vaster section of noumenal existence in which true reality is visible. Love is a "cosmic phenomenon" which, unlike death, enables us to vision noumena within three-dimensional reality. Procreation is regarded by Ouspensky as the lowest manifestation of love and beauty. But, he goes on to say, the positivist interpretation of love as serving procreation and thereafter ceasing restricts it to the level of matter. There is more energy in love than is required for procreation, and this energy does not disappear. Excess love-energy "transforms itself into instincts, ideas, creative forces on different planes of life; into symbols of art, song, music, poetry; so can we easily imagine how the same energy may transform itself into a higher order of intuition, into a higher consciousness which will reveal to us a marvelous and mysterious world. In all living nature (and perhaps also in that which we consider as dead) *love* is the motive force which drives the creative activity in the most diverse directions" (152). Love is an "eternally burning fire" which purifies and reveals; it is an ocean to which we contribute and which contains us all; its physical manifestation brings us directly to the heart of nature. Between love of an individual and love on the plane of physical desire, there is no basic difference in result: the difference is one of preliminary attitude only. Ouspensky emphasizes the expression of cosmic love by means of sensuous symbols in mystical poetry, citing the poetry of the Mohammedan Sufis and *The Song of Solomon* as examples in which the seemingly-profane symbolism has an underlying mystical significance ("When we read some of the Sufi enraptured poetry, we must remember that the Sufi poets use a number of expressions which have a recognized meaning in their

language. Their *sleep* means meditation; *perfume*—hope
of divine favor; *kisses* and *embraces*—the raptures of piety;
wine means spiritual knowledge, etc." [269]).

Ouspensky had assigned the poet a prophetic role in
the ranks of humanity. Since Crane was to assume the
responsibility of articulating a myth for America after
he had read *Tertium Organum*, we will do well to consider the possible effect which Ouspensky might have had
upon the formulation and realization of the myth. It
would be illogical in a three-dimensional sense to expect
Ouspensky to be concerned with problems of human
welfare in the phenomenal world. After all, whether
or not man eats enough to power his body, sleeps in a
building which keeps out the rain, wears enough clothes
to resist the freezing effects of cold, or is accorded sufficient consideration and status to foster a sense of individuality—these and similar related issues are material
and three-dimensional. Ouspensky does not disappoint
us; he is logical in a way that the positivist would applaud; he categorically states that a concern with these
problems conspires to prevent tne expansion of consciousness and the vision of four-dimensional reality ("A cold
wind blows on us from all those social theories promising
incalculable welfare on earth . . ." [278]). The mystical
feeling of brotherhood for all men is scarcely to be found
in *Tertium Organum*. In its stead Ouspensky displays
an aristocratic bias with strong Nietzchean traces. Ideas
about the equality of all men are fallacious, he says ("the
difference . . . is not an accidental difference of position,
state, and heredity, as materialism tries to assure us; nor
is it a difference between the stages of one and the same
evolution, as theosophy affirms; but it is a deep and IM-
PASSABLE difference . . ." [144]). From doubting human

equality, Ouspensky proceeds to separate humanity into a majority and a minority. The minority consists of those who have achieved the higher consciousness or are attempting to do so. This is the path of true evolution, "the evolution into Superman" (85). To this Superman will belong the future; the present is already his property. The majority is dangerous and must be controlled ("The enormous majority of the population of this globe is engaged in effect in destroying, disfiguring, and falsifying the ideas of the minority. The majority is without ideas . . . left to itself it must inevitably disfigure and destroy" [205]). It follows that the idea of democracy on a political level is to be avoided ("Democratic organization and the nominal rule of the majority guarantee nothing: on the contrary, even now, where they are realized—though only in name—they create without delay, and promise in future to create on a larger scale, violence toward the minority, the limitation of the individual, and the curtailment of freedom" [293]).

WALDO FRANK

The works of Waldo Frank, as well as his friendship, were among the potent influences acting upon Crane's life. From 1919, when he first read Frank's *Our America* (1919), until 1931, their lives are intertwined to a considerable extent. It was early in 1923 that Crane, freshly arrived from Cleveland to make his way in New York, met Waldo Frank at lunch. Thereafter, as one can judge from Crane's correspondence, they were close and sympathetic friends, journeying together for a vacation to the Isle of Pines in May 1926. A year later, Frank's review of *White Buildings* in *The New Republic*, containing as it did a diagrammatic representation of Crane's meaning and a statement to the effect that Crane might always be an obscure poet, appears to have hurt Crane. Nevertheless, their relationship was unimpaired, and they remained on close terms until Crane's death.

The pages of *Our America*, Frank's first volume of American cultural criticism and history, contain many of the germs of the attitudes and beliefs which constitute the core of Crane's ideas. Although transmuted with the passage of time and the impact of other experiences and reflections, they were never fundamentally abandoned by Crane. Crane had been exposed to the central thesis established by Frank in *Our America* before he read the book. The books and articles of Van Wyck Brooks, H. L. Mencken, and Randolph Bourne, as well as Frank's earlier articles in *The Seven Arts*, which caustically raked the Puritan spirit and searchingly probed into the materialism of American life, were familiar to Crane by 1919. Crane's review of Anderson's *Winesburg, Ohio* in 1919 had stated that "The Puritan that stalks through the swamps of 'Spoon River' is manifest also in 'Winesburg' .." Though he thought *Our America* was less lyrical than the writing of Brooks, he wrote Munson that "the meat is there anyway, and the book is stimulaing . . ."

Frank's book was stimulating precisely because he clearly placed his hopes for the future of American life on the literary artist: "The leaders of a to-morrow forced to spiritual discovery are men of letters." And he did so not by ineffectually railing against the barren, arid desert of American reality, but by drawing an extended portrait of American cultural history in which the writer appeared to be a culminating and prophetic factor. According to *Our America*, the dominant figure in American life had been the English Puritan, whose energies were harnessed in the struggle against nature with a consequent materialization of his personality: "It was but natural to find from the beginning a greater part of men's capacity for dream and for creation turned into materialistic channels—into genius for invention, for political manipulation, for accumulation. And it was natural as well that much of men's capacity for faith and piety should have become the slave of the dominant issue: should have evolved that moral tone at the service of wealth . . ." Against this externalizing there were but few rebels, although Thoreau and Poe had weakly and unsystematically flung themselves against the Puritan. Emerson had evaded the entire issue by transcending it, and Hawthorne and James had continued to say "Nay" in their work. With Whitman had arisen the first decisive crack in the powerful Puritan dam. Here was a harbinger of the future greatness of the American spirit: *"Democratic Vistas,"* Frank wrote, "is quite as clearly our greatest book of social criticism as *Leaves of Grass* is our greatest poem." For Whitman had been able to sense the "multitudes" of existence, and had yet continued to probe deeply into the individual "Consciousness." As a "great mystic . . . he saw the movements of men upon the flat planes of mundane life in its relation to all mundane life. He saw the unitary flow of all mundane life in its relation to an Infinite Being of which it was an elementary life." Though Whitman was dead, there were other positive forces in American culture which were continuing his battle for the spiritual individual. From the Middle West came writers like Anderson, Masters, Sandburg, and Dreiser, each bearing a virulent "Hate of Puritan ideals" and a determination to creatively portray their damaging effects: "Against the American doctrine of success with its subsidiary Puritan morale, they bring their gospel of Failure. Meaning only this: that the material ends to which we have reduced the largeness of our lives are shoddy false-hood, and that the glory of truth is but the glory of *being*." From New England came Frost with his revelation of "fertile quality" in the "starved, sick world" of his region, as well as an Amy Lowell who used the traditional and sound intellectual attributes of New England in "the cause of American Expression, rather than American possession." Lurking in the sub-cellar of our cultural heritage were the invigorating "buried cultures" of the American Indians and the ancient Mexicans. All these positive streams said "Yea" as they reached their confluence in New York. There the anti-Puritans poured their intensely individual art into the social conscience of a Randolph Bourne, a conscience composed of political and social currents of advance" fused with a "spiritual viewpoint" derived from the "Logical voices of France, mystical pleadings of Russia, protests of the Celt—Moore and Shaw—against the Puritan at home."

In concluding his argument with the declaration that the "man of letters" was the twentieth-century pioneer, a "spiritual pioneer," Frank closed on a theme which undoubtedly fascinated Crane. Indeed, many of the now mature and middle-aged literary men of the present day were as profoundly impressed with *Our America* as Crane confessed himself to be. There was one important exception, however. Frank stressed the importance of spiritual components in the new pioneering. When he called for realism in literature, it was a realism controlled by spiritual realities and inner searching and not by material factors. Only upon Crane of all his contemporaries did this spiritual necessity postulated by Frank exert a compelling force of its own, and only in his work do we see its flowering to any considerable degree.

The problem of the relationship between science and the individual had been troubling American intellectual life from the early years of the nineteenth century. The War of 1914, with its destructive utilization of scientific knowledge and equipment, sharpened the temper of the issue. A reaction to science which both contributed to and typified the post-war attitude of many artists and intellectuals was contained in Henry Adam's *Education,* which became available for general distribution to the public in 1918: Science had not fulfilled its promise of explaining the universe to man and making it habitable. As Adams wryly wrote in his book: "The child born in 1900 would . . . be born into a new world which would not be a unity but a multiple . . . He found himself in a land where no one had penetrated before; where order was an accidental relation obnoxious to nature; artificial compulsion imposed on motion; against which every free energy of the universe revolted; and which, being merely occasional, resolved itself back into anarchy at last."

Crane felt that sense of bitter betrayal. Born just one year before the turning point, he too ached for that "Order and reason, beauty and benevolence" which Adams' study of Karl Pearson's *Grammar of Science* had unfortunately revealed to be ephemeral "characteristics and conceptions which we find solely associated with the mind of man." Nourished on spiritual conceptions which depended ultimately on a unified universe, Crane began to see in science only a senseless destroyer, a perfidious ally. This view he expressed in his review of Lola Ridge's poetry. The "finer, harder line" which science had promised was still forthcoming. In this broken promise, Crane discerned a "cruelty . . . a kind of desperation that is dramatic." The responsibility for the desperate situation it engendered he laid squarely upon science. Even more indicting, he felt, was science's destruction in its forward march of that classical harmony which had hitherto balanced the minds of men and which it had promised to supplant with a new scientific harmony. Now science reigned master in the field, and there was no one to deny its tyranny: "Science, grown uncontrollable, has assumed a grin that has more than threatened the supposed civilization that fed it; science has brought light,—but it threatens to destroy the idea of reverence, the source of all light. Its despotism recognizes no limits. In one sense, it has become a gargoyle."

Waldo Frank made the same plaint in *Our America*, though he went further and postulated a need for mysticism in the solution of the predicament: "Science has levelled knowledge to an exacter cognizance that knowledge does not exist. It has wiped out the myths of causation and effect, put a clear light on the impenetrable dark of Chaos: and added the compulsion of its own deliberate discourse to the human need of mystical experience." As a result, Frank arrayed himself against the chief product of science, the "Machine." In the machine, Frank found a symbol for the mechanistic ugliness which was overwhelming modern man. The machine was a monster which crushed and destroyed personality and body. It shackled people to its wheels and levers, changed the organic rhythm of the living being to conform with the mechanical pulsation of a soulless device, brought about a "denial of experience . . . the mechanization of Desire."

Nevertheless, Frank admitted that the machine might be used to express the creative insight of the artist. Such an artist he found in Alfred Stieglitz, who as a photographer could of course have used nothing else than a camera to express himself. "The powerful vision which is Stieglitz . . ." Frank wrote in *Our America*, "first . . . found itself through a machine." In this concession by Frank can be found a germ which grew to greater proportions in Crane, the belief that an artistic purpose could strain beyond and transcend the confines created by the machine, so that the machine itself might be utilized for a purpose antithetical to its own nature. It was this theory which later in 1922 Crane saw concretely expressed in the writings of Gorham Munson, who had transmuted the doctrines upheld by the machine-loving Dadaists of Europe.

Crane had not yet arrived at a spirit of reconciliation with the machine by 1921. His antagonism to science, like that of Frank, transferred itself to the machine as the single, most concrete personification of scientific achievement. Science in the abstract was too vast and intangible a figure against which to tilt. All about him, however, were the signs and symbols of a tangible industrialism . . . in the "rolling Ohio hills" polluted with "smoking hills" of factories, in the "monkey wrench" which had displaced "the plough, the sword, the trowel," in the "shift of rubber workers" which eddied sullenly through Akron "with the stubbornness of muddy water . . . absorbing and conveying weariness." So that when he was offered the opportunity of writing a critical sketch of Sherwood Anderson's achievements for the July 1921 issue of *The Double-Dealer*, a magazine published in New Orleans, it was only natural that Crane should have unleashed his most virulent language against:

"the 'machine' of modern existence,—the monster that is upon us all. No one who treats however slightly of the lives of the poor or middle classes can escape the issues of its present hold on us. It has seduced the strongest from the land to the cities, and in most cases made empty and meaningless their lives. It has cheapened the worth of all human commodities and even the value of human lives. It has destroyed the pride and pleasure of the craftsman in his work . . . character is bent, blunted, regulated, diverted, or lacerated by the 'machine'."

By 1922, however, Crane was so engrossed in problems of spiritual experience and reality, that a mystical reconciliation with the "Machine" became a possibility. Frank, as we have shown, had seen the "Machine" as an evil necessity which man must master in order not himself to be crushed by it. In order to maintain stability, however, he had also stipulated a renewed sense of unity with a single Godhead. Frank did not by any means advocate the recoil of man from the machine as from an abhorrent pest. But his platform offered no sound approach for a reconciliation with the accomplished fact of mechanization. The dichotomy between man and machine, in Frank's opinion, was fated to continue.

Younger men like Gorham Munson found it much less difficult to accept and even welcome the machine as an integral and desirable part of their lives. To many of them it may even have appeared absurd to consider an existence without the steamships that conveyed them over the ocean to Europe, or the looms, assembly lines, and cement mixers which provided the income to sustain them without employment once they arrived on the Continent. During the early 1920's, Munson and other intellectuals of his age expatriated themselves to Europe in search of eternal values. They found a tremendous interest in American technology and the speedy tempo of American life, its vulgarized culture, its advertising, and its lust for possessions permeating the writing and opinions of the young

Europeans of their generation and similar experimental temper in art and literature. Thus they turned to look back at the United States with a new vision, for the first time realizing the wonders of its science and the permanence of its accomplishments in industry and business. Overwhelmed, they found themselves compelled by their new awe and admiration to seek for ways and means of reconciling science and the machine with the future; both seemed equally durable and inevitable.

A combination of these ideas came to fruition in Munson's mind after his return from Europe in early 1922, and took form in the study of Waldo Frank which he had just undertaken. When he visited Crane in Cleveland later in the year during the month of July, Munson carried with him a draft of the book. Those days when Crane was away at work, Munson spent in polishing its pages for the printer. In the study, which was finally published in 1923, Munson's critical evaluation of Frank was tempered with considerable regard for his achievement as a writer and thinker. Its argument made a profound impression on Crane, who had not been overly enthusiastic with Frank's work even after his acceptance of *Our America*'s "pessimistic analysis." The "propagandistic" strain which Crane felt to be a fatal flaw in an artist and which he thought he detected in Frank, had kept him from reading Frank's novel, *The Dark Mother*, in 1920. Now Munson proved to be the double agent who re-awakened Crane's flagging interest in Frank, while simultaneously enabling him to pass beyond Frank's conception of the "Machine."

Munson's book (*Waldo Frank: A Study*), as well as the discussions which accompanied the two friends' joint reading of completed passages from the manuscript, was therefore instrumental in the basic shift of Crane's attitude to a mechanized world. Writing to Munson about his book shortly after the latter had returned to New York from Cleveland, Crane said: "I have since wanted to read it over again, say fresh in the morning to better absorb its many compact and rich allusions toward your esthetique." Undoubtedly his anticipations with regard to the book had been heightened by the knowledge that Frank himself had liked the book after a reading despite Munson's insistence on a new and different approach to the machine and its attendant phenomena. When Crane received a complete version in January 1923, and was able to see it as a whole instead of in the fragmentary form he had read in the Summer of 1922, his enthusiasm led him to offer his advertising services in writing the dust-jacket blurb. For the book appeared to him to be "a criticism that, besides being quite exact and fair, is dramatic—and very constructive beyond the actual boundaries of the man and subject concerned."

According to Munson, who took *Our America* as his point of departure, the history of human culture had always involved the reconciliation of man with the fact of nature. This reunion was responsible for the production of great works of art in which were embodied the peace of mind achieved by the reunion. Spiritual harmony of the kind achieved in the past, Munson went on to say, is no longer possible for the modern artist. In the midst of the harmonious relationship established between man and nature a disturbing factor had appeared. This was "Machinery," with which the artist must cope more adequately than he had been able to. The negative ways in which the problem had hitherto been treated—either by an impotent flight to nature, or Frank's acceptance of mechanized evil and spiritual resistance thereto—had failed to organically and satisfactorily adjust the artist. The implied result was that great art works could not germinate in such a neurotic atmosphere. Consequently, Munson called for a new recognition that man, nature, and machinery must be united in spiritual fraternity, and he cited the Italian futurist Marinetti who saw new aesthetic values in pure speed, as well as the Dadaist Tzara who rebelled against literary expression itself, as "the agents of a new recognition." Their characteristic violence had arisen, he implied, solely because of an organic necessity for union with the "Machine." And the results of their activity— the collages, montages, typographically-distorted poems and stories, public demonstrations, phonograph recordings, and minor riots with which they titillated a war-ravaged Europe—were "a species of mechanized art." But this species could only give "minor esthetic thrills." Still needed were the "emotional profundities . . . love and desire and religion." And these could, with the recognition of the new spiritual unity of man, nature, and machinery, be grafted into the existent Dadaist art. For, Munson went on to say, "we are in the childhood of a new age, we are, by the chronological accident of our birth, chosen to create the simple forms, the folk-tales and folk-music, the preliminary art that our descendants may utilize in the vast struggle to put positive and glowing spiritual content into Machinery."

The ringing note of optimism in Munson's aesthetics appealed to Crane with special intensity. Combined in it were all the factors that he was most concerned with, and it satisfied his ever-present desire for spiritual unity and harmony. The "skyscrapers, bridges, motion pictures, jazz music, vaudeville, electric light displays, advertising" which Munson considered to be splendid manifestations of the American character, and which Crane so heartily disliked at the same time that he recognized their immediacy and their undoubted permanency, could now be positively incorporated into the substance of his poetry. At last this young poet, thoroughly immersed in the Whitmanian literary tradition of glorious America as well as in the material environment of America, touched by European culture only in an indirect literary and artistic way, could apply himself best to that field of experience and reflection with which he possessed the greatest familiarity. And for a poet who was so conscious of his powers, so determined to stand forth as the most important poet of his times, here was an opportunity to exploit an original and untouched vein of matter. Gone was the self-consciousness, the sense of preliminary defeat, with which a young writer might formerly have approached the universal themes of love, death, God, and birth which Donne, Keats, Shakespeare, and other old masters had so consummately treated in their lines. But meanwhile he had still to write the poem in which he explored his technique and philosophy—"For the Marriage of Faustus and Helen." *The Bridge* would come later.

8. "FOR THE MARRIAGE OF FAUSTUS AND HELEN"

I T TOOK CRANE ALMOST TEN MONTHS TO WRITE "FOR the Marriage of Faustus and Helen." In May 1922, he composed a few lines which he thought would serve as a tentative beginning. With very few changes, the first three lines took their place as the opening of the first stanza of Part I, and the remaining five lines became the opening lines of the second stanza:

> The mind has shown itself at times
> Too much the baked and twisted dough,
> Food for the accepted multitude.
> The mind is brushed by sparrow wings;
> Rebuffed by asphalt, numbers crowd
> The margins of the day, accent the curbs,
> Convoying diverse dawns on every corner
> To druggist, barber, and tobacconist.

More than a year before, he had written the quatrain fragment in which the consciousness was portrayed submerged in darkness. In contrast to the impotent anticipation there revealed, the tentative opening of the new poem was declarative. Crane had been broken loose from the darkness, and was able to comment on the predicament of a chained consciousness. Darkness gave way to a more explicit statement of its constituents: the mind had literally been unveiled before the light.

175

Part I was abandoned for a time, however. After jotting down the opening lines, Crane abruptly let them rest and swung into the heart of the second part of the poem. "Let us invent an idiom for the proper transposition of jazz into words!" he wrote while working on this section. "Something clean, sparkling, elusive!" When Part II was completed early in June, he was more than satisfied with his accomplishment: "I have been at it for the last 24 hours and it may be subjected to a few changes and additions, but as I see it now in the red light of the womb it seems to me like a work of youth and magic. At any rate, it is something entirely new in English poetry so far as I know." Although the poem was praised by Munson, Crane was not thereby stimulated to complete the first and third parts as rapidly as he had written the second. Part II had been concrete and Dionysian. The other two parts were to be abstract and exhortatory. The treatment and mood of Part II had come easily to Crane, whereas now his imagination seemed to lie dormant. In order to place himself in the proper state for working, he goaded himself into excitement with alcohol and music. With their aid in stirring his faculties into action, he managed to finish Part I by the early part of August, and to send Munson a version containing the epigraph from Jonson's *The Alchemist* and seven stanzas (the present seventh stanza was added in late September).

Part III was first concretized in four lines which Crane sent Munson in early August:

> Corymbulous formations of mechanics
> Hurried the breezes, spouted malice
> Plangent over meadows, chipping
> Delicate recesses into death.

To Crane's dismay, this section also could not be hurried, even though he applied the methods which had produced such satisfactory results for Part I. In its meaning and in its movement, he wanted to comment vividly on speed. He was also striving to expand the range of his vocabulary, and we see this in the use of a word like "corymbulous." But both aims required more thought and attention than he could provide, and his poetic difficulties were made even more unpleasant since he was leaving his place of employment for a new job at the time. Finally, he abandoned the concept of speed as an important motif in an effort to simplify the problem of composition. Since he had not planned the structure of this part in sufficient detail, except to decide that it should include a reference to war, he could not proceed with genuine confidence in any direction. He wrote some new lines which he hoped would be satisfactory as the opening of the section, but he was unable to work them out to their conclusion. With Part I standing as a satisfactory embodiment of his intentions, he came to the conclusion that it would be unwise to force himself to work any further on Part III. Accordingly, he put the poem aside temporarily. In the lull created by this cessation, he wrote "Sunday Morning Apples" and "Belle Isle."† Despite his respite from Part III, Crane was unable to cope with it when he tackled it again after a month. Ten more lines were composed for incorporation into Part III, but in disgust he inserted them instead into Part I as the seventh stanza. By this time, Crane was so discouraged by his evident inability to bring the poem to a triumphant unity that he decided to forget about the triadic structure of his conception entirely: Part I was to stand alone under the title "For the Marriage of Faustus and Helen," since he believed that there was an intrinsic unity and power in the lines which did not re-

† *See Appendix.*

quire subsidiary support; Part II became a separate poem entitled "The Springs of Guilty Song"; and projected Part III was tucked away in a drawer until a more propitious time might arise.

Spurred on in October by his need for money and his conviction that he could not bring the poem to a successful conclusion, Crane began to send out Parts I and II as separate poems under their new titles to various magazines. Part II had been previously sent to Matthew Josephson by Crane as a sample of his progress. Josephson, who was a staff member of *Broom*, replied to Crane with high praise. The Josephson letter arrived shortly before *The Dial* rejected Part I under its new title. Prompted by Josephson's interest, Crane immediately sent a draft of Parts I and II on a journey to the Berlin office of *Broom*, where Josephson was now stationed. Before very long, Crane received a letter from Josephson in which the latter accepted both poems for publication. Unfortunately, Josephson did not know that they had originally been planned as sections of a large work, and indeed there was no way in which he might have realized the connection unless he was clairvoyant or Crane had made it clear to him.

Stimulated by his "carousing on New Year's Eve," Crane began work on Part III in January 1923 with more enthusiasm. But now he did not intend to court failure by letting his ideas peter out slowly; the poem was to be written while the lines were still white-hot in his mind. Another important reason for finishing the poem as quickly as possible was his deliberate intention to set up a counter-balance to Eliot's *The Waste Land*, which had appeared in *The Dial* a few months earlier. Thus impelled, in little more than a week he wrote a major portion of Part III and constructed a thematic outline of the entire poem in its three parts. Once again the same "kind of ecstasy and power for WORK" which had impelled him to complete Parts I and II fused ideas, music and language for him. Upon its completion before the end of January 1923, Crane's confidence and pride were renewed. When *Broom* appeared at the same time with "The Springs of Guilty Song" (Part II) in solitary state, however, the event was a serious disappointment to Crane, especially since he had been able finally to integrate and complete the poem to his satisfaction as a triad. Moreover, the enthusiastic response which he received from Allen Tate, Waldo Frank, and others who had read isolated Part II in *Broom* convinced him that his success would have been much greater if all three parts of the poem had appeared together. But it was not until the Winter 1924 issue of *Secession* that "Faustus and Helen" appeared as Crane had intended. An attempt by Munson to present the poem in an earlier issue of the magazine had been so frustrated by editorial innocence, monkey-shines, and typographical manglings on the part of Munson's associates that the pages on which it was printed had to be removed from the magazine.

The epigraph from Jonson's *The Alchemist* which introduces the three parts of the poem performs a dual function. On the one hand, considered as a genuine poetic fragment, it crystallizes Crane's intention to devote himself to the preservation of beauty against the attacks of Philistines. Jonson's references to the Greek mystery rites and the Hebrew Kabbalah are appropriate in a poem where the alchemist and necromancer Faustus is a major symbol, and where the medium of preservation and ennobling is to be language. But there is a more complex level of meaning on which this quotation is to be understood. In Jonson's play, the lines are spoken by a whore, Dol Common, who feigns distraction and utters hysterical speeches whenever philosophical problems are mentioned in her presence. The sensual character Sir Epicure Mammon, greedy for gold, jewels, and the whore whom he has been misled into believing a noblewoman, induces this particular outbreak by talking about the philosopher's stone. In its outline and in the similarity of Mammon's speeches to those which Faustus speaks in praise of Helen in Marlowe's play, *Doctor Faustus*, the entire episode is a comic parody of the Faustus-Helen relationship which Marlowe portrayed. On the plausible assumption that Crane read *The Alchemist* with understanding, and there is no reason to believe otherwise, it becomes evident that the quotation was placed at the head of the poem for an ironic purpose. Mammon—misunderstood, ridiculed, sensuous, anxious for beauty and wealth—is none other than the poet who persists in his role despite the abuse and contempt which are heaped upon him. The irony is a continuation of the mood of "Chaplinesque," and is Laforguean in spirit. Thus the tone of the poem which follows the epigraph is set.

Part I of "Faustus and Helen" is thoroughly Platonic, partaking of the belief that the passage of the mind from the concrete and the particular to the abstract and the ideal will release the consciousness into a world where the archetype of beauty may be seen as a tangible reality. The movement of the poem is based on this progression. The poet reflects on the sterotyped status of the mind, nourished by newspaper columns and other sources of stimulation which have a dulling effect on the consciousness. But there are times when the pattern of commonplace routine is broken. The sparrow is a symbol of those moments: its sooty wings place it within the orbit of metropolitan life and the pattern that stifles . . . the wings of a bird serve also to remind us of the spatial freedom which is its privilege and which only man's spirit shares. For the majority, the poet continues, these "equivocations" are of no avail. The three-dimensional world, which is reality to most men, is adequate enough for those who are not driven to a reconciliation of their aspirations on a higher level. Travelling in a "street car," the poet is suddenly transported from the mundane; all motion and time, its prerequisite, cease; a girl sitting in the vehicle is converted by the poet's ecstasy into Helen, the prototype of female beauty. Helen having been evoked, she arouses a magnificent flood of sexual imagery in the poet, and the poem concludes with a statement of the poet's eternal devotion to beauty:

> The earth may glide diaphanous to death;
> But if I lift my arms it is to bend
> To you who turned away once, Helen, knowing
> The press of troubled hands, too alternate
> With steel and soil to hold you endlessly.
> I meet you, therefore, in that eventual flame
> You found in final chains, no captive then—
> Beyond their million brittle bloodshot eyes;
> White, through white cities passed on to assume
> That world which comes to each of us alone.
>
> Accept a lone eye riveted to your plane,
> Bent axle of devotion along companion ways
> That beat, continuous, to hourless days—
> One inconspicuous, glowing orb of praise.

These last stanzas recapitulate the earlier lines. From the "steel and soil" of Cleveland the poet has turned and dedicated his imagination and vision to Helen, the symbol of beauty who dwells in that timeless world of "hourless days" where death does not appear.

The poet returns in Part II from the supernal world, the "plane" on which abstract beauty can be experienced, to the "quotidian" world of twentieth-century life. Beauty is now seen in its earthly form, the lowest manifestation of its perfection. The poet reacts to it with lust, the antithesis of the devotion expressed in Part I. The "I" in this section performs in two roles. As poet, he observes the desecration of beauty by modern man. As modern man, he is the ravisher and defamer of beauty. This conflict between desire and understanding is the high point of the section, for wantonness leads to "metallic paradises" and "the divine grotesque." The poem opens with nervous blare in a skyscraper night club. A jazz orchestra flings its syncopated rhythm into the air while tipsy dancers whirl about to its strains in Bacchanalian glee. Shadowy figures move across the floor; spotlight rays are broken and deflected by the wild movement; laughter, song, and music vibrate in the ear; the carousing continues without a halt through the night and into the dawn. The Dionysian ecstasy induced in the poet by this revelry drives him to passionate sexual union with the tarnished spirit of jazz. The compulsion under which he acts leaves him with a sense of guilt and fatality.

In the two previous sections, death had been briefly dismissed. He is met face to face in Part III as the "gunman" who must destroy and harass us in order that we may be cleansed and purified of our sins: "Capped arbiter of beauty in this street/That narrows darkly into motor dawn . . ." With a consciousness of guilt, mankind has welcomed death at the same time that it has feared him. "Let us unbind our throats of fear and pity," the poet says. Let us permit death, the most extreme form of tragedy of which we can conceive, to excite us. Only by allowing our emotions to become agitated will our fear and pity be purged from us in catharsis. The World War is recalled, and with it the terrible use to which man's scientific achievements were put when airplane bombs and machine-guns "shook down vertical repeated play of fire." Horrible as the war was, humanity did not lose its faith in the future: "We did not ask for that, but have survived/And will persist to speak again . . ." The poet mocks those who have been overwhelmed by tragedy into insensibility, and have lost their capacity for experiencing absolute beauty through love:

> Laugh out the meager penance of their days
> Who dare not share with us the breath released,
> The substance drilled and spent beyond repair
> For golden, or the shadow of gold hair.

The closing lines sound the renascent not animating Crane. Far beyond the capacity of compromise, cries, and pleas, the imagination will transcend hopelessness and reveal the satisfaction which our lives can give us:

> Distinctly praise the years, whose volatile
> Blamed bleeding hands extend and thresh the height
> The imagination spans beyond despair,
> Outpacing bargain, vocable and prayer.

The major symbols of the poem are literary, although in a limited sense. Faustus and Helen were undoubtedly suggested by Crane's reading of Marlowe's *Doctor Faustus*. But Crane's treatment of these symbols has expanded them beyond the bounds to which Marlowe took them. The Doctor Faustus of Marlowe's play aspires to forbidden knowledge and experience, among which is included the sight and enjoyment of Helen. Like Icarus, who is alluded to in the opening chorus of *Doctor Faustus*, Faustus is destroyed because of his overwhelming desires. Although it may be conjectured that Marlowe did not believe fully in the moral conclusion of his play, Doctor Faustus is nonetheless eternally damned for his presumption. Had Crane not developed his symbol further, he would have been satisfied to conclude his poem with Part II, to which he would have appended the lines about World War I. But Crane felt it requisite to pass beyond Marlowe in concluding on a note of hope. His Faustus is not destroyed by tragedy, but rises ennobled from the flames like a phoenix. This is the type of literary debt which is transcended to such a degree that it is no longer a debt. It has become a starting point.

Crane chose the symbols of Faustus and Helen because, as he wrote in 1925, he could find "no formulated mythology yet for classic poetic reference" in the "many divergent realities of our seething, confused cosmos of today." Although the mythologies of the past appeared hollow at the core to him, "their traditions are operative still—in millions of chance combinations of related and unrelated detail, psychological reference, figures of speech, precepts, etc. These are all a part of our common experience when it defines or extends itself." By 1925, when Crane wrote this, he had already decided to utilize the Brooklyn Bridge as the major symbol of a new long poem. That decision would indicate that in 1925 he had discovered a weakness inherent in his choice of Faustus and Helen as symbols, or else that he did not profoundly believe in the modern and non-classical symbol of the bridge. The first possibility bears the greatest portion of truth. Crane was not unaware that the writer can create new symbols so powerful in their conception and execution that they force themselves upon the flux of their age in an unforgettable manner. Eliot's "Prufrock" and "Melville's "Ahab" are examples of that creative strength which invents its own integers of meaning, and these Crane knew and admired. Yet there is a portentous overtone in the second possibility that bodes no good for *The Bridge*, Crane's second major venture into symbolism.

Having chosen his symbols through lack of confidence in contemporary culture and in himself, Crane redeemed himself by immediately disregarding them. His description of these symbols in a letter written to Waldo Frank in February 1923 adds nothing to the lines of the poem in which the protagonist "I" and the protagonist "Helen" are handled: "Helen, the symbol of this abstract 'sense of beauty,' Faustus the symbol of myself, the poetic or imaginative man of all times." Helen and Faustus appear as beings in a purely contemporary setting or in a universal realm, unrestrained by the "scaffolding" and "correspondences" between 1920 and Greek days which he so laboriously contrived. Although the name of Helen appears twice in the body of the poem, once in Part I and once in Part II, she could just as easily be any other woman who symbolizes abstract beauty. It is in the title of the poem that these symbols exist with any validity in their own right.

The superfluity of the symbols is matched by the superfluity of the "correlatives" between Paris' seduction of Helen and the metropolitan seduction, between the Trojan War which followed Helen's abduction to Troy and the first World War. How flimsy the structural relationships are may be seen in an examination of one of them. According to Greek myth, the Trojan War was caused by united action of the Greek kings who had pledged themselves to defend Helen in case of harm. When Paris abducted Helen from Sparta and took her to Troy, the famous long war began which ended only with the destruction of Troy. This may be viewed as retribution visited on the Trojan kingdom for its participation in Paris' besmirching of Helen, most beautiful of women and therefore the symbol of beauty. But Crane does not show us in Part III that the great War of 1914 was caused by a comparable descration of the ideal of beauty. Certainly the use of airplanes in combat is not such an action, and it could only be a peculiar egoism or blindness which would so analyze the cause of the war. The war stands for tragedy pure and simple in Crane's poem, then, and on *that* basis may be said to have a proper place in the work. Eliot's influence, both in *The Waste Land* and in earlier poems, had much to do with this unnecessary attempt to create, as Crane wrote to Frank, "a kind of fusion of our own time with the past." It did not have a good effect upon Crane, for he had much to offer in his own right as a contemporary consciousness with a brilliant sensibility.

Considered on its merits as a poem and not as an attempt to display a scholastic erudition comparable to that possessed by Eliot, "Faustus and Helen" is a superb expression of an idealistic temperament. Its spiritual vibrancy and its passage beyond tragedy are revelations of the sustaining courage which the workings of the artistic imagination offered Crane, and continue to offer all artists after him. Its rich language, evocative imagery, and fusion of iambic pentameter with free verse, rhymed couplets, and assonance represent Crane's assumption of a mature style.

9. "MYSTICAL SYNTHESIS"

STIMULATED BY THE ENTHUSIASTIC RECEPTION OF HIS "Faustus and Helen," Crane early in February, 1923 began to think about another long poem. It was to be called *The Bridge*, and was to continue the philosophical attitudes of the earlier poem. The conception was still hazy in his mind, but even his first thoughts made it seem so vast a project that he was certain it would require considerable time and work. By the middle of February, with the final version of "Faustus and Helen" completed and out of the way, all of Crane's thoughts were gathered together to cope with the problem of the new project. He decided that the poem was to be a revelation of the motive-forces behind the spirit of the United States, an expression of the deepest inclinations and drives which characterize the phenomenon of America and its people. These forces, beginning with their earliest manifestation in time, were to be yoked together and released in the unifying symbol of a "bridge" which concentrated within its idea and structure the secret essence of those forces. The poem was not to be developed on the realistic level of a narrative discourse such as the historical poems of Longfellow, but would function on an abstract plane in order that the American character might

be presented in a form closely allied with its experience
on a metaphysical level, before its aspects are linked with
the facts of history and matter.

"Very roughly," he wrote Munson on February 18th about the poem,
"it concerns a mystical synthesis of 'America.' History and fact, location, etc., all have to be transfigured into abstract form that would
almost function independently of its subject matter. The initial impulses
of 'our people' will have to be gathered up toward the climax of the
bridge, symbol of our constructive future, our unique identity, in
which is also included our scientific hopes and achievements of the
future. The mystic portent of all this is already flocking through my
mind (when I say this I should say 'the mystic possibilities,' but that
is all that's worth announcing anyway) . . ."

Clearly the intuition of the theme had already been
achieved, but the fleshing of its core was another matter,
as Crane realized. Although he had written a dozen or
so lines, the poem was still in its gestatory stage, and with
no further knowledge of its actual scope than that he
concluded that its length would approximate that of
"Faustus and Helen."

The genesis of *The Bridge* reveals its intent. Crane did
not intend the poem to be a panegyric of American
nationalism, as some of his contemporaries later said, nor
was it planned as a glorification of twentieth-century
United States. These statements are a total misrepresen-
tation of Crane's purpose. When he had first been presented in November 1919 with the thesis of Frank's *Our
America*—"America is a promise and a dream,"—his reaction
had been negative. Referring to Frank's optimism about
the future of America, he wrote at that time to Munson:
"This extreme national consciousness troubles me. I
cannot make myself think that these men like Dreiser,
Anderson, Frost, etc. could have gone so far creatively
had they read this book in their early days." As the years

of frustration sped by for him in Ohio, the possibility of
a reconciliation with the realities of American civilization
became fainter and fainter. It was then that he began to
experience that sense of belonging, not with the externals
of society, but with the ideals which that society was
suppressing and which he believed it was fully capable
of supporting in an organic fashion. The synthesis of
himself with the society in which he found himself, therefore, proceeded along the path previously cleared by Frank.
These ideals were of an eternal nature, far closer to the
truth of being than the businessmen, cultural prostitutes,
and other material frauds who debased these ideals. It
was as a visionary ("The modern artist needs . . . *vision*"),
a prophet of old, that he would call these ideals into being,
very much as Whitman had done so many years before
("I begin to feel myself directly connected with Whitman"). This was the meaning of the few lines of poetry
which he wrote early in February 1923 and revised in
July of the same year:

> So on this structure I would stand
> One moment, not as diver, but with arms
> That open to project a salient disk
> That winds the noon and midnight in one face.
>
> Water shall not stem that disk, nor weigh
> What holds its speed in vantage of all things
> That tarnish, creep, or wane; and so in laughter
> Blessed and posited beyond even that time
> The Pyramids shall falter, slough into sand,—
> Fiercely smooth above the wake and claim of wings
> And figured in that radiant field that rings
> The whispered cosmos, we hold consonance
> Kinetic to a poised and deathless dance.

Crane's repetition of the word "future" in the prose section quoted in paragraph I above is an index of his desire

to surmount the present; his placing of quotation marks about the words "America" and "our people" stresses the literarl distance between himself and the particularity of the present. It was because of this abstracting purpose that Crane reposed his faith in "our scientific hopes and achievements of the future," why he conceived of himself as "a suitable *Pindar* for the *dawn* of the machine age, so-called."†

† *I have italicized the word "dawn"* (B. W.).

III

"THE ARTIST
MUST HAVE ... CONFUSION"

10. "TURNING, TURNING ON SMOKED FORKING SPIRES"

CRANE'S SETTLEMENT IN NEW YORK IN MARCH 1923 released a flood of radiance and peace which had been previously submerged in his personality. It was as if he had suddenly been released from confinement into the living world, and in the joy of his freedom he must embrace the whole universe. The very flow of life became sweet, as if he had never been able to savour the fullness of a moment before: "Everything is FINE ... I never before felt TIME as I do now. It is the most precious thing in the world." The sights and sounds of New York ("so various, noisy and rich") carried him out of himself, and he turned his attention to "the intense and interesting spectacle of the streets and all the various people." But the welter of new experiences overpowered him at times, and he found himself restless mentally and physically. He wanted to fuse himself completely with the essence of reality, to become one with primal existence in a state of childlike innocence. Thus he regretted the absence of that "freedom" which children possess "to join the rhythm of life." "Older people" like himself could only yearn nostalgically for the simple bliss of childhood. Meanwhile, they had to think realistically about earning a living, about living quarters, and the myriad details of a complicated existence.

Upon his arrival, Crane moved into the Grove Street apartment of Gorham Munson. For several weeks, the novelty of his surroundings and the resumption of his personal contacts with old friends kept him from looking very seriously for a job. When he finally bestirred himself, the deep-felt confidence he possessed in his copywriting talents was unable to transmit itself to the executives of the advertising agencies to whom he applied for work. He kept postponing the moment when he would have to make a decision about his future until, when May arrived, he lacked sufficient funds to "get new clothes, shoes fixed, hair cut . . ." In June, however, with the assistance of friends, he managed to obtain a clerical position in a large advertising agency. Although the work did not call for the full utilization of his talents, he was overjoyed that the uncertainty of the past few months was dispelled and that he would not have to return defeated to Cleveland.

While the weeks of unemployment had been slipping by rapidly, Crane's poetry lay dormant within him, and he exhausted his expressive and emotional needs with a hectic round of social activities and explorations. Except by a few intimate friends, he was not encouraged to proceed further with his writing. The recognition which he had previously received from Frank, Munson, and Tate for "Faustus and Helen" had spent itself in its capacity to arouse him to new effort by the time he arrived in New York. He had expected that his poem would evoke an identical enthusiastic response from other critics and poets in his new home. But its positive Ouspenskian spirit was unappreciated by younger men dominated by the pessimism of Eliot's *The Waste Land* and the nihilism which the expatriates were bringing back from Europe. The older generation might have been expected to appreciate the fact that Crane partook of the Whitmanian substance, but they couldn't understand his poetry and unthinkingly relegated him to the camp of Eliot. Of these Crane wrote bitterly to the Rychtariks in April: "Most of them are very disagreeable and don't talk the same language as we do, they are not concerned with the same problems. I read 'Faustus and Helen' to a group of people last evening, and very few of them, of course, understood anything that I was talking about." Those literary figures who remembered Crane from his earlier pre-1920 stays in New York confused him with the ungainly, insecure Midwestern youth that he had been, or else were repelled by his new self-confidence and his powerful poetry. This confidence lost some of its vitality, therefore, and Crane became less sanguine about the task which lay before him in the development of his poetic destiny and the propagation of his mystical creed. "This 'new consciousness' is something that takes a long while to 'put across' . . ." he wrote.

Temporarily rebuffed, Crane made no additions to the few existent lines of *The Bridge* for several months. The period of inactivity was broken in June when he obtained employment and was able to move into a room of his own. Still another factor contributed to the upsurge of his desire to complete the poem. His friends, notably Frank, had been tirelessly publicizing "Faustus and Helen" to other writers and critics, and many of them who heard the poem read aloud by Frank or saw it in manuscript were beginning to recognize Crane's talent. This heartening news at last demonstrated to Crane that his faith in that poem had not been unfounded, for he was unable to rely upon his own conception of the poem's merit. "Really," he wrote the Rychtariks, "it looks as though that poem were going to make a reputation." With this new development, the world became a brighter place, the mental equilibrium for creative work appeared, and he optimistically foresaw the end of *The Bridge* in sight. "I shall be glad to stay here all summer working at my job and writing," he wrote Richard and Charlotte Rychtarik. "I feel that I am getting now just where I have longed to be for so long. I can have absolute quiet and seclusion when I want it, wine when I need it, and the intense and interesting spectacle of the streets and all the various people." During June, therefore, Crane devoted himself ecstatically to *The Bridge*, revising the thirteen or so lines already written and composing thirty-seven new lines to precede them. "It was written verse by verse in the most tremendous emotional exaltations I have ever felt," he wrote the Rychtariks. So engrossing was the process of composition that he rushed home at the close of each day's work to strike down the lines, writing and re-writing in a state of intense happiness—"carried . . . out of myself and all personal interests from the dot of five until two in the morning sometimes . . ."

Unfortunately, this exuberance and appetite for creation was short-lived. The more absorbed Crane became in the composition of his poetry, the more unbearable became his new-found equilibrium. For one, he had not dispensed with the parties, visits, and discussions which took up so much of his time. In addition, his firm had rewarded Crane for industry on their behalf with a promotion to the copywriting department; this new position required him to travel out-of-town and visit the factories of the clients for whom he wrote copy. This left still less time for him in which he could proceed with his poetry, and Crane began to long desperately for a period of freedom undisturbed by daily stints in an office. Indeed, he began to conceive of himself as a martyr spreadeagled on a cross of suffering, unable to unite his powers in a concentrated drive. "All that means *more* work there," he wrote the Rychtariks about his promotion, "and even *less* time for what I want to do. I am forced to be ambitious in two directions, you see, and in many ways it is like being put up on a cross and divided . . . I would like to have the days twice as long as they are—for all I want to do." The problem was the same one which had aggravated him in Cleveland and Akron.

The truth of the matter is, however, that Crane was not being forced to be ambitious by anyone but himself; the experiences of his past employment had taught him very little about how to get along as an employee. He could not reconcile himself to regard his job simply as a means of livelihood, and involved himself emotionally in its atmosphere and conditions. He let himself become enmeshed in a vortex wherein his balance was disturbed at the slightest fluctuation of events in the firm. This would not be so important were it not for Crane's ambition as a poet. He had come to New York to realize this ambition, yet by his negligence let it fade into unimportance in the face of the petty intrigue and economic considerations which almost inevitably conspire to keep the employees of most business and industrial organizations in a state of utter demoralization.

One of the pitfalls into which employees wander in any business, for example, is that of being continually preoccupied with the issue of salary increases, and Crane immediately fell a victim to it in the agency. There is no denying that his wages were low in relation to the services he performed, but in his own words they were sufficient for "the bare necessities of life all the time." By neglecting to automatically raise his pay, the firm managed to extort increased effort and time from him, for he was deluded by the belief that by cooperating he would become more valuable and thereby be granted the additional pay. Thus he became both aggrieved and fretful, and his bitterness could not be filed at the close of day in the office but continued to poison his thoughts at all times. Had he been less "ambitious," he would have been able to concentrate more of his passion and energy in his poetry. Another pitfall was his entanglement in the office intrigue prevalent in any organization. Acutely aware of his lack of education, he smarted under the patronizing condescension of the wealthy college men who predominated in the agency (a "stylish and snobbish set of educated people . . . they are very lofty and certainly seem to think that the social superiority of the place is enough to make up for low salaries"). When the atmosphere and low pay of the agency became intolerable, he consoled himself with the thought that the occupational experience he was gaining would undoubtedly simplify the problem of locating "higher paid positions in other places after a while." He completely ignored the fact that as long as two years earlier the convention of working one's way up the bourgeois ladder of success had proved itself meaningless and illusory to him.

The significance of Crane's optimistic temperament and his mystical faith in this pattern of repetitive and limiting behaviour must not be under-rated. "I want to keep saying 'YES' to everything and never be beaten a moment, and I shall, of course, never be really beaten," he wrote the Rychtariks in the fall of 1922. All the spiritual strains of his life, despite their immersion in painful happenings, combined to make him consider the flux of events as the expression of forces more powerful and true than himself, and therefore to be welcomed rather than rejected. There was also a masochistic flavor to this optimism, as if the experience of pain and sorrow promised greater understanding of reality than did joy and satisfaction. " 'No one has ever begun to really appreciate life, or lived, until he has recognized the background of life as essentially Tragedy.' It is from this platform of perception that I conceive every artist as beginning his work." So Crane had written earlier in 1922. With this idea in the foreground of his thinking, it was as a profound fatalist that Crane did not engage in a serious effort to deflect those things which promised to involve him in turmoil and unhappiness.

"My mother has had her full share of suffering," he wrote in this vein in July 1923, "and I have had much, also. I have had enough, anyway, to realize that it is all very beautiful in the end if you will pierce through to the center of it and see it in relation to the real emotions and values of Life. Do not think I am entirely happy here,—or ever will be, for that matter, except for a few moments at a time when I am perhaps writing or receiving a return of love. The true idea of God is the only thing that can give happiness,—and that is the identification of yourself with *all of life*. It is a fierce and humble happiness, both at the same time, and I am hoping that my Mother will find that *feeling* (for it need not be a conscious thought) at some time or other. She must accept *everything* and as it comes (as we all must) before she can come to such happiness, glorious sorrow, or whatever you want to call it."

But Crane's enthusiasm for complete acceptance of all phases of experience did not prevent him from succumbing to depression and melancholy, perhaps even more abyss-like than is experienced by most people. That he was receiving an over-dose of suffering which paralyzed rather than enriched his creative faculties and his morale became evident in the fall of 1923. The tremendous spiritual desire to complete *The Bridge* petered away, and Crane could only work on smaller poems and fragmentary efforts which did not require long-sustained devotion and self-assurance. But what was he to do now? Though his last few years had been the traditional battle-ground on which the artist struggled against bourgeois society, he had never set himself the task of explicitly evolving a design for living by which the incompatibles of his life might be harmonized. As we have seen, the trend of his reconciling efforts had been to escape from his father first, and thereafter to escape from society itself. Unable to leave for Europe, which symbolized the oasis of art, he had fled to New York instead. Now in New York, he realized that he had not solved the most important of the basic issues motivating his migration to New York. The conflict between his economic needs and his poetry was still raging with undiverted fever.

"The situation for the artist in America," he wrote in September, "seems to me to be getting harder and harder all the time. Most of my friends are worn out with the struggle here in New York. If you make enough to live decently on, you have no time left for your real work.—and otherwise you are constantly liable to starve. New York offers nothing to anyone but a circle of friendly and understanding brothers,—beyond that it is one of the most stupid places in the world to live in. Of course, one's friends are worth it,—but sometimes when you see them so upset by the fever and crowded conditions, the expenses and worries—you wonder whether or not there is much use in the whole business."

Just a month earlier, Crane had almost reached an understanding of the course of action which he ought to follow in order to be able to resolve his impasse and devote himself exclusively to poetry. "I shall certainly break loose and do only such simple labor for my room and board as will not come into my consciousness after 'working hours'," he wrote to Alfred Stieglitz. "Streams of 'copy' and ad layouts course through my head all night sometimes until I feel like a thread singed and twisted in the morning." But this idea evaporated because of his desire to earn enough money so as to be able to bring his mother and aged grandmother to New York to live with him; while it was a laudable sentiment on the part of a son, it was overly-sentimental insofar as his own career was involved.

Unable to adjust the exigencies of existence in a planned fashion, Crane once again thought of leaving them behind. The flight from Ohio was to be repeated, this time from New York, and the inspiration for the move was derived from several factors. Most important, of course, was his job, which became more and more intolerable. The turmoil which it aroused in him, coupled with the tremendous emotional drain which his writing enforced, completely destroyed his capacity for continuing with *The Bridge*. The energy with which he had created so furiously in June declined and disappeared. In July, for example, he added only six new lines to those already written. Yet it was something more than this that made it impossible for Crane to proceed with *The Bridge*. He was uncertain of the direction which the poem ought to take, and a structural outline which would guide him in his writing was impossible to arrive at. In a real sense, this uncertainty was a reflection of his unsettled over-all intellectual beliefs, although Crane's perplexity was limited to the poem alone. The idea of the poem had been grasped by Crane as an implicit apprehension, so that its purpose was clear and details were vague. For this reason, he had naturally turned to the composition of the lines which form its climactic close. Now he faced the problem of developing the preliminary movements for which the lines he had already written would serve as an inevitable finale. Were the "vision" which had supplied his purpose not exhausted now, he would still have faced the necessity of constructing a systematic inspiration. "I've been in such despair about this latter for some time!" he wrote Stieglitz about *The Bridge* in August, "—not seeing my way to introduce it in the way I want (the end and climax . . . is all that's done so far) and not getting the needful hours to ripen anything in myself." He had estimated in July that it would take him another year to complete the poem, which would then be approximately 250 lines in length. More than two years were to elapse before Crane again felt sufficiently sure of himself to tackle the completion of the poem, and at that time it assumed vaster proportions than he had ever believed possible. Meanwhile, it was put aside.

A third cause of Crane's approach to the breaking-point was the expatriation movement in which so many writers participated in the early 1920's. The exodus of artists and intellectuals from the United States to Europe in search of a sympathetic atmosphere, a hegira which had begun with post-war disillusionment, was in active swing. Daily on the New York piers one might have seen the eager faces of the expatriating hopefuls as they waved fare-well to the uncourageous who would not make the trip and to the impoverished who could not. At the same time, those who had left earlier were debarking from the transatlantic liners; among them were Crane's friends, and those whom he knew by name and reputation only. Munson had returned in 1922; Josephson came back shortly thereafter; in August 1923, Malcolm Cowley, whose poetry Crane had been admiring for several years in various little magazines, landed in New York harbor. There were many others, and before long Crane became an intimate member of the little group which they formed in the city. They had returned with a sentimental attachment to France, Italy, and other continental lands, and were determined to recreate in this country the favorable climate which they had enjoyed in Europe, a congenial environment in which, as now too, the artist could exercise individuality and scope. From these men, Crane received his fill of entrancing tales, enough to justify his envy of past years when he had been hearing of one writer after another who was leaving for Europe. Nor had these writers yet tempered their memories with the realization that as artists they had fared no better abroad than had the artists who remained in the States, and that indeed they had cut themselves off from a subject-matter which they understood and could write about. They returned with their original contempt for the American cultural scene, and hurriedly attempted to secret themselves in the country away from the large cities in which they had to earn a living. Some bought farms; those who had less money rented shacks and cottages where they could spend week-ends and summers; and the hardiest lived in the country all-year-round as best they could. Agreeing with these writ-

ers in their repudiation of bourgeois America, Crane was
shown a practical solution to his problem. He could escape and find himself a personal refuge in a non-urban environment. But where?

In the middle of October, Crane suddenly remembered
the family plantation on the Isle of Pines in Cuba, which
he had visited many years before as a boy. Gradually
it assumed the shape of a happy island on which he could
live cheaply, finish *The Bridge*, "drink gallons of orange
juice, bathe and play tennis," and generally at one swoop
bring to an end the miseries of his New York life. Without waiting to hear from his mother, whom he had written about his plan to live on the island, he resigned his
position at the advertising agency. This move had the
approval of Waldo Frank, as Crane wrote Munson. In
addition, Crane's departure from the agency was encouraged by a second friend, a woman familiar with psycho-
analysis who had been analyzing Crane's disturbed emotional life. It was her opinion that Crane needed less,
rather than more inhibitions. In the face of his genuine
distress ("the impact between reality and the consciousness around me threatens to shatter my nerves and health,"
he wrote at this time), she also emboldened him to resign
his job and take the remedial steps which he thought necessary. A few days after he quit the agency, however, his
mother wrote him that the plantation had been put up on
the open market for sale. To go there now was manifestly impracticable, for his constant apprehension that the
plantation was being sold from under him would not be
conducive to creative feelings. Again he was faced with
an uncertain future, though he was convinced that it had
been absolutely necessary for him to follow the course he
had taken.

"I am not at all regretful for what I have done, it being a purely organic necessity," he wrote. "I should have been 'flat' if I had tried to keep up that damned lying hypocrisy of advertising much longer—at least for the time being." To Stieglitz he wrote: "I hardly know how to begin—such confusion reigns at present. It's the usual state, however, with the additional complication that my nerves are a little frazzled. In fact they got so on edge writing that damned advertising under the pseudo-refined atmosphere of the office I was working in that I had to resign the other day to save my mind . . . as things stand at present, haven't got the money to carry me through the rest and contemplation that I need. Rather wound up, you see!"

Since Crane's employer had promised to re-hire him upon his return from the Isle of Pines, he decided that he might as well take a vacation in the country in order to regain his health and composure. Early in November, therefore, he left for the Woodstock, New York cottage of Slater Brown and Edward Nagle.

Crane at first felt very happy in Woodstock. "So quiet it is here!" he wrote the Rychtariks. "No cats fighting, people quarreling or subways beneath you to make the ground tremble." He was glad to be away from the city, to breathe the country air, and to do the simple chores required to keep the Brown-Nagle establishment in living condition. But his escape was merely superficial and temporary. The most pressing of his problems was still the financial one. By December, his money was exhausted, though he had been expending it at the rate of only a dollar a day for food. There were no prospects of employment in New York. He entertained the notion of staying in Woodstock for the entire winter as the caretaker of a summer hotel located on top of a mountain near the town. In exchange for taking care of the estate as well as a group of assorted livestock including horses, a cow and chickens, the hotel owner offered forty dollars a month and expenses. Crane was aware that a winter spent on top of a mountain would involve considerable "Loneliness amid hurricanes and drifts," but it was preferable to a tiresome job in the city with its "scattered prostitutions." "The prospect so far as money goes is so threatening and hopeless as I see it in New York," he wrote Munson, "that I may take this strenuous means of asserting myself against the traditional conflicts of my past." The caretaker job, however, failed to materialize. He sent two poems and a letter requesting some reviews to a new managing editor of *The Dial*, but did not elicit a favorable response. In desperation, he wrote asking his family in Cleveland for money; they sent him only half as much as he had asked for and needed. Family complications, as usual, added their tortuous effect to his emotional life. His mother had accepted a job in a store which sold antiques and expensive furnishings, and in view of the sacrifice which this entailed she could hardly regard her son's decision to take a sudden vacation with equanimity. But Crane, although he sympathized deeply with his mother's plight, for it was reported to him that she returned home at the end of each working day "so exhausted and wrecked that she cannot hardly speak," felt that she had taken the job without any real necessity for the step. "Everything is being sold as soon as possible," he wrote with scarcely-repressed fury and bitterness to the Rychtariks. "Only I refuse to sell myself any longer than I absolutely have to. I shall beg and steal when necessary to avoid it." Meanwhile, he learned that he had not been fortunate enough to win the annual *Fugitive* prize of $100, an award which he had been counting on to relieve him of some of his worry. The result of his self-questioning and his other hopes and tentative decisions came to nought in the knowledge that he had no alternative to returning to New York and begin-

45 Gove Street
Aug 11" '23

Dear Stieglitz:

The imagination dwells on frangible boughs! In ten days' now I've been travelling through the middle west on business for the company. Investigating certain sales fact and figures among hardware and paint dealers on "Barreled Sunlight", a kind of white paint! My mind is like dough — and "The Bridge" is far away, your card was a warm signal to me on the morning of my joyful return. I never saw the Venus in her sphere before — looking on the world with the wind from sulphos in her hair! How do you do it?! You have the distinction of being classic and realistic at once. That, of course, is what real classicism means. You don't know how much I think about my essay on and your work! Please don't think me faithless. I fly in a rage when I think of the sacrifices I pay just to feel myself in the hope of time — a rightful heritage of all of us — and it takes time to say and think out the things I feel in your photographs. I'll try and write you more soon, but don't misunderstand any silences from me. I am your brother always —

Hart Crane

LETTER TO ALFRED STIEGLITZ, 1923

CRANE AND THE BROOKLYN BRIDGE, 1930

CRANE IN MEXICO, 1931

ning the long hunt for a job. "I shall stave off my landlady as long as possible," he wrote Munson, "and then take up a bench in Battery Park or embark on a ship." In Christmas, just before returning to New York, he wrote Munson: "I hope that '24—well, what shall we *hope* for? I don't think I know enough to hope for anything. So I won't inflict details on others—of that category."

There have been critics who have called Crane a poet of the city, the celebrant of American urban life. Lest his concern with a metropolitan symbol, the bridge, be confused with his basic attitude to the modern city of business and industry, it might be well at this point to affirm that Crane's feeling about the city in his life and in his poetry appears to be almost exclusively one of negation. Part VII of *The Bridge*, "The Tunnel," is Crane's extended treatment of metropolitan life, and its total effect is one of fierce revulsion. Beginning with "Porphyro in Akron," this mood predominates in the poems wherein Crane treated the city: "Repose of Rivers" with its vision of "scalding ungents spread and smoking darts"; "Possessions"; "Recitative" with its human beings suspended "from atrocious sums/Built floor by floor on shafts of steel that grant/The plummet heart, like Absalom, no stream . . ."; "Faustus and Helen"; and among others, the rejection of megapolitan civilization embodied in "Key West":

> Because these millions reap a dead conclusion
> Need I presume the same fruit of my bone
> As draws them towards a doubly mocked confusion
> Of apish nightmare into steel-strung stone?

These poems, bearing in mind Crane's honesty, could not have been written unless the city had not indeed been a place of horror for him. As in Woodstock during 1923, the country, whether that of New York, Connecticut, Cuba, or France, was always more stimulating and pleasing to Crane. There he temporarily escaped from the nightmare alleys within which his days and nights were entangled, "searched the hill/Blue-writ and odor-firm with violets, 'til/With June mountain laurel broke through green/And filled the forest with what clustrous sheen!"

Yet even in the country, as we have said, Crane could not genuinely throw off the conflicts of his existence. An index to his mental status at the close of 1923, while in the Catskill mountain country surrounding Woodstock, may be derived from consideration of an incident unmentioned in any of his letters. Mrs. Isabel Lachaise, wife of the sculptor Gaston Lachaise and the mother of Edward Nagle, was a frequent visitor to the Brown-Nagle establishment while Crane was staying there. She was able to observe Crane intimately, and with great pity saw him undergoing such transitory and extreme changes of emotional mood, from acute depression to ecstatic joy, that it was quite obvious to her that he was emotionally disturbed and unstable. One evening, indeed, this torture reached a climax for Crane. The Lachaises had been invited for dinner and, after the meal was finished, were sitting together with Brown, Nagle, and Crane and talking Crane suddenly burst from the room, caught up an axe used for woodchopping on his way out, and ran out of the cottage into the surrounding woods. Nagle and Brown, familiar with Crane's suicidal frame of mind, were very much alarmed and followed after to find and restrain him. It was probably impossible for Crane to kill himself with a long-handled axe; nevertheless, they feared that he might maim himself with it. Fortunately, Crane was found before he had had an opportunity to accomplish any drastic action. It is possible to regard this incident as a dramatic effort to arouse pity, and there is no reason to doubt that many of Crane's later violent actions more and more partake of this character. Whether one adopts this view, which has an element of truth, or believes that Crane really intended to destroy himself, one cannot avoid the tragic element in both possibilities. It throws new light on Crane's concern with death during 1922 and 1923, and negates somewhat the effect of his dance with death in Part III of "Faustus and Helen." It comes as a startling prelude to the actual achievement of his death little less than a decade later. In this obsession with death, literally a wish for death, is to be found the secret of his disagreement with Eliot, who overtly welcomed death in his poetry, as well as Crane's almost frenzied efforts to convince himself and others that he had a deep and abiding pleasure in life, that he was not pessimistic and self-destructive.

The pattern of Crane's life was cooling into finality. Having been unable to adjudicate between the claims of poetry and the need to earn his living, Crane found that he could obtain relief by evading the issue. He failed to avail himself of intellectual choice and decision, and trusted in the natural benevolence of circumstances as they revealed themselves and passed by. The suffering derived from the resultant chaos was made tolerable only by his optimism and acceptance of evil as a necessary component of reality. The devices which he had originally employed as tools for innocent purposes—alcohol to stimulate his poetic gift, sexual indulgence for the love which it engendered—became narcotics, less adequate as their grip over Crane grew progressively more overpowering. Crane had achieved the highest level of social and emotional maturity which he would ever reach. One more adventure was necessary before he became complete, a voyage over the ocean of intellectual belief.

11. "PITEOUS ADMISSIONS . . . SPILT UPON THE PAGE"

THE YEAR 1924 SAW CRANE'S CONSCIOUS ASSUMPtion of the garment of confusion which was to be his for the remainder of his life. This development was brought to a climax by the publication of an article by Ernest Boyd in the first issue of *The American Mercury* (January 1924). Under the generic title of "Aesthete: Model 1924," Boyd uncritically lumped together a group of articulate young writers whose magazines and writings had brought them to the baneful attention of vested literary interests. Boyd's outright accusations of ignorance and posing covered by innuendo Waldo Frank, Gorham Munson, Crane, Malcolm Cowley, Kenneth Burke, Matthew Josephson, and numerous others who had contributed to little magazines like *Broom*, *Secession*, *S4N*, and *The Dial*, and were attempting to penetrate into more sedate organs.

The writers whom Boyd spattered with abuse were superficially alike, but basically dissimilar. Untangling the fluid and evanescent ideas which enveloped these writers into some semblance of order is a Herculean task requiring far greater space than is here available, and I enter the arena with some trepidation. They were linked to-

213

gether, broadly speaking, by their common interest in the formal aspects of literature. Beyond this point, they were divided. (How divided they were, and how seriously they took this division, the forthright paragraphs of their manifestoes and magazine articles reveal all too obviously. Boyd's intransigent statements were no novelty to them.) On the one hand, Frank, Munson, and Crane represented a group which hoped to tap new levels of spiritual consciousness. Cowley, Josephson, Burke, Slater Brown, and Harold Loeb formed a second group which, under the influence of formalistic French criticism and the Dadaists, was more concerned with integrating the indigenous externals of modern American life into its poetry and fiction. Yet even this division into two large groups is inadequate. If we probe more deeply into their constituents, finer lines of division are discovered. Munson, for example, was able to submit freely in the spring of 1924 to the physical and mental disciplines required by the Russian mystic Gurdjieff; whereas Crane adhered to a doctrine of ecstatic personal mysticism and rejected Gurdjieff's practices. Both Munson and Crane, furthermore, believed with the members of the second group that the contemporary English language was decayed and that the skyscrapers, billboards, and other contrivances of a mechanized era provided raw materials for an enriching poetic vocabulary and imagery.

Temperamental differences played almost as important a part in the formation of these two groups as did any conflict of ideas. Munson, although agreeing almost wholeheartedly with the aesthetic values of the Cowley-Burke-Josephson group, was older, and more serious about questions of principle and performance than the members of that group. The light-hearted behaviour of those writers, especially when it involved tampering with the publication of *Secession*, which Munson had organized, created a store of resentment which found itself directed against the American Dadaists. These gentlemen retaliated by personal cat-calls in their own magazine, *Broom*. A typical example of the repartee which flew about was Cowley's personal call to Munson in the November 1923 issue of *Broom* for "a more passionate apprehension of life," probably a reference to Munson's statement in his 1923 study of Waldo Frank that the Dadaists had ignored emotional and religious values. Munson was anxious to discover new themes and approaches in mysticism, but as late as October 1924 wrote in "The Single Portent of Carl Sandburg" (*The Double Dealer*) that he was reluctant to assume the title of a mystic since his personal experiences had failed to convince him that he could undergo a mystical rapture. Crane, on the other hand, sincerely considered himself a mystic; unlike Munson, he shared the gay abandonment and exuberance of the second non-mystical group. The result was that Munson kept himself pretty much apart in a personal sense from the *Broom* group, whereas Crane veered back and forth between Frank-Munson and Cowley-Burke-Josephson-Brown. Such a course of action was eventually bound to arouse imputations of opportunism and intellectual nihilism against Crane, and these were not long in forthcoming. The manner in which Crane reacted to these charges reveals a significant aspect of his mentality.

Before the Boyd article had performed the seemingly-impossible feat of merging into one imaginary corpus all the advance-guard writers, Cowley had attempted to accomplish the task by means of a meeting of *Broom-Se-*

cession contributors in October 1923. " 'If we can get together in one room,' " he wrote in his letter of invitation to Kenneth Burke (*Exile's Return*, 189), " 'we can at least define our separate positions, whether or not we can make plans to go ahead.' " The meeting was a decisive failure, and it is not too difficult to see just why. Verbal brickbats had strained the tempers of many of the invited to a point at which any reconciliation was out of the question. Josephson, for example, had attacked Frank in the December 1922 issue of *Broom* on the grounds of vagueness of language, poor diction and prose rhythm; he linked Frank with Anderson and James Oppenheim as "exponents of mystical or unconscious behaviour"; his praise of Frank was double-edged when he declared that Frank's language experiments deserved commendation for he was then less concerned with meaning, implying that Frank's ideas were valueless. Beyond a desire to infuse European respect for culture into American philistinism, and an adulatory regard for the mechanical products of the philistines, the combined brains who attended had little to offer in the way of a consolidated position which might attract other writers, make literary history, and unite their ranks. Frank did not attend the meeting; Munson, who was convalescing from a serious illness in Woodstock, sent a letter attacking both Josephson and Loeb. Although Crane attended as "the only delegate from the higher spaces," he had, as he apologetically wrote Munson, only "a very slight interest in the meeting, and [I] am unconcerned with its issues. I am really going only for a gesture of affability. Very likely I'll play the most contrary role—make a scene or something before we get through." As the progress of the session is described in *Exile's Return* Crane was not the only one to make a scene, and the conclave finally dissolved without purpose after a good deal of noise, argument, and drinking.

The Boyd article, although its implied purpose was to destroy those invited to attend the October 1923 conclave, also failed to unite the younger writers into a common front. They recognized the threat of philistinism to their progress and welfare, but none of the more vociferous warriors, Munson and Josephson particularly, cared to compromise a fraction of their differences. Throughout 1924 the gap widened. One of the opening guns fired in the campaign of 1924 was an article written by Waldo Frank in the fall of 1923. Entitled "For a Declaration of War," it appeared in *Secession No. 7* in the spring of 1924 and was reprinted in *Salvos* (1924), a collection of Frank's essays and reviews. The article was essentially a challenge to the young writers of the opponent group who had returned from Europe with the disintegrating philosophy of the Dadaists, Joyce, Eliot, and Pound. Frank diagnosed the prevailing spirit of the 1920's as one lacking in philosophical synthesis, without a feeling of unity and wholeness in itself, without any shared religious or ideological beliefs which might tend to unify the age. The advance of science had destroyed all basic philosophical convictions; matter had been proved destructible; time and space had been shown to be dynamic, not static; reason was not independent of outside controls. Despite this destruction of the traditional groundwork upon which man functioned, Frank went on to say, man must not sacrifice the conviction that "Unity is truth. This is a universe, not a multiverse." This conviction "is the categorical imperative of any culture, the expression of the social will to survive. It is a conviction whose mechanics in the individual man is analogous to the instinct of the

atom or the cell to adhere in the major organism." Frank
condemned the Dadaists for rejecting this belief, and by
extension he condemned those who followed their doctrines in America; the result of such rejection he wrote,
is disintegration, the fragmentation of life into unrelated
atoms. Acceptance of such fragmentation is inertia,
Frank continued, and "apologists of inertia" attempt to
convince us that art and life are inevitably "three-dimensional . . . [that] Art's function is to subserve . . . as
documentation, criticism, exposition, explanation, corroboration, decoration . . . the *status quo* spiritual, intellectual and ethical, in which man finds himself at the moment
of encountering it." This inertia must not be allowed to
continue, Frank added, for there are "intimations of
values and dimensions of life" beyond the grasp of the
mind, and art must bring these values and dimensions into
the consciousness. An art which does not perform this
task, or a criticism which does not understand and explain such an art, "is idle, irrelevant, impotent and anti-
social." The grounds upon which Frank based his belief
in super-intellectual certainties were not far removed from
Ouspenskian metaphysics:

"Inspired intellects have glimpsed certain truths still largely alien from
human experience. As that a. Our sense of matter, space, time, thought
is subjective, inadequate and untrue. b. Only the relativity of time,
space, matter, etc., is true. c. And true as measures not of Being, but
of our consciousness of being. d. Hence the laws of cause and effect,
the laws of logic the laws of scientific research and experiment, the
laws of mathematics are *sub specie aeternitatis* null and void. e. What
has been accepted as cause and effect and absolute sequence in time
is mere juxtaposition in some superintellectual direction. f. Hence these
laws governing the mechanics and forms of art are to be superseded.
g. Our convictions of limits and individuals are merely the limits of our
present consciousness and may be superseded."

Art must, therefore, carry out its function of conquering and discovering new forms of life without limitation by logic, language, and other empirical restrictions.

The basic arguments in Frank's essay were repeated by Munson a few months later in an article on Eliot's *The Waste Land*, which appeared in the first issue of *1924* (July 1924), a literary magazine edited by Edwin Seaver. According to Munson, Eliot symbolized spiritual bankruptcy. This condition was reflected in *The Waste Land*, about whose form Munson wrote: "I am compelled to reject the poem as a sustained harmoniously functioning structural unit." In his opinion, Eliot was guilty of deliberate obscurity in an endeavour to give synthetic philosophical depth to his static and directionless outlook: "It is artificially concocted by omissions, incompletions and unnecessary specialization in the assembling of those circumstances which ought to evoke in the reader the whole effect of the given emotion." Only the exploitation of "a new slope of human consciousness" would enable the artist to integrate his work, Munson wrote, and this new consciousness could only be apprehended by mysticism, a mysticism in harmony with the most advanced discoveries of science. The intelligence and sensibility of Eliot were inadequate tools in the absence of spiritual vision.

Munson's article was followed in the third issue of *1924* (Fall 1924) with a specific attack on Dadaism by Frank. Dadaism, he reiterated, was a "surrender to environment." The Dadaist artist's passivity in terms of adopting a constructive attitude to society was reprehensible because his nihilistic disregard of social issues was actually conducive to a perpetuation of those ills which had driven him to embrace Dadaism. Dadaism may have been applicable to the predicament of Europe, where order and form had dominated for centuries; in America, Frank pointed out, life was already so disorganized that the disintegrating tendencies of Dadaism were unnecessary. The artist in America must strive to create works which would express a unitary nature: "A healthy reaction to our world must of course be the contrary of Dada; it must be ordered and serious and thorough." By adopting "a literally religious temper," Frank concluded, the centrifugal and the chaotic could be ordered and dominated.

In response to Frank's latest article, Malcolm Cowley wrote a letter in which he announced his proud willingness to be called "the American Dada" (*1924*, December 1924). He accused Frank of imitating the unanimist doctrines of Jules Romains, and implied thereby that Frank was also under the influence of a foreign philosophy. Cowley derogated mysticism by quoting directly from Bertrand Russell, who had said, according to Cowley, that mysticism was " 'contemplative'," possessed no understanding of the reality of time, and was " 'essentially a lazy man's philosophy'." Thus, the charge of "inertia" with which Frank had decried the Dadaists was reversed into a return salvo against Frank's mystical philosophy. Cowley was defiant, too, about the positive value of Dadaism: "But Dada was also a discovery: that nonsense may be the strongest form of ridicule; that writing is often worst when it is most profound, saintly or devoted and best when it is approached in a spirit of play; that associational processes of thought often have more form than the logical; that defiance carried to the extremes of bravado is more to be admired than a passive mysticism." Although both Cowley and Frank discarded logic, the former was content to mirror life in a disorganized manner, whereas Frank sought for order on a supernatural plane.

As an intimate spectator at the quarrels between the younger writers, Crane was not unaware that the gap between the Frank-Munson group, of which he was ostensibly a member, and the *Broom writers* had widened into an unbridgeable gap. Shortly after the failure of the October 1923 meeting called by Cowley, Crane wrote Munson: "We really have two groups to the former ONE of Secession, and there is no use trying to evade that fact,—as obviously, you are not trying to do." The arguments and principles of Frank and Munson were in harmony with his own thoughts, based as they were in great part on an agreement with Ouspenskian tenets and a firm appreciation of mysticism as a way of life and art. Frank's "For a Declaration of War," which Crane had read in manuscript in October 1923, before the meeting already described, pleased him as "really a whizz of a challenge." Its implications and propositions were perfectly apparent to him. He had read Munson's article on Eliot with approbation before it appeared, and after he re-read it in *1924* he wrote Munson: "I may congratulate you again on some very accurate estimates and constructive motives." There were, in addition, close personal ties linking him to both Munson and Frank. Munson had been his most sympathetic correspondent for over a period of three years, as well as a firm admirer of his poetry; it was Munson who continually undertook to publicize Crane's poetry and to place it in the various magazines with which he came in contact: *Gargoyle, Secession, 1924,* and others. Frank, although a more recent friend, had become before

long the one man in whom Crane confided his most
secret emotions and ideas without fear of ridicule or re-
buff. With Frank, more than with any other man whom
Crane knew, he did not feel compelled to play the buffoon
or to parody his most profound beliefs. But almost as
a direct counterpoint to the serious attention which he
received from Munson and Frank, Crane craved a friendship in which his boisterous humour and capacity for
drinking could find their complete and tolerated expression. This outlet he had found in most of the writers
of the *Broom* group, many of whom combined a talent
for fiction and poetry with a seemingly-unfathomable
liquid bottom and formed an ideal substitute for the
Cleveland-Akron friends from whom Crane was now separated.

Although the group seems on the whole to have been
contemptuous of mysticism and impregnated with the pessimism of Eliot and Spengler, Crane apparently was able
to subdue the philosophical and religious aspects of his
thinking in their presence. Another reason that he felt
himself attracted to these writers was that, like himself,
the majority were younger poets who shared his literary
enthusiasms and encountered similar problems of craft
which could be discussed with joint profit and interest.
Although both Munson and Frank had published a few
poems, their main vehicles of literary expression were criticism and fiction. Attached as Crane was, therefore, to
the writers who, with varying degrees of fever, were com-
batting each other, he was in an unenviable position. One
can imagine how he must have suffered during this movement from camp to camp and back again, for the en-
gagements related in the preceding paragraphs are only a
fractional representation selected to highlight the main

Se

issues of contention and hardly convey the passionate emotional temper of the disputants.

Crane returned from Woodstock to New York in January 1924 in an improved physical condition. But the anticipated mental rehabilitation, which had been his prime reason for fleeing to the country, had failed to materialize. With unhidden envy he saw about him friends who, like Jean Toomer, had set themselves a rigorous program of self-integration and maturation. Unlike them, he was neither integrating himself nor was he slowly becoming "solid and undismayed . . . steady and direct." "I somehow feel about as solitary as I ever felt in my life," he wrote Munson. "Perhaps it's all in the pressure of economic exigencies at present—but I also feel an outward chaos around me—many things happening and much that is good, but somehow myself out of it, between two worlds. Of course none of this would be, were I creating actively myself."

Actually Crane had been writing, but the cessation of active work on *The Bridge* since August 1923 was a depressing reality. It occurred to him that a cause of his inability to push his major project to a successful completion might be the expansive nature of his temper, the floridity of which resulted in a rich but diffused poetry ill-adapted to the thematic nature of *The Bridge*. The lines which he had already written for *The Bridge* were undoubtedly the cause of this train of thought. A week before he left his job in October 1923, Crane had sent Munson a copy of a new poem entitled "Recitative." During his Woodstock stay, he carefully revised the poem in the interests of concision, pruning away all that seemed prolix. "I have been very lazy, but am growing more tight and particular," he wrote Munson from Woodstock, and enclosed as a sample of his intentions a new version of the poem:

> Regard the capture here, O Janus-faced—
> As double as the hands that crash this glass:
> Such eyes at search or rest you cannot see—
> Reciting pain and glee, you cannot bear.
>
> Twin shadowed halves: the second's glancing holds
> In each the skin alone, and so it is
> I crust a plate of vibrant mercury
> Borne cleft to you, and brother in the half.
>
> Resist this much-exacting fragment smile,
> Its drums and darkest blowing leaves decline
> In favor, only, of your tears—reserved
> Communicant to greet an ancient sign . . .
>
> In alternate bells have you not heard
> All hours clapped dense into a single stride?
> Forgive me for an echo of these things,
> And walk through Time, yourselves, in equal pride.

A few months later "Recitative" appeared in *The Little Review* (Spring 1924), bearing some additional changes made by Crane in the third quatrain:

> Resist this much-exacting fragment smile,
> Its drums and darkest blowing leaves deny
> In favor, only, of your listening tears
> Reserved to greet an ancient common sign.

Two other experimental products of the months spent in Woodstock were "Interludium," which was printed in *1924* (July 1924), and "Possessions," which appeared in *The Little Review* together with "Recitative." "Interludium" is reprinted in the appendix; *The Little Review*

MANUSCRIPT PAGE OF "THE BRIDGE", 1926

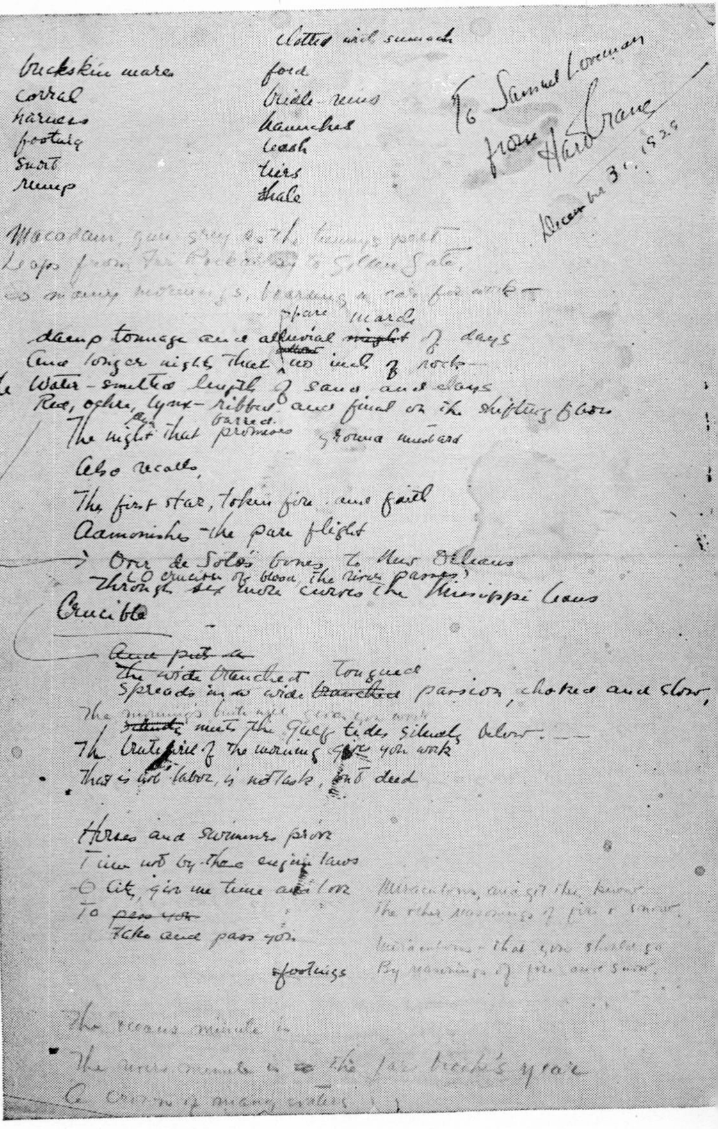
dotted with sumach
buckskin mare
corral
harness
footing
snort
rump
ford
bridle reins
haunches
leash
tiers
shale
To Samuel Loveman from Hart Crane December 31, 1929
The night that promises
Also recalls,
The first star, token fire and faith
Admonishes the pale flight
Over de Soto's bones to New Orleans
Crucible
Horses and swimmers prove
O City, give me time and love
footings

MANUSCRIPT PAGE OF "THE BRIDGE", 1927

version of "Possessions" differs in some respects from the
version of the poem which finally appeared in *White
Buildings,* and the variant *Little Review* stanzas are quoted
below:

> Accumulate such moments to an hour:
> Account the total of this trembling tabulation.
> I know the screen, the distant flying taps
> And stabbing medley that sways—
> Rounding behind to press and grind;
> And the mercy, feminine, that stays
> As though prepared.
>
> And I, entering, take up the stone
> As quiet as you can make a man . . .
> In Bleecker Street, still trenchant in a void
> But dabbling sure possessions in new reach,
> I hold it up against a disk of light—
> I, turning, turning on smoked forking spires,
> The city's stubborn lives, desires.
>
> Tossed on these horns, who bleeding dies,
> Lacks all but piteous admissions to be spillt
> Upon the page whose blind sum finally turns
> Controllable to blended voices stripped
> Of rage, catastrophy and partial appetites.
> The pure possession, the inclusive cloud
> Whose heart is fire shall come,—the white wind rase
> All but bright stones wherein my smiling plays.

In February, still searching for tightness, Crane wrote
"Lachrymae Christi," of which two early versions are
quoted below:

> Recall to music
> and set down at last
> what stain could hold mine eyes
> so long in perjury . . .
>
> What have I asked
> but silence that containd'st

Thee, newly bright to bear
no penitence—but song,
as these, thine everlasting fountains here!

Yea,—every margin wide
with fear, with scorn or terror
clasps no more now, nor rends
my substance (thine
in wakefulness).

Stream, Thou,—
most flowing, and best knowing
what call the rose
obtains in thee,—flower
most bright—Rose, waiting,
of most clear attendance, white.

—Names falling from thine eyes,
whisper and spell out at last
through undiminished flames, thy call,
thy praise and thy prevail, which,

dropping,
Christus, is thy Grail!

•   *   •

Recall to music and set down at last
What stain could hold my eyes
From joy so long in perjury . . .

What, by Thy silence shall I ask, that holds
Me, newly bright to bear no penitence
But song, as these, Thine everlasting fountains here,
While every margin, wide
With fear, with scorn or terror,
Clasps no more now, nor rends.

Stream, Thou,—most effluent,
And knowing best what call the earthly rose
Obtains in Thee, Whose auspices
Are of most clear and vast attendance, white!

—Names falling from Thine eyes
And their undimming lattices of flame,
Whisper and spell out in palm and pain
Translation of Thy praise and Thy prevail,—
Compulsion of the Cross, at last
In liquid, perfect, stricken spheres,—the claim
And shining message, Christus, of Thy Grail.

Crane sought another cause for his poetic stalemate with *The Bridge* in the condition of his language resources. The quality of his language and his capacity to use words as tools of expression first, the total value of his poetry finally—all were in doubt. "My approach to words is still in substratum of some new development—the same as it was when we talked last together—and perhaps merely a chaotic lapse into confusion for all I dare say yet," he wrote Munson in January 1924. Crane's concern with words was a reversion to the months of 1922 and early 1923, to a period when his technique had been under control and able to spring into action whenever commanded. Then, with a vocabulary expanded in range and enriched with the solid music of the Elizabethans, he had created the beauties of "Faustus and Helen." Obviously, this new doubt was occasioned by Crane's introduction to the poems of Samuel B. Greenberg which, when he had read them in Woodstock a few months earlier, struck him as being a cruder version of Rimbaud's more brilliant work: "This poet, Greenberg, whom Fisher nursed until he died of consumption at a Jewish hospital in NY was a Rimbaud in embryo. Did you ever see some of the hobbling yet really gorgeous attempts that boy made without any education or time except when he became confined to a cot. Fisher has shown me an amazing amount of material, some of which I am copying and will show you when I get back. No grammar, nor spelling, and scarcely any form, but a quality that is unspeakably eerie and the most convincing gusto. One little poem is as good as any of the consciously conceived 'Pierrots' of Laforgue."

Samuel B. Greenberg had died in 1917 at the age of twenty-three, leaving behind a mass of manuscript poems which the art critic, William Murrell Fisher, had in his possession and showed Crane in his Woodstock home. In the course of writing his biography of Crane, Philip Horton came upon a typescript of Greenberg's poems which Crane had made from the manuscripts and carried about with him until the summer of 1926, when he left them in Cuba. Horton demonstrated, in an article published in *The Southern Review* in 1936, that "Emblems of Conduct" was almost a complete transmutation of lines taken from several Greenberg poems, and that early drafts of "Voyages II" had also contained Greenberg lines which were eliminated in the course of Crane's writing of the poem. Crane has been accused, directly and indirectly, of plagiarism on this account. Further fuel has been added to this fire by the revelation that Crane did not wish to include "Emblems of Conduct" in *White Buildings*, and only did so upon the urging of Allen Tate and Malcolm Cowley; furthermore, "Emblems of Conduct" is one of the two poems in *White Buildings* which do not seem to have appeared in magazines. These facts demonstrate an unusual reticence on Crane's part insofar as "Emblems of Conduct" is concerned.

It has already been implied that Crane did not obviously regard the poem as entirely his own; nevertheless, it finally appeared in *White Buildings*. It appeared there with good reason, quite as logically as Eliot's transmutation appeared in his first volume of poems and in *The Wast*

Land; the reason being that Crane completely rewove the fragments he had borrowed and stamped them with his own character. In doing so, he accomplished a task which the weaker talent of Greenberg had been unable to complete. The mosaic method of composition which Crane used in writing "Emblems of Conduct" was, as has been shown, a method he had used for many years, even before 1920. It was perfectly natural for him, therefore, to extract fragments from a manuscript collection which, as the mention of Greenberg in his letter shows, he regarded as the unfinished product of a poetic "embryo." Undoubtedly, he considered the writing of "Emblems of Conduct" a practice operation, justified by the unpublished nature of Greenberg's work as well as by the eternal impossibility of its ultimate perfection by Greenberg himself. Since he was neither a scholar nor an editor, he did not append a footnote to "Emblems of Conduct" citing his debt to Greenberg, nor did he edit a volume of Greenberg's poetry. The important aspect of this matter is really the effect of Greenberg upon Crane, and the causes thereof. It has been stated that Crane was already conscious of the importance of new words combined with the old in non-logical patterns which evoked a broad range of connotative meanings. The poetry of Rimbaud and the writings of Ouspensky, at the very least, had convinced him of the necessity for a new language in a superlogical arrangement. Crane had been able to read Rimbaud, however, with difficulty in French and there were few English translations of adequate quality available as supplement. Greenberg had written in English; whatever the reason, he had disregarded syntax, laws of usage, spelling, almost all the rules which govern the language. What affected Crane primarily was Greenberg's resemblance to Rimbaud; he was, in 1923, the most Rimbaldian poet who had used the English language. Here was a cogent illustration to Crane of the brilliance which his own application of the method might achieve. Ouspensky and Rimbaud had prepared the way for his adoption of the method; his drinking and spiritual exaltation would assist in the destruction of the logical; in order to acclimate himself, he worked directly with Greenberg's lines so as to fuse with the heart of the method. If the Greenberg affair means anything at all it is that Crane was a discoverer and not an inventor. The recent publication of a carefully edited selection of Greenberg's poems by Holden and McManis has enabled us to see that there is actually very little of Greenberg in Crane.

The tight watchfulness and the verbal self-consciousness with which Crane wrote after October 1923 did not bring about a renewed feeling of mastery; he was apprehensive still about a possible "lapse into confusion." This, of course, was a major problem for Crane, and there is no doubt of his realization, conscious or subconscious, that the question of subject rather than the issue of faulty technique had caused his personal and poetic doubts and brought *The Bridge* to a halt. By "confusion" Crane did not mean to refer to ideas; yet his comment on the complexity of "Recitative" indicates that it was primarily idea, and not technique, which was disturbing him. "I cannot help thinking that more of 'Recitative' will get over better at some later date if you happen to re-read it," he wrote Allen Tate in March. "It *is* complex, exceedingly,—and I worked for weeks, off and on, of course,—trying to simplify the presentation of the ideas in it, the conception." However, he could hardly have deemed himself successful in execution when a reader as acute as Tate found

it a difficult task to unravel the poem. The four poems—
"Recitative," "Possessions," "Interludium," "Lachrymae
Christi"—written during these months of indecision were
far more difficult to comprehend than any Crane had written previously, including "Faustus and Helen." As in the
case of that poem, Crane continued to employ metaphors
in which the relationship between ideas and objects was
either so single and precise or else so multiple and arbitrary that it could only be unveiled fortuitously. Furthermore, these elusive metaphors were linked together by
contiguity, not by Aristotelian principles of logical reference, while the tightening-up process cut away a good
many syntactical links which might have facilitated the
sequential fusion of the metaphor groups. It is important to keep in mind that Crane did not consciously aim
to be obscure, or difficult, in his poetry. This miscon-
ception, derived from unreasoning exasperation with the
impenetrable nature of many of Crane's lines, must be
demolished if we are to have a true picture of Crane's
problem, or ever be able to read his poetry. When
Tate wrote Crane that he appreciated "Possessions" and
understood the meaning of the fourth stanza of "Recitative," Crane was overjoyed. "It's encouraging," he replied to Tate, "that people say they get at least some
kind of impact from my poems, even when they are honest in admitting considerable mystification. 'Make my dark
poem light, and light,' however, is the text I chose from
Donne some time ago as my direction. I have always
been working hard for a more perfect lucidity, and it
never pleases me to be taken as wilfully obscure or esoteric." Why did these poems, then, result in uninten-
tional obscurity?

In addition to the problems of metaphor and syntax mentioned, another part of the answer will be found in the existence of several layers of plausible meaning in the poems. Crane's explanation of "Recitative" furnishes us with evidence that he intended at least several meanings to be derivable at one and the same time from a single set of lines:

"Imagine the poet, say, on a platform speaking it. The audience is one half of Humanity, Man (in the sense of Blake) and the poet the other. ALSO, the poet sees himself in the audience as in a mirror. ALSO, the audience sees itself, in part, in the poet. Against this paradoxical DUALITY is posed the UNITY, or the conception of it (as you got it) in the last verse. In another sense, the poet is *talking to himself* all the way through the poem, and there are, as too often in my poems, other reflexes and symbolisms in the poem, also, which it would be silly to write here—at least for the present."

The poet is half of humanity looking into an audience . . . looking at himself . . . looking at his reflection in a mirror; he talks to an audience . . . to himself . . . to a mirror . . . or is engaged in reverie. If this seems superficially confusing, it should be remembered by the reader of "Recitative" or other poems of Crane that any one of these pictures derived from the poem is a satisfactory result. The fact that, after additional readings, new interpretations become feasible, is a complimentary reflection upon the richness and depth of the poems. Like experience itself, and one might consider love as an example, the repetition of its complex events stratifies its implications. The poem partakes of this texture of life, which can be enjoyed by some as a superficial surface pattern and by others as a multi-dimensional complexity.

Certainly another factor leading to obscurity was Crane's lack of spiritual and intellectual confidence in the future of America and the other ideas which had prompted him to conceive of *The Bridge*. If it had been the influence of Whitman and Waldo Frank which fostered in him a mystic faith in the secret potentialities of the American nation, it was the more powerful grip which Ouspensky had upon him that led him to doubt the validity of the Whitmanian ideal. At the very least, it would appear that Ouspensky's contempt and disregard for the idea of progress and the future of the world was more in harmony with a mystical annihilation of the concept of time and the existence of a "real" supernatural world than Whitman's socio-spiritual ideas. A strong and stable personality might have been able to cling to Whitmanian beliefs under the impact of the adverse material and psychological forces pressing down upon Crane. But the fundamental disunity of Crane's personality prohibited that type of toughness. "Recitative," which Crane called a "confession" in a letter, is an expression of the terrible fear which his dualism evoked in him. This dualism was far more than an abstract conflict between ideal and reality, between matter and spirit, good and evil, lust and love. It was a dualism that extended through every fiber of his being, sending him in agony from one extremity to another, always in turmoil and never at rest. Regardless of how one visualizes the scene of "Recitative," the speaker's account of indestructible dualities—schizoid self, pain and glee, pair of hands, halves, cleft mercury, joy and sorrow—is indicative of overpowering despair. It is significant in gauging Crane's permeation by Ouspenskian ideas that the unity achieved in the last stanza is presented in the by-now familiar conception of eternal time: past, present, and future "clapped dense into a single stride." Reconciliation is achieved on a plane far removed from the American scene, and the hope to be derived from scientific achievement is non-existent. But

Crane did achieve a temporary unity, and that leads us back to "Possessions."

"Possessions" is a poem in which the torture of Crane's spirit is presented with greater intensity and more genuine catharsis than in "Recitative." The literal narrative of the poem is not important. I happen to think that it concerns visits made by Crane to a friend who lived in New York City during 1923, and who was a collector of fine art. Be that as it may, the poem is undeniably a piece of sexual symbolism, with lust and excess gripping the poet and directing him into paths of anguish. From this suffering and tragedy, the solution is two-fold: first, the poem; second, the cleansing by "fire." Yet this does not lead to amelioration, only to compensation. Here I think we may hit upon another cause of Crane's torment, and that is his realization that he could not adhere to Ouspensky's major tenet, one which most mystics share. Although Ouspensky had shown that the symbolism of love, passion, and wine had figured in mystical poetry, it was as symbolism only and not as goal in itself. The goal was always the annihilation of the self, even though Ouspensky had paradoxically postulated the expansion of emotional consciousness as a step toward knowledge of the supernatural. ("The sign of the growth of the emotions," Ouspensky wrote, "is the liberation of them from the *personal* element, and their sublimation on the higher planes . . . only by withdrawing from *ourselves* do we begin to comprehend the world as it is" [199].) Tossed on the horns of this dilemma, Crane could only doubt that "the pure possession, the inclusive cloud/whose heart is fire shall come . . ." "The white wind" of purity and peace was a mirage.

"Lachrymae Christi" is a poem in which the means of adjustment, temporary though it may be, are saluted by Crane. The poem is a song of thanksgiving, a hymn of praise. The fear, scorn, and terror which racked his spirit were gone when he wrote it. We may ask ourselves: what caused Crane to feel himself in a state of redemption? One answer might be that Crane identified himself with Christ, sharing His agony on the Cross and bleeding with Him.† Possibly Crane's deliverance, in his own mind, had been effected by virtue of his belief in the sacrifice of Christ. Yet the poem states clearly that Crane had won this joy and harmony not because of "penitence," but that he brought "song, as these, Thine everlasting fountains." The answer, of course, is that the cloud of fire had swept over him—Crane had fallen in love. In the intensity of this love, all thoughts of his intellectual doubts and conflicts were swept from his mind. It was a regression to a period when *The Bridge* had been undreamed of, a period in which his emotional consciousness was vibrant and consuming. The problems of intellectual decision could be suppressed beneath the excitement and beauty of a relationship which promised him affection, protection from affliction, and the Dionysian dance of ecstasy which he craved. To Waldo Frank he wrote on April 21, 1924:

"For many days, now, I have gone about quite dumb with something for which 'happiness' must be too mild a term. At any rate, my aptitude for communication, such as it ever is!, has been limited to one person alone, and perhaps for the first time in my life (and, I can only think that it is for the last, so far is my imagination from the conception of anything more profound and lovely than this love). I have wanted to write you more than once, but it will take many letters to let you know what I mean (for myself, at least) when I say that I have seen the Word made Flesh. I mean nothing less, and I

† *One should not overlook Crane's earlier remarks, which have been quoted above, about being crucified on a cross; "Lachrymae Christi" in final form, wherein Christ and Dionysus are merged; also Crane's drunken statements in his last year of life that he was Christ.*

know now that there is such a thing as indestructibility. In the deepest sense, where flesh became transformed through intensity of response to counter-response, where sex was beaten out, where a purity of joy was reached that included tears. It's true, Waldo, that so much more than my frustrations and multitude of humiliations has been answered in this reality and promise that I feel that whatever event the future holds is justified beforehand. And I have been able to give freedom and life which was acknowledged in the ecstasy of walking hand in hand across the most beautiful bridge of the world, the cables enclosing us and pulling us upward in such a dance as I have never walked and never can walk with another.

"Note the above address, and you will see that I am living in the shadow of that bridge. It is so quiet here; in fact, it's the moment of the communion with the 'religious gunman' in my F and H where the edge of the bridge leaps over the edge of the street. It was in the evening darkness of its shadow that I started the last part of that poem. Imagine my surprise when E— brought me to this street where, at the very end of it, I saw a scene that was more familiar than a hundred factual previsions could have rendered it! And there is all the glorious dance of the river directly beyond the back window of the room I am to have as soon as E—'s father moves out, which is to be soon. E will be back then from S America where he had to ship for wages as ship's writer. That window is where I would be most remembered of all: the ships, the harbor, and the skyline of Manhattan, midnight, morning or evening,—rain, snow or sun, it is everything from mountains to the walls of Jerusalem and Niniveh and all related and in actual contact with the changelessness of the many waters that surround it. I think the sea has thrown itself upon me and been answered, at least in part, and I believe I am a little changed—not essentially, but changed and transubstantiated as anyone is who has asked a question and been answered.

"Now I can thank you for the wisdom of your last letter to me and most of all for your confidence in me. (It is strange, but I can feel no place for paragraphs in this letter!) (Yet one goes on making paragraphs.) It came at the very moment of my present understanding and it is as though it, in some clairvoyant way, included it. Only, so much wish you were here these days for you are the only one know who quite encircles my experience. I shall never, of course, be able to give an account of it to anyone in direct terms, but you will be here and not so far from now. Then we shall take a walk across the bridge to Brooklyn (as well to Estador for all that!). Just now feel the flood tide again the way it seemed to me just before I le

Cleveland last year, and I feel like slapping you on the back every half-hour."

Together with the letter, Crane enclosed a "Sonnet."† Revised later into "Voyages III," it was the first poem celebrating his love affair.

The letter to Frank had been written from a rooming house on Columbia Heights in Brooklyn, New York. The pleasure of living in his own private quarters without fear of being unable to pay his room rent was a luxury which Crane had not enjoyed for many weeks. Having been unemployed since October 1923, he was in dire need of money to meet the cost of the bare necessities of life when he returned to New York in January 1924. Although he tried to return to his old position at the advertising agency, the man who had promised to re-hire him turned out to be unavailable when Crane tried to see him. The management of a magazine called *Machinery* were interested in adding Crane to its staff, but there were no openings. At the publishing house of Harcourt, Brace, an old friend seemed "to be neither sufficiently interested in me or my work" to do anything for him. The other firms he approached likewise turned him away. Although his father offered him a position as travelling salesman, however, he rejected the offer. He also refused to take advantage of his mother's plea to return to Cleveland, which she had accompanied with the promise of money to cover the cost of his train fare. The bitterness that suffused him against a society which despised the independent artist and reduced him to a position destruc-

† *See Appendix.*

tive of his imaginative powers had become a fixed attribute
of his personality. "What I said about 'prostituting my
mind,' etc.," he wrote the Rychtariks, "I really meant I
do resent it—and because so many others as good and
better than myself must also do the same in order to live
and breathe doesn't help things at all. I shall keep right
on talking that way—and probably not practice what I
preach at all."

By some good fortune, Crane managed to find a job;
but was fired in February after a few weeks because the
man who hired him had exceeded his authority in doing
so. For the next few weeks, Crane moved from one room
to another, forced to leave his original room on Grove
Street because the man who had sublet it to him wished
to return, evicted from another room because he had no
money to pay the rent. He lived for a time, as he wrote
the Rychtariks, "out of a suitcase . . . books, pictures and
clothes all divided into bundles and stored here and there
and everywhere with different friends all over the place."
Were it not for the generous aid extended to him by
various friends, he unquestionably would have had to return to Cleveland despite his wishes. In early April, finally,
Malcolm Cowley helped him obtain a position with
Cowley's employer, a publishing firm engaged in preparing comprehensive catalogues for the use of purchasing
agents in business and industry. Crane's new work involved a methodical exactitude and a knowledge of technical terms used in architecture and engineering. Although somewhat familiar with these fields, Crane was
not really at ease with this material. Nevertheless, he
preferred it to a return to advertising copy with its
synthetic drama and its distorted conception of human
values.

Having laid low the terrors of economic and personal insecurity, it was strange that Crane's proximity to Brooklyn Bridge and his daily labours with scientific terminology did not stimulate him to think again of *The Bridge*. Actually, of course, all events had conspired to place that poem in limbo. It was absolutely necessary for his peace of mind that the problems and issues which it raked up in him be obliterated from his consciousness. This might have transpired with less pain than he was to receive were it not for the literary events of 1924, the year in which the disagreements of the younger writers who were his friends were aired with increasing violence.

At the close of 1924, several of the writers opposing Frank and Munson decided to complete three pending tasks which could no longer be postponed. Cowley has written in *Exile's Return* of the deeds which he had hoped would result from the October 1923 meeting:

"We planned, for example, to hire a theatre some afternoon and give a literary entertainment, with violent and profane attacks on the most famous contemporary writers, courts-martial of the more prominent critics, burlesques of Sherwood Anderson, Floyd Dell, Paul Rosenfeld and others—all this interspersed with card tricks, solos on the jew's harp, meaningless dialogues and whatever else would show our contempt for the audience and sanctity of American letters. We planned to pass out handbills in the theatrical district and make defamatory soap-box orations in Union Square. We planned to continue *Broom* as long as its capital or credit lasted; we hoped to make it an organ for good prose, experimental verse and violent polemics."

This had not yet been accomplished. Second: the insinuations and accusations of Ernest Boyd had been perpetuated in book form by their inclusion in Boyd's volume of essays, *Portraits: Real and Imaginary*, issued during the year. A review by Josephson rebutting the book had been rejected by the magazine for which it was written. Third: Frank's and Munson's critical articles deserved a sharper reply than Cowley's little rejoinder in *1924*. A bombshell which would simultaneously annihilate Boyd, Frank, Munson and effectuate some of the unrealized hopes of Cowley and his friends thus became the order of the day.

All through the month of December, the conspirators hatched their plans. One weekend in January 1925, everything was ready. Cowley, Burke, Josephson, John Wheelwright,† Crane, Tate, and several others gathered in a hotel and wrote the material included in *Aesthete, 1925*. Designed as a magazine, *Aesthete, 1925* was unveiled to the waiting world in February. Addressed primarily "To The Editors and Critics of New York," it was dedicated to H. L. Mencken, George Jean Nathan, D. H. Lawrence, Boyd, Walt Whitman, Thomas Babington Macaulay, St. Paul, and a host of others living and dead. Its satire ranged over a vast field, and can be sampled from the listing of a fictitious article in its table of contents: "The Hard Professional Joy of the American Public (Rhapsodic Criticism with 39 metaphors and no ideas, by Paulina Roseyfield.)" Literary critics were rated in the following order of descending merit: 1) academic critics with excessive reverence for moral and scholarly standards; 2) psychological and sociological critics who "can tell you why Poe took to drink, but not why he took to greatness"; 3) compromising commercial editors and literary publicists; 4) "the impressionists, the 'I feel' critics of all types." Percentages purporting to reflect the merit of

† *Wheelwright was involved in the mutilation of Crane's "Faustus and Helen" in* SECESSION.

various critics were assigned to them. Once again, a representative few are worth quoting: Paul Elmer More—71.3 percent; George Santayana—70 percent; Eliot—70 percent; Van Wyck Brooks—49 percent; Conrad Aiken—35 percent; Frank—11.8 percent; Munson—6.43 percent. Brooks was attacked for using sociological data as literary criticism; Munson's low rating was accompanied by the quotation, from his Eliot article in *1924*, with which he had rejected *The Waste Land* as an integrated poem. Several pages were devoted to an attack by Kenneth Burke against Waldo Frank's Dada article in *1924*. Burke accused Frank of intellectual confusion, and ridiculed him for stating that a "religious temper" was necessary or could combat the so-called destructive effects of Dadaism. "Dadaism is perception without obsession," Burke went on to say. "Frank's programme threatens to be less a process of integration than a deliberate ruling out of certain predominant factors in life, where we must halt the talk of supernal beauty until the brass band goes by." At another point, Burke enunciated the attitude which Frank had very properly labelled inert: "The artist does not run counter to his age; rather, he refines the propensities of his age, formulating their aesthetic equivalent, translating them into terms of excellence. The artist, as artist, is not a prophet; he does not change the mould of our lives: his moral contribution consists in the element of grace which he adds to the conditions of life wherein he finds himself." It would be pleasant to dismiss both the serious and the jocular in *Aesthete, 1925* as the sportive pastimes of high-spirited young gentlemen. Instead, I regard the magazine and the ideas enunciated therein as the genuine expression of a reasonably thought-out position on literature and its functions. The presence in the magazine of a poem attributed to Crane, therefore, raises fundamental questions about him.

The poem under consideration appeared with the name "Walter S. Hankel" appended to it.† "Walter S. Hankel" was a fictitious person created to be the editor of *Aesthete, 1925*. The Princeton University Library copy of the magazine, which was the only copy available for my inspection, bears the name "Hart Crane" written across the lines of the poem. Since this particular copy was presented to Princeton University by Allen Tate without correction, it may be assumed that Crane is actually the author of the poem. The omission of Crane's name as author indicates that he was not completely enthused about the magazine and its contents. A look at the poem shows us that it is mocking Munson, with a specific reference to his statement on Eliot in *1924*, the same statement ridiculed elsewhere in the magazine. As we have seen, Crane had taken the trouble to praise this very article in a letter to Munson. Either he had never really agreed with Munson's critical remarks, or else he had by this date (seven months later) changed his mind about the validity of the article. Furthermore, the comments by Burke and others in the magazine anent Frank's views on the function of literature were in disagreement with Crane's approval of Frank's "For a Declaration of War" article. Once again, Crane had never agreed, or else since then had reversed his position. These questions must have occurred to Crane; his thoughts about them, as we shall see, and the circumstances under which his poem appeared, permit us to conclude that Crane could not have been very happy about this affair.

† *See "Chanson" in the Appendix.*

If Crane was not already feeling uncomfortable, he was helped to an awareness of the implications of his partici-pation in *Aesthete, 1925* by Munson, who had in some way been informed of the impending coup early in December. The two letters which follow below were written by Crane to Munson on the fifth and eighth of December re-spectively. They are self-explanatory on the whole, al-thought it might be pointed out that the Wyndham Lewis dictum mentioned in the first letter had originally appeared in a 1917 number of *The Little Review*:

"Dear Gorham:

"I'm extremely sorry to have caused you such doubts and misunder-standings by what I said yesterday at lunch and I'm further glad to say that I do not deserve all of them. In fact before your letter reached me I suddenly remembered my mention of the proposed attack on you and Waldo, and that I had given you a very incomplete account of it.

"When this came up at the coffee house a week since yesterday I at once interrupted it by offering to withdraw from any participation in the issue whatever. Allen Tate was there at the time, and as a fairly neutral party I think you can rely on him to check my statement as a fact. At any rate I hope you will ask him about it when you next see him. I have so consistently defended you and Waldo in that particular company that I have so far derived little from the meetings but an unnecessarily aggravated state of nerves and feelings.

"From your standpoint, I have long been aware, there is no excuse for my association with people whose activities are questionable from sev-eral angles. And especially since I have been as strong in denunciations of them as anyone. (And let me add that I have taken no pains to conceal these opinions from anyone whatever.) Yet, at the same time, and whether fortunately or otherwise, I have not been so situated that I could possibly maintain the complete isolation which it has been your desired good fortune to maintain. While there is danger and a good deal of it I dare say, in my position, I have also felt that in yours, Gorham, lurked the possible blindfolding of certain recognitions, which, attached personalities being removed you would have naturally found interesting and worthy. I can summon very little that is definite to support my feelings about this at the present time. Issues are not at all clear, and I am disgusted most of the time. You have set yourself a rigorous program, part of which I subscribe to in action. a larger part of which I applaud you for as a critic, and another part of which I feel is unnecessarily unwieldy, limited and stolid. Perhaps all this assurance-plus is necessary in fighting as stringently as you have done and are doing, but so far I am not crystallized enough, as it were, to accept the whole lock-stock-and-barrel of it. To a certain extent, as Wyndham Lewis says, one must be broken up to live. Which I defend myself by interpreting—the artist must have a certain amount of 'confusion' to bring into form. But that's not the whole story, either.

"Regardless of these issues you will be assured, I hope, that I have so far found nothing in either your work or Waldo's which I would wish to attack. Your generosity, meanwhile, certainly deserves my thanks for appreciating the sometimes necessary distinctions between a personal friendship with a man and one's opinion of his work.

"My rewards or discredit from participation in a magazine issued by your enemies will be bound to be, to a certain extent, somewhat embarrassing, yet, as you recognize, I still feel that I can owe myself that freedom on a clear responsibility. I am growing more and more sick of factions, excoriations and the whole literary she-bang right now. A little more solitude, real solitude, on the part of everyone, would be a good thing, I think.

"Let us have lunch together soon. I won't take absolute 'vows' before that, for this letter is a very crumb of my feelings."

*   *   *

"Dear Gorham:

"Reflecting on our conversation at lunch today I have come to feel bound to suggest that you take whatever decisions or formalities are necessary to 'excommunicate' me from your literary circle. How much further you wish to isolate me depends entirely on your own personal feelings, but I am not prepared to welcome threats from any quarters that I know of—which are based on assumption of my literary ambitions in relation to one group, faction, 'opportunity,' or another.

The conclusions to be drawn from these letters and the events which preceded them are inevitable. Crane did

not agree or disagree with the philosophical beliefs of
Frank and Munson (it may be well to add that Crane's
friendship with Munson was not severed as the second
letter might imply); he did not agree or disagree with
the Dadaism and pessimism of the *Broom* writers. All
these ideas were within him—spiritual and rational, optimistic and pessimistic—to issue whenever the environment
called them forth from him. If we accept this interpretation, we can well understand why work on *The Bridge*
was at a stand-still during the closing months of 1923
and throughout 1924. It was shown on earlier pages of
this book that Crane's reaction to his environment was not
based on a rational evaluation of the factors with a resultant reasoned decision. As the factors changed from good
to bad, from bad to good, in terms of their immediate effect
upon him, so did he react favorably or unfavorably. There
is no need to deny that an undercurrent of uncompromis-
ingness was always present in Crane, but he suppressed it
most deeply whenever the world looked particularly rosy.
He had left Cleveland in 1923 with the illusion that New
York City was in some way a paradise in which he would
flower as poet and individual. It had not worked out as he
had anticipated, and he could foresee no other solution.
Hereafter, he would be characterized by confusion, by lack
of confidence in the ideas which he valued most highly.
Only in his emotional consciousness would he feel secure,
and there would be moments, too, when he would seek to
blot out even this last vestige of self-awareness.

12. *WHITE BUILDINGS*

WHATEVER SUSTENANCE CRANE HAD DERIVED from the love affair which had stimulated him creatively in the "Voyages" and helped him to swallow the burden of doubt and confusion which had been bothering him, seems to have been exhausted by the spring of 1925. The long months of office work were beginning to show their effect in irritability and discontent, too.

"The usual bacchanale of life around here and among my friends still occupies me a good deal," he wrote the Rychtariks in April. "Some of it is sweet and clarifying—but as time goes on I tire of certain repetitions that occur in it and seem to be developing certain reactionary tendencies toward solitude and more austere examinations of myself. Above all, with the regular amount of highly detailed work I have to do every day at the office,—the 'grind' in other words, and all the tempting other activities outside my real self, I feel worn out most of the time and so distracted that I lack the reflection and self-collection necessary to do the work, the *real* work that ultimately concerns me most."

In June, the opportunity was opened for Crane to move out to the country. His friend Slater Brown had just bought a farm in Patterson, New York, and Crane was invited to help put the house and grounds in order. With considerable alacrity, Crane resigned his job and left for

Patterson. He broke away with a violence which was intense, willing to "trust to fate" for the future. "It was either that—or a complete breakdown," he wrote.

The first few days in the country gave birth to what appeared to be a miraculous change in Crane's mental and physical being, "Things couldn't be better," he wrote his grandmother. "I have great quantities of fine Guernsey milk every day from a neighboring farm, the finest butter and eggs and fresh vegetables—and so much outdoor exercise that I am brown as a nut already with the sun and all greased up at the joints. Sleep nights like a top and the uric acid trouble has disappeared completely—at least for the time being." There was a great deal of physical labor to be accomplished before the farm was habitable—rubbish to be removed; furniture to be built, repaired, and cleaned; the garden to be planted; and the house to be painted. The kindness of the Browns added considerably to Crane's state of well-being, and the tone of his letters indicates that, for the first time in many years, he was feeling secure and happy in a simple, quiet fashion. It was, in its way, a re-birth for Crane, but this time in a new home where he was cherished for himself and in which the atmosphere was peaceful rather than stormy.

The first few stanzas of "Passage," written during the course of these weeks in Patterson, reflect his welcome of "an improved infancy," his discarding of "memory . . . casual louse that tissues the buckwheat . . . wakens alleys with a hidden cough." But even in the midst of renaissance, the complaints of his adult life followed him . . . time, the measure of memory, was too insidious, no matter how much he tried to pass beyond it. The freedom and joy of the wind were his, but looking over the hills and valleys he saw smoke rising from buildings and knew himself tied to and destroyed by human experience and its charring effects ("the wind/ Died speaking through the ages that you know/ And hug, chimney-sooted heart of man!/ So was I turned about and back, much as your smoke/ Compiles a too well-known biography.") Thus death was welcome ("smiling an iron coffin"), for it involved the destruction of matter ("from the Ptolemies/ Sand troughed us in a glittering abyss")† and its fusion of time (the serpent) with the creative brightness of sun and space.

In July, Crane was called to Cleveland to assist his mother and grandmother in packing and selling their household goods and equipment. The family house on Euclid Avenue had been sold, and the two women were planning to move into an apartment. This summons came as an unwelcome requisition to him. Most of his time in the country had been devoted to pursuits other than writing, and he felt guilty about his failure to do more than begin "Passage." Furthermore, his mother had not been writing to him for a time, and her neglect, which eventually turned out to be preoccupation with the the sale of her home, was preying on his mind. "I wish that 'wile' and 'guile' were easier instruments for my imagination to use!" he wrote explosively to Frank. "There is always some other immediate duty or requirement for me to perform than creation. I've had only about five hours at the writing table since I came out here . . ." There is also reason to believe that the breaking-up of the family

† *This is a reworking of a discarded line from an early version of* "Atlantis".

home represented a symbolical destruction of the last remnants of his childhood, the last tie with his family, a refuge to which he might have returned at some time. Now this sole remaining source of security had disintegrated, and his sense of isolation increased. There is much poignancy in a postcard bearing a photograph of the house which Crane sent to Munson from Cleveland in August, bearing the comment: "Perhaps you would like a picture of the 'departing' tower—in which you worked for a while." It was the tower room in which Crane had lived from 1919 until 1923, where he had written "Chaplinesque," "Faustus and Helen," and many other poems in a spirit of high hope. From the mass of material removed from the house, Crane managed to extricate his books, his desk and chair, and a trunk filled with dishes, pictures, bedding, and other objects. These were sent on to the Brown farm in Patterson, thus completing in a literal manner the symbolic dissolution of his childhood and youth.

Before Crane went to Patterson in June after resigning from his job, he had filed an application for a shipboard job with a South American steamship company in New York and had anticipated getting a job in July. The trip to Cleveland made it impossible for him to complete the necessary negotiations. Meanwhile Munson had written him about an opening as publicity man at a book company, but Crane was unable to obtain the position. When Crane returned to New York in September from Cleveland, therefore, his funds were so low that he had just enough money to pay for his railroad fare to Patterson. There he stayed on for several weeks until the middle of October, relishing the autumn crispness and color, the manufacture of ale and apple jack from the fruits which abounded on the farm, and the building of tables and cupboards in which to store his possessions. But his inability to contribute financially towards meeting common household expenses rankled within him, and he left for New York. There he made an effort to get the ship job for which he had applied earlier, and was actually approved at the steamship office and sent out to the ship to be hired. Through some mishap, however, another man had also been approved for the job; he managed to reach the ship and the job before Crane arrived to learn the sad news. All through the remaining months of 1925, he was unable to find any employment.

"The facts are hard but true," he wrote the Rychtariks in December. "I have not yet succeeded in finding myself a job, and even after trying every sort of position, like selling books in stores during the Christmas rush, ship jobs, etc., etc., and I have just been kept going by the charity of my friends. The nervous strain of it all has about floored me, and I feel as though the skin of my knees were quite worn off from bowing to so many people, being sniffed at (to see whether I had 'personality' or not) etc."

The unrealized publication of a volume of Crane's poems, under the title of *White Buildings*, during 1925 added its aggravating touch to Crane's spirits. Although he had intended to withhold publication of a book of poems until *The Bridge* was completed and ready for inclusion, it was obvious that that poem would require many more months of work before it would be available, and Crane did not want to delay publication of the poems he had written. He had come across a printer who was willing to publish the book at his own expense, and this, of course, was too good an opportunity to forego. But the printer, although willing, soon found himself in financial difficulties even before the poems had been set up in type, with the result that it was too late for Crane to submit the manuscript to a regular publisher for fall 1925 publication. Nevertheless, he sent the volume to the firm of Harcourt, Brace, which rejected it in July. While the book thus languished, Waldo Frank became interested in seeing to its publication, and volunteered to bring it to the attention of his own publishers, the firm of Boni and Liveright. Under the impression that Eugene O'Neill, the playwright, with whom Crane had become friendly during 1923, was willing to write an introduction to the book, Crane informed Frank that O'Neill was ready to provide the necessary piece. "O'Neill thinks my poetry is better than that of any other American writing today," Crane had written the Rychtariks in March 1924, and probably the playwright had agreed to write some opening remarks for a volume by Crane whenever it appeared. Towards the end of October, Frank was able to report some success, having importuned and obtained Liveright's consent to accept Crane's poetry for publication on the basis of its high merit. Liveright, however, set up the prior condition that O'Neill must contribute a preface or foreword to the volume before he would definitely agree to sign a contract for publication. Unfortunately, Crane had been unable to get in touch with O'Neill, who was variously reported to him as being in Nantucket or Bermuda. When O'Neill was finally reached, and agreed to proceed with the foreword, Liveright decided that he no longer wanted to publish the book. Thus the matter rested in December 1925.

The adventures of *White Buildings* were interlaced with other factors calculated to shake Crane's confidence in his work. For one thing, the energy which had spurred him on to creation during 1924 and the early months of 1925 had practically left him. Coupled with the dissatisfaction he felt about the conditions of his life, the decline of creative impetus, though by this time a recurrent phenomenon, raised doubts in his mind about the value of the work he had hitherto completed. "I cannot profess to any real ability in measuring it," he wrote Rychtariks in April 1925. "One struggles along blindly most of the time."

Any pleasure he may have derived from the composition of "Passage," furthermore, was destroyed when he received the rejected manuscript of *White Buildings* from Harcourt, Brace. Accompanying the package was a letter stating that, as Crane put it to Frank, "They couldn't make anything out of most of the poems. My 'obscurity' is a mystery to me," he continued in the same letter, "and I can't help thinking that publishers and their readers have never heard of Sir Thomas Davies, Donne, Baudelaire, Rimbaud, Valery or even Emily Dickinson."† Before long, "Passage" itself fell under the baneful stare of a publisher, this time the editorial hand of *The Dial's* Marianne Moore, who rejected the poem in August with a combined boost and knock. " 'We could not but be moved,' " she wrote to Crane, " 'as you must know, by the rich imagination and the sensibility in your poem, 'Passage.' Its multiform content accounts I suppose, for what seems to us a lack of simplicity and cumulative force. We are sorry to return it.' " In the letter to Frank which related the tale of this rejection, Crane appended the following remark to Miss Moore's comments: "It seems almost as though

† *Crane is probably referring to Sir Thomas Browne or Sir John Davies.*

Miss Moore might be rather speaking of her own poems with such terms . . ." But this flippancy was superficial, for actually Crane was deeply affected by the impact of both rejections as is shown by his query to Frank: "To me it is still the most interesting and conjectural thing I have written . . . I'm particularly anxious to know what you think of its form."

In October, Crane completed "The Wine Menagerie," a poem even more difficult than "Passage" and which he also seems to have begun during the summer, and both poems were sent off to T. S. Eliot at *The Criterion* in London. Both were rejected, and Crane thereupon sent "The Wine Menagerie" to Miss Moore in November. This time, instead of rejecting the poem outright, she went to the trouble of salvaging that which appealed to her as imagination and sensibility, and placed it into a simple form which she believed had cumulative force. In order to accomplish this feat of editorial arrogance, Miss Moore found it necessary to revise the title to "Again," as well as to delete numerous lines. In short, the poem was re-written. This demonstration of pedagogy was not received by Crane with the enthusiasm of a shining-faced schoolboy. "What it all means now I can't make out," Crane wrote the Rychtariks in December, "and I would never have consented to such an outrageous joke if I had not so desperately needed the twenty dollars.—Just one more reason for getting my book published as soon as possible!" The only event which dispelled the darkness for Crane during these months, in addition to the generosity of Frank and the Browns, was Allen Tate's decision to write a short essay on four of the "Voyages," which were scheduled to appear together with the essay in *The Guardian*, a literary monthly published in Philadelphia. But when the October issue, which also happened to be the last one, appeared without the note or the four poems, it was an addition to the series of disappointments to which Crane had been falling a victim.

IV

"TAKE THIS SHEAF OF DUST"

13. *THE BRIDGE* IS SUBSIDIZED AND CLARIFIED

IN DECEMBER 1925, CRANE'S ECONOMIC PROBLEMS WERE temporarily solved by the philanthropy of Otto Kahn who, as Crane wrote William Wright, "was interested in forwarding the particular poetic theme that I'm endeavoring to formulate . . ." A friend of Crane had received a large sum of money from Kahn in order to be able to study painting in Paris, and this had inspired Crane to write Kahn directly for a loan. On the basis of a personal interview with Crane, which took place after Kahn had spoken about Crane to Frank and O'Neill, Kahn presented him with a thousand dollars and the promise of another thousand for a year's work on his poetry.

The gift enabled Crane to leave the city almost immediately for Patterson, New York, where he was to share a farmhouse rented previously by Allen and Caroline Tate. It also bore with it the connotations of recognition by the forces which his father represented, and this was a triumph of great importance. "You can mention this to anyone you like, as I think it may do my reluctant father some good to have it known—after all his indifference," he wrote the Rychtariks. The extent to which Crane was a victim of the values which he detested is obvious in this

257

pathetic effort to impress his father, and it is another indication of his inability to reconcile himself to exclusion from a middle-class world.

Upon his arrival in Patterson, Crane began in earnest to work on *The Bridge*. By mid-January, he was able to send Frank eighty lines of the final section, which he developed far beyond the more limited scope of his earlier drafts.†
But he could not progress rapidly with the other sections while the outline of the poem was still nebulous, and he realized that he must finish that all-important task before proceeding further.

During the remainder of January and all of February 1926, therefore, Crane fashioned the structure of the poem. In January, he first referred to it vaguely as "Columbus conquests of water, land, etc. Pokahantus, subways, offices etc. etc. . . ." By the middle of March, however, he had developed a fuller outline as well as a thematic statement of the over-all purpose of the poem. Six sections were listed, of which the third and fourth have never been completed or else have been lost. Although the poem's structure was to be considerably changed and expanded, Crane's purposes as expressed in this outline help to clarify his final product.

Crane intended the theme of the poem to be man's "conquest of space and knowledge," a typically Ouspenskian theme. The poem was to revolve about the symbol of "Cathay," which bore the dual burden of referring to the "riches" in that land, thereafter "transmuted" into the re-

†*See Appendix.*

ligious doctrines which the voyage to Cathay was intended to disseminate, the intellectual knowledge achieved, and the feeling of union with God. The poem, then, was to move in alternation between matter and spirit. In that sense, it becomes possible to fix the nature of the bridge symbol. Like Cathay, it is first of all a symbol of material progress, the spanning of two shores. But it also serves as a symbol of the extension of spiritual knowledge. The sections of the poem will be discussed in accordance with the outline form set up by Crane in a letter written to Otto Kahn on March 18, 1926:†

"I. Columbus—Conquest of space, chaos."

Columbus symbolizes the opening phase of man's mastery over space in modern times. Although he possessed a compass, the sextant and the telescope were unavailable to him. The Copernican heliocentric theory of the solar system was still unknown. But despite the inadequacy of his navigational instruments and charts, Columbus courageously sailed through unknown seas to undiscovered lands. Thus he surmounted the confused and chaotic knowledge of his time. On a more literal plane, Columbus was the discoverer of America under the illusion that he had found Cathay. The first contact of Western man with America stamps the new-found land with the duality which underlies the theme of Crane's poem.

"II. Pocahontas—The natural body of American-fertility, etc."

This section follows naturally from the discovery of America. When Columbus landed on the shores of the new world, he was amazed at the abounding natural resources of the land. The land lay before him like a woman, ripe, waiting to be taken.

† *The Hound and Horn* (July-September 1934).

"III. Whitman—The Spiritual body of America (A dialogue between Whitman and a dying soldier in a Washington hospital; the infraction of physical death, disunity, on the concept of immortality)"

When the natural body perishes, is there any future for the soul? Whitman had answered: "I swear I think there is nothing but immortality!" This question and its answer were to form the theme of Section III, the action of which is reminiscent of Whitman's "To One Shortly to Die" and scenes from his *Specimen Days*. A synopsis of this section, written at a later date under the title "Cape Hatteras," states a more elaborate approach and suggests that Section III was transformed into the present "Cape Hatteras" section of *The Bridge*:

"Whitman approaches the bed of a dying (*southern*) soldier—scene is in a Washington hospital. Allusion is made to this during the dialogue. The soldier, conscious of his dying condition, at the end of the dialogue asks Whitman to call a priest, for absolution. Whitman leaves the scene—deliriously the soldier calls him back. The part ends here before Whitman's return, of course. The irony is, of course, in the complete absolution which Whitman's words have already given the dying man, before the priest is called for. This, alternated with the eloquence of the dying man, is the substance of the dialogue—the emphasis being on the symbolism of the soldier's body having been used as a *forge* toward a state of Unity. His hands are purified of the death they have previously dealt by the principles Whitman hints at or enunciates (without talking up-stage, I hope) and here the 'religious gunman' motive returns much more explicitly than in F & H. The agency of death is exercised in obscure ways as the agency of life. Whitman knew this and accepted it. The appeal of the scene must be made as much as possible independent of the historical 'character' of Walt."

Death leads into life Whitman had said: "Death, Immortality, and a free entrance into the Spiritual world." The physical body of America is left behind like the "excrementitious" corpse of the soldier, rotted by the sort of materialism which corrode its surface. The spiritu-

body of America, product of the union of Columbus with Pocahontas, moves forward in time to a realization of the greatness which Whitman foresaw.

"IV. John Brown (Negro porter on Calgary Express making up berths and singing to himself (a jazz form for this) of his sweetheart and the death of John Brown alternately)"

The meaning of this projected section can be derived more easily from a synopsis written by Crane under the title "Calgary Express":

"The 'scene' is a pullman sleeper, Chicago to Calgary. The main theme is the story of John Brown, which predominates over the interwoven 'personal, biographical details' as it runs through the mind of a Negro porter, shining shoes and humming to himself. In a way it takes in the whole racial history of the Negro in America. The form will be highly original, and I shall use dialect. I hope to achieve a word-rhythm of pure jazz movement which will suggest not only the dance of the Negro but also the speed-dance of the engine over the rails."

The synopsis bore an epigraph consisting of four lines from a Negro song:

"Well, don't you know it's mournin' time?
Wheel in middle of wheel;
He'll hear yo' prayers an' sanctify,
Wheel in de middle of wheel."

It becomes apparent that this section was intended as a recapitulation of sections II and III. The Negro's history from slave to freedman makes him an admirable vehicle to encompass American growth from the primitivism of Pocahontas to the civilization of Whitman. The theme of fertility is invested in the Negro's sweetheart; the combined theme of spirituality-death is represented by John Brown, who heeded God's call to free the slaves and received death and immortality as his reward. Although

this section was never developed, it was probably superseded by "The Dance." Crane's interest in John Brown
was the residue of a never-completed desire to write a
play about the abolitionist martyr after reading Oswald
Garrison Villard's biography in 1921; the Negro, of course,
had already served him as a subject for "Black Tambourine." The Negro became an important symbol of primitivism during the first few decades of the twentieth century, especially after African art had become a source
of inspiration for modern artists like Picasso, and Crane
was sufficiently interested in the subject to have ordered
a book containing photographic reproductions of Negro
sculpture from a German dealer in 1922. It is significant
that the African Negro artist, like Crane, did not concern
himself with the conventional logic of perception; parts
of the human body were treated individually, rather than
as parts of a unity subordinated to laws of visual perspective.

"V. Subway—The encroachment of machinery on humanity; a kind of purgatory in relation to the open sky
of last section."

The theme of this section is self-explanatory. There
appears to be no connecton with the preceding sections
however, unless Crane intended to imply that the primitive (Negro) can maintain his spiritual faith under the
impress of machinery (railroad), whereas the urban city
dweller is repressed and distorted by machinery (subway). Another interpretation of the section within the
framework of Crane's outline might be that the suffering
inflicted upon man by the machine is transitory yet deserved, such being the nature of punishment in purgatory.
This view gains credence if we consider the next section, where machinery (bridge) becomes a benevolen

agency symbolizing the expanded consciousness of man and the acquisition of absolute knowledge through union with the eternal.

"VI. The Bridge—A sweeping dithyramb in which the Bridge becomes a symbol of consciousness spanning time and space."

This section sets up a contrast to the hell presented in the subway tunnel. The bridge is a symbol of heaven, an affirmative statement that the machine is an agency of good as well as evil. Though the machine torments the physical body, it fortifies and purifies the spiritual body. Thus the seed with which Columbus impregnated Pocahontas comes to full bloom, and the future is assured.

While Crane plotted the structure of his poem in a systematic exposition, its actual execution began to assume proportions which frightened him. The lines completed in January had been written under the exaltation induced by the freedom which the Kahn gift permitted; in addition, they had treated the bridge, and the emotion which the symbol aroused in him was still powerful. Beyond that point, however, he could not go. Periods of despondency occurred in which the whole project began to seem hopeless; alternating with them came gusts of creative vigor which blew away his fears. Under the give and take of such fluctuating emotional states, Crane's belief in "the theme and substance of the conception" was slowly ebbing away. To Munson he wrote early in March: "In a way it's a test of materials as much as a test of one's imagination." His demoralization gave rise to self-mockery in which the ambitious scope of his plans

simply enlarged the enormity of the failure he saw loom-
ing ahead. "At least, *at worst*," he wrote the Rychtariks,
"the poem will be a *huge* failure! if you get what I mean."

Although Crane received enthusiastic support for his
work from Waldo Frank, the attitude of many of his other
friends, including the Tates, was unfavorable to a project
like *The Bridge*. "People like Waldo Frank will probably like it," Crane wrote about the poem, "—that is,
they'll be interested in the content and presentation, but
most of my younger associates and friends will probably
be pretty doubtful about it." In the summer of 1926,
for example, Allen Tate was to write in his "Foreword"
to Crane's *White Buildings* that America in the 1920 s,
unlike Whitman's America, was static, and that it was no
longer possible for a poetic myth to be constructed on the
American theme: "The great proportions of the myth
have collapsed in its reality. Crane's poetry is a concentration of certain phases of the Whitman substance, the
fragments of the myth." Crane could cope with the
doubt of his friends only by opposing to it an unarticu-
lated faith.

"I am concerned with the future of America," he had written earlier
in 1925, "but not because I think that America has any so-called pa
value as a state or as a group of people . . . . It is only because I fee
persuaded that here are destined to be discovered certain as yet un
defined spiritual quantities, perhaps a new hierarchy of faith not to b
developed so completely elsewhere. And in this process I like to fee
myself as a potential factor; certainly I must speak in its terms an
what discoveries I may make are situated in its experience."

Or else he displayed utter contempt for what he believe
to be the sophistical reasoning of his friends. In a vei
reminiscent of Rimbaud's attack upon the "functionarie
writers" who revive antiquities but fear to grapple wit
the future, he wrote sarcastically of them to Munson: "(

the admired beauty of a casuistical mentality! It is finally content with twelve hours sleep a day and archaeology." These fundamental disagreements had the effect of driving Crane into a corner; the death wish was strong within him, because of his inability to defend his belief in Whitman and the American myth, his chaotic life, and his difficulty in composition; with desperate hope, he nevertheless deluded himself into thinking that it was he who had faith in the future whereas his friends and their intellectual and artistic mentors were welcoming death, mistakenly confusing the pessimism they expressed with a disinterest in the potentialities of life.

"*Is* the last statement sentimentally made by Eliot," he wrote Munson,

> 'This is the way the world ends,
> This is the way the world ends,—
> Not with a bang but a whimper.'

is this acceptable or not as the poetic determinism of our age? I, of course can say no, to myself, and believe it. But in the face of such a stern conviction of death on the part of the only group of people whose verbal sophistication is likely to take an interest in a style such as mine—what can I expect? However, I know my way by now, regardless. I shall at least continue to grip with the problem without relaxing into the easy acceptance (in the name of 'elegance, nostalgia, wit, splenetic splendor') of death which I see most of my friends doing."

14. "THE LOGIC OF METAPHOR"

ALTHOUGH CRANE DROVE HIMSELF TO CONTINUE working on *The Bridge*, he had completed no more than a few lines of "Ave Maria" when a new distraction arose early in March. This was an essay which Gorham Munson had written in 1925 in an effort to evaluate Crane and his work.† During March, Munson sent the essay to Crane, and Crane agreed to read it and return it to Munson with his comments.

Munson granted that Crane was "a poet of great creative force and potentiality," but tempered this praise with criticism of his "highly specialized subjectivity and . . . 'metaphysical' guessing" and implied that Crane's poetry would not endure the test of time. He held that Crane had reached maturity in an age and in a country sterile insofar as thought was concerned; had it been otherwise, he said, Crane would be more concerned with the communication of thought and less satisfied with presenting the "private feelings and associations and magnifications" which supposedly obfuscated his poems. Munson then went on to state that Crane's " 'mysticism' " was unsystematic. Crane's reliance upon intuitions without assurance that

† *This essay appears in Munson's* DESTINATIONS *(1928).*

they were proper instruments of cognition, or without troubling to find out whether they were not "mistaken or even diseased," invited "the risk of bringing back a distorted and poorly glimpsed vision" as well as the likelihood of being emotionally overwhelmed and blinded rather than spiritually illumined by the vision. Observing that Crane's personal life was wretched, a condition made bearable at intervals by "moments of supernal beauty" in which Crane "accidentally tapped some potential reservoir of emotions, purer and higher than those with which we are ordinarily familiar," Munson characterized Crane's existence by adding that "He drops off until fortune gives him another ecstasy after which in turn he slumps." In conclusion, Munson contended that " a genuine metaphysical poetry" could not develop unless poets were inspired by "knowledge [rather] than speculations."

Having received the essay from Munson, Crane read it very carefully. He then replied to Munson with a long letter written on March 17, 1926.† Crane occupied himself primarily with two questions in his letter: first, he disputed Munson's assertion that he had ever attempted to be a metaphysical poet; second, he upbraided Munson for writing about his personal life without demonstrating by direct reference to his poetry that these personal observations bore a legitimate relationship to his poetic production. The first point of issue concerns us most in this book.

Without any necessity to proceed back much further than 1925, it is possible to demonstrate that Crane was mistaken about the poetic role he had chosen for himself. In an essay written in 1925 to assist Eugene O'Neill in the preparation of a foreword for *White Buildings*, Crane

† *See Appendix.*

had defined himself as a poet striving to encounter and reveal metaphysical realities.† "It is my hope to go *through* the combined materials of the poem, using our 'real' world somewhat as a spring-board, and to give the poem *as a whole* an orbit or predetermined direction of its own," he had written, clearly implying that the three-dimensional world was unreal.   Earlier in the same essay, he had described the impressionist poet in contrast to the " 'absolutist' " poet as one who does not realize the importance of knowing "the *causes* (metaphysical)" of his poetic materials, thus stating indirectly that the poet of the absolute (and in this essay Crane declared himself to be such a poet) is preoccupied with a search for the realities of an absolute world more " real' " than the world of three-dimensional reality.   By freeing the poem from his own as well as the reader's perception and judgment as much as possible, Crane hoped to release it from the bondage of the temporal into that absolute universe.   "Such a poem," he wrote, in a sentence which clinches the assertion that Crane thought of himself as a poet of metaphysical inquiry and presentation, "is at least a stab at a truth, and to such an extent may be differentiated from other kinds of poetry and called 'absolute'." The error into which Crane fell when he wrote Munson in his letter that he had "never really attempted to fulfill the functions therein [Munson's essay] attributed to the poet" was magnified when his next paragraph declared that poetry in relation to "absolute knowledge . . . is simply the concrete *evidence* of the *experience* of a recognition (*knowledge* if you like).   It can give you a ratio of fact and experience, and in this sense it is both perception and thing perceived according as it approaches

† *See Appendix A in Philip Horton's HART CRANE* (1937).

a significant articulation or not." A poetry that can give us the "thing perceived" of "absolute knowledge" is a metaphysical poetry, and Crane was literally attempting to skip out from under Munson's charge that he could not be a metaphysical poet without acquiring more knowledge. Crane both considered himself and was a metaphysical poet.

Now it seems to me that both Munson and Crane were wrong in this controversy about metaphysical poetry, for reasons which I will give at a later point in this section. At the moment, it is necessary to see how Crane came to adopt the philosophical theory which justified him in writing a metaphysical poetry, as well as to briefly outline the aesthetic principles which he established to guide himself in its composition. Both the philosophy and the aesthetics may be grouped under the over-all title of the "logic of metaphor," a phrase which Crane employed for the first time in his 1925 essay to explain the rationale of his poetry. He wrote then that his poetry was emotionally motivated, and that its "emotional dynamics" were expressed by the associational relationships of words in metaphor rather than by their denotative ("logical [literal]") meanings in conventional syntax. The association of words and the metaphors formed thereby was "raised on the organic principle of a 'logic of metaphor' . . . which antedates our so-called pure logic, and which is the genetic basis of all speech, hence consciousness and thought-extension." In his 1926 letters, Crane's definition of "the logic of metaphor" was extended to exclude "knowledge" such as "exact factual data (a graphic map of eternity?), ethical morality or moral classifications, etc. from poetry . . ." By linking Crane's philosophy and aesthetics, we arrive at the following conception of his art: a poetry which expresses metaphysical truths without any concern with the verifiable nature of these truths.

The formulation of Crane's conception of poetry naturally involves the literary and personal development which has been detailed until this page. It was greatly influenced by his personal characteristics, although Crane undoubtedly was not aware of this cause for some time. Crane was neither formally nor systematically educated; the elementary training and discipline which high school and college impart to their students, and which many men construct for themselves, was not a part of his makeup. His religious background, including Christian Science with its renunciation of matter as subjectively-constructed sense-data, had encouraged him to disregard so-called surface reality. On the other hand, he possessed a developed emotional life and a vivid imagination. It was natural, therefore, that as a mature individual he would turn to theories which made the most of his assets and little of that which he lacked. Thus, the arguments of Ouspensky previously outlined, as well as those of the other writers whom Crane studied, all tended to substantiate him in his determination to continue as the individual that he irremediably was. We have seen that T. S. Eliot's criticism affected Crane profoundly. No doubt Eliot's belief that there is no such person as a poet who thinks, only a poet like Shakespeare who can express "precise emotion" in contradistinction to a poet like Swinburne who can only express "vague emotion," left its mark upon Crane.

There were two other men, scientists and philosophers primarily, whom Crane read in his early twenties and who provided him with further justification for his view of emotion as an epistemological instrument and metaphor as the realization of emotional inquiry. A. N. Whitehead, whose *Science and the Modern World* Crane read early in 1926, bolstered the Ouspenskian substratum of Crane's thoughts. Whitehead viewed the Romantic movement in literature as a rebellion against a mechanical conception of the universe which had been erected upon Newtonian principles, cause and effect logic, and non-pantheistic science, all of which factors had revealed themselves as being incapable of organically relating man to the universe. I. A. Richards, like Ouspensky and Whitehead, impressed Crane because he knew so much about science and yet was able to adjudicate between science and art so that poetry ended up with a legitimate function in human affairs. The extent of Crane's esteem for Richards may be gauged from a comment he made in December 1927: "Richards' *Principles of Literary Criticism* is a *great* book. One of the few—perhaps the only one in English excepting stray remarks by Coleridge— that get to bed rock." Over a year before, in the letter to Harriet Monroe, Crane had cited Richards' article entitled "A Background for Contemporary Poetry" (*The Criterion*, July 1925) as a justification for his "logic of metaphor"; in his 1925 essay, Crane had utilized Richards' terminology to explain his work: "The statement is pseudo in relation to formal logic—it *is* completely logical in relation to the truth of the imagination . . ." In 1929, Crane referred to Richards again, although indirectly, in his essay "Modern Poetry"; at least two ideas were similar to those expressed by Richards in the *Criterion* article, not only in content but in language too.† "The poet's concern must be, as always, self-

† *"Modern Poetry" is to be found in Crane's COLLECTED POEMS.*

discipline towards a formal integration of experience," Crane wrote. And Richards had written: "The business of the poet is to give order and coherence, and so freedom, to a body of experience." Crane's contention in the essay that poetic truth is vastly different from scientific truth seems to stem as well from the similar conclusion drawn by Richards.

A recapitulation of Richards' arguments in his *Criterion* article will serve to sketch in more of the groundwork which prepared the way for Crane's theories. Richards is best known, of course, for his distinction between scientific statement and poetic statement or "pseudo-statement," a distinction he drew in his article. Scientific statement conveys a meaning the truth of which can be verified by means known to man; "pseudo-statement" is not intended to be true in that sense, scorns logic except as a subordinate to emotion, and employs words as sensory stimuli and emotive symbols without regard for their denotative meaning. "It is not the poet's business to make true statements," Richards said. The poet is primarily concerned with feeling which he shows and attitudes which he does not prove but merely suggests. True knowledge, consequently, is an unnecessary prop for the poet either before or after he writes his poems. How, one might ask, does the poet evoke within himself the feeling and attitudes which he incorporates in his poetry? Richards' Rimbaldian answer is that he values experience as pure experience so that it may call forth emotional responses from him. The poet may have attitudes toward this experience; so long as he does not turn his back upon contemporary experience, it does not matter how scientifically untrue such attitudes are. Those who read Crane' critical prose will observe how solidly the ideas of Richards are woven into it.

A metaphysical poetry which searches for truths other than those located in the universe about us, truths which we do not have the possibility of knowing in the course of human existence, is unnecessary except for those who believe in the immortal soul. At the same time, the truths which we can know are not, I believe, to be known "spiritually," nor by the casting aside of human knowledge as a superfluity. On these counts, Munson was wrong in asserting that a transcendent metaphysical poetry was possible and valid on the groundwork of knowledge, for the reality of transcendent truths cannot be verified or demonstrated by human effort. Furthermore, Munson's failure to specify the type or quantity of knowledge which the metaphysical poet requires reveals the inadequacy of his advice. Other thinkers have not been able to remedy this failure, before or after Munson wrote his essay. On the other hand, I think Crane made a drastic error, first in deciding to be a *transcendent* metaphysical poet, and thereupon in dissociating himself from the only source of inspiration which might have given a shred of credence to his inquiries and conclusions, an organized and theoretical system of knowledge. The root-cause for Crane's misconceptions, as well as Munson's, was an inadequate understanding of the content of reality, the means by which that content can be known, and the function of poetry and the other arts in the knowing of that content.

The writings of F. S. C. Northrop seem to me to provide a valuable answer to these problems, problems which

embrace the value and survival of art.† Northrop holds
that there are two aspects of reality which can be known
by man: the "aesthetic component" and the "theoretic
component." The first component consists of particular
sensuous factors and their relationships; it can be known
by a process of immediate apprehension, and involves the
formulation of a "concept by intuition." The "theoretic
component" consists of those factors in reality which are
universal and eternal, not capable of being directly observed; it can be known by a process of theoretical speculation and formulation, which theory is then experiment-
ally verified . . . this means of knowing involves the construction of a "concept by postulation." The relationship
between the "aesthetic component" and the "theoretic
component" is not one of identity. The painter who sees
a color knows something different than the physicist who
looks at the same color. There is a way of relating the
two components of reality without destroying the individuality of either, and this is by means of an "epistemic
correlation." This correlation is a one-one relationship
thereby preserving intact the nature of each component
while at the same time it may also unite them. Because
the reality which is intuited or aesthetically known is as
true as the reality which is theoretically known, the
"epistemic correlation" makes it possible for art to have
two functions:

"By distinguishing concepts by intuition from concepts by postulation
and thereby preventing the identification of reality as scientifically
and truly thought with reality as immediately and aesthetically intuited
the epistemic correlation permits the aesthetic, purely empirical component of reality to be treated by itself without any dependence upon

† A fuller explication of the ideas in this paragraph will be found
in Northrop's THE MEETING OF EAST AND WEST (1946) and
his "The Functions and Future of Poetry" (FURIOSO, Summer 1941

or reference to scientific theory or philosophical, political, or religious doctrine. By relating, but not identifying, concepts by intuition with concepts by postulation the epistemic correlations also indicate that the aesthetic component of reality points beyond itself to the theoretically-postulated. Thus, providing the epistemic correlations are made one-one, they permit the poet to convey analogically in terms of immediately-experienceable materials, the unobservable theoretical component of reality which can be literally expressed only by the technical concepts by postulation of science and scientifically-formulated philosophy. Thus arises art in its second function as the instrument or handmaid for metaphorically and analogically conveying a theoretical doctrine, the truth of which can be determined correctly only outside of art by some other subject or science."†

The philosophy which has been compressed into the preceding paragraph provides a function, a subject, and a dignity to art which it can hardly afford to neglect in a world almost entirely dominated by ideas of utility. At the same time, it removes from art the robes of universal knowledge with which it clothed itself in order to justify its seemingly-unessential activity. The artist is equipped to know the world intuitively: emotion, color, sound, texture, mobility, etc. are justifiably his concern, and in expressing his aesthetic reactions to these factors of reality the artist is discovering truth and performing a sound function. There need be no sense of inferiority either hidden or overt in the artist because he has not mastered the science of physics, or a similar theoretical field. Should the artist understand physics, however, he must be aware that the physicists and not he have developed the knowledge of physical reality; he, however, can convey his knowledge by means of the aesthetic bridges which form the substance of his art.

It becomes clear that the compulsion which Crane felt to make a "mystical synthesis" of materials he was incapable

† *Reprinted from FURIOSO (Summer 1941), by permission of the Editors.*

of understanding because of his needless anti-intellectual-
ism, was a mistake which eventually proved ruinous to
him in his major work. Mysticism is nothing more than
the individual's direct apprehension of the aesthetic factors of reality (it is no accident that so many mystics are
emotionally upwrought and see intense light) without the
artist's ability to embody his apprehensions in form; it can
discover no more and no less than non-mystical art. It
cannot take the place of science and philosophy, and cannot achieve the universal truths for which the mystic
traditionally strives. It is particular, sensuous, non-theor-
etical, aesthetic. In assigning himself a mystical poetic
role, therefore, Crane was laboring under a lack of understanding of the nature of mysticism; this misunderstanding would not necessarily have harmed his poetry. He
was decidedly on the wrong track, however, when he
sought for eternal theoretic truths without the aid of
scientific and philosophical knowledge and method. Here
is where Crane's mysticism positively misled him.

Crane tried to perform the function of scientist and
philosopher when he set himself up as a modern myth-
maker. The myth-maker agrees with Jung that he serves
as "the collective *man*, the carrier and former of the
unconsciously active soul of mankind." Though he may
seek to evade responsibility for his myth, as Crane did
when he wrote in his 1929 essay that "Poetic prophecy
in the case of the seer has nothing to do with factual
prediction or with futurity," he has indeed constructed
an object which is actively related to both. No one will
deny that the unconscious has a positive relationship with
the conscious, so that the formation of the former must
obviously affect the latter. What is at stake is the responsibility of the poet for his work. In ancient days,

when science and philosophy were the prerogative of the bardic prophets, it was to them that the people turned for an interpretation of reality. The role which Crane wished to assume, however, required a primitive function without a modern understanding of the world. His prophetic utterances, therefore, were unrelated to the twentieth century, and were in essence repudiations of his expressed intention to immerse himself in contemporary experience. The utilization of a twentieth century vocabulary is no substitute for understanding. When Crane set himself up as unconcerned with modern science and philosophy, he automatically ruled himself out of consideration as a poet who could deal with those questions of reality which require scientific and philosophic knowledge.

Were Crane to have limited himself in his poetry to the "emotional dynamics" which make up the best lines in his *Collected Poems*, there would not be much reason to quarrel with his theories or with the *"rationale* of metaphor" as he expressed it in his letter to Monroe. Crane as a poet would undoubtedly have achieved a splendid fruition in the pursuit of the primary function of poetry. He had begun his career as a mature poet in the 1920's with the laudable ambition of expressing his emotional reactions to experience, and was ready for success. As he soon realized, however, his emotions had a tragic contour, and no amount of induced ecstasy could eradicate that complexion. Since Crane was in almost every way excluded from the dominant pattern of his times, he longed for social recognition and status. The quiescent expression of his tragic moods, so contrary to the exultant prosperity temper of the period, would have alienated him still further.

Precisely because Crane was an alienated figure, he attempted to assume a role in life which by its very scope and achievement would counteract those elements in himself which society found negative. Very early in life, futhermore, he had found it impossible to comprehend the world in a systematic manner. He recognized, however, that as a poet who concerned himself primarily with the aesthetic he might not be as great a poet as someone like Dante who encompassed both the theoretical and the aesthetic in his work. By adopting an optimistic and mystic mode, Crane believed that he could dispense with science and philosophy; he could rest assured that he had not actually dispensed with knowledge, only with that knowledge which he considered temporal and unreal. The logic and verification which science and philosophy find requisite was thus replaced with a super-logic, and Crane could proceed in the comfortable belief that he was enabled to play the part of a major writer on his own terms.

15. COLLAPSE OF THE MYTH

IN APRIL, THE TENSION UNDER WHICH CRANE WAS living broke forth into a quarrel between the Tates and himself over domestic issues, and he left for New York. After a few days of indecision, Crane determined to transplant himself to the family plantation on the Isle of Pines in Cuba. On the first of May, therefore, he sailed for the island in the company of Waldo Frank.

While Frank was with him, Crane did not accomplish much on *The Bridge*. After Frank's departure, he could still do no work, and in the first week of June took a schooner trip to Grand Cayman Island in order to stimulate his outlook and refresh his spirits.

Crane returned from Grand Cayman the third week of June in more vigorous physical condition. "In spite of all," he wrote Frank the day after his return, "I find myself rather toughened and well." Inspired by the voyage and the scenes he had encountered, he completed two poems: "Tampa Schooner" (published in *The Dial*, September 1926; later in *White Buildings* as "Repose of Rivers"), and Kidd's Cove" (published in *Poetry* and *transition* in 1927, and in *Collected Poems*, as "O Carib Isle"). It might have been expected that this burst of creative energy would have been further intensified by the reception of news that Edgell Rickword, the biographer of Rimbaud who was now editing *The Calendar* in London, had bought "Praise for an Urn," "Passage," and "At Melville's Tomb." Acceptance of the last poem was in the nature of a triumph for, as Crane wrote Frank, "not one magazine in America would take it." But the state of Crane's temper was such as to prohibit the resumption of work on *The Bridge*. The terrible vision of the American city of the damned in "Repose of Rivers" ("After the city that I finally passed / With scalding unguents spread and smoking darts"), the racked spirit and the anguished desire for death manifested in the final stanzas of "O Carib Isle" (*transition* version):

> Under the poinciana, of a noon or afternoon
> let fiery blossoms clot the light, render my ghost,
> sieved upward, black and white along the air—
> until it meets the blue's comedian host.
>
> Let not the pilgrim see himself again
> bound like the dozen turtles on the wharf
> each twilight,—still undead, and brine caked in their eyes,
> huge, overturned: such thunder in their strain!
> And clenched beaks coughing for the surge again!
>
> Slagged of the hurricane,—I, cast within its flow,
> congeal by afternoons here, satin and vacant . . .
> You have given me the shell, Satan,—the ember,
> Carbolic, of the sun exploded in the sea.

these symptoms of turmoil and depression are indicative of the mental condition in which he struggled. The symbolic explosion of the life-radiating sun in the death-dealing sea, which occupies the last line quoted from "O Carib Isle!," is the mood which dominates the "Voyages" and their years of composition (1924 and 1925) in Crane' life, the coveted extinction of light in dark waters.

The most obvious causes for Crane's inability to forge into *The Bridge*, and for the agonized state of his feelings after Frank's departure from the Isle of Pines at the end of May, were the further series of complications that arose as though designed to forestall the publication of White *Buildings*. Although Liveright had finally agreed to publish the book provided O'Neill wrote the foreword, the difficulties surrounding the arrangements were not ended. A letter written by Crane a day or so after Frank had left for the United States adequately conveys the emotional tension which this situation evoked in Crane:

"Today frequent downpours and your card from Havana. Also a letter from O'Neill—more mysterious than ever. I'll quote exactly and all the words pertaining to the Liveright matter: 'There seems to be a misunderstanding about this Liveright matter somewhere. He isn't waiting for any foreword from me *yet*—at least not according to what he said when I saw him last before I wrote you the last time. He was waiting for more stuff from you apparently. And he spoke of having talked about you with Otto Kahn and so forth. However, I expect to be back in New York within a month and I will see him then and get this matter straightened out.' You will remember my descriptions of this situation up to this point with sufficient accuracy without further repetitions; I can only say with regard to it all that Gene has either misinformed me in his previous letters or else is suffering from a lapse of memory. At any event, I hope that the conversation with Kahn alluded to, hasn't twitched Liveright into the decision to hold up my book until the Bridge shall be completed. If he doesn't really want the book of course nobody can force him to take it,—in which case I hope it won't be too much trouble for you to return the mss to the Boni Bros. There seems no end to the complications with L. The mysterious 'yet' in Gene's statement (my underlining) is simply inexplicable."

Upon his return from Grand Cayman, Crane again wrote to Frank about the matter:

"I am not writing to O'Neill about 'White Buildings'—and do not expect to write him until I hear directly from him. He is supposed to be in NY by this time, and in his last letter he said that he expected to see Liveright on his return and talk things over. He knows that I have prepared in mss all the poems which are to be included in the book and that all that can now hold it back is the lack of his fore-word. It was hard for me to ask him to write such a thing for my book, and it has been harder and more embarrassing still for me to have kept trailing him with letters of urgence. It's impossible for me to address him again on the subject. I'm sorry that what-ever-it-was made him feel constrained to promise the favor initially."

Crane's worries over the publication of *White Buildings* were aggravated, too, by distracting ear abscesses which afflicted him as the result of over-exposure to the sun on the schooner trip.

Yet more insidiously demoralizing than either of these two factors, devastating as they may have been at the time to Crane, was the full maturation of his disbelief in the meaning of *The Bridge* and ipso facto in the validity of his poetic existence. In the same letter in which Crane had declared that he would never write to O'Neill again about the foreword to *White Buildings*, a letter written the day after he returned from the Grand Cayman trip, the following paragraph appeared directly after the quoted one dealing with his book:

"It will be just as well for me to forget publishers for awhile, I think though I can't forget how steadfastly you have persevered in helping me whatever the results have amounted to. And don't think too much about me; my judgments are too unsettled these days to make me feel that I deserve much attention, much less the faith that you assure me of. The situation is really unique with me; it is absurd to say that one is battling indifference; but neither does one build out of an emptied vision. Mere word-painting and juggling, however fastidious,—a prospect of this doesn't excite one very much. At times it seems demonstrable that Spengler is quite right. At present I'm writing nothing—would that I were an efficient factory of some kind!† It was unfortunate in a way to have been helped by our friend, the banker,—with my nose to the grindstone of the office I could still fancy that free

---

† *Crane is referring here to* THE BRIDGE, *since the same letter mentions that he was working on "Tampa Schooner" and "Kidd's Cove".*

dom would yield me a more sustained vision; now I know that much
has been lacking all along. This is less personal than it sounds. I think
that the artist more and more licks his own vomit, mistaking it for
the common diet. He amuses himself that way in a culture without
faith and convictions—but he might as well be in elfin land with a hop
pipe in his mouth . . . . No, the bridge isn't very flambouyant these
days."

Before Frank had an opportunity to consider the implications of these emotional remarks, a second letter, written the day after the first, arrived with a lengthy explanation of the reasoned background of ideas which had
prompted his despairing lines.

The follow-up letter revealed even more than the first
had done that Crane had been overtaken at last by the
conflict which he had been struggling to ignore ever
since the exalted emotion which struck off the lines of
"Atlantis" in 1923 had first begun to dwindle. This emotion had been the substitute for a rational evaluation of
the symbol of the bridge and the many meanings which
it represented. But the "confusion" which was its bedrock militated against a stable emotion, one which could
gather itself together and carry Crane forward in the
completion of his project. Now Crane faced an overwhelming doubt in the poem's purpose and form. The
desire to complete the poem still existed, but "intellectually judged the whole theme and project seems more
and more absurd," he wrote.

The artist, Crane wrote further in the same letter, must
believe in the truth of that which he expresses in his
work. This truth is full trust that his expression is rooted
in society "as an actively operating principle of communal works and faith." Such a belief could only exist
when society regarded the artist as prophet and maker
whose "intuitions were salutary and . . . [whose] vision

either sowed or epitomized 'experience' (in the Blakeian sense)." The artist must know that his work communicates to an audience which will regard him seriously and listen to him: 'Even the rapturous and explosive destructivism of Rimbaud presupposes this, even his lonely hauteur demands it for any estimation or appreciation. (The romantic attitude must at least have the background of an age of faith . . .)" Although he had once possessed this confidence in society and in his expression, Crane went on to say, he no longer did. The present was unworthy of the past's "worth and vision"—the future could not be built upon a fusion of the past with an ignoble and materialistic present: "If only America were half as worthy today to be spoken of as Whitman spoke of it fifty years ago there might be something for one to say—not that Whitman received or required any tangible proof of his intimations, but that time has shown how increasingly lonely and ineffectual his confidence stands." The materials and major symbol which he had selected for *The Bridge*, all of which he had believed "to be (articulate or not) at least organic and active factors in the experience and perceptions of our common race, time and belief," were now seen by him to be part and parcel of the same delusion which had misled him with regard to society and its future: "however great their subjective significance to me is concerned—these forms, materials, dynamics are simply non-existent in the world . . . The bridge as a symbol today has no more significance beyond an economical approach to shorter hours, quicker lunches, behaviourism and toothpicks." On the basis of such disbelief, to continue work on *The Bridge* was "evading a recognition and playing Don Quixote in an immorally conscious way." An alternative was to limit himself to the "word-painting" of which he had spoken in his first letter, but this descent from the high public level on which he had placed himself and his work was intolerable:

"Rimbaud was the last great poet that our civilization will see—he let off all the great cannon firecrackers in Valhalla's parapets, the sun has set theatrically several times since while Laforgue, Eliot and others of that kidney have whimpered fastidiously . . . There always remains the cult of 'words," elegancies, elaborations, to exhibit with a certain amount of pride to an 'inner circle' of literary initiates. But this is, to me, rivalled by numerous other forms of social accomplishment which might, if attained, provide as mild and seductive recognition."

It would be a serious misinterpretation of Crane's previous development if responsibility for the profound depth of his hopelessness were to be assigned to factors which coexisted with the expression of this hopelessness. The *White Buildings* misunderstanding . . . his physical distress . . . the reading of Oswald Spengler's first volume of *The Decline of the West*—these should not be misunderstood, neither over-rated nor under-rated. The fiasco ending of the first attempt to publish *White Buildings* at the close of 1925 had not prevented Crane from continuing to plan and develop *The Bridge* in Patterson. Illness and pain had not previously produced such extensive soul-sickness. As for the effect of Spenglerian theory upon Crane, several pertinent observations may be made. These days upon the Isle of Pines did not see Crane's first acquaintance with Spengler. Through his friendship with Kenneth Burke, whose translations of excerpts from Spengler appeared earlier in *The Dial*, Crane was familiar with, but he was also undismayed by Spengler's pessimism at least as early as 1923. Thus he wrote to Alfred Stieglitz in December 1923 with a full faith: "Burke (between us only) keeps fighting off a true spiritual revelation which is really his birthright, though he can't consciously recognize it. So he falls a prey to Spengler and the cynics of more reasonable tongue—and lives in a rather unhappy and delicate state of scepticism. He sees the surface of your work and admires it intensely, but he simply thinks I'm cucu when I remain unconvinced that he has really SEEN one picture of yours." The effect of a single book, whether Spengler, Ouspensky, or Hitler's *Mein Kampf*, is not a matter of simple causation. It is more often a highlight—originating, substantiating, or concluding—in the multip'e chain of ideas and events which surround an individual and form the history of his growth. Numerous artists have read and understood, like Crane, Spengler's analysis of cultural growth and decay with its contempt for modern art as "sport," its advice to artists "to devote themselves to technics instead of the paintbrush," its contempt for historical optimism, and its underlying conclusion that Western culture was dying instead of living. Yet not all of these artists have as quickly and spontaneously as Crane been plunged into the abyss, and many indeed have survived the experience entire'y. There are reasons why Crane found himself peculiarly drawn to Spengler. One of these was Spengler's high regard for the technique of analogy as a means of understanding; another was Spengler's corollary contempt for "reason and cognition" and the importance he attached to 'intuitiv perception" as the only means of comprehending meta physical reality and the human future. These are but indications of affinity, however, and no more. Crane' ideas as contained in the two letters to Frank emerged or ganically from the course of his development, and the expression at this time was in the nature of a coda to h steady loss of faith. Spengler served as a systematize compilation of all the doubts and questions which had been disturbing Crane hitherto, and the larger meaning of *The Decline of the West* was one that had been forced upon Crane by his own experiences. How slightly the book's arguments themselves overpowered his thoughts may be seen in a letter written to Frank six months later in January 1927: "Thank you so much for having the *Menorah* people send me out your review of Spengler. It's a magnificent rebuttal of the man's psychology. I don't need to know your philosophical references well enough to check up on them to feel that."

Despite his thoroughgoing repudiation of *The Bridge* and its implied and explicit meaning, within little more than a few weeks Crane was hard at work again on the poem. For an artist with the integrity and temperament of Crane, such a complete about-face with its tinge of hypocrisy must have involved an excruciating period during which he literally forced himself into a state conducive to writing on a theme in which he had no faith. The reasons for continuance undoubtedly appeared overwhelming to him. Of these, pride and a mistaken sense of honor were the most important. The receipt of Kahn's money the previous December had been a vindication of his determination to live as a poet, and particularly so with regard to the contempt he believed his family felt for him. On the New Year's Eve preceding 1926, for example, Crane wrote: "Well, the expected results have already been noticed on my family! Long and arardurous letters from uncles, aunts etc. . . . and a fat check from my father for Christmas. They all want me to come out and visit again—which I see no reason for doing at this time. I want to get into my work." After such hallelujahs, a confession of defeat would have been a confirmation of their previous beliefs, an admission of utter uselessness, and in view of Crane's familial concerns an act of the utmost gravity.

The same fear of consequences haunted him with reference to the scepticism expressed by his friends in the likelihood of his success in the myth he was attempting to create. Failure in this instance would denote a repudiation of the philosophical optimism which he had expressed with such conviction in 1923, as well as agreement with Munson that the fundamentals of his literary beliefs were fallacious, that he had been laboring under serious delusions for many years.

In addition to these vital considerations, Crane had to consider the effect of his stalemate upon Otto Kahn, and by extension upon Frank and O'Neill, who had recommended him to Kahn. The first installment of money had been almost exhausted by this time, yet he had nothing to show Kahn for the half-year except incomplete versions of "Atlantis" and "Ave Maria." Since he conceived of his relationship with Kahn as a business venture primarily, aside from any respect which Kahn had for his work, the immediate result of failure to fulfill his obligation would be the impugning of his honor. "I shan't ask for it," he wrote about the next installment of money due from Kahn, "unless I am writing again by that time." And a few weeks later: "In the case of the Bridge I feel enough honor-bound to desire preserve whatever evidence of my industry and effort is forthcoming." This question of honor, indeed, proved to the single greatest influence in persuading him to co tinue in the face of all the contrary evidence which he had gathered. Thus he concluded the second letter about Spengler to Frank with these bitter remarks: "All this does not mean that I have resigned myself to inactivity . . . A bridge will be written in some kind of style and form, at worst it will be something as good as advertising copy. After which I will at least have done my best to discharge my debt to Kahn's kindness."

It is possible at this point to be more critical of the conception that underlay *The Bridge*. Crane was a victim of the confusion which marked the 'twenties and distorted the values of the most sensitive individuals. Against his knowledge of the fictitiousness of the American way of life, gained through experiences that had embittered his emotional existence, he was subtly and ingeniously led to an enthusiastic and uncritical reconciliation with the tawdriness and fraud which he essentially abhorred. His understanding of the framework of American life was sharp, but underlying it was a tendency to welcome integration with even its most despised features. It is difficult to say specifically just what made Crane in 1923 bridge the gap between a yearning distaste for capitalist society and culture and his final role of enraptured American bard. Ouspensky must be considered, like Spengler, as the source of an attractive, systematic summation of a set of ideas which spiritualized and rationalized the transition. Probably Crane's success as an advertising copywriter had much to do with his assumption of the Whitmanian mantle, for the advertising business not only sold but was itself sold on the great and glorious accomplish-

ments of American business and industry. A good deal of
the advertising business' success is based on auto-intoxica-
tion, and it has resulted in the justifiable confidence that
anything can be sold so long as a single consumer remains
alive to be baited. Having driven himself to "sell" heaters
and rubber tires, Crane was himself sold on those products and the order which produced them. (A year or so
later, Bruce Barton began the great campaign which re-
stored Christ to His rightful rank with the American
businessman by writing his book about the man nobody
really knew B. B., Before Barton.) The idea was not
so strange, since the prosperity of the period had already
convinced the nation of the essential soundness of his product and its radiant future. It is not insignificant that
the year 1923 saw the rise of the prosperity index to
its highest point since 1920, and that *The Bridge* dragged
its way to a weary conclusion simultaneously with the
crash of October 1929 and the deflation of the capitalist
myth. I don't mean to question the high-mindedness of
Crane's purpose nor the sincerity of his feelings. But it
is poignantly and tragically symbolic that, at the very
moment when Crane faltered and *The Bridge* might have
passed into limbo unwritten, or at the very least have
been written as a critical tragic poem, it was revivified
by a debt of honor to a banker closely identified with
the materialism which had destroyed Crane's faith—a banker who, and I am not unmindful of Kahn's interest in
and generosity to the arts, must have been gratified that
the twentieth-century America he was helping to shape
would be shown in epic poetry to possess a continuous tie
with the spiritual unity of its past and the splendors which
would be its future.

The will to complete *The Bridge* being still alive within Crane, a cable received from Frank in the first few days of July which stated that Liveright had finally decided to publish *White Buildings* was effective "in piercing the miasmas of these tropics." It might be added that Frank's encouragement in his letters to Crane also played a significant part in enabling Crane to reorient himself toward working again on his poem. An accessory factor in Crane's ability to reverse himself so completely was that characteristic of his, already mentioned in these pages, which permitted him to welcome all experience, good and evil, as necessary and desirable. This form of rationalization served Crane well now.

"Yes, I read the whole of Spengler's book," he wrote Frank two months after his initial mention of the German philosopher. "It is stupendous,—and it was perhaps a very good experience for ripening some of the Bridge, after all. I can laugh now; but you know, alas, how little I could at the time. That book seems to have been just one more of many 'things' and circumstances that seem to have uniformly conspired in a strangely symbolical way toward the present speed of my work. Isn't it true,—hasn't it been true in your experience, that beyond the acceptance of fate as a tragic action—immediately every circumstance and incident in one's life flocks toward a positive center of action, control and beauty . . . . I have never been able to live *completely* in my work before. Now it is to learn a great deal. To handle the beautiful skeins of this myth of America—to realize suddenly, as I seem to, how much of the past is living under only slightly altered forms, even in machinery and such-like, is extremely exciting."

Carried away by the ecstasy of composition, it seemed that nature and the elements had joined with him in seeking release for their hidden thoughts and passions.

"Here, too," he wrote, "is that bird with a note that Rimbaud speaks of as 'making you blush.' We are in the midst of the equatorial storm

2HART CRANE

season; every day, often at night, torrents engulf us, and the thunder rods jab and prospect in the caverns deep below that chain of mountains across. You can hear the very snakes rejoice,—the long, shaken-out convulsions of rock and roots. It is very pleasant to lie awake—just half awake—and listen. I have the most speechless and glorious dreams meanwhile. Sometimes words come and go, presented like a rose that yields only its light, never its composite form. Then the cocks begin to crow."

As Crane's feeling of well-being grew steadily intrenched, his love found itself directed outwards to other people. One of these persons was his housekeeper, Mrs. Simpson ("the very elf of music, little wrinkled burnous wisp that can do anything and remembers so much . . . reads Dante and falls to sleep, her cough has become so admirably imitated by the parrot that I often think her two places at once"), who appears in "The River." Another was the idiot who inspired lines in two of his poems, the wine-glass-shaped "Lenses" (see Appendix)† and "The Idiot."

The composition of *The Bridge*, and of several of the poems in the "Key West" collection, proceeded at a rapid pace during these days. "I feel an absolute music in the air again, and some tremendous rondure floating somewhere," he wrote Frank in the last week of July 1926, and the reference to Whitman's "Passage to India" is unmistakable:

> O vast Rondure, swimming in space.
> Cover'd all over with visible power and beauty,
> Alternate light and day and the teeming spiritual darkness . . .
> With inscrutable purpose, some hidden prophetic intention,
> Now first it seems my thought begins to span thee.‡

† *An undated typescript of this poem indicates that Crane at one time intended "Lenses" to be part of THE BRIDGE, in a position directly preceding "The Tunnel." It may have been written at this time, since its lines are developed more fully in "The Idiot."*

‡ *From*: LEAVES OF GRASS *by Walt Whitman, copyright*, 1924 *by Doubleday & Company, Inc.*

Accompanying the letter was the final seventh stanza of "To Brooklyn Bridge," with the comment that its completion was "going to swing me back to San Cristobal again. . . ." Two days later Frank received "Ave Maria," and in his accompanying letter Crane wrote: "You have the last section ('*Atlantis*,' as I have decided to call it) haven't you? I have discovered that it IS the real Atlantis, even of geology! My plans are soaring again, the conception swells . . . Last night a wonderful breeze came up—and you can wa'k singing through the grove with a great moon simply bending down." Before long, a revised version of "Atlantis" had arrived in Frank's mail. As *The Bridge* unfolded itself on paper, its structure began to change from the outline which Crane had submitted to Kahn in March. New sections forced their way into plan or reality; as they gripped Crane's attention, he could not restrain himself from working on all sections simultaneously, new and old. "All sections moving forward at once!" he wrote. "I didn't realize that a bridge is begun from the two ends at once. . . . I skip from one section to another now like a sky-gack or girder-jack." By the end of July, "Cutty Sark" was ready. There was a brief lu'l in early August while Crane mulled over "Powhatan's Daughter," formerly "Pokahantus," which was now scheduled to include "Indiana" and "The Dance." These were begun when suddenly, as Crane wrote Frank, "Two or three songs have just popped out . . . which come after 'Cutty Sark' "; these were "Southern Cross," "National Winter Garden," and "Virginia."† By the

† "*To Liberty*" (*see Appendix*) *is an undated poem which, judging from Crane's description of "Virginia" (in a letter to Frank dated August* 12, 1926) *as "virgin in process of 'being built'," may be the original version of "Virginia."*

close of August, most of "The Tunnel" (incorporating lines from an early version of "Atlantis") and "The Dance" was completed.

It was to be expected that this form of collective composition, if one may so use the adjective when speaking of a group of poems written concurrently rather than of one poem written by a group of poets, would invite repetitions that might have the effect of weakening the individual force and beauty of single sections. A beneficial effect might be the unification of all sections into a coherent unity by means of threads run through the entire structure. The latter possibility was the one which Crane thought he had realized: "Are you noticing how throughout the poem motives and situations recur—under modifications of environment, etc? The organic substances of the poem are holding a great many surprises for me . . . Greatest joys of creation."

The creative energies which had enabled Crane to write with such furious intensity on the Isle of Pines had shown signs of disappearance in July under the impact of the heat. By the close of August, they had given out almost entirely. In October, he left the island for the United States, hurried along by a hurricane which had destroyed much of the island plantation. From this point on, the despair which he had sublimated for a few weeks assumed a dominating and ineradicable position in him. "My present quandaries, that extend to every detail of my life, personal and artistic, have brought me near lunacy," he wrote in February 1927 to Tate. This alternation of depression and elation became more feverish and pronounced than it had been during earlier years. Each state became shorter in duration, and more extreme in tendency. Economic and personal problems, the same as those which had plagued him since childhood and adolescence, continued to torment him. As problem and reaction continued to act and interact, it became progressively more difficult, and finally impossible, to extricate himself from the "teufels-kreis" in which he whirled. No matter where he went, either for refuge or for inspiration, he could not shake off the difficulties of his life. In 1926, while still on the Isle of Pines, he had begun to study Spanish, having decided then that he must at some later date visit Spain. Towards the end of 1927, the idea appeared again in his mind. It seemed to him, if he could duplicate the "summer by the sea" which he had spent so profitably in Cuba, that he must inevitably be cleansed and rejuvenated. Since he had no money, the trip was postponed. Meanwhile, he had gone as rich man's companion to California where, as happened when he was finally able to go to Europe in 1928, the environment called forth nothing constructive from him in the way of solving his problems, and further increased the rate at which his personality and body were disintegrating. He sought sympathy and affection; those who might have responded were either envious, distorted as he was, or else repelled by his violence and extremity. There was a desperate frenzy in his staggering progress toward collapse. At times, it even drove him to prefer the role in which he had seen himself during the early 1920's, that of clown. "I envy buckandwing dancers and the Al Jolsons of the world sometimes . . ." he wrote Tate in March 1927. "They're able to do some 'good' to somebody. And when they laugh people don't think they are crying . . . there is no place left for *our* kinds of minds or emotions . . . we must apprehend some element of truth in our mock ceremonies or even our follies aren't amusing." The condition he had reached toward the end of his life was such that he distrusted himself as an organism and questioned the possibility of regeneration. A close friend advised him in 1930 to undergo psycho-therapeutic treatment, on the assumption that the complex effects of Crane's predicament could be alleviated in the vacuum of a psycho-analyst's office. Crane dismissed the suggestion with the reply that he doubted whether it could possibly have a curative effect upon him. Even if such a procedure were to introduce order into his life, Crane added, he could not be certain that disorder was not indeed responsible for his past poetic achievements, and that its absence might not irrevocably destroy what genius remained.

The continued disorder of his life did not keep Crane from poetry. In the fall of 1926, he set forth into "The River" but, as he wrote Stieglitz, the poem would not "spill" out and its "organic form (there is always just *one*)" eluded him. Nevertheless, by sheer will power he managed to continue working. By July of next year, "The River," "Van Winkle," and "Harbor Dawn" were finished; and he had also been able to revise "The Dance." He wrote several new poems (among them "To Emily Dickinson" in November 1926), and during the latter part of 1927 developed and completed many of the poems based on his West Indian experiences. The magazines were buying those portions of *The Bridge* already done, as well as many of his shorter poems. (A few of these include "March," *Larus* [March 1927]; "Old Song," *The New Republic* [August 10, 1927]; "The Tunnel," *The Criterion* [November 1927]; "The Hurricane," "Bacardi Spreads The Eagle's Wings," and other "Key West" poems, *transition* [December 1927]; "The Air Plant," *The Dial* [February 1928]; "The Mermen," *The Dial* [September 1928]; "A Name for All," *The Dial* [April 1929]). However, the satisfaction which this would have given him in previous years was not forthcoming now, since he was obsessed with the need for completing *The Bridge*. It was not until the fall of 1929, pressed into action by his commitment to furnish Harry Crosby and The Black Sun Press in Paris with the final sections of *The Bridge*, that he was able to bring it to a conclusion. "Cutty Sark" was revised and the punctuation improved "in order to promote clarity"; "Indiana," "Quaker Hill," and "Cape Hatteras" were in the French printer's hands by the end of December. The difficulty with which Crane ended his work, and the mood which predominated, is symbolized by a correction of a line in "To Brooklyn Bridge" which he sent to Paris with the last pages of his manuscript:

"–And elevators heave us to our day"

changed to . . .

"–Till elevators drop us from our day"

The Bridge concluded, he felt himself cut adrift from the purpose which, while it had haunted him, had also held a goal before him. "I really don't want to write any poetry for awhile now," he wrote in February 1930, "but just the same feel somehow depressed that I haven't some ambitious project on hand to take the place of the Bridge."

Though Crane had reached a low point of morale by the summer of 1926, he did not completely abandon the search for a stable groundwork on which he could survive. However, he was still unable to reconcile himself to a complete abandonment of the optimism and mystic faith which had motivated him in 1923. Thus, he flung himself between pessimism and hope, but was not strong enough to tie himself firmly to one or the other. At one moment, it seemed that he might be genuinely converted to Spenglerian ideas. In March 1927, for example, he suddenly developed the desire to write a biography of John Roebling's son Washington, who took over responsibility for construction of the Brooklyn Bridge when his father died in 1869, and brought it to completion in 1883. Crane spoke of Roebling in terms which were far removed from spiritual conceptions of the bridge: "The man was a genius—and his accomplishment stupendous at 'that time.' There might be only slight public interest in his work. Nevertheless, he was a true Spenglerian hero—and his efforts brought tremendous wealth to his family." Almost at the very same time, he was also writing: "We all must have some kind of incantation, I suppose. Though I'd rather adopt some of Blake's aphorisms. They're abstract enough. And a lot truer than the latest combinations of scientific terms." This basic uncertainty dominated him.

A year later, while in California, Crane made an effort to find a lifetime in the theories of those writers in England and France who were asserting reactionary values, including those of royalism, Catholicism, and classicism. Among the men he read were Ramon Fernandez (*Messages*), Wyndham Lewis (*Time and Western Man*), and, of course, Eliot in the columns of *The Criterion*. But he was unable to subdue the involved speculation with which these writers covered their pages, and flung up his hands in despair.

"Beginning with Spengler and Wells," he wrote Frank in March 1928, "this age seems to be typically encyclopedic. This may assist the artist in time—by erecting some kind of logos, or system of contact between the insulated departments of highly specialized knowledge and enquiry which characterize the times—God knows, some kind of substantial synthesis of opinion is needed before I can feel confident in writing about anything but my shoestrings . . . . These Godless days! I wonder if you suffer as much as I do. At least you have the education and training to hold the scalpel."

He wrote in very much the same vein to Munson a month later:

"The spiritual disintegration of our period becomes more painful to me every day, so much so that I now find myself baulked by doubt at the validity of practically every metaphor that I coin. In every quarter . . . . a thousand issues are raised for one that is settled and where this method is reversed—as with the Neo-Thomists—one has nothing as substitute but an arbitrary dogmatism which seems to be too artificial to have any permanence or hold on the future."

Since Munson had sent him a copy of his book *Destinations* (1928), which contained the essay written on Crane by Munson in 1925, Crane commented on the volume to a considerable extent. The tone of his remarks was resigned: "As for Hart Crane, I know him too well to disagree on as many points as I once did two years ago when I first read the essay. I am certainly grateful for such expert attention, and especially on the technical side I think you express my intentions with a very persuasive gusto that has recently revived in me some conviction of 'reality' here and there in my scrap heap." There was a flash of Crane's old fire, however, when he stated that

he could pick no quarrel with Munson's expression of the
need for "spiritual knowledge and direction . . . more
order," but that Munson had certainly not begun to
"articulate the concrete values" which he should have set
up. "Scepticism may stop there and still claim gratitude
and respect," Crane wrote, "but I am not exactly satisfied
by that, and I doubt if you are. I still stake some claims
on the pertinence of the intuitions; indeed some of Blake's
poems and Emily Dickinson's seem more incontrovertible
than ever since Relativity and a host of other ideologies,
since evolved, have come into recognition."

For a brief period, Crane felt that there was a "luminous
impulse and essential direction . . . a 'Way' " in a series
of articles by Waldo Frank which were appearing serially
in *The New Republic*, and were later released in book
form as his important *The Re-Discovery of America*
(1929). In his articles, Frank re-affirmed the strength of
the mystical method in art, and stated that the artist
should neither "reflect nor . . . reject the world; but . . .
accept and transform it." "To our tragic artists," Frank
went on, "there remains only the *apocalyptic method* . . .
literally make the plastic form of their vision from the
plasmic substance of their experience—without obedience
to conceptual heritage or aesthetic tradition." Yet Frank's
words made but little effect upon Crane for, three months
later, in June, he wrote Frank: "I'm hardly qualified to
give you any fair report on my reactions to your New
Republic series." Crane followed this with several lines in
which he stated that he had read the articles under adverse
circumstances, mentioned the series' "painful condensation
of material and opinion," and concluded with his desire to
read the whole book before passing judgment.

The next mention of Frank's book came in a letter from Paris dated February 7, 1929. "Don't forget to send me your *Re-Discovery of America* now, as soon as possible," he wrote Frank. "I need it as a balance against the seductions of Europe . . . I now need more strength than ever." But it was too late. In Europe, he wrote hardly any poetry, except possibly for some fragmentary efforts. But he did manage to affix his name, together with more than a dozen or so writers, to the "Proclamation" announcing the emancipation of the word which appeared in the June 1929 issue of *transition*. Some of its points deserve quotation, if only for their relevance to the ultimate import of Crane's aesthetic theories and for their striking parallel to his deification of the word, although Crane later said that he had signed while drunk and regretted his action: "2. The imagination in search of a fabulous word is autonomous and unconfined . . . . 5. The expression of these concepts can be achieved only through the rhythmic 'hallucination of the word.' 6. The literary creator has the right to disintegrate the primal matter of words imposed on him by textbooks and dictionaries. 7. He has the right to use words of his own fashioning and to disregard existing grammatical and syntactical laws."

While Crane's confusion, and there is no other word to describe it, proceeded in its intricate and painful festering, he was not encouraged to integrate himself by the critics upon whom he might have depended for guidance. We have already considered Crane's reaction to Munson, who closed his *Destinations* with a call for new investigations into the cultural past as a starting-point for the

formation of values, and detailed his own labors over the
Indian *Mahabharata*. Yvor Winters was at first a staunch
supporter of the poet, although his writings of the past
seventeen years would seem to indicate that the name
"Hart Crane" has almost the same effect upon him that
the words "heretic" and "Jew" had upon Inquisitor-Gen-
eral Torquemada. His review of *White Buildings* in
Poetry (April 1927) was accompanied by an editorial note
dissociating the magazine from the extreme praise which
Winters gave to Crane, among which was his belief that
Crane was "a rare phenomenon in these latter days—a
poet who accepts his age in its entirety, accepts it with
passion, and who has the sensitive equipment to explore
it." It is either amusing or discouraging, depending on
one's mood, to read now in Mr. Winters' books the bar-
rage of invective and critical comment which he un-
leashes against the method of Crane, and specific poems
such as *Faustus and Helen*, all of which he praised with
his usual precision to such an embarrassing extent in
1927. It appears, however, that although Crane thought
enough of Winters in 1929 to ask the Black Sun Press
of Paris to send a review copy of *The Bridge* to Winters, the latter had grown so incensed at Crane as man and
poet that he completely shocked Crane with the personal
criticism he interspersed between passages of literary analysis in his review (*Poetry*, June 1930). The review appears further to have hurt Crane more than it might have
because, as he later related to William Wright, Winters
had previously expressed considerable approval of portions of *The Bridge* which he had seen in magazines and
in manuscript.

Allen Tate's review of *The Bridge* in *The Hound and
Horn* could not have surprised Crane as much as Win-

ters' review did. For, as long ago as July 1926, when
Crane had read the manuscript of Tate's introduction to his
White Buildings, he was aware from its lines that Tate
disapproved of the theme of *The Bridge*—the myth of
America—and doubted the vitality of the Whitmanian
spirit in a static America, although Tate referred to *The
Bridge* by insinuation only. In January 1929, *The Bookman* published an article by Tate entitled "American Poetry Since 1920." Here Tate, while introducing the acute
observation that Crane lacked a set of values and his poetic
genius was therefore undisciplined and in process of being
dissipated, amplified his earlier contradictory remarks
about the absence of a theme and the invalidity of the
presumably-absent theme which, apparently, Crane had
chosen to develop. Tate's main argument was that it
was impossible to put one's finger on a "positive attitude
that we may describe as national, as peculiarly our own,"
and that this was so because there was "no homogeneous
body of beliefs and feelings" in America which could sustain the poet. As a son of the Middle West, from which
had arisen the crude nationalism of Lindsay, Masters, and
Sandburg, Crane, according to Tate, stemmed from a region which lacked unity under the impress of industrialism. Because of its own divided nature, it mistook itself
for the spirit of America, and instead of developing form
and style speeded along in a noisy clamor of self-adver-
tisement which it disguised as poetry. As a result, Tate
concluded, "Hart Crane's effort in this direction is more
ambitious than Lindsay's or Sandburg's, and because he
is a poet of the first order the publication of *The Bridge*
will be an important event in contemporary letters. Of its
success in creating a national myth it is our privilege to
be sceptical in advance." What did Tate advise, then,

for the future of American poetry? First, the discarding of the belief that an American myth is necessary. Second, retirement to the provinces where "a group of craftsmen—of painters, of philosophers, of poets" would accidentally congregate and refresh themselves by drinking water at the roots of "local culture." If we consider the applicability of this advice for the directions it might have offered Crane, we are forced to conclude that it consigned him to an asylum where he might go on cutting poetic dolls. I have no way of knowing just what private opinions were ventured by people like Tate, Winters, and others to him. I can only guess from the content of available documents, as well as from letters written by Crane himself, that there was not much difference. In the case of Tate's article, it would appear that his advice could not possibly apply to Crane in the light of his lack of psychological and social roots in the Middle West or anywhere else. Its effect could only have been exclusive, and destructive of the confidence which Crane needed to bring his project, however ill-conceived, to completion.

Frank, Munson, Tate, and Winters—these critics, the first sympathetic to Crane's mystical inclination, were all enthusiastic about Crane's technical achievements. There were, however, a number of critics who, without devoting much space and attention to Crane's poetry, dismissed it from the standpoint of both theme and technique. The most pernicious demonstration of critical irresponsibility was furnished by William Rose Benet, himself a poet like the other critics I shall mention, who in *The Saturday Review of Literature* produced some parodies of Crane's style and themes which represented in their use of traditional "poetic" devices a complete lack of understanding of that which he satirized, as well as an inability to rise to Crane's level either in jest or seriousness. *The Dial* of May 1927 contained a brief unsigned mention of *White Buildings,* supposedly written by Conrad Aiken, who conceded that Crane had "ability." This ability, however, he found to be overwhelmed by Crane's "affectations of idiom . . . a straining and self-conscious and disingenuous preciosity; partly . . . by an unreflecting indulgence in what one might call high-class intellectual fake," with the result that few of the poems in the book seemed to him complete and unified.

Although Edmund Wilson in *The New Republic* of May 11, 1927 was not as blunt as the two reviewers cited just above, his article on modern poets had a more depressing effect upon Crane than either Aiken or Benet, whom Crane was able to laugh off in his letters. Wilson found Crane "careless and wilful," although he felt that Crane possessed "something like a great style"; it was his comparison with Rimbaud that hurt: "Rimbaud is inconsecutive and confused. Yet, with Rimbaud, whom Mr. Crane somewhat resembles, we experience intense emotional excitement and artistic satisfaction; we are dazzled by the eruption of his images, but we divine what he is saying. But, with Mr. Crane, though he sometimes moves us, it is in a way curiously vague." But more important than Wilson's discussion of style were his observations on poets like Eugene Jolas and James Rorty who, according to him, were attempting to establish a harmonious relationship with society in the spirit of Sandburg and Whitman. Both Jolas and Rorty had failed, Wilson believed, one because he seemed absorbed with geographical detail, the second because he concerned himself with the skyscrapers and other mechanical productions well-loved by the Dadaists. In short, these men were "still preoccupied with the phenomena of the surface," and America as composed of individuals and aspirations remained untouched by them. The applicability of these remarks to much of *The Bridge* is inescapable, and when Wilson prefaced his consideration of Jolas and Rorty by remarking that most of the younger American poets were isolated from society, he accidentally hit upon a combination of factors which was also troubling Crane. That is to say, the portions of *The Bridge* which were already written had a predominance of geographical detail, revolved about an external symbol, and were not inspired by the world from which the imagery and symbolism were derived. Unfortunately for any good which Wilson's article might have done for Crane, it overlooked the fact that most artists including Crane are not isolated from society through their own volition, and the insensitivity revealed by this omission aroused a passionate response from Crane which Wilson's more intelligent remarks might have evoked had there not been such a gross personal provocation.

Malcolm Cowley's sympathetic review of *The Bridge* (*The New Republic*, April 23, 1930) contained the cryptic remark that the faults of the poem, which he did not enumerate, were obvious but that he preferred to "leave [them] to other reviewers." Insofar as Crane was concerned, Cowley need not have refrained. A few pages earlier, I referred to Crane's disinterest in writing after the poem was published. More cognizant than anyone of the lack of genuine intention in the work and of the effort which had been expended to write "Cape Hatteras" and the other concluding parts of *The Bridge*, he was haunted by his knowledge and readier than most to turn his back upon the poem. When Paul Rosenfeld asked Crane in the spring of 1930 to submit an up-to-date version of a letter written in 1927 to Otto Kahn about *The Bridge*, he was unable to do so, not only because of alcoholic excess and mental strain, but because he could not bring himself to enunciate ideas in which he had had no faith for so many years. Yet a few days after writing Rosenfeld about his difficulties, he did send to Eda Lou Walton, the poet and critic who had included a study of *The Bridge* in a modern literature course she taught at New York University, a copy of the 1927 letter "as a fairly accurate chart of certain purposes in the poem which I may or may not have succeeded in accomplishing." It was as if he could not trust himself any longer to express with the old fervor the words about "an epic of the modern consciousness." The sense of failure as a poet was thus linked with the sense of failure as a myth-maker. This explains why he wrote to Tate in September 1930: "I was glad to get your 'Three Poems.' The distinguished diction throughout reminds me of the little advance I have ever made in essential flexibility and the finer intonations." Yet I think it is a mistake to assume that Crane's doubt of his inability to write poetry was as deep-rooted as the conviction that he had written without sincerity, and that he was *therefore* unintegrated. It is true that he wrote to Solomon Grünberg on January 10, 1931: "No writing is being done yet—or even in prospect. Can't fool myself that way, as you know." Yet this is not much different in tone from Crane's statement in an earlier letter of 1927 to Tate that "I seem to be going through an extremely distrustful mood in regard to most of my own work lately . . ." The publication of *The Bridge* precipitated a reasoned balancing of his accounts because it was a public revelation of a conflict which had been kept private, to the extent at least that Crane's friends only gossiped about the situation with their own friends, and that therefore only a small percentage of the American people were ever actually aware of his predicament. The letter which Crane wrote Tate after reading the latter's review of *The Bridge* in *The Hound and Horn*, a review for which he had been looking with anticipation more than six months since December 1929, when he had enthusiastically sent Tate a manuscript version of the poem as an advance copy, shows that he was inclined to accept the failure of his theme as postulated by Tate. But he still had faith in the quality of his writing, as indicated by the determination expressed in the Tate letter to write future poetry in the style and scope of *White Buildings*:

"***I shall be humbly grateful if the Bridge can fulfill simply the metaphorical inferences of its title . . . . You will admit our age (at least our predicament) to be one of transition . . . . If the Bridge, embodying as many anomalies as you find in it, yet contains as much authentic poetry here and there as even Winters grants,—then perhaps it can serve as at least the function of a link connecting certain chains of the past to certain chains and tendencies of the future . . . . Taggard, like Winters, isn't looking for poetry any more. Like Munson. they are both in pursuit of some cure-all. Poetry as poetry (and I don't mean merely decorative verse) isn't worth a second reading any more. Therefore—away with Kubla Khan, out with Marlowe, and to hell with Keats! It's a pity, I think. So many true things have a way of coming out all the better without the strain to sum up the universe in one impressive little pellet. I admit that I don't answer the requirements. My vision of poetry is too personal to 'answer the call' [of Taggard *et al*]. And if I ever write any more verse it will probably be at least as personal as the idiom of *White Buildings* whether anyone cares to look at it or not.

"This personal note is doubtless responsible for what you term as sentimentality in my attitude toward Whitman. It's true that my rhapsodic address to him in the Bridge exceeds any exact evaluation of the man. I realized that in the midst of the composition. But since you and I hold such divergent prejudices regarding the value of the materials and events that W. responded to, and especially as you, like so many others. never seem to have read his Democratic Vistas and other of his statements sharply decrying the materialism, industrialism, etc. of which you name him the guilty and hysterical spokesman, there isn't much use in my tabulating the qualified, yet persistent reasons I have for my admiration of him, and my allegiance to the positive and universal tendencies implicit in nearly all his best work. You've heard me roar at too many of his lines to doubt that I can spot his worst, I'm sure."

A good test of the genuine significance of a person's attitude is to see how well he tried to carry out the intention, particularly when there is no compulsion urging him to deviate from it. Such is the case with Crane's so-called disbelief in his powers. No one made Crane write poetry after he put the finishing touches on *The Bridge* in December 1929, yet it must be granted that, on the basis of subject matter at least, the following poems give indication of having been composed after that date: "To the Cloud Juggler," "The Sad Indian," "The Circumstance," "Purgatorio," "Havana Rose," possibly "By Nilus Once I Knew," and definitely "The Broken Tower," which we know to have been written in the spring of 1932.

Sufficient evidence relating to Crane's mental condition is available to warrant amateur diagnoses of paranoia, manic-depressive disorder, alcoholic dementia, etc., but it is enough for us to realize that the neuroticism of Crane's early years had developed into a psychotic condition accompanied by a progressive debilitation of the physical organism. In cases such as these, there is rarely a sudden change in the manifestations, mental or physical, which have characterized the mental disorder all along. Some-

times a decisive event occurs which accelerates the conclusion to be expected from a combination of symptoms.
The publication and reception of *The Bridge* played the
role of catalytic agent for Crane. But the symptoms had
by no means disappeared, for if they did the conclusion
would not have taken place. Now I have tried to show
that optimism and pessimism in unreasonable quantities
were properties of Crane's make-up. Since Crane put an
end to himself by suicide in 1932, it would be justifiable
to conclude that these two attributes, among others, continued to operate within him. Such was indeed the case.
Crane continued to write; he continued to have moments
in which the world appeared bright and worthwhile. At
such a time, his will to live was still strong and manifested
itself in the belligerent tone which marks portions of the
letter to Tate wherein Crane replied to the review of *The
Bridge*. There were other concretizations of this desire
as in August 1930, when he applied for a John Simon
Guggenheim Memorial Foundation fellowship, and the
statement of his plans for work expressed a wish to study
"characteristics of European culture, classical and romantic, with especial reference to contrasting elements implicit in the emergent features of a distinctive American
poetic consciousness." During the summer of 1930, Crane
made "a devout and satisfying study of the *Commedia* of
Dante"; in January 1931 he wrote from Chagrin Falls,
Ohio, that "Spinoza (Einstein's grandpop) furnishes plenty
of discipline" and that he could see "certain recoveries and
gains in poise" with himself; after he received the Guggenheim fellowship in March 1931, he wrote to Grünberg from Havana that he intended to "study and write
in Mexico for a whole year—on my Cortez play. Feel
as though I were starting out again fresher than ever!"

But there were also periods of depression, as sincerely and genuinely experienced as periods of happier nature.

"These are bewildering times for everyone, I suppose," he wrote Frank in February 1931. "I can't muster much of anything to say to anyone. I seem to have lost the faculty to even feel tension. A bad sign, I'm sure. When they all get it decided, Capitalism or Communism, then I'll probably be able to resume a few intensities; meanwhile there seems to be no sap in anything. I'd love to fight for—almost anything, but there seems to be no longer any real resistance. Maybe I'm only a disappointed romantic, after all. Or perhaps I've made too many affable compromises. I hope to discover the fault, whatever it is, before long . . . Present day America seems a long way off from the destiny I fancied when I wrote that poem The Bridge. In some ways Spengler must have been right."

The months Crane spent thereafter in Mexico were dominated by his inability to achieve a harmonious synthesis which would help him cope with "the chaotic values and frightful spiritual depression" which he felt oppressing the world. Although he defended Whitman against the accusation that the earlier poet was, consciously or otherwise, a bedfellow of those who had brought America to its expansive material heights in the nineteenth century, he, like Whitman, had early turned away from capitalist materialism and found hope, not for the present but for the future, in the concept of spiritual democracy. Since the factors which had turned him from the social world were real in the sense that they were composed of matter and not of spirit, the development of a spiritual faith proceeded in a vacuum into which the material supposedly did not enter. Once this spiritual faith was broken, the world of matter could offer no replacing faith; it had for too long been unimportant.

"Most all the letters we get from the north are pretty damned blue and dubious in tone," he wrote Grünberg on April 13, 1932. "Well, no wonder, of course. I sometimes wonder if I shouldn't go back and wail around the grave of capitalism myself, adopt sackcloth and ashes too, instead of the beautiful bright woolen serape worn around here on cold evenings. All my friends are turning at least a violent pink lately, and I'm almost convinced myself. In fact—by all the laws of logic I *am* convinced. But it goes so against my native grain—seeing nothing but red on the horizon."

Whereas Whitman had been able to subsidize his spiritual democracy with a persistent belief in humanity, Crane's paranoia prevented him from doing the same. Furthermore, since Crane had allegedly and in practice been more concerned with supra-logic than with conventional logic, it mattered little whether or not capitalism or communism were each correct or incorrect. Crane's reaction to one of the most important problems of his day was not one of indifference; it was more likely, and this is in a piece with his history, an inability to take it as seriously as it deserved. Vachel Lindsay's suicide by poison in December 1931 must have been a severe blow to Crane, for it marked the death of the most vocal of those old-guard poets— Sandburg and Masters complete the trio—who arose in the heyday of the Whitmanian renaissance, now so drastically deflated in the reality of breadline America and the symbolic death of Lindsay.

Crane made an error in judgment when he deviated from the aims of *White Buildings* and set himself the vastly more-complex task embodied in *The Bridge*. In other words, Crane did both himself and poetry less good when he underestimated the expression of personal emotion as a legitimate phase of art and attempted to create single-handed a philosophical and sociological myth in which, as it happened, personal emotion predominated when it should not have. He was equipped to write "Passage" and "Recitative," poems of great tragic character, and should have been content with being a poet of the negative. It was ironic that as late as November 1931 he could write to Eda Lou Walton: "These are dull times for poetry . . . I can't derive any satisfaction in the spinning out of mere personal moods and emotions." Although he had decided in 1930 to write poetry in this vein, he could not reconcile himself to a less-heroic role than his mind had conjured up for him in 1924. Yet when he was caught up once again a few months later in a love affair which promised him a social and physical re-alignment, "the old confidence" had him in its grip and he wrote "The Broken Tower," which he called "the most impressive poem I've started on in the last two years." This poem is as personal as any poem could be; it is unquestionably one of Crane's most magnificent pieces; and it reveals both in itself and in the way in which Crane developed it from an early draft that his powers were at their prime.

This time, however, it was too late for rebirth. "Have we the patience to endure? I say YES!" Crane wrote in February 1932. But when "The Broken Tower" was finished by Easter, he was abysmally unsure of it. He sent the poem to *Poetry* and to his friends Malcolm Cowley and Samuel Loveman, imploring Cowley to let him know what he thought of the poem—"prose or nonsense—whatever it may seem." His last days in Mexico were tragic. "If we're drunk enough," he wrote two weeks before his death, "someone dances a *jarabe*, a dance that is all vibrant gristle, emphasis and exhausting grace." That was how Hart Crane lived and died.†

† *Hart Crane committed suicide on April* 27, 1932, *by jumping into the sea from the deck of a steamer bearing him from Mexico to the United States.*

V
"THAT GREAT BRIDGE,
OUR MYTH, WHEREOF I SING"

16. TWO BRIDGES

I T IS A REMARKABLE COINCIDENCE THAT I SHOULD years later, have discovered that another person, by whom I mean you, should have had the same sentiments regarding Brooklyn Bridge which inspired the main theme and pattern of my poem." Thus Crane wrote to the Italian-American painter Joseph Stella in January 1929, and he demonstrated the depth of his feeling by arranging for the publication of Stella's essay, "The Brooklyn Bridge," in the Spring 1929 issue of *transition*. Actually, of course, Crane could not have avoided being acquainted with the work of one of the most important American artists of the early twentieth century and, in a later letter to Stella, Crane recalled having met him at a party given early in the 1920's by the editors of *The Little Review*. Creator of the futurist-cubist painting "Brooklyn Bridge" (1918), Stella enjoyed a considerable reputation as artist and interpreter of the American scene in the 1920's and the closing years of the preceding decade. Since he was an outstanding modern artist, criticism and reproductions of his work were featured in many of the advance-guard literary and art magazines which Crane regularly read. In 1921, for example, Hamilton Easter Field's *The Arts* carried an article on Stella and a reproduction of "Brooklyn Bridge"; the first issue of *Broom* (November 1921) contained "Brooklyn Bridge", and the second issue included more Stella works as well as a verbatim transcript of a speech on art made by Stella in New York. An entire issue of *The Little Review,* the one of Autumn 1922, was dedicated to Stella, and sixteen of his paintings, including "Brooklyn Bridge," were reproduced in its pages; the same number contained a letter by Crane, and there is good reason to suppose that Crane would have read the whole issue.

Whether or not Crane derived the symbol of the bridge from Stella's painting is an interesting speculation, and it may be that he did. But of greater import is a striking analogy to be drawn between the two men and their work which sets off Crane's poem in vivid highlight. Personally, both men were alike in various respects. Each was highly emotional, impressible by color and music, nurtured on art rather than theory, spontaneous in behaviour, and absolutely devoted to his craft. Both were moved by the grandeur and vitality of American industry, as well as by sympathy for outcasts and unfortunates, and incorporated the substance of American life in their work. Yet their artistic response to American life was not dominated by the superficial. "My chief concern . . ." Stella wrote about his early work, "was to catch life flowing unaware with its spontaneous eloquent aspects, not stiffened or deadened by the pose." Stella was as impressed with Pittsburgh as Crane with Akron in 1919: "It was a real revelation. Often shrouded by fog and smoke, her black mysterious mass cut in the middle by that fantastic, tortuous Alleghany River and like a battlefield, ever pulsating, throbbing with the innumerable explosions of its steel mills, was like the stunning realization of some of the most infernal regions sung by Dante." Like Crane, Stella too found inspiration for his artistry in the color, rainbows, trees, sea, and sky of West Indian islands, as well as in the lights, skyscrapers, harbor, and amusement palaces of metropolitan Manhattan.

Crane and Stella found a suitable symbol to embody the essence of America in the Brooklyn Bridge, both called upon Poe and Whitman to sustain them in the course of wrestling with the problem of expression, and both were imbued with religious emotion and awe before the bridge. The lines in which Stella recounts his experience while painting "Brooklyn Bridge" bear an occult resemblance to the imagery, spirit, and themes of *The Bridge*:

"My artistic faculties were lashed to exasperation of production. I felt urged by a *force* to mould a compact plasticity, lucid as crystal, that would reflect—with impassibility—the massive density, luridly accentuated by lightning, of the raging storm, in rivalry to the POE'S granitic fiery transparency revealing the swirling horrors of the Maelstrom . . . . Meanwhile the verse of Walt Whitman—soaring above as a white aeroplane of Help—was leading the sails of my Art through the blue vastity of Phantasy, while the fluid telegraph wires, trembling around, as if expecting to propagate a new musical message, like aerial guides leading to Immensity, were keeping me awake with an insatiable thirst for new adventures. I seized the object into which I could unburden all the knowledge springing from my present experience—'THE BROOKLYN BRIDGE.'

"Seen for the first time, as a weird metallic Apparition under a metallic sky, out of proportion with the winged lightness of its arch, traced for the conjunction of WORLDS, supported by the massive dark towers dominating the surrounding tumult of the surging skyscrapers with their gothic majesty sealed in the purity of their arches, the cables, like divine messages from above, transmitted to the vibrating coils, cutting and dividing into innumerable musical spaces the nude immensity of the sky, it impressed me as the shrine containing all the efforts of the new civilization of AMERICA—the eloquent meeting point of all the forces arising in a superb assertion of their powers, in APOTHEOSIS . . . . I felt deeply moved, as if on the threshold of a new religion or in the presence of a new DIVINITY."

"Brooklyn Bridge" is truly the product of the fury raging in Stella's lines. The canvas is non-representational; one sees dark tunnels studded with red and green lights at the bottom, skyscrapers standing geometrically at the rear of the composition, bolts of light leading upward along the mobile cables to the bridge tower, and above the blazing tumultuous scene a wide arc swinging across the very top of the canvas suggests the sky. Stella's painting is an admirable plastic representation of the "Atlantis" section of *The Bridge*, and Crane was so enthused with the affinity between the painting and his poem that he persuaded the Crosbys to include "Brooklyn Bridge" in full color as a frontispiece for their Black Sun Press edition of *The Bridge*; for technical reasons, however, the painting was never used and photographs by Walker Evans were substituted in its place in the printed volume.

Though "Brooklyn Bridge" and *The Bridge* were generated by the same emotional forces and attempted to express the same concept of American greatness and technological perfection, the scope of *The Bridge* was both larger and more impure than that of the painting. Stella broke up his object into geometrical and color patterns, but never to the extent of forsaking the bridge itself. Although his painting has a more limited symbolical significance as a result, the aesthetic responses which it evokes are firmly and clearly linked to the bridge, ultimately leading to the enhancement of the real bridge and audience-participation in Stella's emotional reaction to it. Crane, on the other hand, uses the bridge as a stepping-stone to all reality, and his original symbol is diffused and never again reconstituted as a whole. The bridge meant more to Crane than to Stella and, because it did so, it required the framework of a system of values to control it as it moved forth into time and space.

17. THE MYTH

THE READER OF CRANE'S ESSAY ON MODERN
poetry, which is appended to his *Collected
Poems*, will be struck with the emphasis which
it places on science and the machine. Seen
in any light, Crane's attention to science seems excessive.
Seen in the context of the 1920's, however, when the literary man emerged into the confusion and chaos which resulted from and contributed to the breakdown of the
established order of spiritual and material relationships
which the war of 1914 accelerated, it assumes a relative
importance which marks Crane's sensitivity to his age. It
also reveals the ambiguity of his response to scientific
theory and its practical application.

Crane feared science at the same time that he understood
the ineradicable position of importance it occupies in
modern life. This fear is indicated in the subordination of
plastic art and literature to mechanics and science which
threads the essay. According to Crane, it was the influence of science which led the artist to devote himself to
"analysis and discovery, the two basic concerns of
science . . ." Crane quite forgot that artists had been
analyzing and discovering long before the perfection of
the steam engine by Watt or the construction of the
dynamo by Faraday in the 1830's. The result of this un-

321

natural obeisance before science was his crowning of science as "the uncanonized Deity of the times," and his decision to "surrender, at least temporarily, to the sensations of urban life"; a decision which presumably expresses his intention to experience as intimately as possible the effects of science and the machine.

Crane's attitude invalidated the field of activity which he had assigned to poetry in a "Machine Age." "Its capacities for presenting the most complete synthesis of human values remain essentially immune from any of the so-called inroads of science," he wrote in his essay. Now if by "human values" Crane meant absolute guides which motivate our judgments independently of the temporal circumstances enveloping us, it would seem to be as unnecessary for the modern poet to "surrender" himself to twentieth-century machinery as it was for Wordsworth or Coleridge to subject themselves to the power looms operating in English textile mills. But since we are aware that Crane's philosophical idealism was a shaky affair, it is also likely that he realized that values are considerably influenced by the temporal aspects of an age, and that he therefore wished to encompass all the contemporary factors which produce our values. But how, we may well ask, is a poet to synthesize the values of an age if he surrenders to their causative factors? Is he not then in a position where he is dominated by them and rendered incapable of that understanding which must precede the process of synthesizing? Except for his ability to use the technical devices of poetry, such a poet would find himself in the same position as the mass of men who do not attempt to write poetry or to understand what is taking place in the world about them. The impasse which was thus created for Crane explains why early in the essay he states that the poet can synthesize human values, essen-

tially a philosophical task, and towards its close doubts
"That the modern poet can profitably assume the roles
of philosopher or theologian . . ." In other words, Crane
is setting himself up to be both thinker and non-thinker.

The same quandary is faced by Crane when he tackles
history in *The Bridge*.

"It seemed altogether ineffective," he wrote Otto Kahn in 1927 about his
treatment of history in the poem, "from the poetic standpoint, to approach this material from the purely chronological historic angle—
beginning with, say the landing of *The Mayflower*, continuing with a
résumé of the Revolution through the conquest of the West, etc. One
can get that viewpoint in any history primer. What I am after is an
assimilation of this experience, a more organic panorama, showing the
continuous and living evidence of the past in the inmost vital substance of the present."

As with machinery and science, Crane surrendered himself to history. But he neglected to evolve an attitude towards this history based upon critical examination. First
he decided that the past was fine, and then he concluded
that the present which had come forth from this past was
also fine. Having arrived at this position, the sequential
picture which a chronological study of history gives
seemed unnecessary, almost a source of possible confusion
for him. Because Crane made no effort to grasp the meaning of American history, *The Bridge* does not fulfill its
assigned task of organic assimilation, of relating the historical past and present in emotional terms; it could not be
expected to do so, because Crane did not attempt to arrive
at any mastery over the subject. Those parts of the poem
which seem to deal most obviously with history—"The
Dance," "Ave Maria," "Cutty Sark," "Indiana"—are actually studies of emotional consciousness, and the historical facts are little more than decorative trappings. This
is not to imply that Crane did not make a serious effort

to obtain genuine historical information: "Ave Maria" is constructed about extracts from Columbus' journal; the names recalled in "Cutty Sark" are those of actual clipper ships which made the long voyage from New England to Asia and Africa; "Indiana" refers to the mid-nineteenth century gold rush.

But often the historical background of the poems is not the result of contact with first-hand sources. It seems obvious, for example, that William Carlos Williams' *In the American Grain* (1925) furnished Crane with some of the facts and emphases of *The Bridge,* and we know from Crane's admission in a letter that he had read the book. As Horace Gregory has indicated in his introduction to the New Directions edition of the book, this indebtedness may be seen in "Ave Maria" and in "The Tunnel." But Williams approached American history directly, that is to say he read the documentary material of the times, and was thereby enabed to formulate a consistent viewpoint which integrates and strengthens his book. (This procedure in lieu of direct participation in the past.) The basic difference between Crane and Williams may be illustrated by considering a specific passage which occurs in both *The Bridge* and *In the American Grain.* In the April 1927 issue of *transition,* Kay Boyle reviewed Williams' book and in the course of so doing abridged a passage quoted by Williams from Strachey's history of colonial settlement in Virginia. This abridgement appears in *The Bridge* as the epigraph preceding "Powhatan's Daughter," which title is itself derived from the fuller passage of Strachey to be found in Williams. By satisfying himself with the inclusion of a third-hand reference, Crane not only demonstrated his uncertainty before the materials of history when the problem of selection arose, but also revealed how intrinsically unimpor-

tant the materials of history were to him. Under these
circumstances, it would have been impossible, as *The
Bridge* shows it to have been, for Crane to demonstrate
convincingly that the past with its glory and its ideals
lives in the present.

Crane wrote further to Otto Kahn in 1927: "What I
am really handling, you see, is the Myth of America."
And again in the same letter: "I am really writing an
epic of the modern consciousness . . ." But Crane was not
qualified to undertake the first part of his self-imposed
assignment. In a moment of misplaced enthusiasm, Frank
had praised Amy Lowell in 1919 for "the first serious
attempt to link the historic pasts of our several American
races to our own potential and emotional present. A real
cultural background, a quick sensory experience and a
firm conscious grasp of both must go into such work."
(*Our America*, 165.) Now this passage may have been
one of the factors which inspired Crane to launch forth
into *The Bridge*. Despite the desire that Crane might
have had to carry out the prescription, however, the pattern of his life prohibited the rational handling of theoretical material. Yet history and science were the two most
important ingredients in a project which united past and
present, ideas with machinery. Because he was unable to
cope with these subjects, *The Bridge* was fated to fall
to pieces as an organic structure. In his choice of a symbol
for the American myth, Crane was fortunate. What more
fitting symbol is there of American culture than a mechanical construction, the essence of expansion in its form, the
warmth of aesthetic life replaced by a levelling stream-
lining? Malinowski has written in his *Myth in Primitive
Psychology* (1927) that "the function of myth . . . is to
strengthen tradition and endow it with a greater value

and prestige by tracing it back to a higher, better, more supernatural reality of ancient events." This purpose could be served by the symbol of the bridge, but Crane did not know enough about it, pro or con, to make it function as the unifying integer of the poem. As a result, *The Bridge* could not become a critical myth. Because Crane did not believe in America, its culture and its values, he could not wholeheartedly embrace it. He lacked the naive faith of an Eddie Guest or an Elbert Hubbard, but he also lacked, and fortunately so, the ability to rationalize his dislikes so as to enable him to exclude them from an imaginary America which might then be satisfactory as a totality. Thus *The Bridge* does not present a myth buttressed by blind faith, and only a reader who is already convinced of America's manifest destiny will find a valid myth in the poem. Crane is not a myth-maker. Because there is no strong yea or nay in *The Bridge*, the poem is not an epic as well. The understanding and faith which Crane did not possess were requisite in the construction and maintenance of a central narrative, idea, or hero, one of which is necessary at the very least to provide the structural unity of an epic. The theology of Dante and the politics of Virgil, to consider but two epic myth-writers, are absent from *The Bridge* and are not replaced by a suitable substitute. The figure of the poet which moves through the poem is diffused and shadowy, receptive and negative rather than affective and positive, and conflicts with the symbol of the bridge as a unifying factor. The bridge symbol itself is inorganic as compared to the religious and political ideologies of Dante and Virgil. Life must be breathed into the bridge, it cannot be discovered therein. For this reason, perhaps, Crane was content to treat the bridge at length in only two poems,

"Proem" and "Atlantis." In each of these, it is not the Brooklyn Bridge which lives, but rather Crane's feelings about the bridge. But these feelings are not powerful enough to integrate the bridge with the symbolic references which Crane has attached to it. Much more stimulating and believable are the descriptive passages relating to the bridge in sunlight or moonlight. Thus, however, the bridge could not be a unifying factor in the poem.

The inadequacy of *The Bridge* as formal myth and epic is seen in its failure to stand as a unity. From one poem to another, there is often the loosest of transitions or else no transition at all. Neither the symbol nor the poet's faith are so sustained that they can span the large gaps of time, place, and theme which separate most of the poems in the sequence. As a result, *The Bridge* might be divided into four main groups of poems rather than the nine divisions set up by Crane. The first, consisting of "Proem" and "Atlantis," is devoted to a mystical consideration of the bridge. One poem complements the other, but "Proem" is far superior to "Atlantis" in organization, emotional intensity, and related imagery. The second group is generally devoted to the American past, and includes "Powhatan's Daughter," "Cutty Sark," and "Cape Hatteras." On another level, this group explores earth, sea, and air respectively. "Three Songs" forms a third group, with no thematic relationship to the poems which immediately precede or follow. But the theme of this little trilogy is related to the sexual content of the "Powhattan's Daughter" poems, and as such raises an interesting speculation. How did these poems find their way into *The Bridge*? The reader of the volume will observe that the climax of Crane's exploration of the earth in "Powhattan's Daughter" comes in "The Dance," when Crane merges with the

Indian chief and in his being is united with the earth, mother and symbol of fertility. It is necessary to stress the relationship of this search and consummation with Crane's Oedipus complex. Peculiarly enough, in the poem which follows "The Dance," "Indiana," the pioneer mother is seen saying goodbye to her son. If we follow the sexual implications, we can now appreciate the importance of "Three Songs" in *The Bridge*. They are related to the theme of frustration in "Indiana," and survey the failure of Crane's love for woman. The fourth group of poems in *The Bridge* contains "Quaker Hill," a bitter glance at the decay of Yankee tradition and the onslaught of bourgeois standards, and "The Tunnel"; both poems are Crane's comments on twentieth-century America, and in each case they are unhappy and disillusioned. If there is one over-all impression to be derived from *The Bridge*, it is that of overwhelming depression. Love is a failure in "Quaker Hill," "The Tunnel," and "Three Songs." In "The Dance," love ends in death. Death, indeed, is victor in *The Bridge*.

Nothing useful can be accomplished, therefore, by persisting in the consideration of *The Bridge* as a unified poem. It must be recognized that Crane, despite his ambition, was unqualified by virtue of his aesthetics, his life, and his lack of knowledge to handle a didactic poem or a poem of faith. *The Bridge* is a collection of individual lyrics of varying quality, and Crane's readers will derive greater pleasure and mete out more justice if they will cease mourning the failure of *The Bridge* as a whole, and begin acclaiming Crane for the poetic achievements which are lavishly strewn throughout its length. This approach would not be completely contrary to the intentions of Crane. He wrote Otto Kahn in 1927:

"Thousands of strands have had to be searched out, sorted and inter-woven . . . . It has taken a great deal of energy—which has not been so difficult to summon as the necessary patience to wait, simply wait much of the time—until my instinct assured me that I had assembled my material in proper order for a final welding into their natural form. For each section of the entire poem has presented its own uni-que problem of form, not alone in relation to the materials embodied within its separate confines, but also in relation to the other parts, *in series*, of the major design of the entire poem. Each is a separate canvas, as it were, yet none yields its entire significance when seen apart from the others. One might take the Sistine Chapel as an anal-ogy."

Crane's "instincts" were not powerful enough to success-fully cope with the problem of weaving the threads of symbolism throughout the poem. Thus he failed in part of his task. But the individual poems are separate can-vases as well, and many of these are completely or frag-mentarily great poetry.

18. "I'VE HEARD HIS SONG ABOVE ALL REASON LIFTING"

THE POEMS OF *The Bridge* ARE IMPORTANT contributions to the artistic heritage of man. They perform an all-significant function in increasing our apprehension and understanding of the aesthetic and emotional qualities of experience. In this respect, they are not dissimilar from the other pieces in the *Collected Poems*, the poems of *White Buildings, Key West*, and *Uncollected Poems*, and much of what I say here is equally applicable to them. The natural history of "Cape Hatteras":

> O, early following thee, I searched the hill
> Blue-writ and odor-firm with violets, 'til
> With June the mountain laurel broke through green
> And filled the forest with what clustrous sheen!
> Potomac lilies,—then the Pontiac rose,
> And Klondike edelweiss of occult snows!

the metropolitan nightmare of "The Tunnel":

> Performances, assortments, résumés—
> Up Times Square to Columbus Circle lights
> Channel the congresses, nightly sessions.
> Refractions of the thousand theatres, faces—
> Mysterious kitchens . . . . You shall search them all.

Some day by heart you'll learn each famous sight
And watch the curtain lift in hell's despite; . . .

the beauty of mechanisms in "Proem":

All afternoon the cloud-flown derricks turn . . .
Thy cables breathe the North Atlantic still.

* * *

Again the traffic lights that skim thy swift
Unfractioned idiom, immaculate sigh of stars,
Beading thy path—condense eternity:
And we have seen night lifted in thine arms.

the universal desire of "Southern Cross":

I wanted you . . . The embers of the Cross
Climbed aslant and huddling aromatically.
It is blood to remember; it is fire
To stammer back . . . It is
God—your namelessness. And the wash—

the profound human sympathy and love of "The River":

Behind
My father's cannery works I used to see
Rail-squatters ranged in nomad raillery,
The ancient men—wifeless or runaway
Hobo-trekkers that forever search
An empire wilderness of freight and rails.
Each seemed a child, like me, on a loose perch,
Holding to childhood like some termless play.
John, Jake or Charley, hopping the slow freight
—Memphis to Tallahassee—riding the rods,
Blind fists of nothing, humpty-dumpty clods.

passages such as these and poems like "Ave Maria," "The Harbor Dawn," and "Cutty Sark" stimulate and please the emotions, the senses, and finally the intelligence. They enrich our lives by their description, their psychological accuracy, their penetration beneath the surface of the routine, their revelation of that which the deadening influence of stereotyping pressure does its utmost to veil. Crane could do this because he was a man who reacted to experience, possessed physical and emotional intensity and sensitivity, and unsparingly communicated this receptivity with its resultant insight into the causes of experience in his poetry. "It's rather ghastly, almost surgery," he wrote Frank about the composition of "The Tunnel."

Most important of all, he was the fortunate possessor of a craftsmanship which was able to utilize and explore the fullest resources of his medium. Essentially, he was not an inventor of technique; echoes of Eliot, Cummings, Rimbaud, Greenberg, and others stand out in his work because lack of confidence characterizes Crane technically as well as intellectually. But he was aware of the potentialities of innovations, as well as of the wealth of tradition, and these he bent to the needs of his surgical dissection and re-creation. Much like James Joyce, he understood that language is connotative as well as denotative, fluid as well as solidified, and there have been few other poets in whom a word could assume the very essence of life, the plasticity of protoplasm, flowing in all directions with an enriching multiplicity of meanings. Because words were not mechanical counters to him but living organisms, there was no language which he did not make use of in his poetry: slang ("Caboose-like they go ruminating through/ Ohio, Indiana—*blind baggage*—"), colloquialisms ("Puffs from a riven stump far out behind/In *interborough* fissures of the mind . . . ?"), industrial terms ("Down Wall, from *girder* into street noon leaks,/ A *rip-tooth* of the sky's *acetylene*"), "improper" words ("and love/ A burnt match skating in a *urinal*—") (my italics, B. W.). His extreme reverence for words, however, sometimes led him to the use of poetic diction in an effort to achieve greater solemnity and dignity. The sentimentality of " 'til" used instead of "until," "wat'ry" in place of "watery," "grindest," "thine," and other obsolete words depreciates the reverent and religious quality of the passages in which they occur, and stands out in contrast to the genuinely original language which Crane is capable of exploiting.

But probably the most consequential aspect of Crane's language is it ambiguity, at one and the same time the cause of confusion as well as reward in a reader's mind, and it can be illustrated by the consideration of a word employed by Crane in "Cape Hatteras":

> Wheeled swiftly, wings emerge from larval-silver hangars.
> Taut motors surge, space-gnawing, into flight;
> Through sparkling visibility, outspread, unsleeping,
> Wings clip the last peripheries of light . . .
> Tellurian wind-sleuths on dawn patrol,
> Each plane a hurtling javelin of winged ordnance,
> Bristle the heights above a screeching gale to hover;
> Surely no eye that Sunward Escadrille can cover!

The word I have reference to is "tellurian," the adjective describing "wind-sleuths." The definition of "tellurian" as an adjective in *Webster's New International Dictionary* is "Of, pertaining to, or characteristic of, the earth," and the origin of the word is traced back to Tellus, the Roman earth goddess. Since Crane was familiar with earth goddesses as a result of his research for *The Bridge*, he may have come to "tellurian" by way of Tellus, and the adjective may have been intended to show the earthly origin of the planes. Another definition of "tellurian," this time as a noun, is that it is a device used to demonstrate that day and night are caused by the earth's rotation on its axis, as well as similar astronomical theories. In this sense, Crane may have conceived of the planes as explorers of space in the same way that the tellurian probes into the spatial movements of the earth. Finally, the dictionary refers to the chemical element "tellurium." When we are informed that this element has a silvery-white color, it is possible to conjecture that Crane may have coined "tellurian" as an adjective to describe the color of the planes. Either of these implications—origin, function, or color—is applicable to the context. The question of choice will only occur to the reader who is aware of all the possible meanings involved; for him there may seem to be confusion, but when it is seen that all meanings are suitable, the image of "wind-sleuths" will be qualified on three levels, and the airplane will stand revealed as a complex construction rather than a simple device of transportation.

Still another aspect of Crane's attitude to language was his love of ornamental words, just as the painter is entranced with the existence of color quite apart from its relationship to other colors on a canvas. An illustration might be the syllable "qu" as it occurred in two words. In "Ave Maria" Crane recounted the throwing overboard of records in a cask. Although his manuscripts show that the word was spelled "cask" in early versions, the final spelling was "casque," which denotes a military helmet. Crane may have been led to this change by reading in the dictionary that "cask" was an obsolete way of referring to "casque"; this may have induced him to think that "casque" might just as easily be an obsolete term for "cask." But the change was probably not so deliberately planned; he simply liked the look of the word "casque." This hypothesis is substantiated in part by Crane's treatment of the word "Escadrille," which occurs in the passage from "Cape Hatteras" quoted just above. Crane's manuscripts, and "Cape Hatteras" itself, show that he

The reader

made himself familiar with technical aviation terminology before he began writing the poem; yet throughout his manuscripts the word "Escadrille" is mis-spelled "Esquadrille." The cause could not have been ignorance, but was more likely an expression of Crane's love for the ornamental spelling of the word.

The symbolism of Crane is intricate. I think the analysis of a few passages and symbols will show how much we must bring to the poems, and how much we can derive from contact with them. The opening stanzas of the "Proem" are the first lines of *The Bridge* which are read, and they are among the lines which many who admire Crane's work have memorized for their beauty of imagery and music:

> How many dawns, chill from his rippling rest
> The seagull's wings shall dip and pivot him,
> Shedding white rings of tumult, building high
> Over the chained bay waters Liberty—
>
> Then with inviolate curve, forsake our eyes
> As apparitional as sails that cross
> Some page of figures to be filed away;
> —Till elevators drop us from our day . . .

The color "white" is important in this poem because it serves as a transitional surface for the later outpouring of yellow (fire and light) which predominates as the poem builds up passion and devotion. It is only mentioned once. Nevertheless, the sensation of whiteness is overpowering, because the symbols connote whiteness: the dawn is white in contrast to the black night; chillness carries a picture of frosty white; the seagull is a white bird; the motion of his wings in the air creates the illusion of white circles; sails are white, and so is the paper which bears the "figures." Crane is moving from the mundane to the abstract in this poem as he did in *Faustus and Helen*. Such movement is physical and mental: the seagull is a symbol of escape, rising from the cold waters whose ripples suggest chains, and in the course of his flight he draws the poet's eye to the Statue of Liberty, symbol of freedom; the wings of the seagull fuse into the vision of sails which suggest the freedom Crane saw in the sea, as well as the actual forward motion of a boat; the sails are submerged in the "page of figures" constituting the aborting material with which the poet works in order to earn a living, but the act of fusing sails with paper has freed the poet from the emotional and physical grip exercised over him by his workaday task.

The interfusion of color and idea by means of symbols in "Proem" was not an accidental happening. Crane did it deliberately here, and he was as deliberate in other poems. A comment he made to Frank in 1926 about the version of "Atlantis" sent to the latter on January 18th of that year bears that out: "It is symphonic in including the convergence of all the strands separately detailed in antecedent sections of the poem—Columbus, conquests of water, land, etc., Pokahantus, subways, offices, etc. etc. I dare congratulate myself in having found some liberation for my condensed metaphorical habit in a form as symphonic (at least so attempted) as this. The bridge, in becoming a ship, a world, a woman, a tremendous harp (as it does finally) seems really to have a career. I have attempted to induce the same feelings of elation, etc.—like being carried forward and upward simultaneously—both in imagery, rhythm and repetition, that one experiences in walking across my beloved Brooklyn Bridge . . . " The reader does not need this comment to comprehend all the metaphors and symbols in the lines. It is but necessary to understand the method, and a good part of the so-called obscurity will vanish. But much of the difficulty cannot be conjured away. For example, in order to appreciate the fact that the bridge is being envisioned as a harp in "Atlantis," the reader must be aware of the musical hints scattered in the lines and fuse these recognitions with the references to strings which are fairly numerous in the poems; he must then think back over the lines he has read. If he recalls that "Proem" contained a vision of the bridge as a "harp," he will have met Crane's intention face to face. Another example of irremediable difficulty is in order. The Indian chief in "The Dance" is called "Maquokeeta"; Crane wrote to Frank about this name: "It may interest you to know that the name, Maquokeeta, derives from an amusing source,—and may not be exact—but a beautiful rum-drinking, firewater wassailing friend of mine,—a NY taxi-driver (independant!) who hails from Missouri and is part Indian, has a middle name, Maquokeeta, which he alludes to as meaning 'big river.' Some tribal term or other . . ." Unlike the Indian name Pocahontas, the name Maquokeeta has very little denotative or connotative value for most readers. Nevertheless, Crane used it for a purpose related to his poem: it refers back to the symbol of the river in "the River"; just as the river became a serpent in the last stanza, so does Maquokeeta become a serpent. This is personal symbolism as much as some of the esoteric symbolism of *The Waste Land*, and both Eliot's poem and *The Bridge* lack organic unity in part because of it.

Crane was a person to whom music offered a constant delight. This music did not have to be formal; it could be the street songs of children, the ebb and flow of the sea, the movement of dancing bodies, the rhythmic contraction of muscles. This catholicity of aural response is visible in *The Bridge*, where Crane employs meter and rhythm to provide the water flow of "Ave Maria," the playfulness of "Virginia," the dignity of the concluding stanzas of "The River," the staccato confusion of twentieth-century culture in "The River's" opening, the dream quality of "Cutty Sark," and one of the most striking examples of success: the musical transition in the last lines of "The Tunnel" from the desperate hysteria of city life to the ecstatic hope and devotion of the following section, "Atlantis." Crane overlooked few of the devices which subtly unite poetic lines in terms of musical contrast and repetition: assonance, alliteration, consonance, pauses, and other verbal features offer satisfaction in themselves and in their direct effect upon meaning. Crane's proficiency with musical effect is almost always successful, even when it approaches the limit of pure sound, as in the syllabic interplay of "Cutty Sark":

> Pennants, parabolas—
> clipper dreams indelible and ranging,
> baronial white on lucky blue!

> Perennial—*Cutty*—trophied—*Sark!*

> *   *   *

> a long tack keeping—
> > *Taeping?*
> > *Ariel?*

He is equally successful in a more restricted vein, as in the rhymed quatrains of "The Dance" or in the powerful blank verse which studs portions of *The Bridge*. The second stanza of "Ave Maria" reveals Crane's ability to control a formal metrical pattern and to introduce elements of contrast therein. The reader will note how the addition of extra syllables in the second and seventh lines fortifies the change of viewpoint and emotional tone by giving the lines an unexpected emphasis, how the metrical uniformity of the iambic pentameter is varied by means of pauses introduced at different spots in the lines, and how the rigid movement of a line from beginning to end is often exchanged for a flexible flow of sound from the end of a line directly into the following line. Crane's blank verse is powerful, quite unlike the quieter tone of the form as employed by Frost and Eliot. But he was not yet a master of blank verse. If one wanted to set up a comparison, one might say that Crane's blank verse was midway between Milton's "Lycidas," with its irregular rhymes and its heroic couplets, and *Paradise Lost*, with its defiant elimination of "the jingling sound of like endings." Immaturity was not the ultimate reason for Crane's impurity of form. Some critics have properly observed that the structural unity of *The Bridge* was imperiled by Crane's utilization of a great variety of metrical and stanzaic forms. The situation is similar in Eliot's *The Waste Land*, which probably furnished inspiration in this respect for Crane. As a believer in the Coleridgean doctrine of organic form, Crane was consistent in permitting the material to take a hand in shaping the form. The success of the applicability of this doctrine is revealed in "The Tunnel." But even there, the freedom afforded by the doctrine is violated in part by its tendency to allow the poet an unimaginative out. The sixth stanza is a mélange of overheard conversation. But Crane, in reporting it, has added neither music nor imagery with the exception of the simile

" 'like a pigeon's muddy dream'." This is perilously close to the realism of journalism. Another example of uncontrolled form might be the tenth stanza of "The River," with its rhyme royal, heroic couplets, irregular rhymes, and final rhymed quatrain.

19. METHOD OF COMPOSITION

THE PLAN OF THIS BOOK FORBIDS AN EXHAUSTIVE study of Crane's method of writing, yet enough can be said at this time to dispel some illusions and demonstrate some realities. For those who wish to delve further into the problem, I have appended as many manuscript versions of "Atlantis" as I have been able to find; the progress of the poem from 1923 until the final printed version of 1930 may thus be studied. The comments I make from this point on are based on the examination of a considerable number of worksheets of *The Bridge* given by Crane to his friend Samuel Loveman.

Crane appears to have prepared himself for writing by reading books pertaining both directly and indirectly to the theme of his projected poem. In the winter of 1926, while working on "Ave Maria" and "Atlantis," he was reading a diversified list of books: William Prescott's *History of the Reign of Ferdinand and Isabella*, Waldo Frank's *Virgin Spain*, D. H. Lawrence's *The Plumed Serpent*, A. N. Whitehead's *Science and the Modern World*, A. S. Hildebrand's *Magellan*, Herman Melville's *White Jacket*, Aeschylus' *Oresteia*, an edition of Columbus' jour-

341

nal, a book on whaling and whaling ships, and others. Horton has shown how carefully Crane read Columbus' journal and utilized both the facts and language of the journal in "Ave Maria"; the spirit of *Virgin Spain's* final chapter, "The Port of Columbus," also went into that poem. In various ways, too, the other books influenced Crane stylistically, ideologically, or factually.

While in the course of reading, or after his research was completed, Crane wrote an outline which was intended to serve as a compilation of ideas and a guide in the completion of the poem. Sometimes the outline was a sketch of the symbolism, as in the case of "Ave Maria":

"Columbus' will—knowledge
Isabella's will—Christ
Fernando's will—gold

—3 ships
—2 destroyed

1 remaining will, Columbus"

For "Cape Hatteras," Crane prepared an outline of the themes to be treated:

" (1) Cape—land—combustion
conceive as a giant turning
(2) *Powerhouse*
(3) *Offshoot*—Kitty Hawk
Take off
(4) War—in general
(5) Resolution (Whitman)"

Accompanying the outline of a projected poem, Crane jotted down words, phrases, and lines of poetry which he thought might be used in the poem. On the sheet containing the "Ave Maria" outline, the following items occur:

" 'And they who mutinied against her Christ
who gave the jewels (for whom she offered jewels)
went with his lust for gold, alas!
Fernando thou!' "†

" O sun that *point*est Cathay
The Promised Land, the sphere
riddle—ream—adjourn—nearing—bounty
And it is ghostly here
  the watch—man of the watch—strong gales & high seas
    running—made sail—steering by wind—yards braced—
    stood way on the starboard tack—rudder reams the path"
Sun that dost point and prove and leavest not my argument
Thy sphere that droppest back into the sea"

On one of the manuscript sheets containing rough drafts of "The River," the following list of words is to be found:

"buckskin mare—corral—harness—footing—snort—rump—
    ford—bridle reins—haunches—leash—tiers—shale—
    clotted with sumach"

Strangely, Crane did not use most of these words and phrases in the poems: in "Ave Maria," only the nautical term "watch" has been incorporated; "The Promised Land" was finally used in "Quaker Hill," written three years after the note was made by Crane; Crane probably intended to write something about horses in "The River," but never did . . . only the words "shale" and "sumach" are in the poem.

After Crane had absorbed his research data and the special words and phrases which he believed might find a place in the poem to be written, he waited until the form to be used announced itself to him, and the emotion pent-up while he read (and jotted down his notes) grew so overpowering that he could no longer contain it within himself. Then he hastily wrote a first draft, sometimes one

† *Italicized words deleted by Crane.*

line, sometimes two or more lines.   These initial fragments
were then worked and reworked when Crane was calmer
and more deliberate, until finally the completed poem was
evolved. A partial reconstruction of Crane's poetic mind
can be made from his manuscript worksheets. The passage
which follows is an early draft of the opening stanza of
"Ave Maria":

> "*now* Louis de St Angel now
> Be with me, *Don Fray Juan Perez*, for I
>   cannot   more *belie*   deny
> Have seen what courtiers *would not believe*
> Be with me now who rode a donkey to the Queen
> Be witness *with me* now before the tides can *take away*
>   reined my suit   read the world **away**
> O you *rode a donkey* to the Queen that doubtful day"†

Words seem to have been suggested to Crane both audi-
torily and visually: "believe" gives way to "belie" of
similar spelling, and "belie" is in turn superseded by "deny"
of similar sound. Imagery is transmuted: the donkey ride
is replaced by an image which is only one aspect of the
ride, but expresses more strongly the nervous tension of
the ride; in the course of this compression of imagery, the
fact that a donkey is being ridden is lost, and the reader
is required to couple the verb "reined" with the unrelated
noun "suit" . . . by synthesizing the two words, the reader
repeats Crane's process and simultaneously obtains a more
vivid impression of the urgency and nature of the action.

The next passage quoted is an almost final version of
the closing stanza of "Ave Maria":

> "Spun toil of heaven's cordons mustering
> In panic rings all sails charged to the far
> Hushed moveless fields and pendant seething wheat

† *Italicized words deleted by Crane.*

> Of knowledge,—now across Thy brows the will
> Unhooded moves! Down-*flowing* from the poles   flashing
> Beyond the sea's blue crying towers a-sway
> Yet *And* ceded by white sails, meridians fall,—
> Thy purpose still one shore beyond desire:
>
> *Te Deum Laudamus!*   *Thy hand is fire"* †

Three observations based on these lines are relevant to a consideration of Crane's method. The stanza is fairly well unified and flows logically from beginning to end. It differs from the final version in several respects. The most important difference is the physical and syntactical rearrangement of lines: the sixth line above is the eighth line in "Ave Maria," where it reads: "The sea's green crying towers a-sway, Beyond." Crane obviously wanted to heighten the emotional tension of the stanza, as well as to increase the sense of distance from the "shore beyond desire". The change accomplishes these aims, but it does so at the cost of destroying the logical thread, and is an illustration of Crane's interest in the operation of super-logic. If similar linear arrangements can be recognized as the result of an identical motivation, the reader should be able to traverse the poems with greater ease and enjoyment. Crane changed the color of the water from "blue" to "green"—no element of confusion is added, but it serves as an example of Crane's arbitrary method when an onomatopoeic effect is available: the longer sound of "green" bolstering the wave-rhythm and the "r" sound adding to the verbal repetition of "r's." Such revisions have their danger in the possibility of sound triumphing over sense; fortunately, this does not occur too often. The third observation concerns itself with a matter of punctuation.

† *"And" and "flowing" were deleted by Crane, and italicized by me.*
B.W.

Crane's punctuation, like that of other good poets, is often careless. In the seventh line of the stanza quoted immediately above, we are told that "meridians fall,—", thereby receiving the impression that human limitations and measurements of time and space are being obliterated before the desire for knowledge. In the version as it finally stands in "Ave Maria":

> And biassed by full sails, meridians reel
> Thy purpose—still one shore beyond desire!

Crane has neglected to indicate by a point of punctuation that "meridians" do not "reel Thy purpose," with the result that the original meaning of the image is lost. Coincidentally, the purpose which the dash should serve, interrupting the sentence in order that the infinite nature of the last five words be accentuated by prolonging the reading time, is negated when the words "meridians reel" are run on into "Thy purpose." Much of Crane's so-called obscurity can be brushed aside by the addition of proper punctuation. He himself was not unaware of the need for careful punctuation in his work. While preparing *The Bridge* in 1929 for publication by the Black Sun Press, he wrote Caresse Crosby about a revised version of "Cutty Sark"; "I have changed very little—what little has been only to promote clarity—which includes a more generous sprinkling of punctuation. So please use this instead of the version you've had."

Although many of Crane's poetical effects were the products of mental synthesis before actual writing commenced, others took form after a rough substance had been poured on the page and refined. Some of Crane's extraordinary imagery was fashioned in this manner. For example, "Quaker Hill" contains a line in which the gaze of a bird from eye to object is seen as the stem of a plant: "So, must we from the hawk's far stemming view, . . ." An earlier version of the line was far less exciting: "O from the hawk's far soaring view."

Poe observed in *The Philosophy of Composition* that:

"Most writers—poets in especial—prefer having it understood that they compose by a species of fine frenzy—an ecstatic intuition—and would positively shudder at letting the public take a peep behind the scenes, at the elaborate and vacillating crudities of thought—at the true purposes seized only at the last moment—at the innumerable glimpses of idea that arrived not at the maturity of full view—at the fully matured fancies discarded in despair as unmanageable—at the cautious selections and rejections—at the painful erasures and interpolations . . ."

My purpose in violating Crane's workshop privacy, however briefly, was to break down a myth, more widely accepted than Crane's own *Bridge*, in which Crane is viewed as composing his poetry in a state of hysteria heightened by artificial stimulants. Undoubtedly Crane did find it easier to set his initial versions on paper while gripped by "the logic of ecstasy," and this inspirational tension could be and was often induced in his case by alcohol, sometimes by love. Yet this relates only to the composition of first drafts. Thereafter, like most poets, he went through the painful process described by Poe, revising and polishing until he had attained a version satisfactory to him in every respect. Because the refining process, carried on under more sober conditions, produced the same miraculous results as those achieved under a state of exaltation, Crane must be considered as possessing a poetic genius which did not require artificial stimulation and could have developed without it. There was sufficient imaginative power within him to carry him along as unsensationally as many a more sedate, although less gifted, poet. In making this necessary clarification, I am defending Crane not only from his detractors and from those who have misunderstood him, but also from the misconceptions which his own statements and way of life have buttressed.

Proem: *To Brooklyn Bridge*

THE POEM IS MULTIFUNCTIONAL. MOST OBVIOUSLY, it dedicates the sequence of poems which follow to the Bridge. It is, thereafter, a eulogy of the attributes which Crane finds in the Bridge. And, finally, the poem is an evocation to the Bridge to provide its blessing and its scope to the poem which bears its name. The first seven stanzas contain one of Crane's favorite themes, that of man's blindness to inherent essence, and this is developed to indicate that the Bridge has not been understood. The Bridge, according to Crane, is a "terrific threshold" in which all phases of human and cosmic experience are embodied: love and death; time with its flow of day and night; season and year; eternity with its stars and sun. From this threshold it is possible to fulfill "the prophet's pledge," stepping forward with the Bridge to span the seas, the continent of America, and the universe, thereby creating with this "harp and altar" a myth in which God will be celebrated. The poem is altogether superb in its music, imagery, and most of its structure. Beginning with the description of New York Harbor in a leisurely pace, it follows the slow wheeling of the seagull until suddenly the

bottom drops out of the reverie, just as we have often felt
while descending in an elavator. The movement speeds
up in tune with the motion picture and is subdued in the
majesty of the Bridge. Once again it accelerates in the
fifth stanza until the sky burns its way down the receding edges of the skyscrapers, and then reaches a passionate
crescendo:

> O harp and altar, of the fury fused,
> (How could mere toil align thy choiring strings!)
> Terrific threshold of the prophet's pledge,
> Prayer of pariah, and the lover's cry,—

The last stanzas are solemn and entreating, and close with
the supplication to the Bridge:

> O Sleepless as the river under thee,
> Vaulting the sea, the prairies' dreaming sod,
> Unto us lowliest sometime sweep, descend
> And of the curveship lend a myth to God.

I have already mentioned the change made by Crane in
the last line of the second stanza. This introduces, I be-
live, a confusion in the temporal sequence of the poem
which lessens its structural neatness. The poem flows
from the beginning of a day to its end; dawn (stanza 1),
arrival at work (stanza 2), noon (stanza 6), night (stanza
9). I am leaving out of consideration the movement from
day into year into the simultaneity of past, present, and future which occurs in stanzas 10 and 11.) By substituting
the line which refers to the close of the day's work, as
it now stands, the sequence of time is distorted.

I. AVE MARIA

The poem is a soliloquy by Columbus as his ship nears
Spain; the sun sinking behind him brings up memories of
the Cathay which he has discovered. The lines are a com-

plex interweaving of reflections in which the triumph of Columbus is divested of its material implications—gold and land, political power and riches—and becomes an addition to human knowledge leading to the revelation of the glory of God and the spiritual kingdoms reposing in the uplifted human heart. The opening stanza sounds off on a note of self-vindication and closes with a statement of the fulfillment of his pledges. Columbus observes the sea, and gives way to a feeling of terror before its mystery; he fears lest the ship, which he believes to be the sole remaining of the original three, may be lost beneath the waves. The possibility of shipwreck leads his mind back to the discovery of Cathay, when he stood watch and saw a light on shore. The return voyage is recalled together with the storm that threatened to capsize them . . . Columbus thinks of the written record of the discovery which was sealed in a cask and flung into the sea. But throughout the storm and apprehension, his faith was unshaken. As his fear mounts now, he pleads with the Virgin Mary for her mercy and intercession. The infinite pity of Mary "dissuades the abyss," and a luminous rainbow becomes visible. The brilliant sky reminds Columbus of the lustful Ferdinand, eager for material gain, and he predicts misery for the bountiful new world if Ferdinand forgets the teachings of Christ and rapaciously exploits Cathay. The eighth stanza predicts the successful conclusion of the return voyage as "Some Angelus environs the cordage tree." The last stanzas are a prayer of thanksgiving to God, in which His supremacy over man and the universe is extolled, and He is experienced as a divine revelation. God is lord over the death, birth, and love of man; He orders destruction, but demonstrates His guardianship of the sailor "by the corposant"; faith in Him strengthens the knowledge derived from scientific instruments such as the compass. The last stanza suggests a foresight of the American continent of fruitful fields and wheat which the harmonious marriage of science and faith has produced.

II. POWHATAN'S DAUGHTER

The Harbor Dawn

The poet awakens from his vision of Columbus in a room near New York Harbor, the scene of the "Proem." Sleep still crowds his mind and body. Harbors sounds, dull but insistent, remind him that he must get up into twentieth-century America. But he does not rise. Instead, in the moment when sleep is leaving and before he wakes into consciousness, he imagines that there is a woman beside him. He is passionately stirred, and physical union with this phantasmal woman follows. As he regains his full consciousness, the woman has vanished. The poem closes with the poet's determination to find her.

It is obvious now that the poet is the bearer of the "seed" which Columbus brought to the new world. In "Ave Maria" the poet lost his identity and became Columbus. Now he has again become a modern man.

Van Winkle

The poet has left his room and is on his way to work. Memories of the historical figures of America whom he knew in childhood crowd his mind as the music of a hand-organ frees him of his maturity, and suddenly Rip Van Winkle is walking beside him. Rip helps him forget his job and his responsibilities, and the poet assumes the child-like innocence of the old Dutch figure. Now childhood remembrances become even more vivid, and time loses its clarity to become both "here" and "there." The poet boards the subway on his way to work, a sudden reversion to maturity, but actually no longer bound to the routine of his existence.

The form of this poem is important in understanding the similar movement of "The River." It begins and ends with an adult activity: walking to the subway, which is the means of transportation to the poet's place of employment, and entering the subway. In between, the poet's consciousness returns to childhood and is overpowered by his reflections thereon.

The River

This section is, I believe, the first one to fail in its structural and poetic quality, and I shall endeavour to explain why by considering it in relationship to Crane's expressed intentions for it. In the letter sent to Otto Kahn on September 12, 1927, Crane wrote:

"The subway is simply a figurative, psychological 'vehicle' for transporting the reader to the Middle West. He lands on the railroad tracks in the company of several tramps in the twilight. The extravagance of the first twenty-three lines of this section is an intentional burlesque on the cultural confusion of the present—a great conglomeration of noises analogous to the strident impression of a fast express rushing by. The rhythm is jazz. Thenceforward the rhythm settles down to a steady pedestrian gait, like that of wanderers plodding along. My tramps are psychological vehicles, also. Their wanderings, as you will notice, carry the reader into interior after interior, all of it funneled by the Mississippi. They are the left-overs of the pioneers in at least this respect—that abstractly their wanderings carry the readers through certain experiences roughly parallel to that of the traders, adventurers, Boone and others. I think I have caught some of the essential spirit of the Great Valley here, and in the process have approached the primal world of the Indian, which emerges with a full orchestra in the succeeding dance."

Examination of the poem shows that it falls into three divisions, only the first two of which are marked off one from the other by the poet. The third one begins with the words "And Pullman breakfasters glide."

In the first division, the poet rides the subway, converted into a railroad train, to reach the west. His eyes are assaulted by advertising billboards, and his mind depressed with thoughts of the degeneration of art, religion, and national feeling, and the distortions of science and commerce. From this sophisticated twentieth-century world the poet is suddenly separated, and he finds himself alongside three tramps watching the train dwindle into the distance. The lines impressionistically satirizing the decadence of American culture are anti-climatic here, since "The River" represents a spirit of positive national enthusiasm and geographical expansion; these lines properly belong in "The Tunnel."

The second division finds the poet travelling with the tramps. These men are symbols of rootlessness: children, clowns, social outcasts, wifeless ones; they are honest and emotional, unaffected by industry and science. They are also symbols of the tributaries which feed into the Mississippi River; with them Crane explores the great river basin from the Rockies to the Atlantic coast. In two fine passages, Crane combines his sympathy for the tramps and the quality of his exploration:†

> Yet they touch something like a key perhaps.
> From pole to pole across the hills, the states
> —They know a body under the wide rain;
> Youngsters with eyes like fjords, old reprobates
> With racetrack jargon,—dotting immensity
> They lurk across her, knowing her yonder breast
> Snow-silvered, sumac-stained or smoky blue—
> Is past the valley-sleepers, south or west.
> —As I have trod the rumorous midnights, too, . . .

† *The first stanza of this pair has already been quoted in Section 18, this book. It is the fifth passage of poetry from the beginning of the section.*

Crane goes on to say that the tramps' relationship with the body of America is direct, contemporary, limited: they have no sense of continuity with the past. Thus we are made to understand that spatial exploration is by itself an inadequate way in which to discover Pocahontas, for she is composed of "Time like a serpent down her shoulder, dark,/ And space, an eaglet's wing, laid on her hair." The unity of this division resides in the narrative progression, as well as in the frame provided between the telegraph wires disapprovingly referred to later. But in between there seems to be a good deal of unnecessary and vague writing. The second and third stanzas could be eliminated completely, since they add nothing to the first of the two stanzas in this division. (I am aware of the four lines containing such good imagery as "the elemental gist of unwalled winds.") I do not think, furthermore, that Crane accomplishes much by his references to place-names wherever they occur, since they evoke only sentimental responses. Finally, I fail to be either abstractly or concretely stimulated by the tramps' movements to envision the adventures of pioneers.

The third devision re-introduces the railroad train. This leads the poet to Cairo, where the Ohio River merges with the Missisippi. There is a suggestion that the river-men celebrated in folk song will, like the tramps, help the poet explore the final winding of the river. The closing stanzas establish the meaning of the river—its symbolic encompassing of the temporal flow of American history and human fate (life, death, and immortality). All "feed the River," those "born pioneers in time's despite" and those —"Sheriff, Brakeman and Authority"—who persecute them. The slow rhythms of the opening stanza are tightened, and emerge with full majestic power in brilliant rhymed quatrains describing the river:

You will not hear it as the sea; even stone
Is not more hushed by gravity . . . But slow,
As loth to take more tribute—sliding prone
Like one whose eyes were buried long ago.

The River, spreading, flows—and spends your dream.
What are you, lost within this tideless spell?
You are your father's father, and the stream—
A liquid theme that floating niggers swell.

Damp tonnage and alluvial march of days—
Nights turbid, vascular with silted shale
And roots surrendered down of moraine clays:
The Mississippi drinks the farthest dale.

Finally the river reaches the end of the long journey in
which it has drawn within its waters the soil of over a
million square miles of land, the heart of a continent, and
exultantly raises itself like a serpent (time) to plunge into
the sea:

The River lifts itself from its long bed,

Poised wholly on its dream, a mustard glow
Tortured with history, its one will—flow!
—The Passion spreads in wide tongues, choked and slow,
Meeting the Gulf, hosannas silently below.

The Dance

Like "The River," but more so, this poem is structur-
ally imperfect. It is difficult to keep track of the symbolism and the imagery is extremely elusive. Consequently, I have thought it advisable to consider the poem
in the light of Crane's explanation in 1927 to Otto Kahn:

"Here one is on the pure mythical and smoky soil at last! Not only
do I describe the conflict between the two races in this dance—I also
become identified with the Indian and his world before it is over
which is the only method of ever really possessing the Indian and his
world as a cultural factor. I think I really succeed in getting under the
skin of this glorious and dying animal, and in terms of expression, in

symbols, which he, himself, would comprehend. Pocahontas (the continent) is the common basis of our meeting; she survives the extinction of the Indian who finally, after being assumed into the elements of nature (as he understood them) persists only as a kind of an 'eye' in the sky, or as a star that hangs between day and night—'the twilight's dim perpetual throne'."

"The River" contained a vision of Pocahontas and the myths of the North American Indians. There was also an implication that the pioneers were incapable of appreciating Pocahontas and Indian mythology. "The Dance" brings the poet back directly to the world of the Indian, and he becomes one with them in a Dionysian whirl of music and sacrifice. The variety of references in the poem is great indeed, and in our review we will attempt to name only the most important.

The first two stanzas are intended to be a preliminary summation of that which is to transpire in the poem, as well as a continuation of the vision of Pocahontas. Against the temporal background of the seasons, Pocohontas is united in love with the "winter king," who is the symbol of both time and the white conquering race. From this union of space and time, the earth bears fruit, and seemingly dies at the moment of fruition. The second stanza is obscure, but I interpret it as the failure of the "winter king" to find Pocahontas again in "drouth" and "sands." On the other hand, Crane may be referring to the idea that Pocohontas is not really dead, but has temporarily turned into desert land in the absence of the American Indian. This would seem to tie in with his comment to Kahn about the Indian race's death and Pocahontas' survival. The third stanza indicates that the vision of Pocahontas is receding into time, and supplies motivation for the rest of the poem. The poet then proceeds up a river by boat; this is a counter-movement to the picture of the river in the preceding poem, and we gather that the poet is continuing the recession into time which began in "Van Winkle." The boat is abandoned, and the poet climbs higher into the Appalachians until, like Rip Van Winkle, he finds himself suddenly on the outskirts of an Indian village. An Indian dance seems to be in progress, and the poet is caught up in its passionate music:

> A distant cloud, a thunder-bud—it grew,
> That blanket of the skies: the padded foot
> Within,—I heard it; 'til its rhythm drew,
> —Siphoned the black pool from the heart's hot root!

The next group of nine stanzas are involved; Maquokeeta, an Indian chief, is being burned at the stake . . . the chief is also the plumed serpent, symbol of fused space and time . . . the immolation of the chief is symbolic of the subjection of the Indians to the white man . . . the death-throes of the chief merge with the beat and motion of the dancers, the poet identifies himself physically and psychically with the death of the Indian race, and an ecstatic series of stanzas bring the dance to an exultant climax of death and immortality:

> Spears and assemblies: black drums thrusting on—
> O yelling battlements,—I too, was liege
> To rainbows currying each pulsant bone:
> Surpassed the circumstance, danced out the siege!
>
> And buzzard-circleted, screamed from the stake;
> I could not pick the arrows from my side . . . .
>
> O, like the lizard in the furious noon,
> That drops his legs and colors in the sun,
> —And laughs, pure serpent, Time itself, and moon
> Of his own fate, I saw thy change begun!
>
> And saw thee dive to kiss that destiny
> Like one white meteor, sacrosanct and blent

At last with all that's consummate and free
There, where the first and last gods keep thy tent.

The chief and the Indian race survive only as spirits
in the sky; their frenzied appeal to fetish and medicine man
for restoration to the heyday of their racial existence:

Sprout, horn!
Spark, tooth! Medicine-man, relent, restore—
Lie to us,—dance us back the tribal morn!

is unavailing. The physical remains of the Indians, like the
skins of a serpent, are absorbed into the earth, married to
Pocahontas. The remaining six stanzas are a hymn of praise
to time and space, the Indian chief; earth, Pocahontas; and
God, the "Brave" of Indian religion. The first, second, and
fifth of the group are directed to the chief, and assure him
that his sacrifice has been beneficial to Pocahontas ("Thy
freedom is her largesse, Prince . . ."). The third and
fourth stanzas are lyric expressions of the fertile wonder
and beauty of Pocahontas: the fourth is a magnificent wed-
ding of sense and sound:

West, west and south! winds over Cumberland
And winds across the llano grass resume
Her hair's warm sibilance. Her breasts are fanned
O stream by slope and vineyard—into bloom!

The sixth and last stanza celebrates the union of time and
space in the infinite bliss of God's embrace.

"The Dance," again like "The River," is divided into
several subsections. Of these, only one is indicated by the
poet. Recognition of these subsections facilitates the understanding of the poem, and adds to its beauty. I believe
the following divisions are valid: (1) stanzas 1-2; (2) stanza 3; (3) stanzas 4-9; (4) stanza 10; (5) stanzas 11-20; (6)
stanzas 21-26. If the poem is evaluated in terms of these
subsections, there is meaning and progression from begin-

ning to end. The individual subsections, however, are not all of equal quality. The first, as we have seen, raises too many questions which Crane does not answer. In the second, one wonders why Pocahontas retires "loth, Disturbed and destined"—there is no reason for this description, unless it is supposed to be provocative, in which case we knew as early as "The Harbor Dawn" that Pocahontas is elusive and the poet is determined to find her. The symbolism and imagery of the fifth subsection are so obscurely interwoven, the association of phrases so abrupt, that it would have been difficult to untangle the ideas had not Crane's statement of intentions been available. Few readers, I believe, can discern from these stanzas that Crane is describing "the conflict between the two races." The most that is actually expressed in these lines, not that it is insufficient, is a combination of passionate physical movement and spiritual frenzy, ablaze with fire and bursting from the bounds of the body, which eventuates in the beatitude of death and eternal spiritual life. The final subsection could, I believe, gain in cumulative force and in significance of meaning if the stanzas were rearranged as I have indicated: stanzas 21, 22, 25, 23, 24, 26.

Indiana

The poet has achieved the goal of his search, union with Pocahontas, in "The Dance." Therefore he retraces his steps now to the present. Pocahontas is envisioned here as a pioneer mother, symbol of the maternal fertility of the American earth. The ballad form in which the stanzas are cast appears to have restrained Crane's imagery; the lines are prosaic and probably the worst in *The Bridge*, excepting some of the decorative lines in "Cape Hatteras." When we remember that this section was among the last composed for *The Bridge*, and that Crane was in the depths of despair and disbelief, the results are explicable. Even so, the poem presents an interesting problem as poetic failure.

There is no need to recapitulate the narrative in this poem: it is best to concentrate on Crane's intentions. According to one synopisis which Crane sent to Otto Kahn:

"This monologue of a woman of the 50's is a farewell to her son who is leaving their Indiana farm for the sea. By her story of the encounter with the half-breed squaw woman and her child, passed on the road back from the western gold-fields, I hope to signalize the transference of the role of Pocohontas to the pioneer white, or from another angle, the absorption of this Pocahontas symbolism by the pioneer white woman. The significance of this anecdote is perhaps clearer without further explanation. This section is psychologically a summary of Powhatan's Daughter in its entirety. The entire section is 'framed' by the sea again. In the beginning, Columbus and the Harbor Dawn, —finally the departure of the first-born for a life before the mast."

I submit that it is difficult, if not impossible, for the reader to experience the two points elucidated by Crane: the "transference" and the psychological summation of the preceding sections of the poem from "Ave Maria" through "The Dance." It is worth noting that where Whitman handles the transference theme in "The Sleepers," a poem which may have influenced "Indiana," he is equally unsuccessful and for the same reason: the emotional continuity between mother and Indian squaw is not deeply felt by the poet. It is finally communicated to us in this poem only by the gloss which Crane put alongside the first stanza of the poem. The summary nature of the poem is also completely lacking. Here we have a perfect example of the failure, not of poetic genius, but of belief. It is also organically unsound to sum up one part of the poem, "Ave Maria," in another part of the same poem, "Powhattan's Daughter." The effect is anti-climactic. But the poem also fails to epitomize the preceding sections of "Powhatan's Daughter." We have been presented with the successful

conclusion of the poet's search for union with the organic
heart of the American continent, nation, people.   Suddenly we read in "Indiana" a narrative and an implication
that contradict the emotional triumph which has been developed.   Remembering "Ave Maria" and its warning to
Fernando, symbol of material lust, we are informed that
the American continent has been exploited in the mad
hunt for gold ("those years—But gilded promise, yielded
to us never, And barren tears"), that the manifest destiny
of the nation has evaporated, and that the future of America resides in the sea.   The effect of "Powhatan's Daughter" is completely dissipated, even if we extend ourselves
and assume that Crane was unable to conceive of any other
way in which to introduce the maritime period which followed and is handled in "Cutty Sark."   Perhaps the best
indication of Crane's anti-climactic effect in "Indiana" is
seen in an earlier synopsis of this section which, unfortunately, was never developed: "It will be the monologue
of an Indiana farmer; time, about 1860.   He has failed in
the gold-rush and is returned to till the soil.   His monologue is a farewell to his son, who is leaving for a life on
the sea.   It is a lyrical summary of the period of conquest, and his wife, the mother who died on the way back
from the gold-rush, is alluded to in a way which implies
her succession to the nature-symbolism of Pocahontas."
Although there is an implied social criticism in this outline,
the beauty and ever-present fertility of the soil painted so
lyrically in "The River" and "The Dance" is not cast out,
and the movement to the sea comes as a new form of exploration and not as the result of futility.

III. CUTTY SARK

This section is an extraordinarily brilliant piece of impressionistic poetry, one in which Crane reveals the mas-

tery of music and language at his command. The poet
is back in the twentieth century, in a saloon along the lower New York water-front. He is listening to a drunken
sailor reminisce, and both he and the sailor are drinking
rum. The sailor's eyes are green, the color of the sea;
the recitation of his adventures partakes of the flowing
and ebbing of the sea, or the movement of a boat among
the waves. He seems to represent the spirit of the sea,
its timelessness and its fascination ("I don't want to know
what time it is . . . No—I can't live on land—!"). Interwoven between the description of the action and the
sailor's words is the music of a piano-player, and the song
being played on the machine "weaves" and "wreathes"
visions of undersea creatures and the sunken paradise of
Plato and the ancients:

> *Rose of Stamboul O coral Queen—*
> *teased remnants of the skeletons of cities—*
> *and galleries, galleries of watergutted lava*
> *snarling stone—green—drums—drown—*
>
> •••
>
> *ATLANTIS ROSE drums wreathe the rose,*
> *the star floats burning in a gulf of tears*
> *and sleep another thousand—*

The piano stops playing, and the poet walks across Brooklyn Bridge to his home. The first mention of the Bridge
as a bridge since "Proem" occurs here, and it is obvious
that Crane intended to show it "vaulting the sea"
("Proem") and bringing the vision of the sailing ships
which follow. The introduction of the Bridge is arbitrarily done, however, and is unconvincing as a demonstration of its powers and meaning. I am much more convinced that the rum and the high talk were contributory
to the vision, and the preliminary lines permit the reader

to reach only that conclusion and no other. Crane is bearing down a little too hard on his symbol, and it does not carry its assigned burden. The remaining lines provide a beautiful nostalgic picture of the clipper ships sailing along. Sailor chanteys alternate with descriptions of sails against the sky, flags, rigging, ship movements—all blended with music in which words and ships "weave" and "heave" together:

>   Pennants, parabolas—
> clipper dreams indelible and ranging,
> baronial white on lucky blue!
>   Perennial-*Cutty*-trophied-*Sark*!
> *Thermopylae, Black Prince, Flying Cloud* through Sunda
> —scarfed of foam, their bellies veered green esplanades,
> locked in wind-humors, ran their eastings down;
>   *at Java head freshened the nip*
>   (*sweet opium and tea!*)
>   and turned and left us on the lee . . .

Beginning with "Indiana," the explicit thread of myth began to disintegrate. "Cutty Sark" continues this disintegration, and here the myth becomes fainter in the romantic remembrance of vanished glories. Except for the opening of the poem in the present, there is no relationship between the clipper era and our own which is developed explicitly in the poem. The lines beginning "*ATLANTIS ROSE*," which I have quoted above, indicate that the sea, rather than the American continent and nation, is assuming a dominant position because of its fusion of time and space. Previously, we will recall, it was Pocahontas who had been enriched by this fusion. This new element is a reversion to the spirit of "Voyages," and would seem to indicate that Crane's faith in his myth was weakened while he wrote this poem.

IV. CAPE HATTERAS

This section is a failure, both as complete poem and as a contributory part of *The Bridge*. The first few lines detail a geological history of Cape Hatteras. Having explored land and sea in previous poems, Crane returns home. Whitman is introduced; the reference reinforces Crane's expression of faith that the American continent is "surcharged with sweetness" which the fiery origin of the earth and its subsequent history has promised us. There is a suggestion that the human being cannot read history properly, and alternates between a long-range view and one which is limited to the circle of his own confusions and personality. The conquest of space by the airplane provides man with new hope ("Seeing himself an atom in a shroud—/ Man hears himself an engine in a cloud!"). Whitman is reintroduced; the poet questions Whitman about the possibility of faith in the modern "labyrinth," and reassures himself that the future, despite our materialistic "Exchange" and "stocks," is as inevitably hopeful as the rejuvenating "second timber" which follows in the wake of exploited earth. The fifth stanza reverts to the theme of energy stated in the opening lines. But now man develops his own energy by harnessing the stars in dynamoes; the lines are so excessive and rhetorical that I believe Crane intended to show the absolute ruthlessness of scientific invention and the danger inherent in permitting it to control our lives; the question "Towards what?" implies fear and doubt of the outcome. The following stanzas devote themselves to a discussion of the airplane, a mechanical device powered with machine-made energy. The airplane possesses potentialities for good and evil; man has employed the airplane and the ship for purposes of destruction and war; the tenth stanza would seem to indicate that a civilization which misuses scienific invention must perish. The idea of these stanzas is reminiscent of Ouspensky's belief that science in itself is of no value to the future without the development of a new type of man. The lines describing the airplane's first flight and its participation in aerial warfare are unadulterated fustian for the most part, the outcome of Crane's desire to show his virtuosity and the resultant expansion of a few images to unnecessary lengths. The last subsection (stanzas 11-18) is an apostrophe to Whitman, to whom the poet declares his eternal devotion. Whitman affords faith in the possibilities of the fruitful employment of science, of the continuity of the American earth, of the immortality of the soul. Whitman is envisioned as someone who absorbed the tragedy of destruction and materialism which "from Appomattox stretched to Somme" and who, as idea, bridge, and prophet, points the way to spiritual consummation. With the exception of scattered lines and a few stanzas (4, 10, 11, 13), the poem is an abysmal deterioration from Crane's usual level of writing. The symbolism which Crane employed with controlled genius in "The Dance" and "The River" is dissipated here, and is extremely difficult to untangle. Probably the most important single idea to be derived from the poem as it stands is the welcoming atttude which Crane has for death.

Like "Indiana," this poem was written under the pressure of despair and forced enthusiasm. The bright outlines of the myth had long vanished. The extent to which Crane contrived in the poem is to be seen in the manuscript worksheets which he left behind. Here words and phrases are dashed off, combined, and fused into lines and passages. On several of these sheets I have found lines which were discarded when Crane prepared the final version of "Cape Hatteras." They are poignant evidences of the state of his spirit. "Lead me past logic and beyond the graceful carp of wit," he wrote, in a line following the fourth stanza. And in another, echoing his cry—"Years of the Modern! Propulsions toward what capes?"—he wrote: "What if we falter sometimes in our faith!"

The connection of "Cape Hatteras" with the other parts of *The Bridge* is haphazard. Had Crane been content to limit its theme to the exploration of space, it would have followed "Powhatan's Daughter" with its exploration of the earth and "Cutty Sark" with its exploration of the sea in logical progression. Since Crane was oppressed at the time he wrote "Cape Hatteras" with the question of ebbing faith, he could not resist an expression of his confidence in Whitman. The effectiveness of the last poem, "Atlantis," is lessened thereby, for the organic validity of the bridge symbol should not have to depend upon the significance of Whitman.

V. THREE SONGS

This sequence of poems does not follow "Cape Hatteras" in any logical progression. It would seem more desirable, if it is assumed that Pocahontas, the American continent, is being viewed from several angles, for Crane to have placed these poems in the "Powhatan's Daughter" part which precedes them. Since he obviously did not, they further increase the logical disintegration of *The Bridge*. As with many of Crane's poems, these three songs evoke many responses, some of which Crane planned and some of which he was unaware. As individual lyrics, they rank high among Crane's total production, and go far toward establishing the great stature of Crane's genius.

"Southern Cross," the first, is an expression of intense desire and longing for woman:

> I wanted you, nameless Woman of the South,
> No wraith, but utterly—as still more alone
> The Southern Cross takes night
> And lifts her girdles from her, one by one— . . .

The poet has no specific woman in mind: she is the archetype of womanhood in all her aspects ("Eve! Magdalene!
or Mary, you?"). As the poem develops, it is seen that
Crane is concerned with Eve in this particular poem. Eve
is the mother of mankind, the symbol of innocence tricked
by evil and fated to give birth in sorrow . . . Crane desires
her in life, not in death. But he is unable to have her for
himself, even though she is "docile, alas, from many arms."
A backward glance at his womanless life rouses him into
churning bitterness:

> And this long wake of phosphor,
>   iridescent
> Furrow of all our travel—trailed derision!
> Eyes crumble at its kiss. Its long-drawn spell
> Incites a yell. Slid on that backward vision
> The mind is churned to spittle, whispering hell.

The interweaving of constellation, night, woman, and sea
is masterfully accomplished, making this one of Crane's
best lyrics.

The second song, "National Winter Garden," is a brilliant portrayal of the overwhelming power of sexual lust.
The woman envisioned is a burlesque dancer twisting in
the postures of that animal passion which she hopes to
arouse in the audience:

> Outspoken buttocks in pink beads
> Invite the necessary cloudy clinch
> Of bandy eyes . . . No extra mufflings here:
> The world's one flagrant, sweating cinch.

Strangely enough, however, the poet reacts with revulsion, as though he came from another world:

> Always you wait for someone else though, always—
> (Then rush the nearest exit through the smoke). . . .
> We flee her spasm through a fleshless door. . . .

Finally, in an outburst of ironic contempt, the poet mocks
the erotic relationship between men and women:

> Yet, to the empty trapeze of your flesh,
> O Magdalene, each comes back to die alone.
> Then you, the burlesque of our lust—and faith,
> Lug us back lifeward—bone by infant bone.

The stanza is extremely complex, and has many levels of
meaning. I cannot help feeling that Crane is making very
important observations. One, that sexual union is a combination of physical and spiritual love, which is perverted
by biology into the production of the species. Another,
that the child thus created is but another aspect of the im-
pregnating male. Probably the greatest effect of the stanza is one which gives strength to the entire poem—Crane's
conclusion that lust is no means for absolving us from
the problems of life . . . we return to life from which we
have thought to escape. The relevancy of this poem to
Crane's own life is inescapable.

The trio of poems is closed with "Virginia," a light-
hearted vision of woman as a youthful virgin office-worker
in the Woolworth Building. There are implications of the
Virgin Mary, unapproachable and pure, in the poem which
bring the sequence to a consistent end. There is much
charm in Crane's reference to the Rapunzel story in lines
15 and 16, which he derived from the Grimm Brothers'
collection of folk tales.

VI. QUAKER HILL

This poem can best be considered with Crane's own
estimate of it in mind. "Quaker Hill is not, after all," he

wrote Caresse Crosby on December 26, 1929, "one of the major sections of the poem; it is rather by way of an 'accent mark' that it is valuable at all." The poem is seemingly an afterthought, and Crane probably wrote it to take the place of three projected sections which were never completed—"The Cyder Cask," "The Calgary Express," and "1927 Whistles." Regarded as an integral portion of *The Bridge*, it is as unnecessary as "Three Songs" and anti-climactic as a totality where "The River" and "Cape Hatteras" were anti-climactic only in part. Preceding "The Tunnel" so closely, it robs the latter section of its force and contains material which might much better have been incorporated in "The Tunnel." "Quaker Hill" may be seen, however, as the extension of the opening lines of "The River." Although it is longer than that passage, it is not more developed in scope, and therefore does not form a more revealing contribution.

I think we must agree that "Quaker Hill" achieves its true level as an individual lyric, and as such it is not completely successful either. The failure resides, I think, in the sentimentality of the contrasts which Crane makes. For example, there is a dearth of genuine feeling in the fifth stanza, and it is vividly revealed in the fifth and sixth lines:

> Fresh from the radio in the old Meeting House
> (Now the New Avalon Hotel) volcanoes roar . . .

Surely we are entitled to expect more from Crane than the simple apposition of discordant elements. The same method was applied in the opening passage of "The River," but there it was frankly impressionistic, whereas here we are led to expect a poetic synthesis which does not take place. Another example is in order: ever since Eliot in a typically anti-Semitic way epitomized modern vulgarity

and the decay of tradition in the figure of the Jew—"My
house is a decayed house,/ And the jew squats on the
window sill, the owner, . . . " ("Gerontion")—it has
become fashionable for poets to juxtapose "foreign" names
alongside "native" names for the same purposes.   One
must give Eliot credit at the very least for believing in
his symbols and for being able to develop them in some
detail, as in his poem "Burbank with a Baedeker: Bleistein
with a Cigar."   Others have been content to do no more
than couple "Burbank" with "Bleistein" through lack of
skill or belief, or both.   I think offhand of Cummings'
"FINKLESTEIN (FRITZ) LIVES AT THE RITZ . . ."
as an example; Crane's lines in "Quaker Hill" are just as
inept and unconvincing:

> What cunning neighbors history has in fine!
> The woodlouse mortgages the ancient deal
> Table that Powitzky buys for only nine-
> Ty-five at Adams' auction,—eats the seal, . . .

These contrasts are essential in developing the theme of the
glorious past beclouded by a sorry present, and they drag
the theme with them in their fall.

If the poem is stripped of its historical implications and
treated solely as a reflection upon the tawdriness of life
acting upon a sensitive individual, it assumes a greater tragic significance.   Even so, only the last two stanzas stand
together as an integrated whole, although the first two
stanzas, re-written, might well have been joined to them.
There is a singular poignancy in the closing lines:

> So, must we from the hawk's far stemming view,
> Must we descend as worm's eye to construe
> Our love of all we touch, and take it to the Gate
> As humbly as a guest who knows himself too late,
> His news already told? Yes, while the heart is wrung,
> Arise—yes, take this sheaf of dust upon your tongue!

In one last angelus lift throbbing throat—
Listen, transmuting silence with that stilly note

Of pain that Emily, that Isadora knew!
While high from dim elm-chancels hung with dew,
That triple-noted clause of moonlight—
Yes, whip-poor-will, unhusks the heart of fright,
Breaks us and saves yes, breaks the heart, yet yields
That patience that is armour and that shields
Love from despair—when love foresees the end—
Leaf after autumnal leaf
                       break off,
                                  descend—
                                            descend—

This is undiluted Crane at his best, feeling deeply and conveying his despair and resignation in couplets whose rhythm beautifully matches the varying movements of idea
and action.   When we remember that these were among
the last lines written for *The Bridge*, their tragic import
becomes evident.

VII. THE TUNNEL

"The Tunnel" is one of the four sections completed
by Crane of the six sections of *The Bridge* projected by
him in 1926. It occupies its intended place as a foil to the
triumph and light of the last section ("Atlantis"). From a
traditional point of view, it deals with the underground
cavern into which the living descend in order to receive instruction about the future from the dead. Concretely, it is
a poem about a subway ride from Manhattan to Brooklyn
via the East River tunnel.

It is as a description of an urban experience that the
poem attains its greatest distinction, and it is unquestionably one of Crane's most successfully-integrated pieces.
The horrors of subway transportation—the noise, the brok-
en conversations, the staring eyes, the lights, the spasmodic

stops and starts at stations, the rounding of curves—are masterfully presented. An illustration of Crane's controlled technique in this poem will show how carefully it is managed:

> Be minimum, then, to swim the hiving swarms
> Out of the Square, the Circle burning bright—
> Avoid the glass doors gyring at your right,
> Where boxed alone a second, eyes take fright
> —Quite unprepared rush naked back to light:
> And down beside the turnstile press the coin
> Into the slot. The gongs already rattle.

There is much distinctive imagery and verbal art in these few lines, but I only wish to point out one example. The stanza provides the transition from the street into the subway. The poet cautions himself to avoid the revolving doors in whose plate glass he sees his reflected image; there is a suggestion here that the whirling motion will carry him away into darkness; he manages to avoid the doors and reaches the turnstile leading to the trains. Obviously, the escape from the revolving doors is ironic, for the subway is a whirling plunge into a more devastating darkness. But it sets the tone for the lines that follow. In order to convey this claustrophobic mood, Crane has boldly and vividly ended four lines with identical single rhymes which close off each line and cumulatively provide a barrier for the movement of the entire stanza. Thus the sensitive reader is subtly prepared for the compressing, trapping effect of the subway trip.

The poem does not fulfill its function of being an integral part of The Bridge. The duality of machinery, its capacity for good and its capacity for evil, was already demonstrated in "Cape Hatteras." The subway is not intrinsically more dangerous to humanity, therefore, than the airplane or any other mechanical contrivance. Follow-

ing "Quaker Hill," wherein humanity itself was shown to
be destructive and insensitive, the reader finds himself concluding that the subway passengers who jabber in the
poet's presence are as repulsive as the subway itself. It is
they who lead him to conclude: "The phonographs of
hades in the brain/ Are tunnels that re-wind themselves,
and love/ A burnt match skating in a urinal— . . ." The
contrast of the subway's depth with the height of airplane
and bridge is too mechanical an observation to have much
significance. In the end, the poem reveals the complete
helplessness of man in his mechanical jungle, a situation
comparable to Columbus' predicament when caught by
storm in "Ave Maria." In that section, as in "The Tunnel," God is a "Hand of Fire" who sears us and gathers
from us the "Kiss of our agony." The real issue, then, is
not the destructive potentiality of machinery, but rather
our faith that the deeds and plans of God are always
justifiable. Having furnished us with a concrete picture
of the jungle, as in the vision of Poe:

> Whose head is swinging from the swollen strap?
> Whose body smokes along the bitten rails,
> Bursts from a smoldering bundle far behind
> In back forks of the chasms of the brain,—
> Puffs from a riven stump far out behind
> In interborough fissures of the mind . . . ?

it is difficult for Crane to convince us of God's holy purposes with these lines:

> And yet, like Lazarus, to feel the slope,
> The sod and billow breaking,—lifting ground,
> —A sound of waters bending astride the sky
> Unceasing with some Word that will not die . . . !

It is significant that the stanza in which these lines occur,
and the very image of the new world lifting itself from

the depths, should have been taken in transmuted form from a version of "Atlantis" written long before "The Tunnel." One could almost believe that Crane had written "The Tunnel" and then, appalled at its implications, inserted lines whose occurrence in a later poem could not be relied upon to offset the immediate negative impact of "The Tunnel."

VIII. ATLANTIS

The conclusion of *The Bridge*, strangely enough, literally defeats the background purpose of the whole poem. Crane thought of "Atlantis" as the "mystic consummation toward which all other sections of the poem converge." This seems to be more accurate as a description of the version sent to Waldo Frank on January 18, 1926 than it is of the version which appears in *The Bridge*. As in "Cape Hatteras," Crane's tendency toward ethereal verbosity reaches a peak which strains the reader. Ideas hover on the verge of expression, then float away in a mist of inexactitude. With the meanings of "Quaker Hill," "The Tunnel," and other sections of the poem in mind, it is quite impossible to be carried away by the animistic vision of the Bridge embodied in these lines. Crane was aware of the prime defect of this section, and wrote in January 1926 to Frank: "This section seems a little transcendental in tendency at present,—but I think that the pediments of the other sections will show it not to have been."

Among the most interesting things about this section are its title and tenth stanza. Readers of the Appendix will note that, as late as the summer of 1926, the title of the section was not "Atlantis." Nor, indeed, was the present tenth stanza a part of the poem. But at the end of that summer, Crane had decided to call the last section

"Atlantis," and some time thereafter he wrote the tenth stanza and inserted it into the poem. The significance of the name "Atlantis" is at least twofold. According to Plato, Atlantis was an ideal society in which the people were "great spirits, uniting gentleness with wisdom . . . [who] despised everything but virtue . . . thinking lightly of the possession of gold and other property . . . they were sober . . ." Atlantis was situated on an island fashioned by Poseidon, god of sea and water, and it was physically beautiful and socially harmonious. As described by Plato in *Critias*, Atlantis assumed the proportions of a legendary Utopia, and throughout the ages men have sought to identify one or another island or continent or land as Atlantis. The search for the contemporary equivalent or location of Atlantis was inspired not only by the vision of Atlantis as a Utopian ideal, something superior to reality, but because Plato went on to say in *Timaeus* that the island of Atlantis had sunk back into the sea from which Poseidon had created it. Thus, any new tract of land, or any land for which one had particular attachments, came to be called the original Atlantis. Palestine, for example, was once thought to be the location of Atlantis. When America was discovered, there were many who thought that the new continent was the site of the ancient Atlantis. On the one hand, then, Atlantis may be said to symbolize the ideality of life for which many men strive. The other aspect of Atlantis is dark; it represents corruption and oblivion. *Critias* relates this picture of dissolution well: "By such reflections and by the continuance in them [people of Atlantis] of a divine nature, the qualities which we have described grew and increased among them; but when the divine portion began to fade away, and became diluted too often and too much with the mortal admixture, and the human nature got the upper hand, they then being unable to bear their fortune, behaved unseemly, and to him who had an eye to see, grew visibly debased, for they were losing the fairest of their precious gifts . . ." *Critias* breaks off in the middle of its description of the fate of Atlantis, but *Timaeus* adds the story of Atlantis' imperialistic conquest of much of Europe and Africa and its final disappearance into the sea. It will be remembered that the original ideal land for which *The Bridge* was searching was Cathay, the Cathay for which Columbus had sailed forth, and Crane had said of Cathay in a letter: "Cathay . . . [is] an attitude of spirit, rather than material conquest throughout, of course." The incorporation of Atlantis as a new element of *The Bridge* in 1926, both in "Cutty Sark" and in the last section, introduces a doubt about the spirituality of Cathay. Atlantis, like Cathay, is an ideal. But whereas Cathay is for us an unsullied symbol, Atlantis is a symbol of the triumph of the material over the spirit. The juxtaposition of these two ideals leads to a transference of the fuller implications of Atlantis to Cathay. The doubt which Crane expressed in the final stanza of the section was reinforced:

> Is it Cathay,
> Now pity steeps the grass and rainbows ring
> The serpent with the eagle in the leaves . . . ?

In other words, the value of America is being questioned, and since America and its future is the backbone of *The Bridge*, "Atlantis" negates the myth of which Crane speaks throughout. One can now understand the significance which the vision of Poe plays in "The Tunnel." It is true that Poe was afraid of science, that he wrote "A Descent into the Maelstrom," and that Roderick Usher in Poe's story, "The Fall of the House of Usher," painted a

picture of a fantastic tunnel. But it is more important
to realize that the lines which Crane uses in "The Tunnel" to compare his situation with Poe's are reworked
from Poe's poem "The City in the Sea":

> —And did their riding eyes right through your side,
> And did their eyes like unwashed platters ride?
> And Death, aloft,—gigantically down
> Probing through you—toward me, O evermore!

In that poem Poe described his vision of a city of the dead
sinking into the sea, its towers and riches unable to preserve it from its fate, "While, from a proud tower in the
town／ Death looks gigantically down." In "Cutty Sark,"
Crane had described a sunken Atlantis. Here, in "Atlantis," Crane shows a sinking poet praying to a floating island
for rescue:

> Atlantis,—hold thy floating singer late!

But the island had sunk below the waves many thousands
of years before, and the poet's belief in his myth had likewise been gone for many a year. So in the end "Atlantis"
was not a suitable roof, and the preceding sections did not
serve as supports for it.

APPENDIX

The first part of the Appendix contains twenty-nine poems by Hart Crane which do not appear in his *Collected Poems*. Thirteen poems, including the three translations from the French of Jules Laforgue, appeared in magazines during Crane's lifetime; a fourteenth, "In A Court," was posthumously printed in a magazine. The remaining fifteen poems have never appeared in printed form, and are taken from Crane's manuscripts; approximate dates of composition are indicated wherever known.

Ten of the twelve prose items by Hart Crane which are included in the second part of the Appendix have been reprinted from magazines; the letter written to Gorham Munson and the undated critical fragment have been taken from Crane's manuscripts. A version of the letter to Munson which differs from the one included here will be found appended to Philip Horton's *Hart Crane* (1937). Other prose written by Crane which is available and has not been reprinted includes an unpublished essay of 1925 (appended to Horton's book); the essay "Modern Poetry" (appended to Crane's *Collected Poems*); and two letters to Otto Kahn which were posthumously printed in *The Hound and Horn* (July-September 1934).

379

The lines of poetry which comprise the third part of this Appendix offer an opportunity for a close study of Crane's method of composition. They include all available drafts from 1923 to 1927 of the "Atlantis" section of *The Bridge*; with the exception of the lines sent to Underwood, they were transcribed from manuscript. In order to facilitate reference to these lines, I have italicized all words which Crane deleted; words which were added by him to the first draft of a line, or a group of lines, have been enclosed in brackets. It will be of interest to note that Crane wrote poetry directly on the typewriter, as well as by hand; the illustrations of manuscripts in this book show Crane's typical worksheets (see plates 3, 6, and 7).

A. UNCOLLECTED POETRY

C 33†

HE HAS woven rose-vines
About the empty heart of night,
And vented his long mellowed wines
Of dreaming on the desert white
With searing sophistry.
And he tented with far truths he would form
The transient bosoms from the thorny tree.

O Materna! to enrich thy gold head
And wavering shoulders with a new light shed

From penitence must needs bring pain,
And with it song of minor, broken strain.
But you who hear the lamp whisper thru night
Can trace paths tear-wet, and forget all blight.

† *Bruno's Weekly* (Sept. 23, 1916).

ECHOES‡

I
SLIVERS of rain upon the pane,
Jade-green with sunlight, melt and flow

‡ *The Pagan* (October-November 1917).

Upward again: they leave no stain
Of storm or strain an hour ago.

II

Over the hill a last cloud dips,
And disappears, as I should go
Silently, now, but that your lips
Are warmer with a redder glow.

III

Fresh and fragile, your arms now
Are circles of cool roses,—so . . .
In opal pools beneath your brow
I dream we quarreled long, long ago.

CARMEN DE BOHEME†

SINUOUSLY winding through the room
On smokey tongues of sweetened cigarettes,—
Plaintive yet proud the cello tones resume
The andante of smooth hopes and lost regrets.

Bright peacocks drink from flame-pots by the wall,
Just as absinthe-sipping women shiver through
With shimmering blue from the bowl in Circe's hall.
Their brown eyes blacken, and the blue drop hue.

The andante quivers with crescendo's start,
And dies on fire's birth in each man's heart.
The tapestry betrays a finger through
The slit, soft-pulling:—and music follows cue.

There is a sweep,—a shattering,—a choir
Disquieting of barbarous fantasy.
The pulse is in the ears, the heart is higher,
And stretches up through mortal eyes to see.

† *Bruno's Bohemia* (March 1918).

Carmen! Akimbo arms and smouldering eyes;—
Carmen! Bestirring hope and lipping eyes;—
Carmen whirls, and music swirls and dips.
"Carmen!", comes awed from wine-hot lips.

Finale leaves in silence to replume
Bent wings, and Carmen with her flaunts through the gloom
Of whispering tapestry, brown with old fringe:—
The winers leave too, and the small lamps twinge.

Morning: and through the foggy city gate
A gypsy wagon wiggles, striving straight.
And some dream still of Carmen's mystic face,—
Yellow, pallid, like ancient lace.

INTERIOR†

IT IS a shy solemnity,
  This lamp in our small room.
O grey and gold amenity,—
Silence and gentle gloom!

Wide from the world, a stolen hour
We claim, and none may know
How love blooms like a tardy flower
Here in the curtained glow.

And even should the world break in
With jealous threat and guile,
The world, at last, must bow and win
Our pity and a smile.

† *The Modernist* (November 1919).

LEGENDE‡

THE tossing loneliness of many nights
Rounds off my memory of her.

‡ *The Modernist* (November 1919).

Like a shell surrendered to evening sands,
Yet called adrift again at every dawn,
She has become a pathos —
Waif of the tides.

The sands and the sea have had their way,
And moons of Spring and autumn,—
All, save I.
And even my vision will be erased
As a cameo the waves claim again.

EPISODE OF HANDS†

THE unexpected interest made him flush.
Suddenly he seemed to forget the pain,—
Consented,—and held out
One finger from the others.

The gash was bleeding, and a shaft of sun
That glittered in and out among the wheels,
Fell lightly, warmly, down into the wound.

And as the fingers of the factory owner's son,
That knew a grip for books and tennis
As well as one for iron and leather,—
As his taut, spare fingers wound the gauze
Around the thick bed of the wound,
His own hands seemed to him
Like wings of butterflies
Flickering in sunlight over summer fields.

The knots and notches,—many in the wide
Deep hand that lay in his,—seemed beautiful.
They were like the marks of wild ponies' play,—
Bunches of new green breaking a hard turf.

And factory sounds and factory thoughts
Were banished from him by that larger, **quieter hand**
That lay in his with the sun upon it.
And as the bandage knot was tightened
The two men smiled into each other's eyes.

† *April* 1920.

THE BRIDGE OF ESTADOR†
An Impromptu,
Aesthetic
TIRADE

WALK high on the bridge of Estador,
No one has ever walked there before.
There is a lake, perhaps with the sun
Lapped under it,—or the dun
Bellies and estuaries of warehouses,
Tied bundle-wise with cords of smoke.

Do not think too deeply, and you'll find
A soul, an element in it all.

How can you tell where beauty's to be found?
I have heard hands praised for what they made;
I have heard hands praised for line on line;
Yet a gash with sunlight jerking through
A mesh of belts down into it, made me think
I had never seen a hand before,
And the hand was thick and heavily warted.

High on the bridge of Estador
Where no one has ever been before,—
I do not know what you'll see,—your vision
May slumber yet in the moon, Awaiting
far consummations of the tides to throw
Clean on the shore some wreck of dreams . . .

But some are twisted with the love
of things irreconcilable,—
The slant moon with the slanting hill:
O Beauty's fool, though you have never
Seen them again, you won't forget.
Nor the Gods that danced before you
When your fingers spread among the stars.

And you others—follow your arches
To what corners of the sky they pull you to,—
The everlasting eyes of Pierrot,
Or, of Gargantua, the laughter.

† *April* 1921.

PORPHYRO IN AKRON†

I

GREETING the dawn
A shift of rubber workers presses down
South Main.
With the stubborness of muddy water
It dwindles at each cross-line
Until you feel the weight of many cars,
North-bound, and East and West,
Absorbing and conveying weariness,—
Rumbling over the hills.

Akron, "high place,"—
A bunch of smoking hills
Among the rolling Ohio hills.

The dark-skinned Greeks grin at each other
In the streets and alleys.
The Greek grins and fights with the Swede,—
And the Fjords and the Aegean are remembered.

The plough, the sword,
The trowel,—and the monkey wrench!
O City, your axles need not the oil of song.
I will whisper words to myself
And put them in my pockets.
I will go and pitch quoits with old men
In the dust of a road.

II

And some of them will be "Americans,"
Using the latest ice-box and buying Fords;
And others—

I remember one Sunday noon,
Harry and I, "the gentlemen," seated around
A table of raisin-jack and wine, our host
Setting down a glass and saying, —
"One month —I go back rich.
I ride black horse . . . Have many sheep."

† *The Double Dealer* (August-September 1921).

And his wife, like a mountain, coming in
With four tiny black-eyed girls around her
Twinkling like little Christmas trees.

And some Sunday fiddlers,
Roumanian business men,
Played ragtime and dances before the door,
And we overpayed them because we felt like it.

III

Pull down the hotel counterpane
And hitch yourself up to your book.

"Full on this casement shown the wintry moon,
And threw warm gules on Madeline's fair breast,
As down she knelt for heaven's grace and boon . . . "

"Connais tu le pays . . . ?"

Your mother sang that in a stuffy parlor
One summer day in a little town
Where you had started to grow.
And you were outside as soon as you
Could get away from the company
To find the only rose on the bush in the front yard.

But look up, Porphyro—your toes
Are ridiculously tapping
The spindles at the foot of the bed.

The stars are drowned in a slow rain,
And a hash of noises is slung up from the street.
You ought, really, to try to sleep,
Even though, in this town, poetry's a
Bedroom occupation.

A PERSUASION†

IF SHE waits late at night
Hearing the wind,

† *The Measure* (October 1921).

It is to gather kindnesses
No world can offer.

She has drawn her hands away.
The wind plays andantes
Of lost hopes and regrets,—
And yet is kind.

Below the wind,
Waiting for morning,
The hills lie curved and blent
As now her heart and mind.

LOCUTIONS DES PIERROTS†
(*Translated from the French of Jules Laforgue*)

I
YOUR eyes, those pools with soft rushes,
O prodigal and wholly dilatory lady,
Come now, when will they restore me
The orient moon of my dapper affections.

For imminent is that moment when,
Because of your perverse austerities,
My crisp soul will be flooded by a languor
Bland as the wide gaze of a Newfoundland.

Ah, madame! truly it's not right
When one isn't the real Gioconda,
To adaptate her methods and deportment
For sharing the poor world in a blue funk.

II
Ah! the divine infatuation
That I nurse for Cydalise
Now that she has fled the capture
Of my lunar sensibility!

† *The Double Dealer* (May 1922).

True, I nibble at despondencies
Among the flowers of her domain
To the sole end of discovering
What is her unique propensity!

—Which is to be mine, you say?
Alas, you know how much I oppose
A stiff denial to postures
That seem too much impromptu.

III
Ah! without the moon, what white nights,
What nightmares rich with ingenuity!
Don't I see your white swans there?
Doesn't someone come to turn the knob?

And it's your fault that I'm this way.
That my conscience sees double,
And my heart fishes in troubled water
For Eve, Gioconda and Dalila.

Oh, by the infinite circumflex
Of the archbeam of my cross-legged labours,
Come now—appease me just a little
With the why-and-wherefore of Your sex!

"*A strictly literal translation of Laforgue is meaningless. The native
implications of his idiosyncratic style have to be recast in English
garments.*" (Hart Crane)

THE GREAT WESTERN PLAINS†

THE little voices of prairie dogs
Are tireless . . .
They will give three hurrahs
Alike to stage, equestrian, and pullman,
And all unstintingly as to the moon.

† *Gargoyle* (August 1922).

And Fifi's bows and poodle ease
Whirl by them centred in the lap
Of Lottie Honeydew, movie queen,
Toward lawyers and Nevada.

And how much more they cannot see!
Alas, there is so little time,
The world moves by so fast these days!
Burrowing in silk is not their way—
And yet they know the tomahawk.

Indeed, old memories come back to life;
Pathetic yelps have sometimes greeted
Noses pressed against the glass.

AMERICA'S PLUTONIC ECSTASIES†

(*With homage to E. E. Cummings*)

PREFERRING laxatives to wine
all america is saying
"how are my bowels today?" and
feeling them in every way and
peering
for the one goat (unsqueezable)
that kicked out long ago—

or, even thinking
of something—Oh!
unbelievably—Oh!
HEADY!—those aromatic LEMONS!
that make your colored syrup fairly
PULSE!—yes, PULSE!

the nation's lips are thin and fast
with righteousness and yet if
memory serves there is still
catharsis from gin-daisies as well as

† *January* 1923 (*S4N, issue 26-29*).

maidenhairferns, and the BRONX
doesn't stink at all.

These
and other natural grammarians are ab-
so-loot-lee necessary
for a FREEEE-er PASSAGE—(NOT
to india, o ye faithful,
but a little BACK DOOR DIGNITY)

BELLE ISLE†

THERE was the river;—now there is
Only this lake's reluctant face
For me to search back to an island
Sown by the river at its base.

And remembering that stream of pain
I press my eyes against the prow,
Waiting . . . And you, who with me also
Traced that flood,—where are you now?

An absolute avowal, yet termed
By hours that carry and divide,
You whispered as we passed Belle Isle
And entered this too placid tide.

That sharp joy, brighter than the deck,
That instant white death of all pain,—
How could we keep that emanation
Constant and whole within the brain!

Yet, clearer than surmise,—a place
The water lifts to gather and unfold,
Seen always—is Belle Isle the grace
Shed from the wave's refluent gold.

It is the after-word that holds
Hushed willows anchored in its glow:
It is the unbetrayable reply
Whose accent no farewell can know . . .

† *January-February* 1923.

EUCLID AVENUE†

To be or not to be — ?

BUT SO to be the denizen stingaree—
As sterterous as nations romanized may throw
Surveys by Maytime slow . . . Hexameters
Suspending jockstraps for gangsters while the pil-

Bland (grim)aces Plutarch's perch. And angles
Break in folds of crepe that blackly drape
The broken door . . . Crouch so. Amend

Then; and clinch.

Sweep . . .
Clean is that cloven Hoof. Then reap
Strain, clasp oblivion as though Chance
Could absent all answer save the chosen rant.

Stop now, as never, never. Speak

As telegrams continue, write, strike
Your scholarship (stop) through broken ribs, jail
(Stripe) answers Euclid. Einstein curves, but does not
Quail. Does Newton take the Eucharist on rail
Nor any boulevard no more? I say . . .

For there are statues, shapes your use
Repeals. Youse use. You're prevalent,—prevail!
Youse
Break food once more and souse, like all me under sail.
My friends, I never thought we'd fail.

That dirty peacock's pride, once gory God's own story:
It didn't belong no more; no, never did glory
Walk on Euclid Avenue, as didn't Wm.
Bleached or blacked, whichever 'twas. What milk
We've put in blasted pigs! I says . . . O, well—

But I say, what a swell chance, boys. No more
Cancers, jealousy, tenements or giblets! Death, my boys,
Nor blinkers either—

† *February* 1923.

Four shots at who-knows-how

Many-it-was unsupervised

Grabbed right outa my mouth that final chew—
Right there on Euclid Avenue.

CHILDREN DANCING†

WHERE gables pack the rainless
fulsome sky
permit a song as comes into the street

permit a song that swings with ropes
and skipping feet
above the laughter that rebounds below.

† *April* 1923.

INTERLUDIUM‡

To "La Montagne," by Lachaise

THY time is thee to wend
with languor such as gains
immensity in gathered grace; the arms
to spread; the hands to yield their shells

and fostering
thyself, bestow to thee
illimitable and unresigned—
Thyself
that heavens climb to measure,

thus
unfurling thee untried: until

‡ "1924" (July 1924).

from sleep forbidden now, and wide
partitions in thee goes

communicant and speeding new
the cup again wide from thy throat to spend
those streams and slopes untenanted thou
hast known . . . And blithe

Madonna, natal to thy yielding still
subsist I, wondrous as
from thine open dugs shall still the sun
again round one more fairest day.

An earlier draft of "Interludium"

Thy time is thee to wend
with languor such as gains
immensity in gathered grace, the arms
to spread; the hands to yield their shells

and fostering
thyself, bestow to thee
illimitable and unresigned
(no instinct flattering vainly now)

Thyself
that heavens climb to measure, thus
unfurling thee untried—until
from sleep forbidden now and wide
partitions in thee—goes

communicant and speeding new
the cup again wide from thy throat to spend
those streams and slopes untenanted thou
hast known . . . . And blithe

Madonna, natal to thy yielding
still subsist I, wondrous as
from thy open dugs shall still the sun
Again round one more fairest day.

SONNET†

WHAT miles I gather up unto you
are lost not one stroke ever in your sides:
nor in your breath that overcomes all tides:
nor in your fingers that reside forever here.

What if I turn toward you the gentle and
most terrible of all denials (shall I say
that you can give me) in intimation of the end
and all of praise—It is the light
that you have seen to reel
and whisper out to you upon the wine
and tables (yes, always between us, two).

Now, in the encrusting edge of years,—
the definition of eternity—call
one word back now, that is your name,
that I may still be, as it is, one half to blame!

† *April* 1924.

CHANSON‡

"I"
said Mr. M. as we crossed the street together
"am compelled to reject this
poem . . ."
At that moment a terrific detonation interrupted his
dictum
and Mr. M. soared into space astride
the lid of a
man-hole
The last I saw of him he was miles high
trying to climb off
in suchwise did Mr. M. ride into Heaven.
Hallelujah!

‡ *Aesthete,* 1925 (January 1925).

LENSES

IN THE focus of the evening there is this island with
the buzz of saw mills, the crunch and blast of quarries;
furnaces, chisels and ploughs.

And the idiot boy by the road, with carbonated eyes, laughing or extending a phallus through the grating,—talking to
a kite high in the afternoon, or in the twilight scanning
pebbles among cinders in the road through a twice-opened
tomato can.

And there is work, blood, suet and sweat,—the rigamarole
of wine and mandolines. Midnight; and maybe love . . .

And there is, as Mr. Budge explained before his
chorea took him away—there is the Nine of
three-times-three,   the   hopeful   plasm,
the   vigilance   of   the   ape,   the   repetition   of   the   parrot.   Locks   on
doors   and   lips   of   agony   to
dance upon.   And there is

time for these; time for all these, as cattle and birds
know, Mr.
Budge —
why did
you
die
so
soon
?

There is
this gate of
wrath

TO LIBERTY

OUT of the seagull cries and wind
On this strange shore I build

The virgin. They laugh to hear
How I endow her, standing
Hair mocked by the sea, her lover
A dead sailor that knew
Not even Helen's fame.

Light the last torch in the wall,
The sea wall. Bring her no robes yet.
They have not seen her in this harbor;
Eyes widely planted, clear, yet small.
And must they overcome the fog,
Or must we rend our dream?

Provide these manners, this salute
The birds feed on, anticipate this sanction.
Things become separately final—
While I become more whole,
Infinite—the gradual all,
Which is a laugh at last,

Struggles.

IN A COURT†

HIS hand changed in the kitchen
by the fire: she moved a little,
like wax against his gaze
that followed flame and transfusion,—
every spark meshed white, a part
of his most solemn appetite.

I looked into the kitchen where
they sat.
Breathless I was that peace should come
where fat is to be grasped and lean
is clenched,
and fingers are a teeth that taste
and smell.

† *Literary America* (September 1934).

THE PILLAR AND THE POST

WHAT you may yank up readiest, Yank—
May not so well serve your purpose
              as your plaint,
When you have no one but the devil to thank,
And wouldn't soil your clean-limbed taint—

Of strangling the Argives of the palms;
     Midas of motion—love those lingering
instants that bespeak a careful manure for all
your progeny—and ask the sun what time it
is before your fingers lose their ten—in biological
and betrothed answer to the ambitious monkey synthesis
             that you adore.

TO THE EMPRESS JOSEPHINE'S STATUE
Martinique
(*Image of Constancy*)

YOU WHO contain, augmented tears, explosions,
Have kissed, caressed the model of the hurricane,
Gathered and made musical in feathered fronds
The slit eclipse of moon in palm-lit bonds,
Pelee, whose blackening breath, and ashen shower,
Repealed horizons like a night of blinding snow—
Deny me not in this sweet Carribean dawn!
You, who have looked back to Leda, who have seen the Swan,
The swirling rushes urge the appointed charge,
Out-did our spies and hood-winked spydom—
Now you may compute your lecheries
As well as I, but not with her.

I own it still—that sure deliberation—
Leave,.leave that Carribean praise to me
Who claims a devout concentration,
To wage you surely out of memory;
Your generosity dispose relinquishment and care,
Your death be sacred to all those who share
Love and the breath of faith, momentous bride.
You did not die for conquerors at your side,
Nor for their fruit of mating that is widowed pride.

MIRROR OF NARCISSUS

THEY judge, whose strictures of their sight
Preclude the evidence I speak. And how
Shall I of their dead conscience build the proof
Unto themselves, whereof their birth was God?
Who will but laugh, and lengthily defer
Their heritage, and sneer down all the pain,
And vomit back the incense breathed in vain!
—O minute elegy, pantouffle pain,
O mirror of Narcissus, when is your wane?

His perfect image dies upon the stage
Or gains, it is no matter for the gods.
The water flows, divides his gain—
Loving the Styx, he sees the rain
Speak otherwise in his own tones
Upon the land he lends such dirges to.

Thy repetition freezes thus my pain . . .

THE MASTERS

THEIR brains are smooth machines that colonize
The sun,—their eyes are atoms of a split hereafter.
They must explain away all moan and laughter,
Then ticket, subdivide and over-rule
Each former entity . . . .
I saw them turn old Demos from the stage
And mock their hearts because their hearts spoke better,
Elaborate all, divided school by school.

A PLACEMENT

SHALL I subsume the shadow of the world—
The sun-spot that absolves us all? In fine
There is the wisp, there is the phantom,
"Fantisticon", in the comedy where we meet.

The interlude without circumventation
This, between the speech of shells and battle gases.
I know this effort by the slant of the obdurate moon.
She, at worst, is the chance of our worst reflection.

Immeasurable scope of veins, imprisoned within mood
Whereon the distance thrives—O jealousy of space!
I, these cameos carve—thy caverns limitless achieve—
These arteries explore.   What is the extent of the sod?
And where I, the clod blown up . . . ?

OYSTER

TIME is not to be worn, strapped to the wrist,
Lady, like any buckled jewel or bangle,
That you can lift with cool fingers that untwist
The oyster from its shell.

Lady, though the same fingers that attach it, twist
The oyster from its shell and draw the bow
Across the cool strings of eternity.

B.   UNCOLLECTED PROSE

THE CASE AGAINST NIETZSCHE†

Before the war, Nietzsche's writings were moderately popular in France, where he was hailed by the Sorbonne long before Oxford awoke to his dimensions. But now the French call him the herald of modern Prussianism.

How parodoxical their accusation seems, when we know that Nietzsche was drawn to the French temperament more than to any other. His favorite novelists were French; Pascal and Montaigne were sources which he frequently mentions as potent influences in his development. Goethe and Schopenhauer were the only Germans for whom he had philosophic ears; and these, as he declares, were fundamentally un-German.

And yet again, how can he be called the spokesman of a nation which always affected him with disgust —if not with hatred? His epithets on characteristic "Germania" at times approach the unprintable. He even denied his German origin, and declared himself a Pole in all his views and sympathies. Anyone who can picture him as an inspired leader of legions of "the pig-headed," as he called them, has indeed capacities for self-delusion.

I might refer to Par. 320 in "Menschlich-all-zu-Menschlich" for a direct arraignment of Prussianism, although no names are mentioned in it. Here the autocratic machine is cooly exposed. He cites the direct control by the state over all educational institutions; the inaccessibility to all personal distinction except some service, sooner or later, to the state; compulsory military training; the supremacy of the army; and at the end he ironically observes,—"Then nothing more is wanted but

† *The Pagan* (April-May 1918).

an opportunity for great wars. These are provided from professional reasons (and so in all innocence) by diplomats, aided by newspapers and Stock Exchanges For the 'nation,' as a nation of the soldiers, need never be supplied with a good conscience in war,—it has one already."

Nietzsche, Zeppelins, and poisoned-gas, go ill together. But Great Indra! one may envy Nietzsche a little; think of being so elusive,—so mercurial, as to be first swallowed whole, then coughed up, and still remain a mystery!

A LETTER TO *THE LITTLE REVIEW*†

Joyce and Ethics

The Los Angeles critic who commented on Joyce in the last issue was adequately answered, I realize,—but the temptation to emphasize such illiteracy, indiscrimination, and poverty still pulls a little too strongly for resistance.

I noticed that Wilde, Baudelaire and Swinburne are "stacked up" beside Joyce as rivals in "decadence" and "intellect." I am not yet aware that Swinburne ever possessed much beyond his art ears," although these were long enough, and adequate to all his beautiful, though often meaningless mouthings. His instability in criticism and every form of literature that did not depend almost exclusively on sound for effect, and his irrelevant metaphors are notorious. And as to Wilde,—after his bundle of paradoxes has been sorted and conned, —very little evidence of intellect remains. "Decadence" is something much talked about, and sufficiently misconstrued to arouse interest in the works of any fool. Any change in form, viewpoint or mannerism can be so abused by the offending party. Sterility is the only "decadence" I recognize. An abortion in art takes the same place as it does in society—it deserves no recognition whatever,—it is simply outside. A piece of work is art, or it isn't: there is no neutral judgment.

However,—let Baudelaire and Joyce stand together, as much as any such thing in literary comparison will allow. The principal eccentricity evinced by both is a penetration into life common to only the greatest. If people resent a thrust which discovers some of their entrails to themselves, I can see no reason for resorting to indiscrimin-

† *The Little Review* (July 1918).

ate comparisons, naming colours of the rainbow, or advertising the fact that they have recently been forced to recognize a few of their personal qualities. Those who are capable of being only mildly "shocked" very naturally term the cost a penny, but were they capable of paying a few pounds for the same thinking, experience and realization by and in themselves, they could reserve their pennies for work minor to Joyce's.

The most nauseating complaint against his work is that of immorality and obscenity. The character of Stephen Dedalus is all too good for this world. It takes a little experience,—a few reactions on his part to understand it, and could this have been accomplished in a detached hermitage, high above the mud, he would no doubt have preferred that residence. *A Portrait of the Artist as a Young Man,* aside from Dante, is spiritually the most inspiring book I have ever read. It is Bunyan raised to art, and then raised to the ninth power.

REVIEW: *THE GHETTO AND OTHER POEMS,* BY LOLA RIDGE†

Extremities in the modern world clash in a close proximity, so that there is a finer, harder, line than usual to divide them. There is a cruelty in this,—a kind of desperation that is dramatic. Science, grown uncontrollable, has assumed a grin that has more than threatened the supposed civilization that fed it; science has brought light,—but it threatens to destroy the idea of reverence, the source of all light. Its despotism recognizes no limits. In one sense it has become a gargoyle.

Lola Ridge's volume is eloquent with a dramatic "awareness" or a kind of sharp recognition, of these dominating aspects of her time. Her poems are always vivid:

> "Life thunders on . . . .
>
> Over the black bridge
> The line of lighted cars
> Creeps like a monstrous serpent
> Spooring gold . . . .
>
> Watchman, what of the track?
>
> Night . . . silence . . . stars . . .
> All's well!"

† *The Pagan* (January 1919).

She is seldom immersed in herself,—she never seems to lose con-sciousness of surroundings. Quite naturally this treatment gives a dramatic quality to even such a personal utterance as,—"Submerged"—

> "I have known only my own shallows—
> Safe, plumber places,
> Where I was wont to preen myself.
>
> But for the abyss
> I wanted a plank beneath
> And horizons . . . .
>
> I was afraid of the silence
> And the slipping toe-hold . . . ."

The essential to all real poetry is in Miss Ridge's work,—sincerity. Sometimes the "macabre intensity" of her words suggest a slight theatricality. Sometimes a figure or construction is so amazingly brilliant, that one suspicions it has been used for itself alone, and that Miss Ridge has been tempted toward a barren cleverness. That she has decided capacities for it is certain. I hope only, that if her course swerves still further that way, she will utilize the novel, or some such form, other than poetry.

"The Ghetto" is representative of the best of Miss Ridge's endow-ments. In some aspects it is like a miniature "Comedie Humaine," with the dominant note of sadness that runs through Balzac's narratives so insistently.

I have spoken more of the social significance of Miss Ridge's work than strictly aesthetic canons would probably admit, because I have felt the interpretive aspect of her work to be its most brilliant facet. When work is so widely and minutely reflective of its time, then, certainly, other than questions of pure *aesthétique* must be considered.

REVIEW OF *MINNA AND MYSELF*, BY MAXWELL BODENHEIM†

I think that many of these poems will endure though they will probably not be widely popular for the principal reason that they are

† *The Pagan* (February 1919).

too distinguished,—too peculiar. They will be classed as "minor
poetry," which designation, by the way, is beginning to assume a far
from depreciative connotation in these days of attempted epics in
"the grand style" like Miss Amy Lowell's very journalistic "Can
Grande's Castle."

Bodenheim cultivates a more limited field. His poems are often
little heaps of images in which the verbal element is subordinated,
making for an essentially static and decorative quality. There are,
however, a few that make me think of the swaying plume of tiny
bubbles that an effervescent pill dissolving in a glass of water, will
make. For example:—

> "Grey, drooping-shouldered bushes scrape the edges
> Of bending swirls of yellow-white flowers.
> So do my thoughts meet the wind-scattered color of
> you," etc.

But the static element generally predominates, as here,

> "An old silver church in a forest
> Is my love for you.
> The trees around it
> Are words that I have stolen from your heart.
> An old silver bell, the last smile you gave,
> Hangs at the top of my church.
> It rings only when you come through the forest
> And stand beside it . . . " etc.

Bodenheim believes that "pure poetry is the vibrant expression of
everything clearly delicate and unattached with surface sentiment in
the emotions of men toward themselves and nature . . . True poetry is
the entering of delicately imaginative plateaus, unconnected with human
beliefs or fundamental human feelings." I quote from his article in
the New Republic of December 22nd, 1917. Now this definition seems
to me inordinately precious. Fortunately for all he has not "lived up"
to it, except in rare instances. A reaction to the general abuse of his
art as a vehicle for all kinds of propaganda is responsible for this
extremity of statement, I am sure.

In regard to the plays . . . I should prefer to call them tapestries,
scenic rather than dramatic, in interest. Bodenheim is not a dramatist
in the real sense of the term, and I question his possibilities in this
field. But if he is to insist on incorporating such fine lines as are

included in the conversation in "The Master Poisoner," I think I should easily be won to listening. The most dramatic piece in the book, to my thinking, is the one called "Soldiers," and that is so by virtue of its arrangement,—a painful focus of realities.

REVIEW OF *WINESBURG, OHIO*, BY SHERWOOD ANDERSON†

Beyond an expression of intense gratitude to the author, it is hard to say a word in regard to a book such as Sherwood Anderson's "Winesburg, Ohio." The entire paraphernalia of criticism is insignificant, erected against the walls of such a living monument as this book, so that defense and explanation are soon evident as its only office.

First of all the book is Sherwood Anderson; then humanity, then a certain period in the development of America's "Middle West," so called, and finally, art. It is a great heart, in company with a strong hand, that can elicit the sympathy, or at least, the understanding of his auditor toward each and every one of the characters of his book; and it is in the nature of Sherwood Anderson, as it often was in Balzac, to accomplish it.

The spark that Edgar Lee Masters struck with his "Spoon River" was a mighty seedling of dynamite, cold and intense,—but I might say sporadic, in comparison with the dignity, the "power in repose," and the sustained inner illumination and bloom of this book. There is the same infinite pathos here, but it seems curbed to a finer reticence that is more genuine than many of the portraits by the elder poet which at times almost touch the melodramatic. However, there is no need to diminish the proportions of the adventurous discoverer in order to sufficiently praise the richness of the settler, for this, to me, seems the relationship in outlook, time, and performance, of these two Americans.

The Puritan that stalks through the swamps of "Spoon River" is manifest also in "Winesburg," but he is here a little less gaunt; I will not say more or less historically "true," although I do maintain that Sherwood Anderson, while typifying him strongly in local garments and habits, has nevertheless somewhat modified him with a certain beauty and suggestiveness of his universal recurrence in many

† *The Pagan* (September 1919).

ages. He is alive in a tale called "Godliness," but the beauty and innocence of youth escape him in terror. He plays parts in other episodes, but is by no means a preoccupation of the author. The windows, alleys, and lanes of the village are open to us to find what epics, tragedies and idylls we may. There is everlasting beauty in a scene called "Mother." The ironic humor and richness of "An Awakening" are unmatched in anything I know of. "Queer" is a story that carries De Maupassant into an anti-climax of grating cogs; and "Paper Pills," perhaps the finest and most exquisite thing in the book is so utterly new, that I know nothing with which to compare it, except, perhaps, an idyll of Lucretius.

To end with aesthetic considerations, the style is flawless. I know of no finer selection of "significant material," combined with proper treatment and economy of detail. America should read this book on her knees. It constitutes an important chapter in the Bible of her consciousness.

A NOTE ON MINNS†

An ignorance of the professional technical "elements" of photography, it seems to me, should very slightly, if at all, invalidate one's claim to the appreciation of such work as that of H. W. Minns. In his case, my appreciation can begin only where the fundamental pedagogics of the camera leave off,—at the point where the craftsman merges into the artist,—where the creative element becomes distinct. Some combination of eye and sympathy and hand are subtly responsible for the quality in his work. His "arrangements" are not the empty, obvious contortions of so many modern photographers. He plainly could not content himself with that. There is, in his faces, the urge of an ethical curiosity and sympathy as strongly evident as in the novels of Henry James. Undoubtedly his portraits are deeper, more vivid, than the daily repetitions of his sitters in their mirrors give back to any but themselves, but this is only to mention again the creative element that gives to his portraits such a sense of dramatic revelations.

Mr. Minns has often exhibited in Europe, and has received extensive recognition at Dresden, Vienna, and Copenhagen exhibitions. He

† *The Little Review* (September-December 1920).

began taking pictures when he was considerably beyond thirty, and has since spent some twenty years working in the rather limited and unresponsive locality of Akron, Ohio.

SHERWOOD ANDERSON†

We have come a long way from the pattern-making preoccupations of an Henry James when we can welcome a statement from an artist with as bold a contrasting simplicity as the answer that Sherwood Anderson once gave me to an analysis I had attempted of one of his short stories. "I am in truth mighty little interested in any discussions of art or life, or what a man's place in the scheme of things may be. It has to be done. I suppose, but after all there is the *fact* of life. Its story wants telling and singing. That's what I want,—the tale and the song of it." And it is that Anderson has so pre-eminently captured the "tale and the song of it" that I find his words so acceptable—at least in so far as they relate to his own work.

I spoke of an "attempted" analysis because of being since satisfied that beyond the possibility of a certain uneven surface penetration, Anderson's stories possess a too defiant and timeless solidity,—too much a share of life and clay itself,—to be tagged and listed with mechanical precision. And what a satisfaction this is, to read stories over and again without a bundle of dry bones and cogwheels of "situtions" and "plots" spilling out into one's lap. It must have been because of a surfeit of such disappointments that "Winesburg, Ohio," when it first appeared, kept me up a whole night in a steady crescendo of emotions. Here was "stark realism, but a realism simplified and strangely sophisticated by the inscrutable soil. And by "soil" I mean something much more than a kind of local colour. There is plenty of that quite wonderfully applied, both in "Winesburg" and in "Poor White," but there is also something more important and rare than this, —a contact with animal and earthy life so indefinably yet powerfully used as a very foundation to the stories that it might be compared to the sap that pervades the tree-trunk, branches, and twigs. Let me quote an instance of what I mean from "Poor White."

Clara Butterworth, merging into womanhood, is musing in the shadows of her father's barns . . .

† *The Double Dealer* (July 1921).

"Clara jumped quickly out of the hammock and walked about under the trees in the orchard. Her thoughts of Jim Priest's youth startled her. It was as though she had walked suddenly into a room where a man and woman were making love. Her cheeks burned and her hands trembled. As she walked slowly through the clumps of grass and weeds that grew between the trees where the sunlight struggled through, bees coming home to the hives heavily laden with honey flew in droves about her head. There was something heady and purposeful about the song of labor that arose out of the beehives. It got into her blood and her step quickened. The words of Jim Priest that kept running through her head seemed a part of the same song the bees were singing. 'The sap has begun to run up the tree,' she repeated aloud. How significant and strange the words seemed! They were the kind of words a lover might use in speaking to his beloved. She had read many novels but they contained no such words. It was better so. It was better to hear them from human lips."

This is but one of many remembered paragraphs and pages from which arises a lyricism, deliberate and light, as a curl of milk-weed seeds drawn toward the sun. It is his love for rows of corn on flat lands, fields bending over rolling Ohio hills, and the smell of barns under the warm hours of noon, that has given Anderson's descriptions of modern city life with its mechanical distortions of humanity, such thrust and bite.

In "Poor White," there is the "machine" of modern existence,—the monster that is upon us all. No one who treats however slightly of the lives of the poor or middle classes can escape the issues of its present hold on us. It has seduced the strongest from the land to the cities, and in most cases made empty and meaningless their lives. It has cheapened the worth of all human commodities and even the value of human lives. It has destroyed the pride and pleasure of the craftsman in his work. "Hugh McVey," the son of a tramp of sordid Missouri River life, becomes a "dreamer of the machines" who invents one after another typical practical improvement[s] such as harvesters, potato-planters, etc., which enrich the speculating manufacturers who grasp at them, bow down before them and wrangle about them. McVey goes on inventing and himself making money, but finds himself in time becoming more and more indifferent and disappointed. Most of all he is bewildered by the ever greater rush of the new industrialism with its "booming" towns, its smoke and squalor. He has found no satisfactory foothold. His own machines have robbed him of something and left nothing in its place. He cannot be satisfied with himself as a machine producing machines. Unconsciously he is being

urged by more natural impulses that he has perhaps denied too long.
Like so many others he is lost among cogs and complicated springs.
One sees all through this book how character is bent, blunted, regulated,
diverted, or lacerated by the "machine." There is the perfect episode
of a harness-maker whose love for manual perfection of craft finally
drives him to the murder of an upstart apprentice who had insisted
in over-ruling him by adopting machine made saddles as substitutes for
the carefully wrought saddles of the old man.

Looking back at two earlier books, "Windy McPherson's Son" and
"Marching Men," one can see a great advance in "Poor White." There
has always been the propagandist threatening the artist in Anderson;
and in these first two books the propagandist comes out too dangerously near a victory to satis.y us despite the much brilliant description
these books contain. Since then he has treed himself from much of
this. Not that he has chosen to ignore any fact or problems, but
rather that he has succeeded in treating them more impersonally, incorporating them, less obviously, in character and action. To appreciate
this advance from the seductive stagnations of sentimentality to a clear
acceptance and description of our life to-day for what it be worth, is
to realize how few other Americans have had the courage, let alone
the vision to do anything like it. Norris and Dreiser, and one or two
others of native birth have been the only ones. In Anderson there has
been some great sincerity, perhaps the element of the "soil" itself per-
sonified in him, that has made him refuse to turn aside to offer the
crowds those profitable "lollypops" that have "made" and ruined so
many other of our writers.

Of course, it is patent that people do not like to be told the truth.
Especially our Puritans! "Winesburg" was the first book to tell the
truth about our small mid-western towns. And what a fury it threw
some people into! It seemed to be so much easier for those people
to fling back,—"Neuroticism!" "Obscenity!" and "Exaggeration!"
than to recognize themselves and others there. I could understand
it perfectly myself, having lived for a while in a small town of similar
location and colour. But my real point for admiring it was not because it merely told the truth; it was that "Winesburg" represented a
work of distinct aesthetic achievement, an example of synthetic form,
—not merely a medley of a thousand exterior details such as Lewis's
"Main Street." It takes more than the recognition of facts as facts to
move us in fiction. There must be some beauty wrung from them to
hold us long. We can recognize this quality without having it pointed
out to us if our hearts are not too deadened, our sensibilities too dulled.
In "Winesburg," the windows, alleys and lanes of the place are opened

to us to find what we may. There is an exalting pathos in the episode called "Mother." The ironic humor and richness of "An Awakening" has the vivid and unbroken vitality of a silhouette. "Paper Pills," to me the finest thing in the book, has an idyllic beauty that sets it beside the old legend of "Daphnis and Chloe," and there are other chapters and episodes unmatched anywhere.

During the last two years there have been some short stories published in various magazines, such as "I Want to Know Why," "The Triumph of the Egg" "The New Englander," and "The Other Woman" that I look forward to seeing collected into a volume. I would like to see Anderson handle the Negro in fiction. So far it has not been done by anyone without sentimentality or cruelty, but the directness of his vision would produce something new and deep in this direction. In the winter and spring of '20 Anderson was in southern Alabama near the sea finishing "Poor White," and his interest in the black man became so aroused that he wrote me,—"The Negroes are the living wonder of this place. What a tale if someone could penetrate into the home and the life of the Southern Negro and not taint it in the ordinary superficial way."

The time has already arrived when Anderson is beginning to be recognized as among the few first recorders of the life of a people coming to some state of self-consciousness. He is without sentimentality; and he makes no pretense of offering solutions. He has humanity and simplicity that is quite baffling in depth and suggestiveness, and his steady and deliberate growth is proving right along the promise it gives of finer work. A verse from his "A New Testament" has an oddly personal tone to it:

"My mind is the mind of a little man with thin legs who sells cigars in a store. My mind is the mind of a cripple who died in an alleyway at Cleveland, Ohio. My mind is the mind of a child who fell into a well, the mind of one who cleans the streets of a city, of an actor who walks up and down on a stage."

REVIEW OF *EIGHT MORE HARVARD POETS*†

The main bulk of this collection credits Harvard with little more than an even gait with recent Oxford and Cambridge anthologies of similar intention, and helps to prove that there are as many incipient

† *S4N* (March-April 1923).

'Georgians' in America as in England. The fact would hardly warrant mention if beyond this margin of quietude there were not the more
animated gestures of two poets who have at least convincing manners.
The attenuated Woodberrian echoes still haunt the banks of the
Charles, but beside the fresher reactions of Malcolm Cowley and John
Brooks Wheelwright even the disguise of vers libre fails to rescue
their notes from the embrace of familiar nostalgias and worn allusions.

In this well bred and predominating group (whose tradition certainly needs no present defense) Royall Snow is the only one to
approach an interesting idom. He has a rather true sense for classic
diction, though he fails to carry his expression through to the point of
valor. Like the others, he gives scattered couplets that are pleasant and
all-too-quotable, but there is scarcely a poem from any of the six poets
of this group which is satisfying as a completed statement.

A genial pedestrianism, however, in several of Malcolm Cowley's
poems indicate the possibility of a 20th century 'pastoral' form. A
faculty for fresh record, city and road panorama, and ironic nuance,
all make Cowley's experiments quite valuable. For one who can so
well afford to stick closer to home, he deliberately allows French and
18th century influences to intrude too notably in several instances; yet
practically all of his poems achieve consistent form. I think that its
austerity and sense of timelessness make *Mountain Valley* his best
accomplished poem. Its intonation is suave and deeper than the
graded accents of his other poems; its rhythm is accumulative of something less amiable, yet rarer and more abstract than his usual 'Chaucer-
ian' method of observation includes. Cowley seems to be civilized in
the same sense as the older Chinamen. His alertness is a steady re-
assurance against crudities or bathos wherever his technical facilities
may lead him.

John Brooks Wheelwright has little of Cowley's refinement, but
the stertorous drive in several of his poems carries with it real emotional
significance. The Hamilton poem, which best exemplifies this quality,
is certainly one of the three best poems in the anthology, and the last
verse of *Closing Gesture* is a statement so imaginative and balanced
that it should be quoted: —

> Myself,
> stand against the black drift of storms,
> trustful as the appealing brave, praying with his
>   arms,
> invincible as Hamilton in granite,
> firm as a colossal crucifix upon a mountain trail
> forever changeless against changing sky.

It is good to find a poet with the power of fusing ideas with such subjective intensity that the result is poetry. Wheelwright's stringency is a rare quality in American poetry. We have had it in Robinson; but, unless I am mistaken Wheelwright is emotionally more generously endowed, and, in spite of several second-rate poems, he offers interesting conjectures.

A detailed record of the Muses' bouts at Cambridge is included in Dorian Abbot's able preface. Turning poets loose is a natural privilege of universities, but it will never become, at least in our America, a popular inter-collegiate sport. The Fates are kind in this, even though the idea of the undergraduate anthology seldom gets as much encouragement as it really deserves.

A LETTER TO GORHAM MUNSON†

Dear Gorham:

My rummy conversation last Monday offered, I fear, but a poor explanation of my several theoretical differences of opinion with you on the function of poetry, its particular province of activity, etc. Neither was I able to express to you my considerable appreciation of many accurate distinctions made in your essay which certainly prompt my gratitude as well as applause. It would probably be uninteresting as well as bit excessive for me to enumerate and dwell on these felicitations, however gratifying to myself I may feel them to be. Your essay is roughly divided in two the second half including our present disagreement, and inasmuch as I have never really attempted to fulfill the functions therein attributed to the poet, your theories on that subject can be discussed from a relatively impersonal angle so far as I am concerned. Furthermore, it is *one* aspect of a contemporary problem which has already enlisted the most detailed and intense speculation from a number of fields, science, philosophy, etc., as you, of course, know. I'm not saying that my few hasty notes which follow are conclusive evidence, but the logic of them (added to the organic convictions incident to the memorized experience of the creative "act," let us say) is not yet sufficiently disproved for me by such arguments, at least, as you have used in your essay.

Poetry, in so far as the metaphysics of any absolute knowledge extends, is simply the concrete *evidence* of the *experience* of a recog-

† *March* 17, 1926.

nition (*knowledge* if you like). It can give you a *ratio* of fact and experience, and in this sense it is both perception and thing perceived, according as it approaches a significant articulation or not. This is its reality, its fact, *being*. When you attempt to ask more of poetry,—the fact of man's relationship to a hypothetical god, be it Osiris, Zeus or Indra, you will get as variant terms even from the abstract terminology of philosophy as you will from poetry; whereas poetry without attempting to logically enunciate such a problem or its solution, may well give you the real connective experience, the very "sign manifest" on which rests the assumption of a god-head.

I'm perfectly aware of my wholesale lack of knowledge. But as Allen said, what exactly do you mean by "knowledge?" When you ask for exact factual data (a graphic map of eternity?), ethical morality or moral classifications, etc. from poetry—you not only limit its goal, you ask its subordination to science, philosophy. Is it not equally logical to expect Stravinsky to bring his fiddles into dissent with the gravitation theories of Sir Isaac Newton? They *are* in dissent with this scientist, as a matter of fact, and organically so; for the group mind that Stravinsky appeals to has already been freed from certain of the limitations of experience and consciousness that dominated both the time and the mind of Newton. Science (ergo all exact knowledge and its instruments of operation) is in perfect antithesis to poetry. (Painting, architecture, music, as well). It operates from an exactly opposite polarity, and it may equate with poetry, but when it does so its statement of such is in an entirely different terminology. I hope you get this difference between *inimical* and *antithetical*, intended here. It is not my interest to discredit science it has been as inspired as poetry,—and if you could but recognize it, much more hypothetically motivated.

What you admire in Plato as "divine sanity" is the architecture of his logic. Plato doesn't live today because of the intrinsic "truth" of his statements: their only living truth today consists in the "fact" of their harmonious relationship to each other in the context of his organization of them. This grace partakes of poetry. But Plato was primarily a philosopher and you must admit that grace is a secondary motive in philosophical statement, at least until the hypothetical basis of an initial "truth" has been accepted—not in the name of beauty, form or experience, but in the name of rationality. No wonder Plato considered the banishment of poets;—their reorganizations of chaos on bases perhaps divergent from his own threatened the logic of *his* system, itself founded on assumptions that demanded the very defense of poetic construction which he was fortunately able to provide.

The tragic quandary (or *agon*) of the modern world derives from the paradoxes that an inadequate system of rationality forces on the living consciousness. I am not opposing any new synthesis of reasonable laws which might provide a consistent philosophical and moral program for our epoch. Neither, on the other hand, am I attempting through poetry to delineate any such system. If this 'knowledge," as you call it, were so sufficiently organized as to dominate the limitations of my personal experience (consciousness) then I would probably find myself automatically writing under its "classic" power of dictation, and under that circumstance might be incidentally as philosophically "contained" as you might wish me to be. That would mean "serenity" to you because the abstract basis of my work would have been familiarized to you before you read a word of the poetry. But my poetry, even then,—in-so-far as it was truly poetic,—would avoid the employment of abstract tags, formulations of experience in factual terms, etc., —it would necessarily express its concepts in the more direct terms of physical-phychic experience. If, not, it must by so much lose its impact and become simply categorical.

I think it must be due to some such misapprehensions of my poetic purpose in writing that leads you to several rather contradictory judgments which in one sentence are laudatory and in other contexts which you give them,—put me to blush for mental attitudes implied on my part. For instance, after having granted me all the praise you do earlier in your essay for "storming heaven" as it were how can you later refer to that same faculty of verbal synchronization as to picture me as "waiting for another ecstasy—and then slumping— rather as a baker would refer to a loaf in his oven. Granted your admiration for the "yeastiness" of some of my effusions, you should (in simple justice to your reader and your argument) here also afford the physical evidence (actual quotation or logical proof) of the "slump," the unleavened failure. There really are plenty of lines in this respect which could be used for illustration. What I'm objecting to is contained in my suspicion that you have allowed too many extra-literary impressions of me to enter your essay, sometimes for better, sometimes for worse. The same is true of your references to the "psychological gaming" (Verlaine) which puts the slur of superficiality and vulgarity on the very aspects of my work which you have previously been at pains to praise.—And all because you arbitrarily propose a goal for me which I have no idea of nor interest in following. Either you find my work poetic or not but if you propose for it such ends as poetry organically escapes, it seems to me, as Allen said, that you as a critic of literature are working into a confusion of catagories. Certainly this charge of alternate "gutter sniping" and "angel kissing" is no longer anything more than a meretricious substitute for psychological sincerity in defining the range of an artist's subject matter and psychic explorations. Still less should it be brought forward unless there is enough physical evidence in the artist's work to warrant curiosity in this respect on the part of the reader.

Your difficulties are extra, I realize, in writing about me at all. They are bound to be thus extra because of the (so far as the reader goes) "impurities" of our previous literary arguments, intimacies of statement, semi-statements, etc. which are not always reflected in a man's work, after all. But your preoccupations on the one hand with a terminology which I have not attempted and your praise on the other hand of my actual (physical) representation of the incarnate *evidence* of the very knowledge, the very *wisdom* which you feel me to be only conjecturally sure of—makes me guilty of really wronging you, perhaps. but drives me to the platitude that "truth has no name." Her latest one, of course, is "relativity."

A DISCUSSION WITH HART CRANE†

(CORRESPONDENCE WITH HARRIET MONROE)

Apropos of the poem *At Melville's Tomb*, printed in the verse section of this number, the following correspondence between its author and the editor, printed with the consent of both, may be of interest to our readers.

From the editor to Mr. Crane:

Take me for a hard-boiled unimaginative unpoetic reader, and tell me how *dice* can *bequeath an embassy* (or anything else); and how a calyx (*of death's bounty* or anything else) can give back a *scattered chapter, livid hieroglyph;* and how, it it does such a *portent* can be *wound in corridors* (of shells or anything else).

And so on. I find your image of *frosted eyes lifting altars* difficult to visualize. Nor do compass, quadrant and sextant *contrive* tides, they merely record them, I believe.

All this may seem impertinent, but is not so intended. Your ideas and rhythms interest me, and I am wondering by what process of reasoning you would justify this poem's succession of champion mixed

† *Poetry* (October 1926).

metaphors, of which you must be conscious. The packed line should pack its phrases in orderly relation, it seems to me, in a manner tend-ing to clear confusion instead of making it worse confounded.

But pardon me—you didn't ask for criticism. Of course I should not venture upon these remarks if I were not much interested.

From Mr. Crane to the editor:

Your good nature and manifest interest in writing me about the obscurities apparent in my Melville poem certainly prompt a wish to clarify my intentions in that poem as much as possible. But I realize that my explanations will not be very convincing. For a paraphrase is generally a poor substitute for any organized conception that one has fancied he has put into the more essentialized form of the poem itself.

At any rate, and though I imagine us to have considerable differ-ences of opinion regarding the relationship of poetic metaphor to ordin-ary logic (I judge this from the angle of approach you use toward por-tions of the poem), I hope my answers will not be taken as a defense of merely certain faulty lines. I am really much more interested in certain theories of metaphor and technique involved generally in poet-ics, than I am concerned in vindicating any particular perpetrations of my own.

My poem may well be elliptical and actually obscure in the order-ing of its content, but in your criticism of this very possible deficiency you have stated your objections in terms that allow me, at least for the moment, the privilege of claiming your ideas and ideals as theoretically, at least, quite outside the issues of my own aspirations. To put it more plainly, as a poet I may very possibly be more interested in the so-called illogical impingements of the connotations of words on the consciousness (and their combinations and interplay in metaphor on this basis) than I am interested in the preservation of their logically rigid significations at the cost of limiting my subject matter and per-ceptions involved in the poem.

This may sound as though I merely fancied juggling words and images until I found something novel, or esoteric; but the process is much more predetermined and objectified than that. The nuances of feeling and observation in a poem may well call for certain liberties which you claim the poet has no right to take. I am simply making the claim that the poet does have that authority, and that to deny it is to limit the scope of the medium so considerably as to outlaw some of the richest genius of the past.

This argument over the dynamics of metaphor promises as active a future as has been evinced in the past. Partaking so extensively as it does of the issues involved in the propriety or non-propriety of certain attitudes toward subject matter, etc., it enters the critical distinctions usually made between "romantic," "classic" as an organic factor. It is a problem that would require many pages to state adequately—merely from my own limited standpoint on the issues. Even this limited statement may prove onerous reading, and I hope you will pardon me if my own interest in the matter carries me to the point of presumption.

Its paradox, of course, is that its apparent illogic operates so logically in conjunction with its context in the poem as to establish its claim to another logic, quite independent of the original definition of the word or phrase or image thus employed. It implies (this *inflection* of language) a previous or prepared receptivity to its stimulus on the part of the reader. The reader's sensibility simply responds by identifying this inflection of experience with some event in his own history or perceptions—or rejects it altogether. The logic of metaphor is so organically entrenched in pure sensibility that it can't be thoroughly traced or explained outside of historical sciences, like philology and anthropology. This "pseudo-statement," as I. A. Richards calls it in an admirable essay touching our contentions in last July's *Criterion,* demands completely other faculties of recognition than the pure rationalistic associations permit. Much fine poetry may be completely rationalistic in its use of symbols, but there is much great poetry of another order which will yield the reader very little when inspected under the limitation of such arbitrary concerns as are manifested in your judgment of the Melville poem, especially when you constitute such requirements of ordinary logical relationship between word and word as irreducible.

I don't wish to enter here defense of the particular symbols in my own poem, because, as I said, I may well have failed to supply the necessary emotional connectives to the content featured. But I would like to counter a question or so of yours with a similar question. Here the poem is less dubious in quality than my own, and as far as the abstract pertinacity of question and its immediate consequences are concerned the point I'm arguing about can be bettered demonstrated. Both quotations are familiar to you, I'm sure.

You ask me how a *portent* can possibly be wound in a *shell.* Without attempting to answer this for the moment, I ask you how Blake could possibly say that "a *sigh* is a *sword* of an Angel King." You ask me how *compass, quadrant and sextant* "*contrive*" tides. I ask you how Eliot can possibly believe that "Every street *lamp* that I pass *beats* like a fatalistic *drum!*" Both of my metaphors may fall down completely. I'm not defending their actual value in themselves, but your criticism of them in each case was leveled at an illogicality of relationship between symbols, which similar fault you must have either overlooked in case you have ever admired the Blake and Eliot lines, or have there condoned them on account of some more ultimate convictions pressed on you by the impact of the poems in their entirety.

It all comes to the recognition that emotional dynamics are not to be confused with any absolute order of rationalized definitions; ergo, in poetry the *rationale* of metaphor belongs to another order of experience than science, and is not to be limited by a scientific and arbitrary code of relationships either in verbal inflections or concepts.

There are plenty of people who have never accumulated a sufficient series of reflections (and these of a rather special nature) to perceive the relation between a *drum* and a *street lamp—via* the *unmentioned* throbbing of the heart and nerves in a distraught man which *tacitly* creates the reason and 'logic" of the Eliot metaphor. They will always have a perfect justification for ignoring those lines and to claim them obscure, excessive, etc., until by some experience of their own the words accumulate the necessary connotations to complete their connection. It is the same with the "patient etherized upon a table," isn't it? Surely that line must lack all eloquence to many people who, for instance, would delight in agreeing that the sky was like a dome of many-colored glass.

If one can't count on some such bases in the reader now and then, I don't see how the poet has any chance to ever get beyond the simplest conceptions of emotion and thought, of sensation and lyrical sequence. If the poet is to be held completely to the already evolved and exploited sequences of imagery and logic—what field of added consciousness and increased perceptions (the actual province of poetry, if not lullabys) can be expected when one has to relatively return to the alphabet every breath so so? In the minds of people who have sensitively read, seen and experienced a great deal, isn't there a terminology something like short-hand as compared to usual description and dialectics, which the artist ought to be right in trusting as a reasonable connective agent toward fresh concepts, more inclusive evaluations? The question is more important to me than it perhaps ought to be; but as long as poetry is written. an audience, however small, is implied, and there remains the question of an active or an inactive imagination as its characteristic.

It is of course understood that a street-lamp simply can't beat with a sound like a drum; but it often happens that images, themselves totally dissociated, when joined in the circuit of a particular emotion located with specific relation to both of them, conduce to great vividness and accuracy of statement in defining that emotion.

Not to rant on forever I'll beg your indulgence and come at once to the explanations you requested on the Melville poem:

> "*The dice of drowned men's bones he saw bequeath*
> *An embassy.*"

Dice bequeath an embassy, in the first place, by being ground (in this connection only, of course) in little cubes from the bones of drowned men by the action of the sea, and are finally thrown up on the sand, having "numbers" but no identification. These being the bones of dead men who never completed their voyage, it seems legitimate to refer to them as the only surviving evidence of certain messages undelivered, mute evidence of certain things, experiences that the dead mariners might have had to deliver. Dice as a symbol of chance and circumstance is also implied.

> "*The calyx of death's bounty giving back,*" etc.

This calyx refers in a double ironic sense both to a cornucopia and the vortex made by a sinking vessel. As soon as the water has closed over a ship this whirlpool sends up broken spars, wreckage, etc., which can be alluded to as *livid hieroglyphs*, making a *scattered chapter* so far as any complete record of the recent ship and her crew is concerned. In fact, about as much definite knowledge might come from all this as anyone might gain from the roar of his own veins, which is easily heard (haven't you ever done it?) by holding a shell close to one's ear.

> "*Frosted eyes lift altars.*"

Refers simply to a conviction that a man, not knowing perhaps a definite god yet being endowed with a reverence for deity—such a man naturally postulates a deity somehow, and the altar of that deity by the very *action* of the eyes *lifted* in searching.

> "*Compass, quadrant and sextant contrive no farther tides.*"

Hasn't it ofen occurred that instruments originally invented for record and computation have inadvertently so extended the concepts of the entity they were invented to measure (concepts of space etc.) in the mind and imagination that employed them, that they may metaphorically be said to have extended the original boundaries of the entity measured? This little bit of "relativity" ought not to be discredited in poetry now that scientists are proceeding to measure the universe on principles of pure *ratio*, quite as metaphorical, so far as previous standards of scientific methods extended, as some of the axioms in *Job*.

I may have completely failed to provide any clear interpretation of these symbols in their context. And you will no doubt feel that I have rather heatedly explained them for anyone who professed no claims for their particular value. I hope, at any rate, that I have clarified them enough to suppress any suspicion that their obscurity derives from a lack of definite intentions in the subject-matter of the poem. The execution is another matter, and you must be accorded a superior judgment to mine in that regard.

From the editor to Mr. Crane:

No doubt our theories and ideals in the art differ more or less fundamentally, yet I would not deny to the poet the right to take certain of the liberties you claim. I think he can take as many as he suceeds with without mystifying his particular audience; for mystery is good, but not mystification.

I think that in your poem certain phrases carry to an excessive degree the "dynamics of metaphor"—they telescope three or four images together by mental leaps (I fear my own metaphors are getting mixed!) which the poet, knowing his ground, can take safely, but which the most sympathetic reader cannot take unless the poet leads him by the hand with some such explanation as I find in your letter. I refer to such phrases as my letter quoted, except that I think I was over-exacting in criticizing the "quadrant and sextant" line. Accepting as I do much of what you say about "the illogical impingements of the connotations of words on the consciousness, and their combinations and interplay in metaphor," I must admit that these phrases in your poem are for me too elliptical to produce any effect but mystification (this until you explained them).

I don't get this effect from Blake or Eliot in the lines you quote or others that I have read. I am not familiar with Blake's symbolic poems but now, opening Prof. Pierce's volume of selections from them, I find in their use of metaphor a singular simplicity and clarity. He deals with magnificient mysteries, but presents them in flaming images like

> *"what time I bound my sandals*
> *On to walk forward through eternity."*

I find here no crowded and tortured lines.

My argument comes down, I suppose, rather to your practice than your theory. Or, more specifically, your practice strains your theory by carrying it with relentless logic, to a remote and exaggerated extreme. You find me testing metaphors, and poetic concept in general, too much by logic, whereas I find you pushing logic to the limit in a painfully intellectual search for emotion, for poetic motive. Your poem reeks with brains—it is thought out, worked out, sweated out. And the beauty which it seems entitled to is tortured and lost.

In all this I may be entirely wrong, and I am aware that a number of poets and critics would think so. Yvor Winters for example, in a recent letter, speaks of your *Marriage of Faustus and Helen* in *Secession* 7 as "one of the great poems of our time, as great as the best of Stevens or Pound or Eliot." Well, I cannot grant it such a rank.

The editor would rather not have the last word, but as Mr. Crane contributes no further to the discussion, we must pass it on to our readers.   H. M.

REVIEW OF *GREEN RIVER*, BY JAMES WHALER†
From Haunts of Proserpine

To write adequate biography is one task, but to convey that record convincingly in terms of heroic couplets is a far more delicate achievement. It involves a closer identification of the author with the intimate aspirations of his subject—an even finer apprehension of his very pulse and successive subconscious motivations than most matter-of-fact accounts take into consideration. James Whaler, inspired by the noble vision and tragic frustrations of the Sicilian-American naturalist, Constantine Rafinesque, has taken a life that is all but forgotten, and so illumined it with the intrinsic light of its own Shelleyan pantheism and purity of motive that this long dramatic monologue, in which the aging botanist pours out his recollections, penetrates and transcends the bare recorded facts of his career. And if this results in a characterization imposing enough to take on some of the outlines of a myth, it is all to Mr. Whaler's credit as a poet. In so doing he has been but the more faithful to his subject, whose scientific obsessions were the active manifestations of a poetic imagination.

A beautiful and adulterous wife robbed Rafinesque of his native Sicily and all further hope of earthly love. His courtship of this daughter of a Greek innkeeper, his subsequent struggle between the claims of science and matrimony, and his desperate and lonely departure for the unpoisoned wilderness of the New World form the theme of the first half of *Green River*. But still more disastrous was the storm which foundered his ship in Long Island Sound, swallowing within call of shore his fifty boxes of scientific equipment, his books, manuscripts

† *Poetry* (April 1932).

and funds, the results of years of devoted labor. Later on, while working in a Philadelphia counting-house, he was to hear how his wife —whom he constantly envisages as "Proserpine"—was squandering what remained of his once ample fortune in frolic with an island lover. But the final blow came with the death of John Clifford, his friend and benefactor, for whose sake he had gone west into Kentucky.

It is easy to conceive how this series of calamities could confuse the vision of the staunchest spirit. Rafinesque died, a half-insane pauper in a garret on lower Race Street, Philadelphia, in 1840. During his twenty-five years in America, however, he had been a lecturer— received and remembered with honor—at Transylvania University; had crossed the Alleghanies five times on foot rather than by horse, in order to neglect no possible discoveries of uncharted forms of natural life; and had consistently held the respect, if not always the unbiased understanding, of Audubon and other more fortunate representative scientists of his period. The cave region along the Green River in Kentucky still has mementoes of his wanderings; and it is in his monologue relating his presumable discovery of what is actually named Rafinesque's Cave that his high moral conscience and lyric phantasy unite in a scene (*Section II*) which forms the poem's dramatic apex. There, amidst "Babylons of stalactite"—

> Where pearl-boughs blossoming in bursts of stars
> Show me a jeweled heaven of dead czars,
> And moon-tailed orioles roost wing to wing
> With mocking-birds that only dream they sing—

as this nacreous Plutonian palace unfolds before him, his ecstasy conceives an idealistic prehistoric race of river-men about him, stone-frozen, "paired lovers all, in a dominion where beauty is omnipotent wth death." Before him also looms the mummy-phantasy of his wife, his "Proserpine" of bitter memory, whose beautiful image he there commits to flames, burning her imprint forever from his heart.

The curtain falls on Rafinesque before the tragic breakup of his faculties, but already in his Race Street garret overlooking the shipping on the Delaware. In a stoic refrain he is left in contemplation of the world about him:

> With masts and mariners before
> Your window, street-cries in your ears,
> There lay your bed, there nail your desk,
> There leaven all you know with tears.

Green River contains few of those psychological nuances and moral casuistries abounding in the narrative verse of Mr. Robinson,

Mr. Aiken, and others. Though if often features nature, society and the individual at odds, they are like the more elemental odds that have occupied such themes as Masefield's. *Green River* is often melodramatic with expletives, rhapsodic flights of fancy and bitter invocations. Perhaps any extended monologue must be so rhetorically energized in order to sustain the burden of so long a narrative. But here one occasionally feels a strain in the otherwise vigorous and tough texture of the verse, so felicitously inlaid with a thousand names from field and stream. Rafinesque speaks in this multitudinous world of flowers birds and fish as intensely as an astronomer breathes among the stars. Mr. Whaler's fresh evocation of this natural background (so prettified and sterile in most hands) is almost as fine an achievement as his resurrection of a forgotten hero.

CRITICAL FRAGMENT

A pure approach to any art or creative endeavor must involve the elimination of extraneous elements that through confusion, prejudice or inertia have gained a bastard identification with the ideal subject as determined by its special tendencies. Equally commonplace is the corollary that persistent respect for such a method of precedure leads not only to an ever deeper comprehension of the *medium* of that art and its potentials—it finally forces the subject to yield surprising illuminations and assertions new to our experience, additions to the total of our sensibilities.

As such, the approach to certain irreducible common denominators, called Truth, is evident as a perpetually creative principle. Paradoxically, when seeming most to narrow and confine the subject (to itself) it proceeds to open and extend it by this purification. It may not be until the distinct florescence has been already in large degree achieved that we begin to gather any assurance of a harvest at all, for there are no guide posts or tracks to answer us, seldom even a terminology to follow us. An inward synthesis of past recognitions may apprehend the logic of our pursuit, but it is only when that moving factor in this process, a really scientific honesty, has already connected a new link of realizations to our perceptions that the proper order of relationships is evident. Simultaneously, then, occurs a creation and its recognition and the proof of a deeper logic in the medium and subject than could have been located or perhaps even guessed at before.

C. THE DEVELOPMENT OF "ATLANTIS"

LINES SENT TO WILBUR UNDERWOOD, FEBRUARY 1923

And midway on that structure I would stand
One moment, not as diver, but with arms
That open to project a disk's resilience
Winding the sun and planets in its face.
Water should not stem that disk, nor weigh
What holds its speed in vantage of all things
That tarnish, creep, or wane; and in like laughter,
Mobile yet posited beyond even that time
The Pyramids shall falter, slough into sand,—
And smooth and fierce above the claim of wings,
And figured in that radiant field that rings
The Universe:—I'd have us hold one consonance
Kinetic to its poised and deathless dance.

WORKSHEETS, SPRING 1923

And, steady as the gaze incorporate
Of flesh affords, we turn, surmounting all
With transience straight to that sear arch-head,—
Expansive center, pure moment and ELECTRON
That guards like eyes that must look always down
In reconcilement of our chains and ecstasy
Crashing manifoldly on us as we hear

The looms, the wheels, the whistles in concord
Tethered and welded as the hills of dawn
Whose feet are silvery with speed to tread
And shuttle
Whose feet are shuttles silvery with speed
To tread *our world* and weave our answering world
Recreant and rising resonantly in this dome.

                      [*then*]   [so **we may**]
And, steady as the gaze incorporate
Of flesh affords, we turn, surmounting all
    [keenest]
With *straightest* transience to that sear arch-head,—
That guards like eyes that must look always down
[*The*] [In]
In reconcilement of our chains and ecstasy
   [That crashes]
Crash*ing* manifoldly on us as we hear
The looms, the wheels, the whistles in concord
Tethered and welded as the hills of dawn
Whose feet are shuttles silvery with speed
To tread and weave our answering world
                 [en]
Recreant and resonantly ris*ing* in this dome.
Recreate, and

LINES SENT TO ALFRED STIEGLITZ, JULY 4, 1923

The baited rock precipitate with sound
Of waters bending and astride the sky.
Until, as though an organ pressing doom
Should set this nave of time atremble, we feel
Through brimming clay and signalling upright,
Beneath us lift a porch, a living concourse
Whose alignment rears from equal out to equal,
Yielding mutual assumption on its arches
Fused and veering to the measure of our arms.

O whitest instruments, in pain addressed
And so applied in beams of driven fire,
In ordered sheaves remission gathered up
And multiplied with steps to such a sum,—
That, scathless, we assume and guide
The tempered axis of the world in moving
Sidereal phalanx to that tolling star
That fills us and renews us as a sun. . .

To be, Great Bridge, in vision bound of thee,
So widely straight and turning, ribbon-wound,
Multi-colored, river-harboured and upborne
Through the bright drench and fabric of our veins,—
With white escarpments swinging into light,
Sustained in tears, the cities are endowed
And justified conclamant with the fields
Revolving through their harvest in sweet torment.

And, steady as the gaze incorporate
Of flesh a.fords, we turn, surmounting all
With keenest transience to that sear arch-head,—
Expansive center, purest moment and electron
That guards like eyes that must look always down
In reconcilement of our chains and ecstasy
That crashes manifoldly on us as we hear
The looms, the wheels, the whistles in concord
Tethered and welded as the hills of dawn
Whose feet are shuttles, silvery with speed
To tread and weave our answering world,—
Recreate and resonantly risen in this dome.

So on this structure I would stand
One moment, not as diver, but with arms
That open to project a salient disk
That winds the moon and midnight in one face.

Water shall not stem that disk, nor weigh
What holds its speed in vantage of all things
That tarnish, creep, or wane; and so in laughter
Blessed and posited beyond even that time
The Pyramids shall falter, slough into sand,—
Fiercely smooth above the wake and claim of wings

And figured in that radiant field that rings
The whispering cosmos, we hold consonance
Kinetic to a poised and deathless dance.

LINES SENT TO RICHARD AND CHARLOTTE RYCHTARIK, JULY 21, 1923

(Verses from the last part of "The Bridge")

The hand you carry to the rock knows lime
And all the mineral wariness of earth . . .
Yet, touch its cloudy buried throat where light
Is branched like prayers unspoken that await
Your deepest thrusting agony for answer: strike
Its breast precipitate, its lust-forbidden flanks,
Sleek with your sweat's erosion,—til we hear
The sound of waters bending and astride the sky:
Until, as though an organ pressing doom
Should set this nave of time atremble, we feel
Though brimming clay and signalling upright,
Beneath us lift a porch, a living concourse
Whose alignment rears from equal out to equal,
Yielding mutual assumption on its arches
Fused and veering to the measure of our arms.

O whitest instruments, in pain addressed
And so applied in beams of driven fire,
In ordered sheaves remission gathered up
And multiplied with steps to such a sum
That, scathless, we assume and predicate
The tempered axis of the world in joined
Sidereal phalanx to that tolling star
That fills us and renews us as a sun!

To be, Great Bridge, in vision bound of thee,
So widely belted, straight and banner-wound,
Multi-colored, river-harboured and upbourne
Through the bright drench and fabric of our veins,—
With white escarpments swinging into light,
Sustained in tears the cities are endowed

And justified, conclamant with the fields
Revolving through their harvests in sweet torment.

And steady as the gaze incorporate
Of flesh affords, we turn, surmounting all
In keenest transience to that sear arch-head,—
Expansive center, purest moment and electron
That guards like eyes that must always look down
Through blinding cables to the ecstasy
That crashes manifoldly on us when we hear
The looms, the wheels. the whistles in concord
Teathered and atiphonal to a dawn
Whose feet are shuttles, silvery with speed
To tread upon and weave our answering world,
Recreate and resonantly risen in this dome.

WORKSHEETS, c. 1926

      [The]   '[of cassions,]
     The cassions' grinding whirr, *the* torrid sledge,
             [realignments]
[of] *New* axle conformations, arctic gongs,
         realignments
     Meridian *displacements* in the throes
   [*The*]   [girdles] [of]   [*eclipses*] [ellipses]
[And] Of aeon *measures in* thy thighs, O bridge;
               [a] [this]
     Dreadful, the blossoms of *the* faith unfold;
     From riven stems into an unrecked sky
     Kiss of our agony thou gatherest.
     Make our love sure, to lift whose song we die!

     To be, Great Bridge, in vision bound of thee,
     So widely chartered, straight and ocean-wound,
     River-harboured, irridescently upborne
     Through the bright drench and fabric of our veins.—
     With white escarpments swinging into light,
     Sustained in tears the cities are endowed
     And justified conclamant with the fields
     Revolving through their harvest in sweet torment.

Serenities, anathema to say,
          [ing]
O Bridge synoptic foliate dome:
Always through blinding cables to our joy
—Of thy release, the square prime ecstasy.
Through the twined cable strands, upward
Veering with light, the flight of strings,
Kinetic choiring of white wings . . ascends.

LINES SENT TO WALDO FRANK,
JANUARY 18, 1926

BRIDGE-Finale

Through the twined cable strands, the arching path
Upwards, veering with light, the flight of strings,—
Clouds sweeping clear amid limpid strokes of moon,
Abeyant canyons of two seas between:
Up the index of night, of steel and stone,
Transparent octaves,—fleckless the farthest naves—
Sibyllines voices flicker, waver and join
As though a god were issue of the strings.

And through the cordage shaking its white call
From arch to arch, from seamless tides below,
Their labryinthine mouths of history
Shaping reply as though all ships at sea
Fleshed in prismatic vibrancy, made cry,
(So seven oceans answer from their dream)
"Make thy love sure, to lift whose feet we die."

Obliquely on and up bright carrier nets,
New music drawn between twin monoliths
Beyond whose frosted capes the moon bequeaths
Two worlds of sleep: O boughs enthralled of song,
Onward and up the crystal-flooded aisles
White tempest sheets file upward, upward ring
With silver terraces the mastiff spars,
The loft of vision, palladium helm of stars.

Strings lifting up in silver inference
That crossing, speak from diamond sequined heights
Through interstitial bars all hails, farewells,
Whose syncopating gulfs the winds careen,
Whose giant knots new hierarchies attain:
Woven antinomies, straits sentinel,
Free embassies to cyclic avatars,—
The fanfare's and the tabor's throbbing way
To latitudes of magi emperies:
O psalms unutterable of ultimate Cathay!

Through the twined cable strands, the arching path
Beyond beginning, termless cradle strings:
Of whitest instruments in pain addressed
And so annealed in beams of driven fire,—
In ordered sheaves remission gathered up,
Avowals to such perfect nadir sum,
—Hymalayan consummations! Til is heard
The sound of waters bending and astride the sky,

Until, as though an organ pressing doom
Should set this nave of time atremble, we feel
Beneath us lift a world, a new concourse
Outspanned of silver parallels that strike
Upward with stitch of stars, with stallion glow
Hereditary autumnal plateaus,—
Upward, til razor paces tilt the slow
Pale rings of rebirth, aureate horns of snow.

The grinding whir of polar cassions, groan
Of axle re-alignment, glacial gongs,
Shivers of meridians in burden throes,—
From glittering thighs this white nativity!
O Bridge! Kiss of our agony thou gatherest.
From riven stems into an unrecked sky
Dreadful, the blossoms of the faith unfold.
Regard our love, to lift whose song we die.

To be, Great Bridge, in vision bound of thee,
So widely curvatured and ocean wound,
River harbored, irridescently upborne
Through the bright drench and fabric of our veins,—

With white escarpments swinging into light,
Sustained in tears the cities are endowed
And justified conclamant with the fields
Revolving through their harvests in sweet torment.

Serenities, anathema to say,
O Bridge, synoptic foliating dome:
Always through blinding cables to our joy
—Of thy release, the square prime ecstasy.
Up through the spires of cordage, pyramids
Veering with light, the flight of strings,
With Easter saliency the naked sheaves—
Kinetic choiring of white wings . . . ascends.

So beyond calendar and forge of noon,
Gathered like spokes to that far telling star
That bleeds infinity, the orphic strings,
Sidereal Argive phalanxes, I see converge:
—One song, O bird of fire! Is it Cathay,—
Now pity steeps the grass and rainbows wind
The serpent with the eagle in the leaves . . . ?
Whispers antiphonal in azure swing.

WORKSHEETS, SPRING AND SUMMER, 1926

Through the twined cable strands, the arching path
Upward, veering with light, the flight of strings,—
        [crest] [arrases]
A brittle *haze* of moonlight syncopates
                        [*wings*]
The whispered rush, telepathy of *wires*:
Up the index of night, of steel and stone,
Transparent octaves,—fleckless the farthest naves—
Sibylline voices flicker, wavering stream
As though a god were issue of the strings.

                        [with] [its]
And through the cordage, notching *its white* call
    [after]
Arch *into* arch, from seamless tides below,

[With]
Their labyrinthine mouths of history
Tumbling reply as though all ships at sea
Enkindled in one vibrant breath, made cry,
"Make thy love sure, to lift those feet we die;"—
          [granite piers]
From blank embankments rolling anarchy
So seven oceans answer from their dream.

And on, obliquely up bright carrier bars
New anthems lift between twin monoliths
Beyond whose frosted capes the moon bequeaths
Two worlds of sleep; O boughs enthralled of song,
Onward and up the crystal-flooded aisles
White tempest sheets file upward, upward ring
With silver terraces the humming spars,
The loft of vision, palladium helm of stars.

          •   •   •

Sheerly the eyes are poured in avenues
          [decrees] [the *threshing*] [winnowing]
Up towering *syncopations, leaning* press
Of blade on tendon blade, inevitably
          [altar]
Whose *verdant* looms and shuttles, drawing love,
          [er] [blazing]
Build shimming up *the* conquering script;
[And terror] [shimmering] [up]   [build]
Lo, confidences of *all youth,* beatitudes
     [th] [testaments]
In sinuous music hewn of mythic words,—
The dance is chosen, the steep ways evoked!

Strings lifting night to deepest inference
Of purest day, from diamond-sequined heights
Through intercrossing bars all hails, farewells
Suspired to winds whose vats thy webs constrain:
Woven antimonies, straits sentinel,
The fanfare's and the tabor's throbbing way
To latitudes of magus empery,—
O psalms unutterable of ultimate Cathay!

[rough]
The cable-crested arbors, sentient paths
Beyond beginning, ceaseless cradle strings
In pain addressed, O whitest instruments,—
And so annealed in beams of naked fire,
Remissions aggregate in sparkling sheaves,
 [Sierras of]
That palisade new hierarchies, acclaim
Hymalayn consummations; til be heard
                    [sounded]
An arc of water *sounding* astride the sky,

 •   •   •

                    [flung *up* and poured]
Sheerly the eyes are *poured in* avenues
That shuttle upward (so the towering press
Of string on string leads on) and so incline
Beyond memory, O verdant cresting tides,
So shimmering of all youth, so dyed with love—
The steep dance chosen and the ways evoked;
Yea, as this shine refers,—beatitudes
In sinuous shafts commemorate of all Spring.

[Sheerly the eyes are poured in avenues]

 •   •   •

          [out]
Sheerly the eyes *are* poured in avenues,
   [Up] [Of]   [and] [*the*] [through]
          Up towering looms, *whose* winnowing sidelong **press**
                              [gleams]
          Of blade on tendon blade some altar *gleans,*
   [Whose]   [love] [wefting]   [rise]
[With] *With* shuttles *fluttering* love and terror, *lifts*
          The scriptural ciphers of *how young* a world [**how young,**]
                    [the]   [swords]
          How old *in* music hewn of mythic *words,*
                              [steeper]
          With dances vowed, *and* still *steep* ways evoked'
                         [some]
   [The aureate violences of *a* new world,
   With dances vowed, still steeper ways evoked
   How old in music hewn of mythic words
   The scriptural ciphers of how old a world!]

•   •   •

[Picked *thread*]   [bightingly]
Sheerly the eyes are poured in avenues—
                        [biting]   [those]
Up towering looms, *the winnowing sidelong* press
Of blade on shuttle blade what *dread subsumes*
                                [sidelong dread]
With blinding love
With love, O wafts of memory
[*And weaves with love*]
[*Woven with*]
[*Catches the*]

•   •   •

Sheerly the eyes are spilled in avenues,
Picked bitingly up towering *avenues* that *crest* rake
Of blade on shuttle blade what sidelong spurs

Picked bitingly up towering looms to guess
What texture topplingly Tomorrows

Sheerly the eyes are spilled in avenues,
Picked bitingly up towering looms press
(In lakes of rime the conquest apples burn!)

Sheerly the eyes are spilled in avenues,
                [looms]
Picked bitingly up towering *avenues* that *crest rake*

Sheerly the eyes are spilled in avenues,
Raked bitingly up towering looms that press
(O sidelong press of blade on shuttle blade)
All themes into that *cipher* that dreadful cipher
All themes into that dreadful cipher soar,
O love, that only you *can guess* may

•   •   •

                [spilled]
Sheerly the eyes are *poured* in avenues,—
Picked bitingly up towering looms whose press

Of blade on shuttle blade what sidelong *dread* spurs
Medley of love and terror ciphers there

Draw love and terror

Of blade on shuttle blade *catches* what deathly catch
Of love and terror ciphers
That only love and death may cipher
That only love or death may cipher

Of blade on shuttle blade what texture time
Tremendously
Tremendously has

Tomorrows draw, what texture, Time, That only love
May cipher

                    *   *   *

Sheerly the eyes are spilled in avenues,
Picked bitingly up towering looms that press
(O sidelong spurs of blade on shuttle blade!)
Tomorrows into yesterdays, all themes,
                          [rime and]
Love,—blended, stung with starlight, soar
                          [*in whose sleeping curves*]
Into terrific cipher, *O minute man*
The laugh of mythic spears
Into the laugh of mythic spears

Sheerly the eyes are spilled in avenues,
Picked bitingly up towering looms that press
[(Swiftly a seagull chides the *rain of* reins of **light**)]
(*O sidelong spurs of blade on tendon blade*)
Tomorrows into yesterdays, all themes
Loveblended, stung with rime and starlight, soar
Into the mythic laugh of spears that leans

It

Sheerly the eyes, like seagull's, stung with rime
                          [black]
And starlight riding the reins of light
Pick bitingly up towering looms that press

(O sidelong spurs of blade on shuttle blade!)
Tomorrows into yesterday, and *soar* [*thread*] [delve]
        [cipher curves]
With *curves* of sleep *into* what *lakes* what skies contain
The mythic laugh of spears

* * *

Sheerly the eyes, like seagulls stung with rime
And starlight, riding *the* black reins of light,
Pick bitingly up towering looms that press
            [*the*]   [with]
(O sidelong flight of blade on shuttle blade!)
(Tomorrows into yesterdays) and delve
[What]   [no traveller reads]
The cipher curves of sleep   *that none may read*
[But who has answered love and death and hailed]
    [who]
[But has answered love and death and hailed
The timeless searching laugh of mythic spears.]

LINES SENT TO WALDO FRANK, AUGUST 3, 1926

BRIDGE—Final Section

Through the twined cable strands, the arching path
Upward, veering with light, the flight of strings,
Taut miles of brittle moonlight syncopate
The whispered rush, telepathy of spires:
Up the index of night, granite and steel,
Transparent octaves,—flleckless the farthest naves—
Sibylline voices flicker, wavering stream
As though a god were issue of the strings . . .

And through the cordage, threading with its call
Arch after arch, from seamless tides below—
Their labyrinthine mouths of history
Pouring reply as though all ships at sea
Engirdled in one vibrant breath, made cry,

"Make thy love sure, to lift whose song we die,"
From blank embankments rolling anarchy
So seven oceans answer from their dream.

And on, obliquely up bright carrier bars
New measures tressel the twin monliths
Beyond whose frosted capes the moon bequeaths
Two worlds of sleep: O boughs enthralled of song,†
Onward and up the crystal-flooded aisles
White tempest sheets file upward, upward ring
With silver terraces the humming spars,
The loft of vision, palladium helm of stars.

Sheerly the eyes, like seagulls stung with rime
And startryst, riding the black fins of light
Pick biting way up towering looms that press
Sidelong with flight of blade on tendon blade
(Tomorrows into yesterday), and delve
What cipher script of sleep no traveller reads
But who through smoking pyres of love and death
Searches the timeless laugh of mythic spears.‡

Like hails, farewells, up diamond-sequined heights
Some trillion whispering hammers glimmer Tyre;
Serenely, sharply up the long anvil cry
Of inchling aeons silence rivets Troy.
And you, aloft there—Jason! hesting shout
Still wrapping harness to the swarming air!
Silvery the rushing wake, surpassing call,
Beams yelling "Aeolus" splintered in the straits.

From gulfs unfolding, terrible of drums,
Tall answer to the voyage, tensely spare,—
Bridge lifting night to cresting inference
Of deepest day, O choir translating time
Into what multitudinous verb the suns
And synchrony of waters ever grind, recast
In myriad syllables,—Psalm of Cathay,
Meridian of motion, Caravan . . . !

† *A variant*: Two worlds of sleep: O strands enthralled of song.
‡ *A variant*: Invades the timeless laugh of mythic spears.

We left the haven hanging in the night,
Sheened harbor lanterns backward fled the keel.
Here at time's other ocean, bearing corn,—
Eyes stammer through the pangs of dust and steel.
And still the fathomless, indubitable frieze
Of heaven's meditation, yoking wave
To kneeling wave, one song devoutly twines,
The vernal passage predicates, O strings.

O Thou, carved cognizance whose leap commits
The agile precints of the lark's return,
Within whose lariat course encinctured sing
In single chrysalis the many twain,—
Upward with stitch of stars and stallion glow
Until as though an organ pressing doom
Should goad this beach of time aside, what love†
From terror lifted, stanchions the heart's pain!‡

Swift peal of savage light, O turning Bridge,
Whose fell unshadow is death's utter wound,—*
O river-throated, irridescently upborne
Through the bright drench and fabric of our veins,—
Wth white escarpments swinging into light
Sustained in tears the cities are endowed
And justified conclamant with the fields
Revolving through their harvests in sweet torment.

Forever Deity's foliate pledge, O Thou
Whose canticle assigns the chemistry**
And calm succession of nativity,—***
Always through blinding cables to our joy—
Of thy white seizure springs the prophecy;
Always through spiring cordage, pyramids
Of silver sequel, Deity's young name
Kinetic of white choiring wings . . . ascends.

So beyond calendar and forge of noon,
Like spears ensanguined of that telling star

† *A variant*: Should goad this realm of time aside—we win
‡ *A variant*: The compass everlasting of all pain!
* *A variant*: Whose steep unshadow is death's utter wound,—
** *A variant*: Whose canticle the chemistry assigns
*** *A variant*: Of calm succession and nativity

That bleeds infinity, the orphic strings,
Sidereal phalanxes, leap and converge:
—One song, O bird of fire! Is it Cathay,—
Now pity steeps the grass and rainbows wind
The serpent with the eagle in the leaves . . . ?
Whispers antiphonal in azure swing.

AN EARLY VERSION OF THE 10th STANZA OF "ATLANTIS"

Migrations that must void the memory,
Inventions that cobblestone the heart,—
Unspeakable Thou Bridge to Thee, O Love
Whose stems inherit gods and drink the sea,
—Thy pardon for this history, whitest Flower,
O Answerer of all,—Anemone,—
Now while thy petals spend the suns about us, hold,
Atlantis, hold thy floating singer late!

SELECTED BIBLIOGRAPHY

POETRY AND PROSE BY HART CRANE

Crane, Hart. *The Collected Poems of Hart Crane*. Edited with an Introduction by Waldo Frank. (Contains *The Bridge, White Buildings, Key West, Uncollected Poems, "Modern Poetry"*.) New York: Liveright, 1933.

——"Two Letters on *The Bridge*," *The Hound and Horn* (July-September 1934).

——"General Aims and Theories," in Philip Horton's *Hart Crane* (1937).

——"Prose Writing," edited with an Introduction by Brom Weber, *Twice A Year* (Double Number XII-XIII, 1945).

BOOKS AND ARTICLES CONSIDERING HART CRANE

Blackmur, R. P. *The Double Agent*. New York, 1935.

Cowley, Malcolm. "A Preface to Hart Crane," *The New Republic* (April 23, 1930).

——"Roaring Boy," *The New Republic* (June 9, 1937).

——*Exile's Return*. New York, 1934.

Deutsch, Babette. *This Modern Poetry*. New York, 1935.

Drew, Elizabeth, with John L. Sweeney. *Directions in Modern Poetry*. New York, 1940.

Eastman, Max. *The Literary Mind*. New York, 1931.

Flint, F. Cudworth. "Metaphor in Contemporary Poetry," *The Symposium* (July 1930).

Foster, Elizabeth. *Arthur Rimbaud and Hart Crane*, 1940. (An unpublished doctoral dissertation, Ohio State University).

Fowlie, Wallace. "The Juggler's Dance," *The Chimera* (Autumn 1943).

442   SELECTED BIBLIOGRAPHY

Frank, Waldo. "The Poetry of Hart Crane," *The New Republic* (March 10, 1927)

Greenberg, Samuel B. *Poems from the Greenberg Manuscripts.* Edited with a Commentary by James Laughlin. Norfolk, Conn., 1939.

——*Poems by Samuel Greenberg.* Edited with an Introduction by Harold Holden and Jack McManis. New York, 1947.

Gregory, Horace, and Marya Zaturenska. *History of American Poetry, 1900-1940.* New York, 1946.

Hicks, Granville. "The Rediscovery of America," *The Nation* (April 30, 1930).

Hoffman, Frederick J., Charles Allen and Carolyn R. Ulrich. *The Little Magazine.* Princeton, 1946.

Horton, Philip. "The Greenberg Manuscript and Hart Crane's Poetry," *The Southern Review* (Summer 1936).

——"Identity of S. B. Greenberg," *The Southern Review* (Autumn 1936).

——*Hart Crane.* New York, 1937.

Larrabee, Ankey. "The Symbol of the Sea in Crane's 'Voyages,'" *Accent* (Winter 1943).

Leavis, F. R. "Hart Crane From This Side," *Scrutiny* (March 1939).

Matthiessen, F. O. "Crane, Harold Hart," *Dictionary of American Biography,* vol. xxi, New York, 1944.

——"American Poetry, 1920-1940," *The Sewanee Review* (January-March 1947).

Munson, Gorham B. "*The Fledgling Years,* 1916-1924," *The Sewanee Review* (January-March 1932).

——*Destinations.* New York, 1928.

Parry, Albert. *Garrets and Pretenders.* New York, 1933.

Peyre, Henri. "American Literature through French Eyes," *Virginia Quarterly Review* (Summer 1947).

Rice, Philip Blair. "Review of Crane, Lewis, Spender," *The Symposium* (October 1933).

Riding, Laura, and Robert Graves. *A Survey of Modernist Poetry.* New York, 1927.

Ridge, Lola. "A Modern Mystic," *The Saturday Review of Literature* (September 1, 1934).

Savage, D. S. "The Americanism of Hart Crane," *Horizon* (May 1942).

Schappes, Morris U. "Notes on the Concrete as a Method in Criticism," *The Symposium* (July 1931).

Shattuck, Roger. "Hart Crane's Other Bridge," *The Yale Literary Magazine* (Winter 1943).

Tate, Allen. 'American Poetry Since 1920," *The Bookman* (January 1929).

——"A Distinguished Poet," *The Hound and Horn* (July-Sept. 1930).

——'Hart Crane and the American Mind," *Poetry* (July 1932).

——"The Whole Image of a Man," *The Hound and Horn* (January-March 1933).

——*Reactionary Essays on Poetry and Ideas.* New York, 1936.

Waggoner, Hyatt Howe. "Hart Crane's Bridge to Cathay," *American Literature* (May 1944).

Walton, Eda Lou. "Hart Crane," *The Nation* (May 3, 1933).

Wells, Henry W. *The American Way of Poetry.* New York, 1943.

Williams, William Carlos. "Hart Crane (1899-1932)," *Contempo* (July 5, 1932).

Wilson, Edmund. "The Muses Out of Work," *The New Republic* (May 11, 1927).

Winters, Yvor. "Hart Crane's Poems," *Poetry* (April 1927).

——"The Progress of Hart Crane," *Poetry* (June 1930).

——"The Symbolist Influence," *The Hound and Horn* (July-Sept. 1931).

——*In Defense of Reason.* New York, 1947.

Zabel, M. D. "Phelps Putnam and America," *Poetry* (September 1932).

——"Book of Hart Crane," *Poetry* (April 1933).

Zinsser, Hans. *As I Remember Him.* Boston, 1940.

INDEX

A

Abbot, Dorian, 413
Aeschylus, 341
Aesop, 132
Aesthete, 1925, 240-42, 243, 244
Aiken, Conrad, 24, 36, 37, 241, 305
Aldington, Richard, 32, 35
American Mercury, The, 213
Anderson, Margaret, 13, 15, 19, 38, 64
Anderson, Sherwood, 42-3, 57-8, 62, 63, 77, 88, 105, 120-23, 124, 125, 130, 134-35, 141-42, 164, 165, 169, 189, 239
Apuleius, 86
Aristotle, 156
Art and Letters, 126
Arts, The, 317

B

Balzac, de, Honoré, 42, 122
Barton, Bruce, 290
Baudelaire, Charles, 27, 29, 89, 95, 107, 127, 133, 140, 252
Beethoven, van, Ludwig, 116
Bessaraboff, Nicholas, 152-53
Bible, 3, 161
Blake, William, 25, 127, 149, 284, 298, 300
Blast, 19
Bodenheim, Maxwell, 13, 31, 40

Bookman, The, 303
Boone, Daniel, 353
Bourne, Randolph, 17, 164, 166
Boyd, Ernest. 134, 213, 214, 215, 217, 239-40
Boyle, Kay, 324
Bragdon, Claude, 152-53
Brancusi, Constantin, 126
Brandes, Georg, 20
Bridges, Robert, 24
Brinton, Crane, 20
Brooks, Van Wyck, 16, 58, 87, 164, 241
Broom, 115, 178, 179, 213, 215, 216, 221, 222, 239, 245, 318
Brown, Slater, 207, 210, 214, 215, 246, 247, 249, 253
Browne, Sir Thomas, 252
Browning, Elizabeth Barrett, 127
Bruno's Bohemia, 33, 34
Bruno, Guido, 13-14, 34
Bruno's Weekly, 13, 33-6
Bunyan, John, 403
Burke, Kenneth, 213-16, 240, 241, 285-86
Butler, Samuel, 60
Byron, Lord, 127

C

Cabell, James Branch, 65, 87, 97
Calendar of Modern Letters, The, 147, 280

444